Solaris™ Operating Environment System Administrator's Guide

Fourth Edition

Janice Winsor

Sun Microsystems Press
A Prentice Hall Title
PRENTICE
HALL
PTR

10 9 8 7 6 5 4 3 2 1

ISBN 0-13-101401-3
Printed in the United States of America
Editorial/production supervisor: Wil Mara
Cover design director: Jerry Votta
Cover designer: Kavish & Kavish Digital Publishing and Design
Manufacturing manager: Alexis R. Heydt
Marketing manager: Debby van Dijk
Executive editor: Gregory G. Doench
Sun Microsystems Press
Publisher: Myrna Rivera

Sun Microsystems Press
A Prentice Hall Title

CONTENTS

2 Using Basic OS Commands   85

4 Understanding Shells   113

11 Administering Printing   387

ACKNOWLEDGMENTS

Many people contributed to the design, writing, and production of the fourth edition of this book. Sun Microsystems Press and the author would like to thank the following people for their contributions.

Gordon Marler for his excellent technical input and many examples. Gordon unpacked his first Sun workstation in 1987 and has been fascinated by UNIX ever since. He has worked as a UNIX System Administrator and Architect in Texas, Washington state, and New York City for various firms in the pharmaceutical, telecommunications, and financial fields, as well as a government contract here and there. He is currently a UNIX System Engineer for a global financial service institution and lives in New Jersey.

Peter H. Gregory, author of *Solaris Security* and *Sun Certified System Administrator for Solaris 8 Study Guide*, for organizing Gordon's help as a technical reviewer.

Bill Lane, Sun Microsystems, Inc., for enabling the author to participate in the Solaris 9 Beta program and to Larissa Brown, Miguel Ulloa, and Beauty Shields, for help with administrative details.

James Litchfield, Senior Staff Engineer, Solaris System Resource Services, Sun Microsystems, Inc., for information about new functionality in the Solaris 9 release.

Gary M. Gere, Sun Microsystems, Inc., for answering questions about Live Install functionality.

Matthew Williamson, Engineering Manager, Solaris Installation Infrastructure, Sun Microsystems, Inc., for answering questions about Live Install functionality and for reviewing Chapter 3, "Understanding the Flash Install and Live Upgrade Features."

The following members of the Solaris 9 Beta team, listed in alphabetical order, who were instrumental in answering questions and responding to my Solaris 9 Beta problem reports: Sally Beach, Tom Hardesty, and Beauty Shields.

Linda Gallops, Sun Microsystems, Inc., for technical help.

Those writers from Sun Technical Publications who contributed to the *Solaris System Administration Guides Volumes I, II, and III*, which were used as a technical reference resource.

The author would especially like to thank Mike Alread and Myrna Rivera of Sun Microsystems Press and Greg Doench, Senior Editor, Prentice Hall, for their unfailing enthusiasm, support, and friendship, Mary Lou Nohr for editing this manuscript with her usual skill and tact, and Wil Mara of Prentice Hall for production.

Thanks to the following people who contributed to the third edition of this book.

Peter Gregory, HartGregory Group, for reviewing the technical information in this book and for useful suggestions about adding new information.

Linda Gallops, Sun Microsystems, Inc., for technical help.

Mary Lautner, Sun Microsystems, Inc., for providing useful information about the Solaris 8 release.

John Stearns, Technical Publications Manager, SSE Group, Sun Federal, Sun Microsystems, Inc., for providing answers to questions about Role-Based Access Control (RBAC) features.

Mary Lautman, Sun Microsystems, Inc., for providing answers to questions about Role-Based Access Control (RBAC) features and providing valuable input to Chapter 5.

Larissa Brown, Sun Microsystems, Inc., for helping put me in contact with the right people to help with new Solaris 8 functionality.

Those writers from Sun Technical Publications who contributed to the *Solaris System Administration Guides Volumes I, II, and III*, which were used as a technical reference resource.

The author would especially like to thank Rachel Borden of Sun Microsystems Press and Greg Doench, Senior Editor, Prentice Hall, for their unfailing enthusiasm, support, and friendship, Mary Lou Nohr for editing this manuscript with her usual skill and tact, and Wil Mara of Prentice Hall for production.

Thanks to the following people, who contributed to the second edition of this book.

Brett Bartow, Acquisitions Editor, Macmillan Technical Publishing, for his enthusiasm and support on this project.

Mary Lautner, Program Manager, Sun Microsystems, Inc., for her invaluable help and assistance in providing the author with documentation and answers to numerous questions. Without Mary's help and the information she provided, the author would have been unable to complete this project.

Those writers from SunSoft Technical Publications who contributed to the *Solaris System Administration Guide*, which was used as a technical reference resource.

Lisa Gebken of Macmillan Technical Publishing for editing this manuscript.

Tobin Crockett, for networking the author's SPARCstation 10 and Macintosh PowerPC and setting up a network printer.

Rob Johnston, System Support Specialist, Sun Microsystems Computer Company, for installing Solaris 2.6 and troubleshooting hardware and software problems.

Tien Nguyen, System Support Specialist, SunSoft, Inc., for help in troubleshooting hardware and software problems.

Linda Gallops, SunSoft SQA, for help in tracking down information about modems.

Ken Erickson of SunSoft, for allowing the author to pester him with occasional technical questions.

The author would especially like to thank Rachel Borden and John Bortner of Sun Microsystems Press for their unfailing enthusiasm, support, and friendship.

Thanks to the following people, who contributed to the first edition of this book.

Connie Howard and Bridget Burke, SunSoft Publications managers, for their support and encouragement.

Randy Enger, SunSoft Engineering Manager, for help in gaining early access to the Solaris 2.1 administration tools. Special thanks are also due to Gordon Kass, Solaris 2.1 Product Manager, and Steve Hanlon, SunSoft Marketing.

Patrick Moffitt, SunOS Ambassador, for providing background information about the Service Access Facility. Patrick Moffitt and Cindy Swearingen, Technical Education Services, for providing a modem procedure that worked.

Rick Ramsey, SunSoft Technical Writer, for source information about NIS+, and for many discussions about good technical writing.

Keith Palmby, SunSoft Technical Writer, for source information about user environments.

Charla Mustard-Foote, SunSoft Technical Writer, for providing source information and the conversion table for Appendix A, and for calmly helping make software available for screen shots.

Bruce Sesnovich, SunSoft Technical Writer, for providing background information about the Service Access Facility and modem procedures.

Tom Amiro, SunSoft Technical Writer, for providing background information about administering user accounts and printers, and for early access to information about the Solaris 2.1 administration tools. Tom also deserves thanks for help in making software available for screen shots.

John Pew, Writing Consultant, for providing information and filters for converting raster files to GIF format.

Bill Edwards, Dave Miner, Jeff Parker, Chuck Kollars, Ken Kane, and Paul Sawyer—SunSoft Engineers in Billerica, MA—deserve thanks for reviewing information about NIS+ security, Administration Tool security, Database Manager, and User Manager.

Sam Cramer, SunSoft Engineer, for help with file system information. Bill Shannon, SunSoft Distinguished Engineer, for help with backup and restore information.

Pat Shriver, SunSoft Engineer, Robin Greynolds, SunSoft System Administrator, and Craig Mohrman, SunSoft Engineer, for technical review.

Karin Ellison, SunSoft Press, for parenting this book and for extraordinary assistance, including providing a Solaris 2.0 system for use on this project.

Thanks are also due to Melinda Levine, our editor at Ziff-Davis Press, and to Cheryl Holzaepfel, Managing Editor, for being so easy to work with.

And lastly, thanks to the engineers, writers, and marketing folks at SunSoft who helped with the SunSoft version of this book.

PREFACE

This book is for beginning system administrators, system administrators new to the Solaris™ Operating Environment, or any user who wants a task-oriented quick-reference guide to basic administrative commands.

A Quick Tour of the Contents

Chapter 1, "Introducing Solaris System Administration," describes basic administration tasks and superuser status. It tells how to communicate with users, start up and shut down systems, and monitor processes. It also introduces some frequently used commands and the new Administration Tools in the Solaris 8 Operating Environment.

Chapter 2, "Using Basic OS Commands," describes basic commands for finding user and environment information, creating and editing files, combining commands and redirecting output, displaying manual pages, and locating basic disk information.

Chapter 3, "Understanding the Flash Install and Live Upgrade Features," describes two installation features new in the Solaris 9 release.

Chapter 4, "Understanding Shells," describes some commands common to all shells and provides basic information about the Bourne, C, Korn, Bourne-Again, `tcsh`, and `zsh` shells.

Chapter 5, "Administering User Accounts and Groups," describes how to add and remove user accounts and how to set up new group accounts.

Chapter 6, "Administering Rights and Roles," introduces the Role-Based Access Control (RBAC) security feature, new in the Solaris 8 Operating

Environment, that enables you to assign a subset of superuser privileges to one or more users.

Chapter 7, "Administering File Systems," describes the types of file systems provided in the Solaris Operating Environment, the default file system, the virtual file system table, and the file system administrative commands. It shows you how to make file systems available and how to back up and restore file systems.

Chapter 8, "Administering Devices," describes how to use tapes and diskettes to store and retrieve files and how to administer disks. It also introduces the Service Access Facility and provides instructions for setting up port monitors for printers and modems.

Chapter 9, "Administering Systems," describes commands to display system-specific information, configure additional swap space without reformatting a disk, and create a local mail alias.

Chapter 10, "Administering Network Services," describes commands to check on remote system status, log in to remote systems, and transfer files between systems. This chapter also introduces the IPv6 Internet protocol, describes how to display network statistics and configuration information, how to use the snoop command, and how to use the Secure Shell.

Chapter 11, "Administering Printing," introduces the LP print service, describes how to set up printing services, and explains how to use the printing commands.

Chapter 12, "Recognizing File Access Problems," provides information on how to recognize problems with search paths, permission, and ownership.

The Glossary contains basic system administration terms and definitions.

Important: Read This Before You Begin

Because we assume that the root path includes the /sbin, /usr/sbin, /usr/bin, and /etc directories, the steps show the commands in these directories without absolute path names. Steps that use commands in other, less common directories show the absolute path in the example.

The examples in this book are for a basic Solaris software installation without the Binary Compatibility Package installed and without /usr/ucb in the path.

CAUTION. If /usr/ucb *is included in a search path, it should always be at the end. Commands like* ps *or* df *are duplicated in* /usr/ucb *with different formats and options from those of Solaris commands.*

This book does not contain all the information you need to administer systems. Refer to the complete system administration documentation for comprehensive information.

Because the Solaris Operating Environment provides the Bourne (default), Korn, and C shells, examples in this book show prompts for each of the shells.

The default C shell prompt is *system-name%*. The default Bourne and Korn shell prompt is $. The default root prompt for all shells is a pound sign (#). In examples that affect more than one system, the C shell prompt (which shows the system name) is used to make it clear when you change from one system to another.

Conventions Used in This Book

Commands

In the steps and the examples, the commands to be entered are in bold type. For example: "Type **su** and press Return." When following steps, press Return only when instructed to do so, even if the text in the step breaks at the end of a line.

Variables

Variables are in an italic typeface. When following steps, replace the variable with the appropriate information. For example, the step to print a file instructs you to "type **lp** *filename* and press Return." To substitute the file named quest for the *filename* variable, type **lp quest** and press Return.

Mouse-Button Terminology

This book describes mouse buttons by function. The default mouse button mapping is shown below.

- SELECT is Left.
- ADJUST is Middle.
- MENU is Right.

Use the SELECT mouse button to select unselected objects and activate controls. Use the ADJUST mouse button to adjust a selected group of objects, either adding to the group or deselecting part of the group. Use the MENU mouse button to display and choose from menus.

Platform Terminology

In this document, the term IA (Intel Architecture) is used instead of x86 to refer to the Intel 32-bit processor architecture, which includes the Pentium, Pentium Pro, Pentium II, Pentium II Xeon, Celeron, Pentium III Xeon processors, and comparable microprocessor chips made by AMD and Cyrix.

Storage-Medium Terminology

In this book, we distinguish between three different types of media storage terminology in the following way.

- *Disc* is used for an optical disc, CD-ROM, or DVD disc.
- *Disk* is used for a hard-disk storage device.
- *Diskette* is used for a floppy diskette storage device. (Note: Sometimes, screen messages and mount points use the term *floppy.*)

Icons

Marginal icons mark information that is new in this edition. The new information is new with the Solaris 9 Operating Environment.

Other new information may have been available in previous releases but was not included in the third edition. Where possible, the text indicates the release number when the command or functionality was added.

Solaris Management Console Tools

This book refers to the *Solaris Management Console Tools* book, by Janice Winsor, published by Sun Microsystems Press and Prentice Hall. The SMC Tools book documents the tools available in SMC release 2.0. The upcoming second edition of the *Solaris Management Console Tools* book will include information about the new tools available in the Solaris 9 SMC 2.1 release.

SPARC and IA Information

This book provides system administration information for both SPARC and IA systems. Unless otherwise noted, information throughout this book applies to both types of systems. Table A summarizes the differences between the SPARC and IA system administration tasks.

Table A   *SPARC and IA System Administration Differences*

Category	SPARC Platform	IA Platform
System operation before kernel is loaded	A programmable read-only memory (OpenBoot PROM) chip with a monitor program runs diagnostics and displays device information. The OpenBoot PROM is also used to program default boot parameters and to test the devices connected to the system.	The basic input/output system (BIOS) runs diagnostics and displays device information. A Solaris Device Configuration Assistant boot diskette with the Multiple Device Boot (MDB) program is used to boot from nondefault boot partitions, the network, or the CD-ROM.
Booting the system	Commands and options at the OpenBoot PROM level are used to boot the system.	Commands and options at the MBD, primary, and secondary boot subsystems level are used to boot the system.
Boot programs	`bootblk`, the primary boot program, loads `ufsboot`. `ufsboot`, the secondary boot program, loads the kernel.	`mboot`, the master boot record, loads `pboot`. `pboot`, the Solaris partition boot program, loads `bootblk`. `bootblk`, the primary boot program, loads `ufsboot`. `ufsboot`, the secondary boot program, loads the kernel.
System shutdown	The `shutdown` and `init` commands can be used without additional operator intervention.	The `shutdown` and `init` commands are used but require operator intervention to type any key to continue the prompt.
Disk controllers	SCSI, IDE.	SCSI and IDE.

Table A   *SPARC and IA System Administration Differences (Continued)*

Category	SPARC Platform	IA Platform
Disk slices and partitions	A disk may have a maximum of eight slices, numbered 0–7.	A disk may have a maximum of four `fdisk` partitions. The Solaris `fdisk` partition may contain up to 10 slices, numbered 0–9, but only 0–7 can store user data.
Diskette drives	Desktop systems usually contain one 3.5-inch diskette drive.	Systems may contain two diskette drives: a 3.5-inch and a 5.25-inch drive.

Solaris System Software Evolution

To help you understand how Solaris is evolving, Table B provides a list of the major system administration feature differences for each release.

Table B   *Solaris System Software Evolution*

Release	New Features
Solaris 1.0	Solaris 4.x contains Berkeley (BSD) UNIX functionality.
Solaris 2.0 (SunOS 5.0)	A merger of AT&T System V Release 4 (SVR4) and BSD UNIX. To facilitate customer transition, Solaris uses SVR4 as the default environment, with BSD commands and modes as an option. Administration Tool provides a graphical user interface Database Manager and Host Manager.
Solaris 2.1 (SunOS 5.1)	Administration Tool adds a graphical user interface Printer Manager and User Account Manager.
Solaris 2.2 (SunOS 5.2)	Volume management integrates access to CD-ROM and diskette files with the File Manager and provides a command-line interface. Users no longer need superuser privileges to mount CD-ROMs and diskettes. Solaris 2.0 and 2.1 procedures do not work with volume management because volume management controls and owns the devices.

Table B   *Solaris System Software Evolution (Continued)*

Release	New Features
Solaris 2.3 (SunOS 5.3)	Volume management changes Solaris 2.2 mount point naming conventions.
	Administration Tool adds a graphical user interface Serial Port Manager with templates that provide default settings, which makes adding character terminals and modems much easier.
	The automounter subsystem is split into two programs: an automounted daemon and a separate automount program. Both are run when the system is booted. The loadable autofs kernel module enables automounted file systems to be part of a virtual file system (VFS). Mount points under the automounter's control are real mount points instead of symbolic links, and the /tmp_mnt mount point is no longer needed. Additional predefined automount map variables are provided. (Refer to the *Solaris Advanced System Administrator's Guide*.)
	Online: Backup 2.1 is included with the release. (Not documented in this book.)
	Pluggable Authentication Model (PAM) is included with the release. PAM provides a consistent framework to enable access control applications, such as login, to be able to choose any authentication scheme available on a system, without changing the login program itself. (Refer to the *Solaris Advanced System Administrator's Guide*.)
	C2 Security is included in this release. (Not documented in this book.)
	The format(1) command changes for SCSI disks. (Not documented in this book.)
	PPP network protocol product that provides IP network connectivity over a variety of point-to-point connections is included in this release. (Not documented in this book.)
	Cache File System (CacheFS) for NFS is included in this release. CacheFS is a generic, nonvolatile caching mechanism to improve performance of certain file systems by using a small, fast, local disk.

Table B   Solaris System Software Evolution (Continued)

Release	New Features
	New NIS+ setup scripts are included in this release. The `nisserver`(1M), `nispopulate`(1M), and `nisclient`(1M) scripts enable you to set up an NIS+ domain much more quickly and easily than if you used the individual NIS+ commands to do so. With these scripts, you can avoid a lengthy manual setup process.
Solaris 2.4 (SunOS 5.4)	New Motif GUI for Solaris software installation is added. (Not documented in this book.)
Solaris 2.5 (SunOS 5.5)	New `pax`(1M) portable archive interchange command for copying files and file systems to portable media is added.
	Admintool is used to administer only local systems. The Solstice AdminSuite product is available for managing systems in a network for SPARC and IA systems.
	New process tools are available in `/usr/proc/bin` to display highly detailed information about the active processes stored in the process file system in the `/proc` directory.
	Telnet client is upgraded to the 4.4 BSD version. `rlogind` and `telnetd` remote login capacity are improved. (Not documented in this book.)
Solaris 2.5.1 (SunOS 5.5.1)	The limit on user ID and group ID values is raised to 2147483647, or the maximum value of a signed integer. The `nobody` user and group (60001) and the no access user and group (60002) retain the same UID and GID as in previous Solaris releases.
Solaris 2.6 (SunOS 5.6)	Changes to the Solaris 2.6 printing software provide a better solution than the LP print software in previous Solaris releases. You can easily set up and manage print clients by using the NIS or NIS+ nameservices to enable centralization of print administration for a network of systems and printers. New features include redesign of print packages, print protocol adapter, bundled SunSoft Print Client software, and network printer support.
	New `nisbackup` and `nisrestore` commands provide a quick and efficient method of backing up and restoring NIS+ namespaces.

Table B   Solaris System Software Evolution (Continued)

Release	New Features
	New patch tools, including `patchadd` and `patchrm` commands, add and remove patches. These commands replace the `installpatch` and `backoutpatch` commands that were previously shipped with each individual patch. (Refer to the *Solaris Advanced System Administrator's Guide*.)
	New `filesync` command ensures that data is moved automatically between a portable computer and a server. (Not documented in this book.)
	The previous flat `/proc` file system is restructured into a directory hierarchy that contains additional subdirectories for state information and control functions. This release also provides a watchpoint facility to monitor access to and modifications of data in the process address space. The `adb`(1) command uses this facility to provide watchpoints.
	Large files are supported on UFS, NFS, and CacheFS file systems. Applications can create and access files up to one Tbyte on UFS-mounted file systems and up to the limit of the NFS server for NFS- and CacheFS-mounted file systems. A new `-o largefiles` option disables the large-file support on UFS file systems. Using the `-o largefiles` option enables system administrators to ensure that older applications that are not able to safely handle large files do not accidentally operate on large files.
	NFS Kerberos authentication now uses DES encryption to improve security over the network. The kernel implementations of NFS and RPC network services now support a new RPC authentication flavor that is based on the Generalized Security Services API (GSS-API). This support contains the hooks for future stronger security of the NFS environment. (Refer to the *Solaris Advanced System Administrator's Guide*.)
	Font Admin enables easy installation and use of fonts for the X Window System. It supports TrueType, Type0, Type1, and CID fonts for multibyte languages and provides comparative font preview capability. It is fully integrated into the CDE desktop. (Not documented in this book.)

Table B   *Solaris System Software Evolution (Continued)*

Release	New Features
	The Solaris 2.6 operating environment is year 2000 ready. It uses unambiguous dates and follows the X/Open guidelines where appropriate. (Not documented in this book.)
	WebNFS software enables file systems to be accessed through the Web with the NFS protocol. This protocol is very reliable and provides greater throughput under a heavy load. (Not documented in this book.)
	The Java Virtual Machine 1.1 integrates the Java platform for the Solaris Operating Environment. It includes the Java runtime environment and the basic tools needed to develop Java applets and applications. (Not documented in this book.)
	For IA systems, the Configuration Assistant interface is part of the new booting system for the Solaris (Intel Platform Edition) software. It determines which hardware devices are in the system, accounts for the resources each device uses, and enables users to choose which device to boot from.
	For IA systems, the `kdmconfig` program configures the mouse, graphics adapter, and monitor. If an `owconfig` file already exists, `kdmconfig` extracts any usable information from it. In addition, `kdmconfig` retrieves information left in the `devinfo` tree by the `defconf` program and uses that information to automatically identify devices. (Not documented in this book.)
	Release is fully compliant with X/Open UNIX 95and POSIX standards. (Not documented in this book.)
Solaris 7 (SunOS 5.7)	Solaris 64-bit operating environment is added (SPARC Platform Edition only). (Not documented in this book.)
	UFS logging improves file system support.
	Lightweight Directory Access Protocol (LDAP) protocol improves management of nameservice databases. (Not documented in this book.)
	Java Development Kit for Solaris significantly improves scalability and performance for Java applications. (Not documented in this book.)

Table B   *Solaris System Software Evolution (Continued)*

Release	New Features
	Dynamic reconfiguration significantly decreases system downtime.
	AnswerBook2 server runs on a Web server. (Not documented in this book.)
	Unicode locales enhanced with multiscript capabilities and six new Unicode locales are added.
	RPC security is tightened with data integrity and confidentiality enhancements. (Not documented in this book.)
	The Solaris Common Desktop Environment (CDE) contains new tools to make it easy to find, manipulate, and manage address cards, applications, e-mail addresses, files, folders, hosts, processes, and Web addresses. (Not documented in this book.)
Solaris 8 (SunOS 5.8)	IPv6 adds increased address space and improves Internet functionality by using a simplified header format, support for authentication and privacy, autoconfiguration of address assignments, and new quality-of-service capabilities.
	The Solaris Operating Environment provides the Naming Service switch back-end support for directory service based on Lightweight Directory Access Protocol (LDAP). (Not documented in this book.)
	The Java2 Software Development Kit (SDK) for Solaris significantly improves scalability and performance of Java applications. (Not documented in this book.)
	The Solaris 8 Installation CD provides a graphical, wizard-based, Java-powered application to install the Solaris Operating Environment and other software. (Not documented in this book.)
	The Solaris 8 Operating Environment supports the Universal Disk Format (UDF) file system, enabling users to exchange data stored on CD-ROMs, disks, diskettes, DVDs, and other optical media.

Table B   *Solaris System Software Evolution (Continued)*

Release	New Features
	The Solaris Smart Card feature enables security administrators to protect a computer desktop or an individual application by requiring users to authenticate themselves by means of a smart card. (Not documented in this book.)
	The PDA Synchronization (PDA Sync) application synchronizes the data from applications such as Desktop Calendar, Desktop Mail, Memo, and Address, with data in similar applications on a user's Personal Digital Assistant (PDA). (Not documented in this book.)
	The Solaris 8 Software CDs and Languages CD include support for more than 90 locales, covering 37 languages. (Not documented in this book.)
	The Solaris Common Desktop Environment (CDE) contains new and enhanced features that incorporate easy-to-use desktop productivity tools, PC interoperability, and desktop management tools. (Not documented in this book.)
	The X Server is upgraded to the X11R6.4 industry standard that includes features to increase user productivity and mobility, including remote execution of X applications through a Web browser on any Web-based desktop, Xinerama, Color Utilization Policy, EnergyStar support, and new APIs and documentation for the developer tool kits. (Not documented in this book.)
	Role-Based Access Control (RBAC) enables system administrators to create specific roles by which they can assign superuser privileges for specific tasks to one or more individual users.
Solaris 8 (SunOS 5.8) 6/00	Mobile Internet Protocol (IP) enables the transfer of information to and from mobile computers such as laptop and wireless communications.
	Removable Media management fully supports removable media such as DVD-ROMs, Zip drives, Jaz drives, CD-ROMs, and diskettes.

New!

Table B Solaris System Software Evolution (Continued)

Release	New Features	
Solaris 8 (SunOS 5.8) 10/00	IP network multipathing provides recovery from single-point failures with network adapters and increased traffic throughput.	*New!*
	Web-Based Enterprise Management (WBEM) includes a description of the system properties that the CIM Object Manager uses and descriptions of the new `Solaris_Printer` and other printing definition classes.	
	You can use Solaris Print Manager to set up a Universal Serial Bus (USB) printer attached to a SPARC system with USB ports.	
Solaris 8 (SunOS 5.8) 1/01	Lightweight Directory Access Protocol (LDAP) is supported in the iPlanet Web Server directory server.	*New!*
	Solaris Management Console 2.0 software provides an integrated, GUI-based, network-aware suite of system administration tools.	
	You can manage role-based access control (RBAC) with the Solaris Management Console graphical interfaces.	
	Web-Based Enterprise Management (WBEM) adds an updated `init.wbem` command, updated security, Solaris Management Console Log Viewer, added descriptions of new `Solaris_Network 1.0.mof` file and `Solaris_Users1.0.mof` file.	
	Support for USB devices for Sun Blade 100, Sun Blade 1000, and SunRay systems.	
Solaris 8 (SunOS 5.8) 4/01	New Berkeley Internet Name Domain (BIND) functionality.	*New!*
	`sendmail` version 8.10 includes new command-line options, new and revised configuration file options, new defined macros, new and revised m4 configuration macros, new and modified compile flags, new delivery flag agents, new equates for delivery agents, new queue features, new uses for LDAP, new rule set features, new file locations, and a new built-in mailer feature.	

Table B   *Solaris System Software Evolution (Continued)*

Release	New Features
	Web-Based Enterprise Management (WBEM) includes the Sun WBEM SDK 2.4, new providers, and an MOF Compiler (mofcomp) description of the system properties that the CIM Object Manager uses, and descriptions of the new Solaris_Printer and other printing definition classes.
	IP network multipathing adds dynamic reconfiguration (DR), which uses IP network multipathing to decommission a specific network device with no impact on existing IP users.
	Mobile Internet Protocol IP enables system administrators to set up reverse tunnels.
Solaris 8 (SunOS 5.8) 7/01	Solaris PPP 4.0 supports both asynchronous and synchronous communications and offers Password Authentication Protocol (PAP) and Challenge-Handshake Authentication Protocol (CHAP) authentication. Solaris PPP 4.0 is highly configurable.
	Solaris Network Cache and Accelerator (NCA) provides a sockets interface through which any Web server can communicate with NCA with minimal modifications.
	IP network multipathing introduces the cPCI Network Interface (IPMP) Reboot Safe feature.
Solaris 8 (SunOS 5.8) 10/01	Dynamic Reconfiguration (DR) 3.0 replaces DR 3.0. DR 3.0 controls DR operations on the domain with the domain configuration server dcs(1M) command. You use the automated dynamic reconfiguration (ADR) commands to perform DR operations.
	USB support for keyboards, mouse devices, printers, and audio devices.
Solaris 8 (SunOS 5.8) 2/02	Sun RPC library extensions provide the Sun ONC+ RPC library with an asynchronous protocol.

Table B   *Solaris System Software Evolution (Continued)*

Release	New Features	
Solaris 9 (SunOS 5.9)	Solaris 9 Resource Manager enables system administrators to allocate computing resources, monitor resource use, and generate extended accounting information about resource use. Full functionality is administered with a command-line interface. Solaris Management Console enables performance monitoring and the setting of resource controls.	*New!*
	Fixed-priority (FX) scheduling class provides a scheduling policy for processes that require user or application control of scheduling priorities.	
	Web Start Flash Install feature that enables you to create a master system and then clone that configuration to other systems of the same architecture.	
	Live Upgrade feature that enables you to create a duplicate boot environment and install a Web Start Flash archive while the system is still running. When you are ready, you activate the duplicate environment and reboot the system.	
	New display options for the df, du, and ls commands that enable you to display disk usage and file or file system sizes in powers of 1024.	
	pargs and preap commands to improve process debugging.	
	Integrated version of the iPlanet Lightweight Directory Access Protocol (LDAP) directory.	
	Nameservice support for LDAP.	
	NIS+ to LDAP migration tools.	
	Solaris PPP 4.0.	
	Sun Internet FTP server.	
	Sun RPC library extension.	
	sendmail version 8.12.	
	Improved Solaris Network Cache and Accelerator (NCA).	
	IP network multipathing link-up and link-down notification support.	

Table B   Solaris System Software Evolution (Continued)

Release	New Features
	Mobile IP agent advertisements over dynamic interfaces.
	Bind version 8.2.4.
	Solaris volume manager.
	Solaris Management Console 2.1 with six new tools.
	smpatch(1M) command you can use to install patches on single or multiple systems, analyze patch requirements, and download required patches.
	Solaris Secure Shell commands that enable you to securely access a remote host over an unsecured network.
	Write CD file systems with the cdrw(1) command.

Freeware

The following freeware tools and libraries are included in the Solaris Operating Environment.

- bash—sh-compatible command language interpreter.
- bzip2—Block-sorting file compressor.
- gpatch—A tool that applies patch files to originals.
- gzip—GNU zip compression command.
- less—A pager similar to more.
- libz—Also known as zlib. A library that performs compression, specifically, RFCs 1950–1952.
- mkisofs—A tool that builds a CD image, using an iso9660 file system.
- rpm2cpio—Transforms a package in RPM format (Red Hat Package Manager) to a cpio archive.
- tcsh—C shell with file-name completion and command-line editing.
- zip—Compression and file packaging command.
- zsh—Command interpreter (shell) usable as an interactive login shell and as a shell script command processor.

1

INTRODUCING SOLARIS SYSTEM ADMINISTRATION

Winchester Mystery House [in San Jose, California] . . . was designed to baffle the evil spirits that haunted Sarah Winchester, eccentric heiress to the Winchester Arms fortune and mistress of the house. With 160 rooms and 2,000 doors, 13 bathrooms, 10,000 windows, 47 fireplaces, blind closets, secret passageways, and 40 staircases, the house is so complex that even the owner and servants needed maps to find their way.

—AAA, California/Nevada TourBook, 1991

Sarah Winchester, listening to the advice of psychics, believed that if she kept adding rooms to the house, she would not die and be subject to the influences of spirits who had been killed with the Winchester rifles manufactured by her husband.

The UNIX operating system is much like the Winchester Mystery House without, we hope, the evil spirits. The original operating system has been continually enhanced and expanded. There are many ways to get about, and, like the owner and the servants in the Winchester house, system administrators frequently need a map to help them get from place to place.

To add to the complexity, there are many versions of the UNIX operating system based on either Berkeley (or BSD) UNIX or AT&T's System V. This book serves as a map to some of the most frequently used "rooms" of the Solaris Operating Environment, which is an enhanced implementation of UNIX System V, Release 4 (usually referred to as SVR4).

Defining the System Administrator's Job

The system administrator's job is to keep the software (and perhaps hardware) functioning for a stand-alone system or for a set of systems on a network so that others can use the systems.

Typical duties of system administrators vary, depending on the number of systems supported and how the duties are divided up. It is not uncommon for system administrators to be experts in administering one or more areas and be inexperienced in others. Some administrators specialize in network administration, others in user accounts, and still others in areas such as printing.

The following list of typical system administration duties are described in part or in full in this book.

New!

- Installing systems.
  - Understanding Flash Install.
  - Understanding Live Upgrade.
- Understanding shells.
  - Using generic shell commands.
  - Using Bourne shell commands.
  - Using C shell commands.
  - Using Korn shell commands.
- Administering user and group accounts.
  - Adding user accounts.
  - Removing user accounts.
  - Changing user account information.
  - Creating new group accounts.
  - Using Solaris User Registration.
- Administering roles.
  - Granting users superuser permissions for specific tasks.
  - Creating, modifying, and deleting roles.
- Administering file systems.
  - Understanding the types of file systems.
  - Mounting and unmounting file systems.
  - Checking file system consistency.
  - Backing up and restoring files and file systems.
  - Creating cache file systems.

- Administering devices.
  - Understanding device autoconfiguration.
  - Allocating devices. *New!*
  - Understanding SCSI and PCI hot-plugging. *New!*
  - Using DVD-ROM devices.
  - Using tape cartridges.
  - Using Jaz or Zip drives. *New!*
  - Writing CD discs. *New!*
  - Understanding Volume Management.
  - Formatting diskettes.
  - Monitoring disk use.
  - Administering disks.
  - Understanding the Service Access Facility.
  - Setting up and using a bidirectional modem.
- Administering systems.
  - Finding system information.
  - Creating local mail aliases.
  - Configuring additional swap space.
  - Administering the system date and time.
- Administering network services.
  - Configuring systems for a network. *New!*
  - Finding network information.
  - Transferring files between systems.
  - Administering NIS+ databases.
  - Displaying network statistics.
  - Displaying network configuration information.
  - Understanding the IPv6 Internet protocol.
  - Displaying packet contents. *New!*
  - Using the Secure Shell. *New!*
- Administering printing.
  - Setting up a print client and print server.
  - Using printing commands.
- Recognizing file access problems.
  - Identifying problems with search paths.
  - Solving problems with permission and ownership.
  - Locating problems with network access.

The organization of this book matches the tasks listed above. To accomplish these tasks, you need to know when and how to perform the following tasks.

- Gain full access to all file systems and resources.
- Communicate with users.
- Shut down and start up systems.
- Monitor processes.

However, information about the following system administration tasks is beyond the scope of this book.

- Installing system software.
- Installing third-party software.
- Setting up and administering network services.
- Setting up and administering mail services.
- Adding and removing hardware.
- Administering security and accounting.
- Monitoring system and network performance.

The rest of the sections in this chapter, which describe how to accomplish the system administrator's tasks, introduce some basic commands and administrative tools.

Understanding Superuser Status

The *superuser* is a privileged user with unrestricted access to all files and commands. The superuser has the special UID (user ID) 0. The user name for this account is *root*. Note that the terms *root* and *superuser* have the same meaning and are used interchangeably in this book. You must be root to perform many system administration tasks, such as mounting and unmounting file systems, changing ownership or permissions for a file or directory you do not own, backing up and restoring file systems, creating device files, and shutting down the system.

You can become superuser in one of two ways.

- When logged in as another user, by typing the **su** (switch user) command and then typing the root password.
- From a login prompt, by typing **root** and then typing the root password.

When you have superuser privileges, the shell provides a special # (pound sign) prompt to remind you that you have extra access to the system. The system keeps a log that records each time the su command is used and who uses it. You can keep track of who is using the superuser account with the `su` command by consulting the `/var/adm/sulog` log file. This log does not track direct root logins.

Become superuser only when it is required, and avoid doing your routine work as superuser. Occasionally, you may need to log out of your user account and log in again as root. When a task in this book requires you to log in as root, you are instructed to do so. You should switch user (**su**) to root, perform the required tasks, and exit superuser status when the tasks are complete.

Because unauthorized access to root can be a serious security breach, always add a password to the root account. For enhanced security, change the root password frequently.

NOTE. The default shell for root is the Bourne shell. See Chapter 4, "Understanding Shells," for more information on shells.

Becoming Superuser (su)

Become superuser only when you need to perform a task that requires root permissions. Use the following steps to become superuser.

1. At the shell prompt ($ or %), type **su** and press Return. You are prompted for the superuser (root) password if one has been set up.
2. Type the superuser password and press Return. If you enter the password correctly, you have superuser (root) access to the system and the root shell prompt (#) is displayed in this terminal window.

```
oak% su
Password:
#
```

NOTE. If you want to use root's environment variables, type **su -** *and press Return.*

Exiting Superuser Status

To exit superuser status, simply type **exit** and press Return. The shell prompt is redisplayed.

```
# exit
oak%
```

Logging In as Root

For you to log in as root, ensure that the system is at a login prompt.

1. At a login prompt, type **root** and press Return. You are prompted for the root password.
2. Type the root password and press Return. If you enter the password correctly, you have superuser (root) access to the system, and the root prompt (#) is displayed in all open terminal windows.

```
login: root
Password:
```

With the Role-Based Access Control (RBAC) security feature, starting with the Solaris 8 Operating Environment, you can assign a subset of superuser privileges to a role and assign one or more users to that role. See Chapter 6, "Administering Rights and Roles," for more information. If you are a member of a role that assigns a subset of superuser privileges, you log in by using the su command with the role name and the password assigned to that role.

New!

Communicating with Users

An important part of your job as a system administrator is communicating with users to let them know that a task you are performing can affect their ability to use a system. Always let users know when you are about to perform a task that affects them, such as rebooting a system, installing new software, or changing the environment in some way.

You can communicate with users by personal visit or phone, but the most common way is by using the system to notify users in one of the following ways.

*   Display a system-specific message at login by using the message of the day.
*   Send a message directly to an individual user's terminal by using the write command.
*   Send a message to all users on a system by using the wall command.
*   Send a message to all users on a network by using the rwall command.
*   Send a message to an individual or a group of users by electronic mail.

Displaying System-Specific Messages at Login (motd)

Each time a user logs in to a system, the message of the day in the file /etc/motd is displayed. The message is not displayed to users who are already logged in and are using the system. Use motd to give users system-specific information that someone logging in would want to know. This information might include the release number of the installed operating system, changes to system software, the name of the newly installed (or deleted) third-party software, or a list of scheduled downtimes.

Be sure to keep the motd file current. If motd displays outdated messages, users may begin to ignore all the messages, thereby missing critical information when it is presented. Keep the message short: If the message is longer than a screenful of information, users won't be able to read the beginning because it will scroll off the top of the screen before they have a chance to read it.

Root should own the /etc/motd file and be the only user who has write permission to it.

```
oak% ls -l /etc/motd
-rw-r--r--   1 root      sys      49 Jan  1  1970 /etc/motd
oak%
```

NOTE. When the system software is installed, several files, including /etc/motd, have a time stamp of "Jan 1 1970." This date is the beginning of UNIX time. When you edit these files, the time stamp is updated.

The default /etc/motd file contains information about the Solaris release level. The following example shows the default /etc/motd file for Solaris 8.

```
paperbark% more /etc/motd
Sun Microsystems Inc.   SunOS 5.8        Generic  February 2000
paperbark%
```

Creating a Message of the Day

Use the following steps to create a message of the day.

1. Become superuser.
2. Use an editor such as vi to edit the /etc/motd file.
3. Delete any existing messages and type the new one.
4. Save the changes.

   The message is changed and is displayed the next time a user logs in to the system.

Sending a Message to an Individual User

You can send a message to the terminal of an individual user by using the `write` command. When a windowing system such as CDE or OpenWindows is used, each window is considered a separate login. If the user is logged in more than once, the message is directed to the console window.

> *NOTE. In the CDE environment, users may or may not use a console window. If the console window is not open, the user never sees the message because it is not displayed if the user opens a console window after the `write` message has been received.*

Typing a Short Message to an Individual User (write)

Use the following steps to send a short, one-time message to an individual user.

1. Type **write *username*** and press Return. *username* is the login name of the user.
2. Type the message you want to send.
3. When the message is complete, press Control-D.

   The message is displayed in the user's console window.

The following example shows a message a system administrator might type.

```
# write winsor
winsor is logged on more than one place.
You are connected to "console".
Other locations are:
pts/3
pts/4
pts/5
pts/6
pts/7
I'll come by at 12:00 to look at your problem.
#
```

As you can see, `winsor` is logged in to more than one place and `write` tells you that it is sending the message to the console window. The message is displayed in the user's console window, as shown in the following example.

```
paperbark%
        Message from winsor on paperbark (pts/6) [ Tue Mar  7 16:40:09 ] ...
I'll come by at 12:00 to look at your problem.
<EOT>
```

New!

However, if you are concerned that the user is not using the console window, you can use the `write` *username terminal* command to send the `write` message to any of the other terminals listed.

Sending a Message from a File to an Individual User (write)

If you have a longer message that you want to send to a number of users, use the following steps to create the message in a file and then use the file name as an argument to the `write` command.

1. Create a file containing the text of the message you want to send.
2. Type **write** *username* **<** *filename* and press Return.

In the following example, the system administrator uses the `cat` command to create a file named `message` that contains a short message and then uses the `write` command to send the message.

```
oak% cat > message
I'll come by at 12:00 to look at your problem.
oak% write ignatz@elm < message
write: ignatz logged in more than once ... writing to console
oak%
```

If the user is logged in to more than one window, the message is displayed in the user's console window, as shown below.

```
Message from fred@oak on ttyp1 at 11:20 ...
I'll come by at 12:00 to look at your problem.
EOF
```

As you can see, the user doesn't see any difference in the output created from a typed message and the message included from a file. The user can initiate a dialogue by using the `write` command to respond, but the dialogue is not truly interactive. Two `write` paths are open, one in each direction. See the `write`(1) manual page for more information. For more information about manual pages, see "Using Manual Pages" on page 94.

Sending a Message to All Users on a System or Network (wall, rwall)

You can use the `wall` (write all) command to simultaneously send a message to every user on a system. You can use the `rwall` (remote write all) command to simultaneously send a message to the console window of every user on a network.

NOTE. In the CDE environment, users may not use a console or a terminal window. If no console or terminal windows are opened, the user never sees the message because it is not displayed if the user opens a window after the `wall` *message has been received.*

Use the following steps to send a message to all users on a system.

1. Type **wall** and press Return.
2. Type the message you want to send.
3. When the message is complete, press Control-D. The message is displayed in the console window of each user on the system.

The following example shows a message a system administrator might type.

```
oak% wall
System will be rebooted at 12:00.
oak%
```

The message is displayed in the users' console window, as shown below.

```
Broadcast message from root on console ...
System will be rebooted at 12:00.
EOF
```

NOTE. Use the rwall *command carefully because it consumes extensive system and network resources.*

Use the following steps to send a message to all users of a group.

1. Type **rwall -n *group*** and press Return.
2. Type the message you want to send.
3. When the message is complete, press Control-D. The message is displayed in the console window of each user on the system.

The following example shows a message the system administrator might type to send to all members of the netgroup Eng.

```
oak% rwall -n Eng
System oak will be rebooted at 12:00.
oak%
```

The message is displayed in the users' console window, as shown below.

```
Broadcast message from root on console ...
System will be rebooted at 12:00.
```

You can also use the rwall command to send a message to all users on a system by typing **rwall *hostname*.**

NOTE. At many security-conscious sites, system administrators disable the rwall *command by commenting out the* walld *daemon line in the* /etc/inetd.conf *file.*

Sending a Message by E-Mail

E-mail is an effective way to communicate some system administration informational messages. However, this book does not describe how to use electronic mail. See the mail(1), mailtool(1), mailx(1), and dtmail(1X) manual pages for information about the mail programs.

Starting Up Systems

Starting up systems is an integral part of performing system administration tasks. This section describes procedures for routinely starting up systems. If a system does not start up gracefully, see your system documentation for information on how to diagnose booting problems.

Choosing an Init State

The init state (also called run level) determines what programs are started or initialized when a system is booted. A system can be in only one init state at a time. The Solaris Operating Environment has eight init states; the default init state for each system is specified in the /etc/inittab file. The default init state for the Solaris Operating Environment is run level 3. Table 1 shows the available run levels and the state of the system at each level.

Table 1   System Init States

Init State	Function
0	Firmware state.
S, or s	Single-user state. All file systems mounted.
1	Administrative state. All file systems mounted and user logins allowed.
2	Multiuser state (resources not exported). All daemons are running except the NFS server daemons.
3	Multiuser state. NFS resource-sharing available.
4	Alternative multiuser state (currently unused).

Table 1   System Init States (Continued)

Init State	Function
5	Power-down state. Shut down the operating system so that it is safe to turn off power to the system. If possible, turn off power on systems that support this feature.
6	Reboot. Shut down the system to init state 0 and then reboot to the multiuser state defined in the `inittab` file.

The `/sbin/init` command is responsible for keeping the system running correctly and is the command you use to change init states. You can also use the init states (with the `-i` option) as arguments to the `shutdown` command. The four types of system states are described below.

- Power-down (run level 5).
- Single-user (run levels 1 and s or S).
- Multiuser (run levels 2 and 3).
- Reboot (run level 6).

When preparing to do a system administration task, you need to determine which init state is appropriate for the system and the task at hand.

The /etc/inittab File

When you boot a system or use the `init` or `shutdown` command to change run levels, the `init` daemon starts processes by reading information from the `/etc/inittab` file. This file defines the following important items for the `init` process.

- The default run level for the system.
- The processes to start, monitor, and restart if they terminate.
- Actions to take when the system enters a new run level.

Each entry in the `/etc/inittab` file has the following fields.

```
id:rstate:action:process
```

Table 2 describes the fields in the `/etc/inittab` file.

Table 2   Fields in the inittab File

Field	Description		
id	A unique identifier for the entry.		
rstate	A list of run levels to which this entry applies.		
action	How the process specified in the process field is to be run. Possible values are listed below.		
	respawn	If the process does not exist, start the process. Do not wait for its termination (continue to scan the inittab file), and when the process dies, restart it. If the process currently exists, do nothing and continue scanning the inittab file.	*New!*
	wait	When init enters the run level that matches the *rstate* for the entry, start the process and wait for its termination. Ignore all subsequent reads of the inittab file while init is at the same run level.	*New!*
	once	When init enters a run level that matches the *rstate* for the entry, start the process and do not wait for its termination. When the process dies, do not restart it. If init enters a new run level and the process is still running from a previous run-level change, do not restart the program.	*New!*
	boot	Process the entry only at init's boot-time read of the inittab file. init starts the process and does not wait for its termination. When the process dies, init does not restart it. For this instruction to be meaningful, the *rstate* should either be the default or match init's run level at boot time. This action is useful for an initialization function following a hardware reboot.	*New!*

Table 2   Fields in the inittab File (Continued)

Field	Description	
	bootwait	Process the entry the first time `init` goes from single-user to multiuser state after the system is booted. If `initdefault` is set to 2, run the process right after the boot. `init` starts the process, waits for its termination, and when it dies, does not restart it.
	powerfail	Execute the process associated with this entry only when `init` receives a power fail signal, `SIGPWR`. (See signal(3C).)
	powerwait	Execute the process associated with this entry only when `init` receives a power fail signal, `SIGPWR`, and wait until it terminates before continuing any processing of `inittab`.
	off	When the process associated with this entry is currently running, send the warning signal `SIGTERM` and wait five seconds before forcibly terminating the process with the kill signal, `SIGKILL`. If the process is nonexistent, ignore the entry.
	ondemand	A synonym for the respawn action. The functionality is identical to respawn but it has a different keyword to divorce its association from run levels. Use this instruction only with a, b, or c values in the *rstate* field.
	initdefault	Scan an entry with this action only when `init` is initially invoked. `init` uses this entry to determine the initial run level. It takes the highest run level specified in the *rstate* field and uses that as its initial state. If the *rstate* field is empty, the value is interpreted as 0123456 and `init` enters run level 6. This interpretation loops the system (it goes to firmware and reboot continuously). In addition, if `init` does

Table 2   *Fields in the inittab File (Continued)*

Field		Description
		not find an `initdefault` entry in `inittab`, it requests an initial run level from the user at reboot.
	`sysinit`	Execute entry before `init` accesses the console (before the `Console Login:` prompt). Use this entry only to initialize devices that `init` might try to ask the run-level question. These entries are executed, and `init` waits for them to complete before continuing.
process		The command to execute.

The following example shows a default `/etc/inittab` file.

```
ap::sysinit:/sbin/autopush -f /etc/iu.ap
ap::sysinit:/sbin/soconfig -f /etc/sock2path
fs::sysinit:/sbin/rcS sysinit              >/dev/msglog 2<>/dev/msglog </dev/console
is:3:initdefault:
p3:s1234:powerfail:/usr/sbin/shutdown -y -i5 -g0 >/dev/msglog 2<>/dev/msglog
sS:s:wait:/sbin/rcS                        >/dev/msglog 2<>/dev/msglog </dev/console
s0:0:wait:/sbin/rc0                        >/dev/msglog 2<>/dev/msglog </dev/console
s1:1:respawn:/sbin/rc1                     >/dev/msglog 2<>/dev/msglog </dev/console
s2:23:wait:/sbin/rc2                       >/dev/msglog 2<>/dev/msglog </dev/console
s3:3:wait:/sbin/rc3                        >/dev/msglog 2<>/dev/msglog </dev/console
s5:5:wait:/sbin/rc5                        >/dev/msglog 2<>/dev/msglog </dev/console
s6:6:wait:/sbin/rc6                        >/dev/msglog 2<>/dev/msglog </dev/console
fw:0:wait:/sbin/uadmin 2 0                 >/dev/msglog 2<>/dev/msglog </dev/console
of:5:wait:/sbin/uadmin 2 6                 >/dev/msglog 2<>/dev/msglog </dev/console
rb:6:wait:/sbin/uadmin 2 1                 >/dev/msglog 2<>/dev/msglog </dev/console
sc:234:respawn:/usr/lib/saf/sac -t 300
co:234:respawn:/usr/lib/saf/ttymon -g -h -p "`uname -n` console login: " -T sun
  -d /dev/console -l console -m ldterm,ttcompat
```

Run Control Scripts

The `init` command uses a different script for each run level instead of grouping all of the run levels together. The files named by a run level are located in the `/sbin` directory.

The following listing shows the default run control scripts in the `/sbin` directory.

```
mopoke% ls -l /sbin/rc*
-rwxr--r--   3 root     sys          2792 Nov  8  2001 /sbin/rc0
-rwxr--r--   1 root     sys          3177 Nov  8  2001 /sbin/rc1
-rwxr--r--   1 root     sys          2922 Nov  8  2001 /sbin/rc2
-rwxr--r--   1 root     sys          2403 Nov  8  2001 /sbin/rc3
-rwxr--r--   3 root     sys          2792 Nov  8  2001 /sbin/rc5
-rwxr--r--   3 root     sys          2792 Nov  8  2001 /sbin/rc6
-rwxr--r--   1 root     sys          9934 Nov  8  2001 /sbin/rcS
mopoke%
```

Run control files are located in the /etc/init.d directory. These files are linked to corresponding run control files in the /etc/rc*.d directories. The files in the /etc directory define the sequence in which the scripts are performed within each run level. For example, the /etc/rc2.d directory contains files, listed below, that start and stop processes for run level 2.

New!

```
mopoke% ls /etc/rc2.d
K03samba          S21perf           S73nfs.client     S90wbem
K03sshd           S30sysid.net      S74autofs         S91afbinit
K06mipagent       S40llc2           S74syslog         S91gfbinit
K07dmi            S42ncakmod        S74xntpd          S91ifbinit
K07snmpdx         S47pppd           S75cron           S92volmgt
K16apache         S69inet           S75flashprom      S93cacheos.finish
K21dhcp           S70sckm           S75savecore       S94ncalogd
K27boot.server    S70uucp           S76nscd           S95IIim
K28kdc            S71ldap.client    S77sf880dr        S95svm.sync
K28kdc.master     S71rpc            S80lp             S96ab2mgr
K28nfs.server     S71sysid.sys      S80spc            S98efcode
README            S72autoinstall    S85power          S99audit
S01MOUNTFSYS      S72directory      S88sendmail       S99dtlogin
S05RMTMPFILES     S72inetsvc        S88utmpd
S10lu             S72slpd           S89bdconfig
S20sysetup        S73cachefs.daemon S89PRESERVE
mopoke%
```

The scripts are always run in ASCII sort order. The names of the scripts have the form [K,S][0-9][A-Z][0-99]. Files beginning with K are run to terminate (kill) some system process. Files beginning with S are run to start a system process. The actions of each run-level control script are summarized in the following sections.

The /sbin/rc0 Script   The /sbin/rc0 script performs the following tasks.

- Stop system services and daemons.
- Terminate all running processes.
- Unmount all file systems.

The /sbin/rc1 Script   The /sbin/rc1 script runs the /etc/rc1.d scripts to perform the following tasks.

- Stop system services and daemons.
- Terminate all running processes.
- Unmount all file systems.
- Bring the system up in single-user mode.

The /sbin/rc2 Script   The /sbin/rc2 script runs the /etc/rc2.d scripts to perform the following tasks.

Local system-related tasks:

- Mount all local file systems.
- Enable disk quotas if at least one file system was mounted with the quota option.

- Save editor temporary files in `/usr/preserve`.
- Remove any files in the `/tmp` directory.
- Start system activity data collecting, system accounting, and system auditing if configured. *New!*
- Start the system logging daemon (`syslogd`), set the default dump device, and rotate the `/var/adm/messages` file. *New!*
- Set the default scheduling class if the `/etc/dispadmin.conf` file exists. *New!*
- Start LP print service (`lpsched`) if a local printer is configured and clean up the print queue. *New!*
- Configure power management if appropriate. *New!*
- Start the `utmpd` daemon. *New!*
- Start `cron` and `vold` daemons.
- Configure serial device stream. *New!*
- Configure WBEM services. *New!*
- Synchronize volumes if required and start the `mdmonitord` daemon to monitor the physical components of the volumes. *New!*
- Start the CDE desktop login process, `dtlogin`, if appropriate. *New!*

Network service and security-related tasks:

- Configure the network interfaces, set `ifconfig` netmask, and configure network routing if appropriate. *New!*
- Start network service (`inetd` and `rpcbind`) daemons. *New!*
- Set the nameservice domain name, start various nameservice daemons, depending on whether the system is configured for a nameservice and whether the system is a client or a server. *New!*
- Start `keyserv`, `statd`, `lockd`, and `xntpd` daemons if appropriate.
- Start the logical link controller (`llc2`) if configured. *New!*
- Mount all NFS entries.
- Configure the Solaris Network Cache and Accelerator (NCA) and NCA logging if appropriate. *New!*
- Start the Solaris PPP server or client daemons (`pppoed` or `pppd`) if configured. *New!*
- Start LDAP cache manager (`ldap_cachemgr`) if configured. *New!*
- Start directory server (`slapd`) daemon if configured. *New!*
- Start DNS (`in.named`) daemon if configured. *New!*
- Start Service Location Protocol (`slpd`) daemon if configured. *New!*
- Configure system resource controls and system pools if the `/etc/rctladm.conf` and `/etc/pooladm.conf` files exist. *New!*

New!
- Start the `cachefsd`, `automount`, and `sendmail` daemons if appropriate.

New!
- Start the `htt_server` process.

New!
Install-related tasks:

- Configure the boot environment for the Live Upgrade software on system startup or system shutdown.
- Check for the presence of the `/etc/.UNCONFIGURE` file to determine whether to reconfigure the system.
- Reboot the system from the installation medium or a boot server if either `/.PREINSTALL` or `/AUTOINSTALL` exists.

New!
Hardware-related tasks:

- Start the Sun Fire 150000 key management daemon (`sckmd`) if appropriate.
- Start the Sun Fire 880 Dynamic Reconfiguration daemon (`sf880drd`) if appropriate.
- Run the flash PROM update script.
- Configure any graphic frame buffers or graphic accelerators.
- Run the FCode interpreter daemon (`efdaemon`) if necessary.

New!
Transition the following services between run-level changes:

- Apache (`tomcat`).
- Boot server (`in.rarpd`, `rpc.bootparamd`, or `rpld`).
- DHCP (`in.dhcpd`).
- Kerberos KDC (`krb5dc`) and Kerberos administration (`kadmind`).
- Mobile IP (`mipagent`).
- NFS server (`nfsd`, `mountd`, `nfslogd`).
- Samba (`smdb` and `nmdb`).
- Secure shell (`sshd`).
- Solstice Enterprise Agents (`dmispd` and `snmpXdmid`).

NOTE. Many of the system services and applications started at run level 2 depend on what software is installed on the system.

The /sbin/rc3 Script   The `/sbin/rc3` script runs the `/etc/rc3.d` scripts to perform the following tasks.

New!
- Start the Apache server daemon (`tomcat`) if configured.

New!
- Start the DHCP daemon (`in.dhcpd`) if appropriate.

New!
- Start Kerberos KDC (`krb5dc`) and Kerberos administration (`kadmind`) daemons if configured.

- Start Mobile IP daemon (`mipagent`) if configured.
- Start the Samba daemons (`smdb` and `nmdb`) if configured.
- Start the secure shell daemon (`sshd`) if appropriate.
- Start the Solstice Enterprise Agents (`dmispd` and `snmpXdmid`).
- Clean up the `/etc/dfs/sharetab` file.
- Start the NFS server daemons `nfsd`, `mountd`, and `nfslogd` if appropriate.
- If the system is a boot server, start `rarpd`, `rpc.bootparamd`, and `rpld`.

The /sbin/rc5 and /sbin/rc6 Scripts   The `/sbin/rc5` and `/sbin/rc6` scripts run the `/etc/rc0.d/K*` and `S*` scripts (in that order) to perform the following tasks.

- Kill all active processes.
- Unmount the file systems.

The /sbin/rcS Script   The `/sbin/rcS` script runs the `/etc/rcS.d` scripts to bring the system to run level S and perform the following tasks.

- Establish a minimal network.
- Mount `/usr` if necessary.
- Set the system name.
- Check the root and `/usr` file systems.
- Mount pseudofile systems (`/proc` and `/dev/fd`).
- Rebuild the device entries for reconfiguration boots.
- Check and mount other file systems to be mounted in single-user mode.

Finding the Run Level for a System

To find the run level for a system, type **who -r** and press Return. The run level, date and time of the last run-level change, process termination status, process exit status, number of times at this run level since the last reboot, and previous run level are displayed.

In the following example, the system named `paperbark` is at the default multiuser run level (3), the date and time of the last run-level change is `May 2 08:34`, the process exit status is `3`, the number of times at this run level since the last reboot is `0`, and the previous run level is `S`.

```
paperbark% who -r
    .       run-level 3  May  2 08:34    3      0  S
paperbark%
```

The next sections describe how you might use each init state.

New!

Using OpenBoot PROM State, Run Level 0

Use run level 0 to shut down the operating system and put the system into OpenBoot PROM (on SPARC systems only).

Using Single-User State, Run Level s and S

Use run level s or S when performing administrative tasks that require you to be the only user on the system with all file systems mounted and accessible. The terminal from which you issue the init s command becomes the console. No other users are logged in.

> *NOTE. In the Solaris 7 release, Bug ID 1154696 was fixed so that you can cleanly bring a system to run level S (or single-user mode) by using the* shutdown -s *or the* init -s *command. The* inittab *file and the* rc *scripts in the* /etc/init.d *directory and the* /etc/rcn.d *directories have been modified to ensure that system run-level transitions are made cleanly and efficiently.*

Using Administrative State, Run Level 1

Use run level 1 as a single user to access all available file systems with no user logins allowed.

Using Multiuser State, Run Level 2

Use run level 2 for normal operations. Multiple users can access the system and the entire file system. All daemons are running except for NFS server and syslog.

> *NOTE. A* daemon *is a special type of program that, once activated, starts itself and carries out a specific task without any need for user input. Daemons typically are used to handle jobs, such as printing, mail, communication, UPS monitors (to shut down a system in case the UPS says that a power outage is imminent), and Web servers.*

Using Remote Resource-Sharing State, Run Level 3

Use run level 3 for normal operations with NFS resource-sharing available.

Using Alternative Multiuser State, Run Level 4

Run level 4 is an alternative multiuser state, currently not used.

Using Power-Down State, Run Level 5

Use run level 5 to shut down the operating system so that it is safe to turn off power to the system. If possible, automatically turn off power on systems that support this feature.

Using Reboot State, Run Level 6

Use run level 6 to shut down the system to run level 0, and then reboot to multiuser level (or to whatever level is the default in the `inittab` file).

Changing Run Levels

Use either the `telinit` or `init` command to change run levels. The `telinit` command takes a one-character argument that tells `init` what run level to use. Although you can use the `init` command directly, `telinit` is the preferred command to use to change system run states.

Use the following steps to change run levels.

1. Become superuser.
2. Type **telinit** *n* and press Return. Replace the variable *n* with the number of the init state you want to use.

The following example shuts down the system and places the focus at the OpenBoot PROM prompt (on SPARC systems only).

```
oak% su
Password:
# telinit 0
```

The following example changes the system to single-user state.

```
oak% su
Password:
# telinit 1
```

The following example changes to multiuser state, with no NFS server daemons running.

```
oak% su
Password:
# telinit 2
```

The following example changes to multiuser state, with NFS server daemons running.

```
oak% su
Password:
# telinit 3
```

The following example shuts down and reboots a system.

```
oak% su
Password:
# telinit 6
```

Using Platform-Specific Booting Protocols

The OpenBoot PROM and Interface (SPARC Platforms)

Each SPARC system has a programmable read-only memory (PROM) chip with a program called the *monitor*. The monitor controls operation of the system before the kernel is available. When you turn a system on, the monitor runs a quick self-test procedure to check things such as the hardware and memory on the system. If the monitor finds no errors, the system begins the automatic boot process.

> *NOTE. Some older systems may require PROM upgrades before they will work with the Solaris Operating Environment. Contact your local service provider for more information.*

The boot process consists of the boot PROM, boot programs, kernel initialization, and system initialization phases. These phases are summarized in Table 3.

Table 3   Description of the SPARC Boot Process

Boot Phase	Description
OpenBoot PROM	The OpenBoot PROM displays system identification information and then runs self-test diagnostics to verify the hardware and memory of the system.
	Then, the OpenBoot PROM loads the `bootblk` primary boot program, which loads the secondary boot program from the default boot device located in the UFS file system.
Boot programs	The `bootblk` program finds and executes the `ufsboot` secondary boot program and loads it into memory.
	After the `ufsboot` program is loaded, `ufsboot` loads the kernel.

Table 3   Description of the SPARC Boot Process (Continued)

Boot Phase	Description
Kernel initialization	The kernel initializes itself and begins loading modules, using `ufsboot` to read the files. When the kernel has loaded enough modules to mount the root file system, it terminates the `ufsboot` program and continues by using its own resources.
	The kernel creates a user process and starts the `/sbin/init` process, which starts other processes by reading the `/etc/inittab` file.
`init`	The `/sbin/init` process starts the run control (`/sbin/rc*`) scripts, which execute a series of other scripts (`/etc/rc*.d/S*`). These scripts check and mount file systems, start various processes, and perform system maintenance tasks.

The OpenBoot firmware on the SPARC PROM not only initiates the boot process but also provides a command-line interface. OpenBoot provides two modes. The restricted monitor mode, which displays the > prompt, provides only three commands. These commands enable you to boot the operating system (b *specifiers*), resume the execution of a halted program (c), or enter the Forth Monitor (n).

The Forth Monitor, also referred to as *new command mode*, is the default mode of the OpenBoot firmware. The Forth Monitor displays the ok prompt. This monitor enables you to access an extensive set of diagnostic commands for hardware and software. Anyone who has access to the system console can access these functions. To access the restricted monitor, at the ok PROM prompt, type **old-mode** and press Return.

Displaying the PROM Release for a System   To display the PROM release for a system, at the ok PROM prompt, type **banner** and press Return. Hardware configuration information, including the release number of the PROM is displayed, as shown in the following example.

```
ok banner
    Sun Blade 100 (UltraSPARC-IIe, Keyboard Present
    Copyright 1998-2002 Sun Microsystems, Inc. All rights reserved.
    OpenBoot 4.5, 128 MB memory, installed, Serial #50640486.
    Ethernet address 0:23:ba:4:b6:66, Host ID 8304b666
```

OpenBoot Configuration Information   OpenBoot configuration parameters are listed in Table 4.

NOTE. Not all OpenBoot systems support all parameters. Defaults can vary depending on the system and the PROM revision.

Table 4   Boot Configuration Parameters

auto-boot?	If true, boot automatically after power-on or reset. Default is true.
boot-command	
	If auto-boot? is true, execute command. Default is boot.
boot-device	
	Device from which to boot. boot-device can contain zero or more device specifiers separated by spaces. Each device specifier can be either a PROM device alias or a PROM device path. The boot PROM tries to open each successive device specifier in the list, beginning with the first device specifier. The first device specifier that opens successfully is used as the device to boot from. Default is disk net.
boot-file	File to boot (an empty string lets the secondary booter choose default). Default is an empty string.
diag-device	
	Diagnostic boot source device. Default is net.
diag-file	File from which to boot in diagnostic mode. Default is an empty string.
diag-level	Diagnostics level. Values include min and max. The default value is min. The values off and menus are no longer available.
diag-switch?	
	If true, run in diagnostic mode. Default is false.
fcode-debug?	
	If true, include name parameter for plug-in device FCodes. Default is false.
input-device	
	Input device used at power-on (usually keyboard, ttya, or ttyb). Default is keyboard.
keyboard-click?	
	If true, enable keyboard click. Default is false.
keymap	Keymap for custom keyboard. There is no default.

New! (beside diag-level row)

New! (beside diag-switch? row)

Table 4   Boot Configuration Parameters (Continued)

`nvramrc`	NVRAM startup script. Default is an empty string.
`oem-banner`	Custom OEM banner (enabled by setting `oem-banner?` to `true`). Default is an empty string.
`oem-banner?`	
	If `true`, use custom OEM banner. Default is `false`.
`output-device`	
	Output device used at power-on (usually `screen`, `ttya`, or `ttyb`). Default is `screen`.
`sbus-probe-list`	
	Which SBus slots are probed and in what order. Default system-specific because different SBus systems have different numbers of SBus slots. Newer Sun systems have a PCI bus instead of an SBus.
`scsi-initiator-id`	
	SCSI bus address of host adapter, range 0–7. Default is `7`.
`security-mode`	
	Firmware security level (options: `none`, `command`, or `full`). If set to `command` or `full`, system prompts for PROM security password. Default is `none`.
`security-password`	
	Firmware security password (never displayed). Can be set only when security mode is set to `command` or `full`.
`ttya-mode`	TTYA (baud rate, #bits, parity, #stop, handshake). Default is `9600,8,n,1,-`.
	Fields, in left-to-right order, are described below.

	`baud rate`	110, 300, 1200, 4800, 9600...
	`data bits`	5, 6, 7, 8
	`parity`	n (none), e (even), o (odd), m (mark), s (space)
	`stop bits`	1, 1.5, 2
	`handshake`	– (none), h (hardware: rts/cts), s (software: xon/xoff)

`ttyb-mode`	TTYB (baud rate, #bits, parity, #stop, handshake). Default is `9600,8,n,1,-`.
	Fields, in left-to-right order, are described below.

New! (beside `nvramrc` row)

New! (beside `sbus-probe-list` row)

Table 4   *Boot Configuration Parameters (Continued)*

	baud rate	110, 300, 1200, 4800, 9600...
	data bits	5, 6, 7, 8
	stop bits	1, 1.5, 2
	parity	n (none), e (even), o (odd), m (mark), s (space)
	handshake	- (none), h (hardware: rts/cts), s (software: xon/xoff)
`ttya-ignore-cd`		
	If `true`, operating system ignores carrier-detect on TTYA. Default is `true`.	
`ttyb-ignore-cd`		
	If `true`, operating system ignores carrier-detect on TTYB. Default is `true`.	
`ttya-rts-dtr-off`		
	If `true`, operating system does not assert DTR and RTS on TTYA. Default is `false`.	
`ttyb-rts-dtr-off`		
	If `true`, operating system does not assert DTR and RTS on TTYB. Default is `false`.	
`use-nvramrc?`		
	If `true`, execute commands in `nvramrc` during system start-up. Default is `false`.	
`version2?`	If `true`, hybrid (1.x/2.x) PROM comes up in version 2.x. Default is `true`.	
`watchdog-reboot?`		
	If `true`, reboot after watchdog reset. Default is `false`.	

You can display and set the list of OpenBoot commands from Solaris by using the `eeprom` command or display the list at the `ok` PROM prompt by typing **printenv** and pressing Return.

The following example uses the `eeprom` command without arguments to display the current settings.

New!

```
mopoke% eeprom
test-args: data not available.
diag-passes=1
pci-probe-list=7,c,3,8,d,13,5
local-mac-address?=false
```

```
fcode-debug?=false
ttyb-rts-dtr-off=false
ttyb-ignore-cd=true
ttya-rts-dtr-off=false
ttya-ignore-cd=true
silent-mode?=false
scsi-initiator-id=7
oem-logo: data not available.
oem-logo?=false
oem-banner: data not available.
oem-banner?=false
ansi-terminal?=true
screen-#columns=80
screen-#rows=34
ttyb-mode=9600,8,n,1,-
ttya-mode=9600,8,n,1,-
output-device=screen
input-device=keyboard
load-base=16384
auto-boot?=true
boot-command=boot
diag-file: data not available.
diag-device=disk net
boot-file: data not available.
boot-device=disk:a disk net
use-nvramrc?=false
nvramrc: data not available.
security-mode=none
security-password: data not available.
security-#badlogins=0
diag-script=none
diag-level=max
diag-switch?=false
error-reset-recovery=boot
mopoke%
```

The following example sets the method for setting the `auto-boot?` parameter to `true`. You may need to enclose the command in double quotation marks to prevent the shell from interpreting the question mark.

```
# eeprom "auto-boot?"=true
#
```

Alternatively, you can precede the question mark with an escape character (\) to prevent the shell from interpreting the question mark.

Commands Used to View or Modify Configuration Variables   Table 5 describes the commands you can use from the `ok` PROM prompt to view or modify the OpenBoot configuration variables.

Table 5   Commands to View or Modify OpenBoot Configuration Variables

Command	Description
help [*category*]	Display a list of help categories. Help for an individual category is displayed if you specify a *category* argument.

Table 5　　*Commands to View or Modify OpenBoot Configuration Variables (Continued)*

Command	Description
printenv [*variable*]	Display the variable, the current value, and the default value. If you specify a variable, the values for that variable are displayed.
setenv *variable value*	Set *variable* to the specified numeric or text value. Changes are permanent but often do not take effect until after you reset or reboot the system.
set-default *variable*	Reset the value of the variable to the factory default.
set-defaults	Reset all variable values to the factory defaults.
password	Set security password.

OpenBoot Firmware Security Levels　　The OpenBoot firmware provides three levels of system security: none, command, and full.

For the none security level, no password is required. Users can change all OpenBoot settings, including the boot disk partition and execute any command. By default, Sun systems are shipped with the OpenBoot security level set to none.

For the command security level, a password is required for all commands except boot and go (continue system operation after a Stop-A, L1-A, or Break sequence).

For the full security level, a password is required for all OpenBoot commands except go.

You can set the OpenBoot security level either while running Solaris or from the ok PROM prompt.

Use the following steps to set the OpenBoot security level from Solaris.

1. Become superuser.
2. Type **eeprom security-mode=*level*** and press Return.

   The security level is set as specified by the *level* argument.

In the following example, the security level is set to command.

```
paperbark% su
Password:
# eeprom security-mode=command
```

To set the OpenBoot security level, at the ok PROM prompt, type
security-mode=*level* and press Return.

In the following example, the security level is set to full.

```
ok security-mode=full
```

For more information, refer to the eeprom(1M) manual page or to the
OpenBoot documentation available from Sun Microsystems.

The PC BIOS (IA Platforms)

For IA platforms, before the kernel is started, the system is controlled by the
read-only-memory (ROM) Basic Input/Output System (BIOS), which is the
firmware interface on a PC.

Hardware adapters can have an onboard BIOS that displays the physical
characteristics of the device and that can be used to access the device. During
the startup sequence, the PC BIOS checks for the presence of an adapter
BIOS and, if it finds one or more, loads and executes each one. The BIOS for
each individual adapter runs self-test diagnostics and displays device
information.

Boot Subsystems

You can make the choices about booting a system at three times during the
Solaris IA boot process, as described below.

- Primary Boot Subsystem (Partition Boot Menu)—This first menu is
  displayed if multiple bootable fdisk partitions exist on the disk. The
  menu enables you to boot from one of the fdisk partitions. By default,
  the active partition is booted if you take no action. Note that if you boot
  a non-Solaris partition, the next two menus are never displayed.
- Interrupt the Autoboot Process—If you interrupt the autoboot process,
  you can access the Configuration Assistant, which enables you to boot
  the Solaris Operating Environment from a different boot device,
  configure new or misconfigured hardware, or perform other device- or
  boot-related tasks.
- Current Boot Parameters Menu—This menu has two forms, one for a
  normal Solaris boot and one for a Solaris installation boot.
    - The normal Current Boot Parameters menu enables you to boot
      the Solaris system with options or to enter the boot interpreter.
    - The install Current Boot Parameters menu enables you to choose
      the type of installation to be performed or to customize the boot.

Table 6 describes the IA Platform boot subsystems.

Table 6   *IA Platform Boot Subsystems*

Boot Subsystem	Description
Primary Boot Subsystem	This menu is displayed if the disk you are booting from contains more than one `fdisk` partition in addition to the Solaris `fdisk` partition.
Secondary Boot Subsystem	This menu is displayed each time you boot the Solaris Operating Environment. The Solaris Operating Environment is booted automatically unless you interrupt it to run the Solaris Device Configuration Assistant.
Solaris Device Configuration Assistant/Boot Diskette	You can access the Solaris Device Configuration Assistant menu by using the Solaris Device Configuration Assistant Boot Diskette to boot the system or by interrupting the autoboot process when booting the Solaris Operating Environment from an installed disk.
Current Boot Parameters Menu	This menu is displayed when you boot from a disk with the Solaris Operating Environment installed or if you want to install the Solaris release from the Solaris installation CD or the network. In either case, this menu presents a list of boot options.

When booting an IA platform, the Configuration Assistant performs the following tasks during the device identification phase.

- Scans for devices installed on the system.
- Displays the identified devices.
- Enables you to perform optional tasks such as choosing a keyboard type and editing devices and their resources.

During the boot phase, the system displays a list of devices from which to boot. The asterisk (*) marks the default boot device. You can perform optional tasks, such as editing autoboot and property settings.

The boot process consists of the BIOS, boot programs, kernel initialization, and system initialization phases. These phases are summarized in Table 7.

Table 7   Description of the IA Boot Process

Boot Phase	Description
BIOS	When the system is turned on, the PC BIOS runs self-test diagnostics to verify the hardware and memory on the system. If the BIOS finds no errors, the system begins to boot automatically. If errors are found, error messages are displayed describing recovery options. BIOS for additional hardware devices are run. The BIOS boot program tries to read the first physical sector from the boot diskette or hard drive. This first disk sector contains the mboot master boot record, which is loaded and executed. If BIOS finds no mboot program, an error message is displayed.
Boot programs	The mboot program contains disk information needed to find the active partition and the location of the pboot Solaris boot program. mboot loads and executes pboot. pboot loads bootblk, which is the primary boot program. bootblk loads the secondary boot program located in the UFS file system. If the disk has more than one bootable partition, bootblk reads the fdisk table to locate the default boot partition and builds and displays a menu of available partitions. You have a 30-second timeout interval during which you can choose an alternative partition from which to boot. This step occurs only if more than one bootable partition is present on the system. bootblk finds and executes either the boot.bin or ufsboot secondary boot program in the root file system. At this point, you have a 5-second timeout interval during which you can interrupt the autoboot to start the Configuration Assistant.

Table 7   Description of the IA Boot Process (Continued)

Boot Phase	Description
	`boot.bin` or `ufsboot` starts a command interpreter that executes the `/etc/bootrc` script, which provides a menu of choices for booting the system. The default action is to load and execute the kernel. You have a 5-second timeout interval during which you can specify a boot option or start the boot interpreter.
Kernel initialization	The kernel initializes itself and begins loading modules, using `boot.bin` or `ufsboot` to read the files. When the kernel has loaded enough modules to mount the root file system, it terminates the secondary boot program and continues by using its own resources. The kernel creates a user process and starts the `/sbin/init` process, which starts other processes by reading the `/etc/inittab` file.
`init`	The `/sbin/init` process starts the run control (`/sbin/rc*`) scripts, which execute a series of other scripts (`/etc/rc*.d/S*`). These scripts check and mount file systems, start various processes, and perform system maintenance tasks.

Booting a System

If a system is powered off, turning it on starts the multiuser boot sequence. The following procedures tell you how to boot in different states from the `ok` PROM prompt. If the PROM prompt is `>`, type **n** to display the `ok` prompt, and then follow the appropriate steps.

NOTE. The PROM prompt description is for SPARC systems.

Table 8 describes commands for booting a system for different reboot reasons.

Table 8   Commands for Booting a System

Reboot Reason	Boot Instructions
Turning off system power because of anticipated power outage.	Turn on system power.

Table 8　　*Commands for Booting a System (Continued)*

Reboot Reason	Boot Instructions
Changing kernel parameters in the /etc/system file.	Reboot to run level 3 (multiuser mode with NFS resources shared) (boot). See "Booting in Multiuser State" on page 34 for more information.
Performing file system maintenance, such as performing a backup or restoring system data.	Use Control-D from run level S to bring the system back to run level 3.
Repairing a system configuration file such as /etc/system.	Interactive boot (boot -a). See "Booting Interactively" on page 34 for more information.
Changing pseudodevice parameters in the /etc/system file.	Reconfiguration boot (boot -r). See "Booting After Adding New Hardware" on page 36 for more information.
Adding or removing hardware from the system.	Reconfiguration boot (boot -r) plus turning on system power after adding or removing hardware. See "Booting After Adding New Hardware" on page 36 for more information.
Booting the kernel debugger to track down a system problem.	Boot kadb. See "Booting the System with the Kernel Debugger" on page 38.
Repairing an important system file that is causing system boot failure.	Recovery boot (SPARC platform, sync; IA platform, kadb). See "Booting a System for Recovery Purposes (SPARC Platform) and "Booting a System for Recovery Purposes (IA Platform)" on page 39.
Recovering from a hung system and forcing a crash dump.	Recovery boot (SPARC platform, sync; IA platform, kadb). See "Booting a System for Recovery Purposes (SPARC Platform)" on page 38 and "Booting a System for Recovery Purposes (IA Platform)" on page 39.

Booting in Multiuser State

To boot in multiuser state, at the ok PROM prompt, type **boot** and press Return. The automatic boot procedure starts on the default drive, displaying a series of start-up messages. The system is brought up in multiuser state.

Booting in Single-User State

To boot in single-user state, at the ok PROM prompt, type **boot -s** and press Return. The system boots to single-user state and prompts you for the root password.

```
ok boot -s

INIT: SINGLE USER MODE
Type Ctrl-d to proceed with normal start-up,
(or give root password for system maintenance)
Type the root password and press Return.
```

NOTE. To continue the process and bring the system up in multiuser state, press Control-D.

Booting Interactively

You may boot interactively if you want to make a temporary change to the system file or the kernel. In this way, you can test your changes and recover easily if you have any problems.

1. At the ok PROM prompt, type **boot -a** and press Return. The boot program prompts you interactively.
2. Press Return to use the default kernel or type the name of the kernel to use for booting.
3. Press Return to use the default modules directory path, or type the default path for the modules and press Return.
4. Press Return to use the default /etc/system file, or type the name of the system file and press Return.
5. Press Return to use the default root file system. Type **ufs** for local disk booting or **nfs** for diskless clients.
6. Press Return to use the default physical name of the root device, or type the device name.

In the following example, the user accepted the default choices (shown in square brackets [ ]) by pressing Return.

```
ok boot -a
(Hardware configuration messages)
rebooting from -a
Boot device: /sbus/esp@0,800000/sd@0,0 File and args: -a
Enter filename [/kernel/unix]:
```

```
Enter default directory for modules [/platform/SUNW,Ultra-2/kernel
 /platform/sun4u/kernel /kernel /usr/kernel]:
Name of system file [/etc/system]:
(Copyright notice)
root filesystem type [ufs]
Enter physical name of root device
[/sbus@if,0/SUNW,fas@e,8800000/sd@0.0:a]:
Swap filesystem type [swapfs]
Configuring IPv4 interfaces: le0
Hostname: paperbark
The system is coming up. Please wait.
(fsck messages)
(Startup messages)
paperbark login:
```

Looking at the Boot Messages

The most recent boot messages are stored in the /var/adm/messages file. To see these messages after you have booted the system, type **more /var/adm/messages** and press Return. The /usr/sbin/dmesg command is obsolete; however, you can still use it to display boot messages.

> NOTE. *You can now view* /usr/sbin/dmesg *text from a CDE terminal window, which was not possible in previous releases.*

Because the /var/adm/messages file is maintained in chronological order, the most current boot messages are at the end of the file. The following example shows the last 30 lines of the /var/adm/messages file.

```
paperbark% tail -30 /var/adm/messages
Mar  7 18:11:15 paperbark swapgeneric: [ID 308332 kern.info] root on
 /sbus@1f,0/SUNW,fas@e,8800000/sd@0,0:a fstype ufs
Mar  7 18:11:16 paperbark sbus: [ID 349649 kern.info] zs0 at sbus0: SBus0 slot
 0xf offset 0x1100000 Onboard device sparc9 ipl 12
Mar  7 18:11:16 paperbark genunix: [ID 936769 kern.info] zs0 is
 /sbus@1f,0/zs@f,1100000
Mar  7 18:11:16 paperbark sbus: [ID 349649 kern.info] zs1 at sbus0: SBus0 slot
 0xf offset 0x1000000 Onboard device sparc9 ipl 12
Mar  7 18:11:16 paperbark genunix: [ID 936769 kern.info] zs1 is
 /sbus@1f,0/zs@f,1000000
Mar  7 18:11:19 paperbark rootnex: [ID 349649 kern.info] ffb0 at root: UPA
 0x1e 0x0
Mar  7 18:11:19 paperbark genunix: [ID 936769 kern.info] ffb0 is
 /SUNW,ffb@1e,0
Mar  7 18:11:19 paperbark unix: [ID 987524 kern.info] cpu0: SUNW,UltraSPARC
 (upaid 0 impl 0x10 ver 0x22 clock 168 MHz)
Mar  7 18:11:22 paperbark hme: [ID 517527 kern.info] SUNW,hme0 : Sbus (Rev Id
 = 22) Found
Mar  7 18:11:22 paperbark sbus: [ID 349649 kern.info] hme0 at sbus0: SBus0
 slot 0xe offset 0x8c00000 and slot 0xe offset 0x8c02000 and slot 0xe offset
 0x8c04000 and slot 0xe offset 0x8c06000 and slot 0xe offset 0x8c07000
 Onboard device sparc9 ipl 6
Mar  7 18:11:22 paperbark genunix: [ID 936769 kern.info] hme0 is
 /sbus@1f,0/SUNW,hme@e,8c00000
Mar  7 18:11:24 paperbark genunix: [ID 454863 kern.info] dump on
 /dev/dsk/c0t0d0s1 size 512 MB
Mar  7 18:11:26 paperbark hme: [ID 517527 kern.info] SUNW,hme0 : Internal
 Transceiver Selected.
Mar  7 18:11:26 paperbark hme: [ID 517527 kern.info] SUNW,hme0 :
 Auto-Negotiated   10 Mbps Half-Duplex Link Up
Mar  7 18:12:01 paperbark pseudo: [ID 129642 kern.info] pseudo-device: pm0
Mar  7 18:12:01 paperbark genunix: [ID 936769 kern.info] pm0 is /pseudo/pm@0
Mar  7 18:12:01 paperbark pseudo: [ID 129642 kern.info] pseudo-device: tod0
```

```
Mar  7 18:12:01 paperbark genunix: [ID 936769 kern.info] tod0 is /pseudo/tod@0
Mar  7 18:12:02 paperbark sendmail[250]: [ID 702911 mail.crit] My unqualified
 host name (paperbark) unknown; sleeping for retry
Mar  7 18:12:03 paperbark pseudo: [ID 129642 kern.info] pseudo-device:
 devinfo0
Mar  7 18:12:03 paperbark genunix: [ID 936769 kern.info] devinfo0 is
 /pseudo/devinfo@0
Mar  7 18:12:06 paperbark sws.smc[290]: [ID 987397 daemon.notice] [1 admin.195
 0 (SW) NOTICE]: Running with SWS Configuration file
 "/etc/ehttp/server.conf".
Mar  7 18:12:10 paperbark sws.smc[290]: [ID 409041 daemon.error] [1
 servlet.353 0 (SW) ERR]: Servlet smc load error.
Mar  7 18:12:10 paperbark sws.smc[290]: [ID 420037 daemon.notice] [1
 servlet.919 0 (SW) NOTICE]: Servlet Engine (with JSDK2.0) started.
Mar  7 18:12:10 paperbark sws.smc[290]: [ID 111395 daemon.notice] [1 httpd.105
 0 (SW) NOTICE]: Sun_WebServer/2.1 server started.
Mar  7 18:12:15 paperbark sws.smc[290]: [ID 329940 daemon.notice] [1 httpd.135
 0 (SW) NOTICE]: Shutting down server.
Mar  7 18:12:18 paperbark sws.smc[368]: [ID 987397 daemon.notice] [1 admin.195
 0 (SW) NOTICE]: Running with SWS Configuration file
 "/etc/ehttp/server.conf".
Mar  7 18:12:19 paperbark sws.smc[368]: [ID 420037 daemon.notice] [1
 servlet.919 0 (SW) NOTICE]: Servlet Engine (with JSDK2.0) started.
Mar  7 18:12:19 paperbark sws.smc[368]: [ID 111395 daemon.notice] [1 httpd.105
 0 (SW) NOTICE]: Sun_WebServer/2.1 server started.
Mar  7 18:13:02 paperbark sendmail[250]: [ID 702911 mail.alert] unable to
 qualify my own domain name (paperbark) -- using short name
paperbark%
```

Booting After Adding New Hardware

New!

A reconfiguration boot tells the system to probe for all connected devices and build the names for them in the /devices and /dev directories. Adding new devices to a system formerly required a complete reconfiguration boot.

New!

With the Solaris 8 release, the devfsadm command manages the special device files in the /dev and /devices directories. The new devfsadmd daemon handles both processing of reconfiguration boot and updating of the /dev and /devices directories and responds to dynamic reconfiguration events. Because devfsadmd automatically detects device configuration changes generated by any reconfiguration event, you no longer need to perform a reconfiguration boot (boot -r) when you add most new hardware to a system. Some device addition and removal scenarios may still require you to perform a reconfiguration boot. For example, adding a USB Zip Drive requires a boot -r before the system can recognize the device. See Chapter 8, "Administering Devices," for more information.

With the OpenBoot PROM, you can use the -r option to the boot command so that the operating system knows to look for new device drivers and incorporate them as part of the boot process.

1. Load the new device driver, following the instructions included with the hardware.
2. Shut down your system and install the new hardware.

3. Type **boot -r** and press Return. A reconfiguration script is run to load all the device drivers listed in the modules directories and to create the corresponding hardware nodes.

Alternatively, if you add another device with the driver already installed, you can use the following commands to tell the system to recognize the new device.

```
# touch /reconfigure
# _INIT_RECONFIG=YES /etc/init.d/drvconfig
# _INIT_RECONFIG=YES /etc/init.d/devlinks
```

Forcing a Crash Dump and Rebooting the System

Sometimes you need to save crash dumps of the operating system. Starting with the Solaris 7 Operating Environment, saving crash dumps is enabled by default.

Starting with the Solaris 8 Operating Environment, the halt command provides a -d option that enables you to force a crash dump before stopping the system.

New!

1. Become superuser.
2. Type **halt -d** and press Return.

   The disk is synchronized and a crash dump is written and the OpenBoot PROM ok prompt is displayed. A message like the following example is displayed:

```
dumping to /dev/dsk/c1t0d0s1 offset 107479040, content: kernel.
100% done: 11207 pages dumped, compression ratio 2.95, dump succeeded
Program terminated
```

Dumps are compressed to improve performance and to fit more information into existing swap partitions.

Typing the dumpadm command with no arguments shows the current settings, as shown in the following example.

```
mopoke% su
Password:
# dumpadm
      Dump content: kernel pages
       Dump device: /dev/dsk/c1t0d0s1 (swap)
  Savecore directory: /var/crash/mopoke
   Savecore enabled: yes
#
```

Refer to the dumpadm(1M) manual page for more information.

The savecore(1M) command works with alternative kernels. In the past, the symbol table was generated from the currently installed kernel. The symbol table is now part of the dump. Before this change, if you patched the Solaris kernel and then crashed before you rebooted the system, the crash dump was useless because the symbol table generated was from the patched kernel, not the running kernel.

savecore supports large files because the file it writes can be greater than 2 Gbytes.

Administering Crash Dumps

You can administer the crash dump facility with the dumpadm(1M) command, which provides the following capabilities.

- Turn on or off saving crash dumps.
- Set up a dedicated dump device (raw partition) or swap entry. The default is the best swap partition.
- Change directory where savecore(1M) puts its files. The default is /var/crash/*hostname*.
- Dump all memory or only kernel pages. The default is kernel.

Booting the System with the Kernel Debugger

Use the following steps to boot the system by using the kernel debugger.

1. Type the stop key sequence for your system.

   The specific sequence depends on your keyboard type. For example, you can press Stop-A or L1-A. On terminals, press the Break key.

2. At the ok prompt, type **sync** and press Return.

   The disk is synchronized and a crash dump is written.

3. When you see the syncing file systems... message, press the abort key sequence again.

4. At the ok prompt, type **boot kadb** and press Return.

5. Review kadb booting messages (starting with Rebooting with command: kadb) to verify that the system is booting with the kernel debugger.

Refer to the kadb(1M) manual page for information about how to use the kernel debugger.

Booting a System for Recovery Purposes (SPARC Platform)

Use the following procedure on SPARC platforms when the boot process fails. The boot process can fail, for example, when an important file such as /etc/passwd has an invalid entry.

1. Boot from the installation CD-ROM (**boot cdrom -s**) or from an installation server on the network (**boot -net -- -s**) and press Return.

2. Type **mount /dev/dsk/** *device-name* **/a** and press Return.

3. Type **cd /a/** *directory* and press Return.

4. Type **TERM=sun;export TERM** and press Return.

5. Remove the invalid entry from the file with an editor such as vi.

6. Type **cd /** and press Return.

7. Type **umount /a** and press Return.

8. Type **init 6** and press Return.

   The system is rebooted.

9. Verify that the system boots to run level 3.

   The login prompt is displayed when the boot process has finished successfully.

The following example shows how to repair the **/etc/passwd** file after booting from a local CD-ROM.

```
ok boot cdrom -s
(Boot messages are displayed here)
# mount /dev/dsk/c0t3d0s0 /a
# cd /a/etc
# TERM=sun;export TERM
# vi passwd
(Remove or edit invalid entry)
# cd /
# umount /a
# init 6
```

Booting a System for Recovery Purposes (IA Platform)

Use the following procedure on IA platforms when the boot process fails. The boot process can fail, for example, when an important file such as /etc/passwd has an invalid entry.

1. Boot from the Solaris 2 installation CD or from the network. Use steps a through g. If you are booting from the network, skip step a.

   a. Insert the Solaris 2 installation CD into the CD-ROM drive.

   b. (Optional) If the disk you are booting from doesn't contain the Solaris 8 Intel Platform Edition or compatible version, insert the Configuration Assistant/Boot Diskette into the primary diskette drive (DOS drive A).

   c. If the system displays the Type any key to reboot prompt, press any key to reboot the system. At this prompt, you can also press the reset button. If the system is shut down, turn the system on with the power on/off switch.

d. At the Solaris Device Configuration Assistant screen, press the F2 key (F2_Continue).

    Device identification is performed, and a screen identifying the devices is displayed.

e. At the Identified Devices screen, press the F2 key (F2_Continue). Bootable drivers are loaded.

f. From the Boot Solaris screen, select the CD-ROM drive or network as the boot device. Then, press the F2 key (F2_Continue).

    The Solaris boot option screen is displayed.

g. At the `Select the type of installation:` prompt, type **b -s** and press Return.

    After a few minutes, the single-user mode # prompt is displayed.

2. Type **mount /dev/dsk/*device-name* /a** and press Return.

    The root file system is mounted.

3. Type **cd /a/*directory*** and press Return.

4. Type **TERM=sun;export TERM** and press Return.

    The terminal type is set and exported.

5. Remove the invalid entry from the file with an editor such as vi.

6. Type **cd /** and press Return.

7. Type **umount /a** and press Return.

8. Type **init 6** and press Return.

    The system is rebooted.

9. Verify that the system boots to run level 3.

    The login prompt is displayed when the boot process has finished successfully.

The following example shows how to repair the **/etc/passwd** file after you boot from a local CD-ROM.

```
Type any key to reboot
SunOS Secondary Boot version 3.00
Solaris Intel Platform Edition Booting System
Running Configuration Assistant...
Autobooting from Boot path: /pci@0,0/pci-ide@7,1/ide@0/cmdk@0,0:a
If the system hardware has changed, or to boot from a different
device, interrupt the autoboot process by pressing ESC.
Press ESCape to interrupt autoboot in 5 seconds.
        .
        .
        .
Boot Solaris
Select one of the identified devices to boot the Solaris kernel and
choose Continue.
To perform optional features, such as modifying the autoboot and property
settings, choose Boot Tasks.
An asterisk (*) indicates the current default boot device.
> To make a selection use the arrow keys, and press Enter to mark it [X].
[ ]   NET : DEC 21142/21143 Fast Ethernet
```

```
on Board PCI at Dev 3
[ ]   DISK: (*) Target 0, QUANTUM  FIREBALL1280A
on Bus Mastering IDE controller on Board PCI at Dev 7, Func 1
[ ]   DISK: Target 1:ST5660A
on Bus Mastering IDE controller on Board PCI at Dev 7, Func 1
[ ]   DISK: Target 0:Maxtor 9 0680D4
on Bus Mastering IDE controller on Board PCI at Dev 7, Func 1
[ ]   CD  : Target 1:TOSHIBA  CD-ROM XM-5602B  1546
on Bus Mastering IDE controller on Board PCI at Dev 7, Func 1
F2_Continue    F3_Back    F4_Boot Tasks    F6_Help
        .
        .
        .
               <<< Current Boot Parameters >>>
Boot path: /pci@0,0/pci-ide@7,1/ide@0/cmdk@0,0:a
Boot args: kernel/unix -r
Select the type of installation you want to perform:
1 Solaris Interactive
2 Custom JumpStart
3 Solaris Web Start
  Enter the number of your choice followed by <ENTER> the key.
  If you enter anything else, or if you wait for 30 seconds,
    an interactive installation will be started.
  Select type of installation:  b -s
        .
        .
        .
# mount /dev/dsk/c0t0d0s0 /a
        .
        .
# cd /a/etc
# vi passwd
(Remove invalid entry)
# cd /
# umount /a
# init 6
```

Aborting a Booting Process

Occasionally, you may need to abort the booting process. The specific abort key sequence depends on your keyboard type. For example, on SPARC systems with a Sun keyboard, you might press Stop-A or L1-A. On TTY terminals, press the Break key.

To abort the booting process, type the abort key sequence for your system. When you abort the boot process, the monitor displays the ok PROM prompt.

```
ok
```

Type **boot** and press Return to restart the boot process, or type **help** and press Return to display a list of help options. If your terminal shows the > monitor prompt, type **n** to get the ok prompt.

Shutting Down a System

The following sections describe how to choose a shutdown and use it and init commands to shut down a system.

The Solaris Operating Environment is designed to be left running continuously so that the e-mail and network software can work correctly. You must, however, halt or shut down a system when performing the following tasks.

- Turning off system power.
- Installing a new release.
- Preparing for a power outage.
- Adding hardware to a system.
- Performing maintenance on a file system.

Choosing Which Shutdown Command to Use

When preparing to do a system administration task, you need to determine which shutdown command is appropriate for the system and the task at hand. The next sections describe how you might use each of the available shutdown commands.

- /usr/sbin/shutdown
- /etc/telinit and /sbin/init
- /usr/sbin/halt
- /usr/sbin/reboot
- /usr/sbin/uadmin

These commands initiate shutdown procedures, kill all running processes, write out any new data to the disk, and shut down the Solaris Operating Environment to the appropriate run level.

shutdown

Use the shutdown command when shutting down a system with multiple users. The shutdown command sends a warning message to all users who are logged in, waits 60 seconds (the default), and then shuts down the system to single-user state. You can choose a different default wait time.

telinit and init

Use the telinit or init command to shut down a single-user system or to change its run level. The init command changes the run level of the system. The telinit command tells init what run level you want. You can use the commands interchangeably, but telinit is the preferred command. You can use telinit to place the system in power-down state (init 0) or in single-user state (init 1).

NOTE. Use telinit/init *and* shutdown *as the preferred method of changing system state. These programs are the most reliable way to shut down a system because they use a number of* rc *scripts to kill running processes.*

halt

Use the halt command when the system must be stopped immediately and it is acceptable not to warn any current users. The halt command shuts down the system without any delay and does not warn any other users on the system. The halt command does not run the rc shutdown scripts and is not the preferred method for shutting down a system.

reboot

Use the reboot command to shut down a system that does not have multiple users and to bring it back into multiuser state. The reboot command does not warn users on the system, does not run the rc scripts, and is not the preferred method for shutting down a system.

Shutting Down a Multiuser System

Before shutting down a multiuser system, inform the other users on the system and give them time to complete critical procedures such as saving changes.

1. Type **who** and press Return.
   A list of all logged in users is displayed.
2. Type **ps -ef** and press Return.
   A list of system activities is displayed. If the activity is acceptable for running shutdown, go to the next step.
3. Become superuser.
4. Type **/usr/sbin/shutdown** and press Return.
   You are asked to confirm that you want to shut down the system.
5. Type **y**.
   A message is broadcast to all users. After a 60-second wait, the system is shut down to single-user state, and you are prompted for the root password.
6. Type the root password.
   The system is in single-user state, and you can perform any maintenance task.
7. Press Control-D to return to the default run system level.

```
paperbark% su
Password:
# cd /
```

```
# shutdown

Shutdown started.    Tue May  2 13:16:57 WST 2000

Broadcast Message from root (pts/7) on paperbark Tue May  2 13:16:59...
The system paperbark will be shut down in 1 minute

Broadcast Message from root (pts/7) on paperbark Tue May  2 13:17:29...
The system paperbark will be shut down in 30 seconds

Do you want to continue? (y or n):  y
Broadcast Message from root (pts/7) on paperbark Tue May  2 13:17:53...
THE SYSTEM paperbark IS BEING SHUT DOWN NOW! ! !
LOG OFF NOW OR RISK YOUR FILES BEING DAMAGED
(Shutdown messages)

INIT: SINGLE USER MODE
Type control-d to proceed with normal startup,
(or give root password for system maintenance):
```

Shutting Down a System: Alternative Ways

To change the default actions of the shutdown command, choose one of the tasks in the following six sections.

Shutting Down a System Without Confirmation

Use the following steps to shut down a system without confirmation.

1. Become superuser.
2. Type **/usr/sbin/shutdown -y** and press Return.

    The shutdown proceeds without asking you to type **y** to confirm.

Changing the Shutdown Grace Period

The default is for the shutdown command to provide a 60-second grace period to enable users to save their changes. Use the following steps to change the shutdown 60-second grace period.

1. Become superuser.
2. Type **cd /** and press Return.
3. Type **/usr/sbin/shutdown -g** *nnn* and press Return.

    The grace period is changed to the number of seconds you specify.

    The following example changes the grace period to 120 seconds.

```
# cd /
# shutdown -g120
```

Shutting Down and Rebooting a Multiuser System

Use the following steps to shut down and reboot a multiuser system.

1. Become superuser.
2. Type **cd** **/** and press Return. You must be in the root directory to run the shutdown command.
3. Type **shutdown** **-i6** and press Return. A message is broadcast to all users and the rc scripts are executed; the system is shut down to power-down state and then brought back up to multiuser state.

Shutting Down a Single-User System

To shut down a single-user system, type **telinit** **0** (or **init** **0**) and press Return. The init command runs scripts that bring the system down cleanly. No warning messages are broadcast.

Shutting Down and Rebooting a Single-User System

To shut down and reboot a single-user system, type **telinit** **6** (or **init** **6**) and press Return. Information is written to the disk, all active processes are killed, and the system is brought to a power-down state. The system is then rebooted to the default level (usually multiuser).

Shutting Down a System in a Hurry

To shut down a system in a hurry, type **uadmin** **2** **0** and press Return. The system displays the OpenBoot PROM prompt.

Monitoring Processes

The programs that are running on a system at any one time are called *processes*. You can monitor the status of processes, control how much CPU time a process gets, find or signal processes, and suspend or halt the execution of a process.

Commands for Monitoring Processes

The ps (process status) command is your main tool for obtaining information about processes. You can use the ps command in combination with the grep command to focus your search for specific information.

You can also use the `dispadmin, priocntl, nice, renice, pgrep,` and `pkill` commands to manage processes. Table 9 lists the commands for managing processes.

Table 9   Commands for Managing Processes

Command	Description
ps	Check the status of active processes on a system and display detailed information about the processes.
dispadmin	List default scheduling policies.
priocntl	Assign processes to a priority class and manage process priorities.
nice	Raise or lower the priority of a timesharing process.
renice	Alter the scheduling priority of one or more running processes.
pgrep, pkill	Find or signal processes.

Refer to the `ps`(1), `dispadmin`(1M), `priocntl`(1), `nice`(1), `renice`(1), `pgrep`(1), and `pkill`(1) manual pages for complete information about these commands.

In addition, the `/usr/proc/bin` directory contains process tools that you can use to display highly detailed information about the processes listed in `/proc`. The `/proc` directory is also known as the process file system (procfs). ProcFS maps process information into the file system, enabling you to manipulate process attributes with a file-access paradigm. For more information about the `/proc` file system, see "Types of File Systems" on page 182.

The process tools are similar to some options of the `ps` command, except that the output provided by the tools is more detailed. In general, the process tools do the following.

- Display more details about processes, such as `fstat` and `fcntl` information, working directories, and trees of parent and child processes.
- Provide control over processes, enabling users to stop or resume them.

Table 10 summarizes the `/usr/proc/bin` commands.

Table 10   Process Tools in the /usr/proc/bin Directory

Command	Description
pcred *pid*	Display credentials.
pfiles *pid*	Display fstat and fcntl information for open files.
pargs	Print the command arguments (argv[]), environment variables, or auxiliary vector. New in the Solaris 9 release. *New!*
pflags *pid*	Show /proc tracing flags, pending and held signals, and other status information for each LWP.
pldd *pid*	Show dynamic libraries linked into each process.
pmap *pid*	Show address map space.
prun *pid*	Restart the process.
psig *pid*	Display signal actions.
pstack *pid*	Display hex+symbolic stack trace for each LWP.
pstop *pid*	Stop the process.
ptime *pid*	Time the process, using microstate accounting.
ptree *pid*	Show process trees containing specified PIDs.
pwait *pid*	Wait for the specified processes to terminate.
pwdx *pid*	Display current working directory.

Starting with the Solaris 8 release, some of the proc tools can also be applied to corefiles. A corefile is a snapshot of a process's state and is produced by the kernel before terminating a process with a signal or with the gcore(1) command. Some of the proc tools may need to derive the name of the executable corresponding to the process that dumped core or the names of shared libraries associated with the process. These files are needed, for example, to provide symbol table information for pstack(1). If the proc tool in question is unable to locate the needed executable or shared library, some symbol information is unavailable for display. Similarly, if a corefile from one operating system release is examined on a different operating system release, the runtime link-editor debugging interface (librtld_db) may not be able to initialize. In this case, symbol information for shared libraries is not available.

For a complete description of the process tools, refer to the proc(1) manual page. For information about how to use the process tools commands to display details about processes and how to start and stop them, see "Using the /usr/proc/bin Commands" on page 55.

Using the ps Command

You can use the ps command to determine which processes are running (or not running) and to get the following detailed information about an individual process.

- PID (process ID).
- UID (user ID).
- Priority.
- Control terminal.
- Memory use.
- CPU time.
- Current status.

The ps command takes a snapshot of system activity at the time you type the command. If you are monitoring system activity by time, be aware that the results are already slightly out-of-date by the time you read them. Table 11 shows the most frequently used options for the ps command. See the ps(1) manual page for a complete list of options.

Table 11　Most Frequently Used Options for the ps Command

Option	Description
-e	Report on all processes.
-f	Show the owner of the process, by name instead of by UID, in the first column. This option turns off -1, -t, -s, and -r and turns on -a.
-1	Generate a long report, which includes all fields except STIME.

What the ps Command Reports

When you type **ps -e** and press Return, you get a report that looks like the following example.

```
mopoke% ps -e
   PID TTY        TIME CMD
     0 ?         0:16 sched
     1 ?         0:00 init
     2 ?         0:00 pageout
     3 ?         0:00 fsflush
   411 ?         0:00 sac
   237 ?         0:00 utmpd
   208 ?         0:00 nscd
    49 ?         0:00 sysevent
    56 ?         0:00 picld
   115 ?         0:00 in.route
   179 ?         0:00 automoun
   133 ?         0:00 rpcbind
   189 ?         0:00 syslogd
```

```
 155 ?         0:00 inetd
 213 ?         0:00 lpsched
 170 ?         0:00 lockd
 176 ?         0:00 statd
 511 ?         0:00 dtfile
 193 ?         0:00 cron
 226 ?         0:00 powerd
 440 ?         0:00 Xsession
 414 ?         0:00 ttymon
 261 ?         0:02 vold
 249 ?         0:00 smcboot
 248 ?         0:00 smcboot
 250 ?         0:00 smcboot
 266 ?         0:00 htt
 268 ?         0:00 htt_serv
 401 ?         0:00 dmispd
 372 ?         0:00 auditd
 283 ?         0:00 dwhttpd
 284 ?         0:23 dwhttpd
 416 ?         0:00 sshd
 434 ?         0:00 sendmail
 454 ?         0:00 speckeys
 432 ?         0:00 sendmail
 439 ?         0:00 dtlogin
 450 ?         0:00 fbconsol
 487 pts/3     0:00 csh
 503 pts/3     0:00 dtsessio
 484 pts/3     0:00 sdt_shel
 485 ?         0:00 dsdm
 584 pts/6     0:00 ftp
 419 ?         0:00 mibiisa
 418 ??        0:00 fbconsol
 402 ?         0:00 snmpXdmi
 415 ?         0:04 Xsun
 395 ?         0:00 dtlogin
 392 ?         0:00 snmpdx
 412 console   0:00 ttymon
 417 ?         0:00 dtlogin
 504 ?         0:00 rpc.ttdb
 502 pts/3     0:00 ttsessio
 510 ?         0:01 dtwm
 537 ?         0:00 rpc.rsta
 513 ??        0:01 dtterm
 514 ?         0:00 sdtperfm
 515 pts/3     0:00 sh
 516 pts/3     0:00 dtpad
 548 ?         0:00 cat
 518 ?         0:00 sdtvolch
 535 pts/7     0:00 csh
 522 pts/4     0:00 csh
 525 pts/5     0:00 csh
 529 pts/6     0:00 csh
 638 pts/4     0:00 ps
 569 ?         0:04 .netscape
 568 ?         0:00 netscape
 570 ?         0:00 netscape
 571 ?         0:00 .netscape
mopoke%
```

The columns are described in Table 12.

Table 12   Columns in the ps -e Report

Column	Description
PID	Process identification number.

Table 12   Columns in the ps -e Report (Continued)

Column	Description
TTY	The terminal from which the process (or its parent) started. If the process has no controlling terminal, this column contains a question mark (?). Processes with question marks usually are system processes.
TIME	The cumulative amount of CPU time used by the process.
CMD	The name of the command that generated the process. Note that for the ps -e command only the first eight characters of the file name are displayed.

When you type **ps -el** and press Return, you get a listing that looks like the following example.

Newl

```
mopoke% ps -el
 F S   UID   PID  PPID  C PRI NI     ADDR      SZ   WCHAN TTY      TIME CMD
19 T     0     0     0  0   0 SY        ?       0         ?        0:16 sched
 8 S     0     1     0  0  40 20        ?     150       ? ?        0:00 init
19 S     0     2     0  0   0 SY        ?       0       ? ?        0:00 pageout
19 S     0     3     0  0   0 SY        ?       0       ? ?        0:00 fsflush
 8 S     0   411     1  0  40 20        ?     216       ? ?        0:00 sac
 8 S     0   237     1  0  40 20        ?     130       ? ?        0:00 utmpd
 8 S     0   208     1  0  40 20        ?     349       ? ?        0:00 nscd
 8 S     0    49     1  0  40 20        ?     268       ? ?        0:00 sysevent
 8 S     0    56     1  0  40 20        ?     367       ? ?        0:00 picld
 8 S     0   115     1  0  40 20        ?     207       ? ?        0:00 in.route
 8 S     0   179     1  0  40 20        ?     475       ? ?        0:00 automoun
 8 S     0   133     1  0  40 20        ?     272       ? ?        0:00 rpcbind
 8 S     0   189     1  0  40 20        ?     414       ? ?        0:00 syslogd
 8 S     0   155     1  0  40 20        ?     297       ? ?        0:00 inetd
 8 S     0   213     1  0  40 20        ?     391       ? ?        0:00 lpsched
 8 S     0   170     1  0  40 20        ?     266       ? ?        0:00 lockd
 8 S     1   176     1  0  40 20        ?     306       ? ?        0:00 statd
 8 S  1001   511   503  0  50 20        ?    1097       ? ?        0:00 dtfile
 8 S     0   193     1  0  40 20        ?     253       ? ?        0:00 cron
 8 S     0   226     1  0  40 20        ?     174       ? ?        0:00 powerd
 8 S  1001   440   439  0  40 20        ?     240       ? ?        0:00 Xsession
 8 S     0   414   411  0  40 20        ?     217       ? ?        0:00 ttymon
 8 S     0   261     1  0  40 20        ?     363       ? ?        0:02 vold
 8 S     0   249   248  0  40 20        ?     215       ? ?        0:00 smcboot
(Additional lines deleted from this example)
```

Table 13 describes the fields in the long listing report.

Newl

NOTE. The ADDR *field is obsolete and contains only question marks.*

Table 13   Summary of Fields in a ps -el Report

Field	Description
F	Hexadecimal flags, which, added together, indicate the process's current state. These flags are available for historical purposes. You should ascribe no meaning to them.

Newl

Table 13   Summary of Fields in a ps -el Report (Continued)

Field	Description	
	00	The process has terminated. Its place in the process table is free.
	01	The process is a system process and is always in memory.
	02	The process is being traced by its parent.
	04	The process is being traced by its parent and has been stopped.
	08	The process cannot be awakened by a signal.
	10	The process is currently in memory and is locked until an event completes.
	20	The process cannot be swapped.
S	The current state of the process, as shown by one of the following letters.	
	O	Currently running on the processor.
	S	Sleeping; waiting for an I/O event to complete.
	R	Ready to run.
	I	Idle; process is being created.
	Z	Zombie. The process has terminated and the parent is not waiting, but the dead process is still in the process table.
	T	Stopped because the parent is tracing the process.
	X	Waiting for more memory.
UID	The user ID of the owner of the process.	
PID	The process identification number.	
PPID	The parent process's identification number.	
C	The process's CPU use (that is, an estimate of the percentage of CPU time used by the process).	
PRI	The process's scheduling priority. Higher numbers mean lower priority.	
NI	The process's nice number, which contributes to its scheduling priority. Making a process "nicer" means lowering its priority so it does not use up as much CPU time.	
ADDR	The memory size of the process. Note that the ADDR field is obsolete and is not displayed with some options.	

New!

Table 13   Summary of Fields in a ps -el Report (Continued)

Field	Description
SZ	The amount of virtual memory required by the process. This is a good indication of the demand the process puts on system memory.
WCHAN	The address of an event for which the process is sleeping. When this field is blank, the process is running.
TTY	The terminal from which the process (or its parent) started, or a question mark to indicate there is no controlling terminal (which usually indicates a system process).
TIME	The total amount of CPU time used by the process since it began.
COMD	The command being run by the process.

Uses for the ps Report

When you need to check on which processes or daemons are running, use the ps -e option. If you need more detailed information about a process, use the ps -el options. See the ps(1) manual page for a complete list of options. With experience, you will know how the report should look and be able to judge what is out of the ordinary.

The following guidelines can help you spot potential problems.

- Look for many identical jobs owned by the same user. This condition may result from someone running a script that starts a lot of background jobs without waiting for any of the jobs to terminate. Talk to the user to find out if that's the case. If necessary, use the kill command to terminate some of the processes. See "Killing Processes" on page 53 for more information on killing a process.

- Look at the TIME field for processes that have accumulated a large amount of CPU time. Such processes might be in an endless loop.

- Look at the C field to find unimportant processes that consume a large percentage of CPU time. If you do not think a process warrants so much attention, use the priocntl command to lower its priority. See the priocntl(1M) manual page for more information.

- Look at the SZ field for processes that consume too large a percentage of memory. If a process is a memory hog, you may need to kill the process. If many processes are using lots of memory, the system may need more memory.

- Watch for a runaway process that uses progressively more CPU time. You can check this by using the -f option to see the start time (STIME) of the process and by watching the TIME field for the accumulation of CPU time.

Signalling a Process

New!

The Solaris Operating Environment provides a way to signal processes. A signal is an asynchronous notification of an event. With signals, you can interrupt a process or a thread within a process as the result of a specific event. Asynchronous signals can result from the current instruction stream. Such signals originate as hardware trap conditions for conditions such as illegal address references (segmentation violation) and illegal math operations (floating-point exceptions).

The system also implements asynchronous signals that result from an external event that may not be related to the current instruction stream. Examples of such signals are job control signals, one process or thread sending a signal to another, or a kill signal sent to terminate a process.

For example, the SIGHUP signal hangs up a process, SIGINT interrupts a process, and SIGKILL kills a process. Refer to signal(3HEAD) for a complete list of signals.

Most signals can be ignored, a signal can be caught and a process-specific signal handler invoked, or a process can permit the default action to be taken. Every signal has a predefined default action.

Killing Processes

You can use the kill command to deliver different signal types to programs. Many of those signals instruct a program to perform some predetermined and normal action. The following section describes how to use the kill command to terminate a process.

You can use the kill command to eliminate a process entirely. The syntax of the kill command is kill *-signal PID*, where *signal* is a number or a name and *PID* is the process ID of the process to which you send the signal.

The usual way to kill a process is to send it a certain signal. The TERM (-15) signal generally cleanly shuts down a process. If TERM (or some other signal you know the process is prepared to accept and act on) doesn't work, then you can send the KILL (-9) signal as a last resort. The KILL (-9) signal may result in loss of data, so you should not use it indiscriminately.

Sometimes processes do not die when you use the kill command. The three most common cases are listed below.

- The process is waiting for a device, such as a tape drive, to complete an operation before exiting.
- The process is waiting for resources that are unavailable because of NFS problems. To kill such a process, type **kill -QUIT** *PID*.

- The process is a zombie, as shown by the message defunct in the ps report. A zombie process is one that has had all its resources freed but has not received an acknowledgment from a parent process, receipt of which would ordinarily remove its entry from the process table. The next time a system is booted, zombie processes are cleared. The Solaris 9 Operating Environment provides the preap(1) command that you can use to force a defunct process to be reaped by its parent.

New!

Use the following steps to kill a process.

1. Become superuser.

   You must be superuser to kill a process that you do not own.

2. Type **ps -e** and press Return.

   A list of the processes is displayed. Use the PID (process ID) number in the first column as input to the next step. If you know which process is causing the problem, you can type **ps -e | grep** ***process-name*** and press Return to focus your search.

3. Type **kill** ***PID*** and press Return.

   When you type **kill** with no signal argument, signal 15 is sent.

4. Type **ps -e** and press Return.

   Check to see if the process has terminated. If it's still there, go to step 5.

5. Type **kill -9** ***PID*** and press Return.

   The process should be terminated. To see a description of the signals used by kill, type **man -s5 signal** and press Return.

In the following example, OpenWindows is frozen on the system oak. You must log in remotely from another system and kill the process.

```
elm% rlogin oak
Password:
oak% ps -e | grep openwin
PID TTY      TIME COMD
2212 pts/0   0:00 openwin
2213 pts/1    0:00 grep openwin
oak% su
Password:
oak# kill 2212
oak# exit
oak% logout
elm%
```

Using the /usr/proc/bin Commands

Starting with the Solaris 2.6 release, you can use a set of commands to display detailed, technical information about active processes. These commands are summarized in Table 14.

Table 14   Process Tools in the /usr/proc/bin Directory

Command	Description
pcred *pid**	Display credentials.
pfiles *pid**	Display fstat and fcntl information for open files.
pflags *pid**	Show /proc tracing flags, pending and held signals, and other status information for each LWP.
pldd *pid**	Show dynamic libraries linked into each process.
pmap *pid**	Show address map space.
prun *pid*	Restart the process.
psig *pid**	Display signal actions.
pstack *pid**	Display hex+symbolic stack trace for each LWP.
pstop *pid*	Stop the process.
ptime *pid*	Time the process, using microstate accounting.
ptree *pid*	Show process trees containing specified PIDs.
pwait *pid*	Wait for specified processes to terminate.
pwdx *pid**	Display current working directory.

*Must be superuser to execute.

> *NOTE. If you use the* /usr/proc/bin *commands frequently, add the process tool directory to your* PATH *variable to make the commands more easily accessible.*

All of the /usr/bin/proc commands use the process ID (PID) as the argument to the command. You can obtain the PID by using the ps -e and the grep commands to search for the name of the process you want more information about. The following example displays the PID for the openwin process in the first column.

```
oak% ps -e | grep openwin
PID TTY      TIME COMD
2212 pts/0   0:00 openwin
2213 pts/1    0:00 grep openwin
oak%
```

Displaying and Controlling Information About Processes

Use the following steps to display and control information about a process.

1. Type **ps -e | grep *process-name*** and press Return.

   The first column of the output displays the PID for the appropriate process name.

2. Become superuser to use pcred, pfiles, pflags, pldd, pmap, psig, pstack, and pwdx commands.

3. Type ***command PID*** and press Return.

   The information for the specified command is displayed.

The following examples show the output for each of the /usr/proc/bin commands for the dtlogin PID of 283.

```
castle% ps -e | grep dtlogin
   283 ?         0:00 dtlogin
   270 ?         0:01 dtlogin
castle%
# /usr/proc/bin/pcred 283
283:    e/r/suid=0  e/r/sgid=0
        groups: 1 0 2 3 4 5 6 7 8 9 12
# exit
castle% /usr/proc/bin/ptime 283

real        0.016
user        0.000
sys         0.016
castle%
# /usr/proc/bin/pfiles 283
283:    /usr/dt/bin/dtlogin -daemon
  Current rlimit: 64 file descriptors
   0: S_IFDIR mode:0755 dev:32,24 ino:2 uid:0 gid:0 size:1024
      O_RDONLY|O_LARGEFILE
   1: S_IFDIR mode:0755 dev:32,24 ino:2 uid:0 gid:0 size:1024
      O_RDONLY|O_LARGEFILE
   2: S_IFREG mode:0644 dev:32,24 ino:326220 uid:0 gid:0 size:49
      O_WRONLY|O_APPEND|O_LARGEFILE
   3: S_IFCHR mode:0666 dev:32,24 ino:406038 uid:0 gid:3 rdev:13,12
      O_RDWR
   4: S_IFIFO mode:0666 dev:171,0 ino:4124779288 uid:0 gid:0 size:0
      O_RDWR|O_NONBLOCK
   5: S_IFREG mode:0644 dev:32,24 ino:326221 uid:0 gid:0 size:4
      O_WRONLY|O_LARGEFILE
      advisory write lock set by process 270
   7: S_IFSOCK mode:0666 dev:166,0 ino:32032 uid:0 gid:0 size:0
      O_RDWR
   8: S_IFDOOR mode:0444 dev:171,0 ino:4124780632 uid:0 gid:0 size:0
      O_RDONLY|O_LARGEFILE FD_CLOEXEC  door to nscd[174]
#
# /usr/proc/bin/pflags 283
283:    /usr/dt/bin/dtlogin -daemon
  /1:    flags = PR_PCINVAL|PR_ORPHAN|PR_ASLEEP [ wait() ]
#
# /usr/proc/bin/pldd 283
283:    /usr/dt/bin/dtlogin -daemon
/usr/openwin/lib/libXmu.so.4
/usr/openwin/lib/libX11.so.4
/usr/dt/lib/libDtSvc.so.1
/usr/lib/libresolv.so.2
/usr/lib/libdl.so.1
/usr/lib/libbsm.so.1
/usr/lib/libauth.so.1
/usr/lib/libsocket.so.1
/usr/lib/libnsl.so.1
/usr/dt/lib/libSDtFwa.so.1
```

```
/usr/lib/libc.so.1
/usr/openwin/lib/libXt.so.4
/usr/openwin/lib/libSM.so.6
/usr/openwin/lib/libICE.so.6
/usr/openwin/lib/libXext.so.0
/usr/lib/libm.so.1
/usr/openwin/lib/libtt.so.2
/usr/dt/lib/libXm.so.3
/usr/lib/libmp.so.2
/usr/lib/nss_files.so.1
/usr/lib/libpam.so.1
#
# /usr/proc/bin/pmap 283
283:    /usr/dt/bin/dtlogin -daemon
00010000      108K read/exec          /usr/dt/bin/dtlogin
0003A000       32K read/write/exec    /usr/dt/bin/dtlogin
00042000       80K read/write/exec     [ heap ]
EEE90000       12K read/shared        dev:32,24 ino:196384
EEEA0000       12K read/shared        dev:32,24 ino:196384
EEEB0000       12K read/shared        dev:32,24 ino:196384
EEEC0000        8K read/write          [ anon ]
EEF11000        4K read/write          [ anon ]
EEF89000        4K read/write          [ anon ]
EF001000        4K read/write          [ anon ]
EF060000       24K read/exec          /usr/lib/libpam.so.1
EF075000        4K read/write/exec    /usr/lib/libpam.so.1
(More information, not shown here)
EF7C0000        4K read/exec/shared   /usr/lib/libdl.so.1
EF7D0000      112K read/exec          /usr/lib/ld.so.1
EF7FB000        8K read/write/exec    /usr/lib/ld.so.1
EF7FD000        4K read/write/exec     [ anon ]
EFFF9000       28K read/write/exec     [ stack ]
 total      5480K
#
# /usr/proc/bin/psig 283
283:    /usr/dt/bin/dtlogin -daemon
HUP      ignored
INT      caught   RESETHAND,NODEFER
QUIT     ignored
ILL      default
TRAP     default
ABRT     default
EMT      default
FPE      default
KILL     default
BUS      default
SEGV     default
SYS      default
PIPE     ignored
ALRM     default
TERM     caught   RESETHAND,NODEFER
USR1     caught   RESETHAND,NODEFER
USR2     default
CLD      default NOCLDSTOP

PWR      default
WINCH    default
URG      default
POLL     default
STOP     default
TSTP     default
CONT     default
TTIN     ignored
TTOU     default
VTALRM   default
PROF     default
XCPU     ignored
XFSZ     ignored
WAITING  default
LWP      default
FREEZE   default
THAW     default
CANCEL   default
LOST     default
RTMIN    default
RTMIN+1  default
```

```
RTMIN+2 default
RTMIN+3 default
RTMAX-3 default
RTMAX-2 default
RTMAX-1 default
RTMAX   default
#
# /usr/proc/bin/pstack 283
283:    /usr/dt/bin/dtlogin -daemon
 ef479154 wait      ()
 ef479154 _libc_wait (0, 3ec4c, 3b000, 12d, ef4e227c, 1e340) + 8
 0001e340 ManageSession (43000, 43000, 482f8, ef001230, 81010100, c) + 454
 00019348 StartDisplay (482f8, 3c954, 43000, 3b224, ef001240, ff00) + 7bc
 0001a324 ForEachDisplay (189a8, 0, 2400, 41800, 42e48, 17ca8) + 1c
 00017d54 main      (0, effffefc, efffff08, 3b000, 0, 0) + 228
 0001541c _start    (0, 0, 0, 0, 0, 0) + dc
#
# /usr/proc/bin/pwdx 283
283:    /
#
castle% /usr/proc/ptime 283

real       0.066
user       0.000
sys        0.032
castle%
castle% ptree 283
270   /usr/dt/bin/dtlogin -daemon
  283   /usr/dt/bin/dtlogin -daemon
    301   /bin/ksh /usr/dt/bin/Xsession
      311   /usr/openwin/bin/fbconsole
      346   /usr/dt/bin/sdt_shell -c unsetenv _ PWD;              unsetenv DT;
        349   -csh -c unsetenv _ PWD;               unsetenv DT;       setenv
 DISP
          366   /usr/dt/bin/dtsession
            373   dtwm
            374   dtterm -session dt0vPI0t -sdtserver
              387   /bin/csh
                407   ./textedit
                528   sh
              390   /bin/csh
              393   /bin/csh
                417   /usr/openwin/bin/cmdtool
                  420   /bin/csh
              531   /bin/csh
                553   ptree 283
            375   dtfile -session dtbfiQD_
              405   dtfile -session dtbfiQD_
            376   snapshot -Wp 781 588 -Ws 326 201 -WP 6 6 +Wi -f snapshot.rs
castle%
```

The Priority Control Command (priocntl)

You can use the priocntl command to display or set scheduling parameters
of specified processes. You can also use it to display the current configuration
information for the process scheduler of a system or to execute a command
with specified scheduling parameters.

Solaris provides several scheduling classes, each with its own scheduling
policy. A process can be assigned to one of these classes; the process priority
can then be adjusted within the boundaries allowed by that particular
scheduling class.

- System (`SYS`).

  Use the system scheduling class to schedule the execution of certain special system processes such as the `swapper` process.

- Interactive (`IA`).

  Use the interactive class to provide good response time to interactive processes and good throughput to CPU-bound jobs. This class gives snappier performance than does `SYS` for GUI programs such as X11, CDE, and OpenWindows that the user interacts with. You can change the processes of the interactive class in the same way as those in the timesharing class, although the modified priorities continue to be adjusted to provide good responsiveness for user interaction.

- Real-time (`RT`).

  Use the real-time class to provide a fixed-priority, preemptive scheduling policy for those processes that need fast responses and absolute user and application control of scheduling priorities.

- Timesharing (`TS`).

  Use the timesharing class to provide fair and effective allocation of CPU resources among processes that have varying CPU consumption requirements.

- Fair-share (`FS`), new in the Solaris 9 release.   *New!*

  Use the fair-share class to provide a fair allocation of system CPU resources among projects independently of the number of processes they own. Processes are given "shares" to control their entitlement to CPU resources.

- Fixed-priority (`FX`), new in the Solaris 9 release.   *New!*

  Use the fixed-priority class to provide a fixed-priority, preemptive-scheduling policy for those processes that cannot handle dynamic adjustments and require that the user or application have control of the scheduling priorities. The fixed-priority class values range from 0–60.

For the timesharing class, the user-supplied priority ranges from –20 to +20. The priority of a timeshare process, referred to as the user-mode priority, is inherited from the parent process. The system looks up the user-mode priority in its timesharing dispatch parameter table, adds in any `nice` or `priocntl` (user-supplied) priority, and ensures a 0–59 range to create a global priority.

In the default configuration, a runnable real-time process runs before any other process. Inappropriate use of real-time processes can have a dramatic, negative impact on system performance.

Creating and Administering Resource Management Pools

New!

Starting with the Solaris 9 release, you can create permanent processor sets, called resource pools, and associate a scheduling class with that set. You can then assign projects to that resource pool. Use the poolcfg(1M) command to create XML-based pool configuration files. The systemwide configuration is stored in /etc/pooladm.conf.

Once you have created a pool configuration file, activate it with the pooladm(1M) command, which is also automatically run at boot time if the /etc/pooladm.conf file is present. You can bind processes, tasks, or projects to a pool with the poolbind(1M) command or query the binding for a process, if you have the appropriate authorizations. You can also specify the binding of a project to a pool with an attribute in the project(4) database. This binding is used when you are logging in or when you use the newtask(1) command.

Solaris 9 also introduces the concept of a task, which is a collection of processes. Tasks remove the limitations of current process aggregates such as process groups and sessions. Tasks are bound to projects whose membership and attributes are described in the project(4) database. The SMC Projects tool is a GUI front end that you can use to administer projects and tasks in addition to the commands. Refer to Sun's *System Administration Guide: Resource Management and Network Services* and the relevant manual pages for more information about creating and administering resource management pools.

Displaying Basic Information About Process Classes

Use the following procedure to display basic information about process classes.

- Type **priocntl -l** and press Return. The process class and scheduling parameters for the system are displayed.

In the following example, all classes except RT are loaded at the moment.

```
paperbark% priocntl -l
CONFIGURED CLASSES
==================

SYS (System Class)

TS (Time Sharing)
        Configured TS User Priority Range: -60 through 60

IA (Interactive)
        Configured IA User Priority Range: -60 through 60
paperbark%
```

Displaying the Global Priority of a Process

You can use the `ps` command to display the global priority of a process. The global priority is listed under the `PRI` column.

With the `-c` option to `ps`, higher numbers in the `PRI` column mean higher priority. Without the `-c` option, higher numbers mean lower priority.

The following example shows the output from the `ps -ecl` command. Data in the `PRI` column shows that `pageout` has the highest priority at 98, and the `dtfile`, `dtpad`, and `dtsession` commands have the lowest at 49.

```
mopoke% ps -ecl
  F S    UID    PID   PPID  CLS  PRI    ADDR       SZ  WCHAN TTY        TIME CMD
 19 T      0      0      0  SYS   96       ?        0      ?          0:13 sched
  8 S      0      1      0   TS   59       ?      150    ? ?         0:00 init
 19 S      0      2      0  SYS   98       ?        0    ? ?         0:00 pageout
 19 S      0      3      0  SYS   60       ?        0    ? ?         0:00 fsflush
  8 S      0    411      1   TS   59       ?      216    ? ?         0:00 sac
  8 S      0    237      1   TS   59       ?      130    ? ?         0:00 utmpd
  8 S      0    208      1   TS   59       ?      347    ? ?         0:00 nscd
  8 S      0     49      1   TS   59       ?      268    ? ?         0:00 sysevent
  8 S      0     56      1   TS   59       ?      367    ? ?         0:00 picld
  8 S      0    115      1   TS   59       ?      207    ? ?         0:00 in.route
  8 S      0    179      1   TS   59       ?      475    ? ?         0:00 automoun
  8 S      0    133      1   TS   59       ?      272    ? ?         0:00 rpcbind
  8 S      0    170      1   TS   59       ?      266    ? ?         0:00 lockd
  8 S      0    155      1   TS   59       ?      297    ? ?         0:00 inetd
  8 S      0    189      1   TS   59       ?      414    ? ?         0:00 syslogd
  8 S      0    213      1   TS   59       ?      391    ? ?         0:00 lpsched
  8 S      1    176      1   TS   59       ?      306    ? ?         0:00 statd
  8 S      0    193      1   TS   59       ?      253    ? ?         0:00 cron
  8 S      0    226      1   TS   59       ?      174    ? ?         0:00 powerd
  8 S      0    414    411   TS   59       ?      217    ? ?         0:00 ttymon
  8 S      0    261      1   TS   59       ?      363    ? ?         0:02 vold
  8 S      0    249    248   TS   59       ?      215    ? ?         0:00 smcboot
  8 S      0    248      1   TS   59       ?      215    ? ?         0:00 smcboot
  8 S      0    250    248   TS   59       ?      215    ? ?         0:00 smcboot
  8 S      0    266      1   TS   59       ?      121    ? ?         0:00 htt
  8 S      0    268    266   TS   59       ?      378    ? ?         0:00 htt_serv
  8 S   1001    416    395   IA   59       ?     3568    ? ?         0:07 Xsun
  8 S      0    372      1   TS   59       ?      227    ? ?         0:00 auditd
  8 S      1    283      1   TS   59       ?     1178    ? ?         0:00 dwhttpd
  8 S      1    284    283   TS   59       ?     1277    ? ?         0:00 dwhttpd
  8 S      0    417    395   IA   59       ?      662    ? ?         0:00 dtlogin
  8 S   1001    483    480   IA   59       ?      184    ? pts/3     0:00 csh
  8 S   1001    446    436   IA   59       ?      292    ? ?         0:00 fbconsol
  8 S   1001    436    435   IA   59       ?      240    ? ?         0:00 Xsession
  8 S      0    435    417   IA   59       ?      662    ? ?         0:00 dtlogin
  8 S   1001    450      1   IA   59       ?      639    ? ?         0:00 speckeys
  8 S   1001    499    483   IA   49       ?      999    ? pts/3     0:00 dtsessio
  8 S   1001    507    499   IA   49       ?     1097    ? ?         0:00 dtfile
  8 S   1001    480    436   IA   59       ?      496    ? pts/3     0:00 sdt_shel
  8 S   1001    481      1   IA   59       ?      295    ? ?         0:00 dsdm
  8 O   1001    555    522   IA   59       ?      138      pts/4     0:00 ps
  8 S      0    419    391   TS   59       ?      288    ? ?         0:00 mibiisa
  8 S      0    401      1   TS   59       ?      384    ? ?         0:00 dmispd
  8 S      0    415      1   TS   59       ?      331    ? ?         0:00 sshd
  8 S      0    402      1   TS   59       ?      439    ? ?         0:00 snmpXdmi
  8 S      0    395      1   TS   59       ?      621    ? ?         0:00 dtlogin
  8 S      0    418    395   IA   59       ?      292    ? ??        0:00 fbconsol
  8 S      0    391      1   TS   59       ?      268    ? ?         0:00 snmpdx
  8 S      0    412      1   TS   59       ?      217    ? console   0:00 ttymon
  8 S   1001    498      1   IA   59       ?      574    ? pts/3     0:00 ttsessio
  8 S      0    500    155   TS   59       ?      427    ? ?         0:00 rpc.ttdb
  8 S   1001    506    499   IA   59       ?     1158    ? ?         0:02 dtwm
  8 S   1001    528    509   IA   59       ?      180    ? pts/6     0:00 csh
  8 R   1001    509    499   IA   59       ?     1004      ??        0:00 dtterm
  8 S   1001    510    499   IA   59       ?      921    ? ?         0:00 sdtperfm
  8 S   1001    518    498   IA   59       ?      137    ? pts/3     0:00 sh
```

```
8 S 1001    512    1    IA  59    ?     239    ? ?        0:00 sdtvolch
8 S 1001    519   518   IA  49    ?     907    ? pts/3    0:00 dtpad
8 S 1001    545   507   IA  49    ?    1097    ? ?        0:00 dtfile
8 S    0    520   155   TS  59    ?     230    ? ?        0:00 rpc.rsta
8 S 1001    522   509   IA  59    ?     180    ? pts/4    0:00 csh
8 S 1001    525   509   IA  59    ?     180    ? pts/5    0:00 csh
8 S 1001    531   509   IA  59    ?     180    ? pts/7    0:00 csh
8 S 1001    544   512   IA  59    ?     122    ? ?        0:00 cat
8 S    0    546    1    TS  59    ?     565    ? ?        0:00 sendmail
8 S   25    547    1    TS  59    ?     561    ? ?        0:00 sendmail
mopoke%
```

You can also use the /usr/sbin/dispadmin -l command to display
process scheduler information.

The following example shows the output from the dispadmin -l
command.

```
castle% /usr/sbin/dispadmin -l
CONFIGURED CLASSES
==================

SYS     (System Class)
TS      (Time Sharing)
IA      (Interactive)
castle%
```

For complete information, refer to the dispadmin(1M) manual page.

Designating a Process Priority

Use the following steps to designate a process priority.

1. Become superuser.

2. Type **priocntl -e -c *class* -m *userlimit* -p *priority
   command-name*** and press Return.

   The -e option executes the command. The -c *class* option specifies
   the class with which to run the process. Valid classes are TS
   (timesharing), RT (real time), IA (interactive), FSS (fair share), or FX
   (fixed priority). The -m *userlimit* option specifies the maximum
   amount you can raise or lower your priority with the -p option. The
   -p *pri* option enables you to specify the relative priority in the RT
   class for a real-time thread. For a timesharing process, you can
   specify the user-supplied priority, which ranges from -60 to +60. The
   command operand specifies the name of the command for which you
   want to change the process priority.

3. While the process is running, in another terminal window, type
   ps -ecl | grep *command-name* and press Return.

4. Review the output of the PRI column to verify that you have changed
   the process status successfully.

The following example starts the `find` command with the highest possible user-supplied priority.

```
# priocntl -e-c TS -m 60 -p 60 find . -name core -print
mopoke%
mopoke% ps -ecl | grep find
 8 S   0   686   682   TS  60       ?    133      ? pts/7    0:00 find
mopoke%
```

Changing the Class of a Process

Use the following steps to change the class of a process.

NOTE. You must be superuser or working in a real-time shell to change the class of a process from or to realtime.

1. Become superuser.
2. Type **priocntl -s -c *class* -i *id-type id-list*** and press Return.

   The -s option enables you to set the upper limit on the user priority range and change the current priority. The -c class option specifies the class, TS or RT, to which you are changing the process. The -i *id-type* and *id-list* options use a combination of *id-type* and *id-list* to identify the process. The *id-type* specifies the type of ID, such as PID or UID.
3. While the process is running, in another terminal window, type **ps -ecl | grep *command-name*** and press Return.
4. Review the output of the PRI column to verify that you have changed the process status successfully.

The following example changes all the processes belonging to user 1001 to timeshare processes.

```
# priocntl -s -c TS -i uid 1001
# ps -ecl | grep 1001
 8 S  1001   496   481   TS  59       ?    137      ? pts/4    0:00 sh
 8 S  1001   497   496   TS  59       ?    152      ? pts/4    0:00 more
 8 S  1001   329   308   TS  59       ?   3801      ? ?        0:35 Xsun
 8 S  1001   350   332   TS  59       ?    241      ? ?        0:00 Xsession
 8 S  1001   408     1   TS  59       ?    590      ? pts/3    0:00 ttsessio
 8 S  1001   360   350   TS  59       ?    297      ? ?        0:00 fbconsol
 8 S  1001   417   409   TS  59       ?   1105      ? ?        0:00 dtfile
 8 S  1001   364     1   TS  59       ?    326      ? ?        0:00 speckeys
 8 S  1001   394   391   TS  59       ?    182      ? pts/3    0:00 csh
 8 S  1001   391   350   TS  59       ?    501      ? pts/3    0:00 sdt_shel
 8 S  1001   392     1   TS  59       ?    300      ? ?        0:00 dsdm
 8 S  1001   409   394   TS  59       ?   1015      ? pts/3    0:00 dtsessio
 8 S  1001   416   409   TS  59       ?   1176      ? ?        0:03 dtwm
 8 S  1001   418   409   TS  59       ?    977      ? ??       0:01 dtterm
 8 S  1001   430   418   TS  59       ?    180      ? pts/4    0:00 csh
 8 S  1001   420   409   TS  59       ?    929      ? ?        0:00 sdtperfm
 8 S  1001   450   417   TS  59       ?   1105      ? ?        0:00 dtfile
 8 S  1001   422   408   TS  59       ?    137      ? pts/3    0:00 sh
 8 S  1001   423   422   TS  59       ?    913      ? pts/3    0:00 dtpad
```

```
8 S  1001   424     1   TS  59      ?    240     ? ?       0:00 sdtvolch
8 S  1001   455   424   TS  59      ?    122     ? ?       0:00 cat
8 S  1001   435   418   TS  59      ?    180     ? pts/5   0:00 csh
8 S  1001   439   418   TS  59      ?    180     ? pts/6   0:00 csh
8 S  1001   442   418   TS  59      ?    182     ? pts/7   0:00 csh
8 S  1001   481   430   TS  59      ?    131     ? pts/4   0:00 man
8 S  1001   545   442   TS  59      ?    517     ? pts/7   0:03 spider.e
8 S  1001   690   439   TS  59      ?    235     ? pts/6   0:00 ftp
8 S  1001   610   608   TS  59      ?   2574     ? ?       0:00 .netscap
8 S  1001   607     1   TS  59      ?    630     ? ?       0:00 netscape
8 S  1001   609   607   TS  59      ?    653     ? ?       0:00 netscape
8 S  1001   608   607   TS  59      ?   3165     ? ?       0:20 .netscap
#
```

Setting Fair-Share Parameters

The valid class-specific options for setting fair-share parameters—new in the Solaris 9 release—are shown in Table 15.

Table 15   Options to the Fair-Share Class of the priocntl Command

Option	Description
-m *fssuprilim*	Set the user-priority limit of the specified process(es) to *fssuprilim*.
-p *fssupri*	Set the user priority of the specified process(es) to *fssupri*.

Setting Fixed-Priority Parameters

The valid class-specific options for setting fixed-priority parameters—new in the Solaris 9 release—are shown in Table 16.

Table 16   Options to the Fixed-Priority Class of the priocntl Command

Option	Description
-m *fxuprilim*	Set the user-priority limit of the specified process(es) to *fxuprilim*.
-p *fxupri*	Set the user priority of the specified process(es) to *fxupri*.
-t *tqntm* [-r *res*]	Set the time quantum of the specified process(es) to *tqntm*. You can optionally specify a resolution.

Use the following steps to assign a fixed priority to a command.

1. Become superuser.
2. Type **priocntl -e -c** *class* **-m** *fxuprilim* **-p** *fxupri* **-t** *tqntm command* and press Return.

The -e option enables you to execute a specific command with the class and scheduling parameters associated with a set of processes. The -c *class* option specifies the class, in this case, FX for fixed priority, to which you are changing the process. The -m *fxuprilim* option specifies the user priority limit of the specified processes. The -p *fxupri* option specifies the user priority of the specified processes. The -t *tqntm* option specifies time quantum of the specified processes. The *command* argument specifies the command to which to apply the fixed-priority options.

The following example executes a command in the fixed-priority class with a user-priority limit of 20, a user priority of 10, and a time quantum of 250 milliseconds.

```
mopoke% su
Password:
# priocntl -e -c FX -m 20 -p 10 -t 250 ps -ef | grep priocntl
    root   701   674  0 01:01:52 pts/4    0:00 grep priocntl
#
```

Setting the Priority of a Process (nice)

NOTE. The `nice` command is supported only for backward compatibility with previous Solaris releases. Use the `priocntl` command to manage process priorities.

New!

The priority of a process is determined by the policies of its scheduling class and by its `nice` number. The global priority of each timesharing process is calculated by adding the user-supplied priority and the system-calculated priority. You can modify only the user-supplied priority. You can view the `nice` number of a process in the NI column of the output of the `ps -l` command.

New!

The range of nice numbers is between 0 and +40, with 0 the highest priority. The default value is 20.

New!

You can use the `priocntl` command (preferred) or the `nice` command to raise or lower the priority of a command or a process. When you use the `nice` command without an argument, the default is to increase the `nice` number by four units, thus lowering the priority of the process.

NOTE. You must be superuser to raise the priority of a process with the `nice` command. Users can lower their own process priorities.

Use the following command to lower the priority of a command by four units (the default).

```
/usr/bin/nice command-name
```

Use the following command to lower the priority of a command by increasing the `nice` number by ten units.

```
/usr/bin/nice -n +10 command-name
```

NOTE. The plus sign (+) is optional for positive numbers. The minus sign (–) is required for negative numbers.

Use the following command to raise the priority of a command by lowering the `nice` number by ten units.

```
/usr/bin/nice -10 command-name
```

Use the following command to raise the priority of a command by lowering the `nice` number by ten units. The minus sign indicates a negative number.

```
/usr/bin/nice -10 command-name
```

Changing the Priority of a Running Process (renice)

If you want to alter the scheduling priority of one or more running processes, you can use the `renice` command. Specify the process IDs of the processes to be affected. If the first operand is a number within the range of priorities (–20 to 20), `renice` treats it as a priority. Otherwise, `renice` treats it as an ID.

Users other than superuser can alter the priority only of processes they own and can increase their `nice` value only within the range 0 to 19.

The following example adjusts the system scheduling priority so that process IDs 987 and 32 have a lower scheduling priority.

```
paperbark% renice -n 5 -p 987 32
paperbark%
```

The `-n` option specifies the system scheduling priority, and the `-p` option specifies the process ID numbers to adjust.

Finding or Signalling Processes (pgrep, pkill)

You can use the `pgrep` command to examine the active processes on the system and report the process IDs of the processes whose attributes match the command-line argument. The simplest way to use pgrep is to type the command with the name of the process as the argument.

```
pgrep process-name
```

Refer to the pgrep(1) manual page for a complete listing of options and arguments.

The following example uses pgrep to find the process ID of the sendmail command.

```
paperbark% pgrep sendmail
2830
paperbark%
```

The pkill command works in the same way as pgrep except that it signals each matching process as would kill(1) instead of displaying the process ID. You can specify a signal name or number as the first command-line option to pkill.

Refer to the pgrep(1) manual page for a complete listing of options and arguments for pkill.

The following example terminates the most recently created xterm.

```
paperbark% pkill -n xterm
paperbark%
```

Reviewing Essential Administration Tools

The Solaris Operating Environment provides two groups of administration tools.

- The usual collection of operating system commands.
- Solaris Management Console (SMC) tools. SMC, introduced in the Solaris 8 1/01 update release, is a collection of network-aware system administration tools. See "Tools in the Solaris Management Console" on page 80 for more information.

New!

Frequently Used Commands

The following sections briefly introduce basic Solaris commands that you are likely to use regularly as part of routine system administration; they are grouped by tasks. See Chapter 2, "Using Basic OS Commands," for additional frequently used commands.

Getting Around in the File System (pwd, cd)

The Solaris Operating Environment has a hierarchical file system. When administering systems, you need to know where you are in the file hierarchy and how to change to a different directory.

Finding Where You Are in the File System   To find out where you are in the file system hierarchy, type **pwd** and press Return. The print working directory command displays the current directory.

```
oak& pwd
/etc
oak%
```

Changing Directories   To change directories, type **cd** *pathname* and press Return. The change directory command moves the focus to the directory whose name you type.

```
oak% cd /usr
oak% pwd
/usr
oak%
```

If you type **cd** and press Return without typing a path name, focus is returned to the login home directory.

Finding Information About Files

With the ls command, you can list the contents of a directory and display permissions, links, ownership, group, size (in bytes), modification date and time, and file name for files. Many user problems related to accessing files can be traced to problems with incorrect permissions or ownership. See Chapter 12, "Recognizing File Access Problems," for more information.

Table 17 shows the options to the ls command.

New!

Table 17   Options to the ls Command

Option	Description
-@	The same as -l except that extended attribute information supersedes ACL information. An at sign (@) is displayed after the file permission bits for files that have extended attributes. New in the Solaris 9 release.
-a	List all entries, including those that begin with a dot (.), which are normally not listed.

Table 17   Options to the ls Command (Continued)

Option	Description
-A	List all entries, including those that begin with a dot (.) with the exception of the working directory (.) and the parent directory (..).
-b	Force printing of nonprintable characters to be in the octal *ddd* notation.
-c	Use time of last modification of the inode (file created, mode changed, and so forth) for sorting (-t) or printing (-l or -n).
-C	Display multicolumn output, and sort entries down the columns. This format is the default.
-d	If an argument is a directory, list only its name (not its contents); often used with -l to get the status of a directory.
-f	Force each argument to be interpreted as a directory, and list the name found in each slot. This option turns off -l, -t, -s, and -r, and turns on -a; the order is the order in which entries appear in the directory.
-F	Mark directories with a trailing slash (/), doors with a trailing greater-than sign (>), executable files with a trailing asterisk (*), FIFOs with a trailing vertical bar (	), symbolic links with a trailing at-sign (@), and AF_UNIX address family sockets with a trailing equal sign (=).
-g	The same as -l, except do not print the owner.
-i	For each file, print the inode number in the first column of the report.
-l	List in long format, giving mode, ACL indication, number of links, owner, group, size in bytes, and time of last modification for each file. If the file is a special file, the size field contains the major and minor device numbers. If the time of last modification is greater than six months ago, it is shown in the format *month date year* for the POSIX locale. When the LC_TIME locale category is not set to the POSIX locale, a different format of the time field can be used. Files modified within six months show *month date time*. If the file is a symbolic link, the file name is printed, followed by -> and the path name of the referenced file.
-L	If an argument is a symbolic link, list the file or directory the link references instead of the link itself.

Table 17   *Options to the ls Command (Continued)*

Option	Description
-m	Stream output format; list files across the page, separated by commas and spaces.
-n	The same as -1, except print the owner UID and group GID numbers instead of the associated character strings.
-o	The same as -1, except do not print the group.
-p	Put a slash (/) after each file name if the file is a directory.
-q	Force printing of nonprintable characters in file names as the character question mark (?).
-r	Reverse the order of sort to get reverse alphabetic or oldest first as appropriate.
-R	Recursively list subdirectories.
-s	Give size in blocks, including indirect blocks, for each entry.
-t	Sort by time stamp (latest first) instead of by name. The default is the last modification time. (See -u and -c.)
-u	Use time of last access instead of last modification for sorting (with the -t option) or printing (with the -1 option).
-x	Display multicolumn output, and sort entries across instead of down the page.
-1	Print one entry per line of output.

Displaying File Information (ls)

To display information about an individual file, type **ls -1** *filename* and press Return. Permissions, links, owner, group, file size in bytes, modification date and time, and the file name are displayed.

```
oak% ls -1 /etc/passwd
-r--r--r--   1 root      sys         659 Feb 24 17:28 /etc/passwd
oak%
```

The mode printed with the -1 option consists of ten characters. The first character is one of the following.

-	The entry is an ordinary file.
b	The entry is a block special file.
c	The entry is a character special file.
d	The entry is a directory.

D	The entry is a door.
l	The entry is a symbolic link.
p	The entry is a FIFO (or named pipe) special file.
s	The entry is an AF_UNIX address family socket.

The next nine characters are interpreted as three sets of three bits each. The first set refers to the owner's permissions; the next, to permissions of others in the user-group of the file; and the last, to all others. Within each set, the three characters indicate permission to read, to write, and to execute the file as a program. For a directory, execute permission is interpreted as permission to search the directory for a specified file.

For user and group permissions, the third position can be occupied by x (execute) or – (deny access). For user permissions, s denotes the set-user-ID bit. For group permissions, it denotes the set-group-ID bit. For example, the ability to assume the same user ID as the program owner during execution is used during login when you begin the process as root but then assume the identity of your user login.

For group permissions, l can occupy the third position. l refers to mandatory file and record locking. This permission describes a file's ability to allow other files to lock its reading or writing permissions during access.

For others permissions, the third position can be occupied by t or T. These refer to the state of the sticky bit and execution permissions.

The permissions are described below.

r	The file is readable.
w	The file is writable.
x	The file is executable.
–	The indicated permission is not granted.
s	The setuid or setgid bit is on, and the corresponding user or group execution bit is also on.
S	Undefined bit state (the setuid or setgid bit is on, and the user or group execution bit is off).
t	The 1000 (octal) bit, or sticky bit, is on (see chmod(1)), and execution is on.
T	The 1000 bit is on, and execution is off (undefined bit state).
l	Mandatory locking occurs during access (the setgid bit is on, and the group execution bit is off) (/usr/bin/ls).
L	Mandatory locking occurs during access (the setgid bit is on and the group execution bit is off) (/usr/xpg4/bin/ls).

New!

When you use the ls -l command, any file that has an access control list (ACL) displays a plus (+) sign to the right of the mode field. See the getfacl(1) and setfacl(1) manual pages or the *Solaris Advanced System Administrator's Guide*, published by Sun Microsystems Press and Prentice Hall, for more information about ACLs.

New!

NOTE. If you specify the -@ option—new in the Solaris 9 release to display extended attributes of a file—the presence of extended attributes supersedes the presence of an ACL and the + sign is replaced with an at sign (@).

To see a complete list of all files in the directory, type **ls -l** and press Return.

See the ls(1) manual page for a complete list of options.

Finding a File (find)

To find a file by searching from the home directory, type **find $HOME -name *filename* -print** and press Return. The $HOME variable starts the search with the home directory. The -name option looks for the name specified in the *filename* variable. The -print option displays the results of the find. If the named file is not found, the prompt is redisplayed.

The following example shows the results of find looking for core files.

```
oak% find $HOME -name core -print
/home/ignatz/core
oak%
```

Table 18 shows some of the options to the find command that you can use to focus your searches.

Table 18   Options to the find Command

Option	Description
-fstype *type*	Find files of the file system type you specify (typically ufs or nfs).
-prune	Limit the search to the specified directory.
-nouser	Find files that belong to a user not in the /etc/passwd database.
-nogroup	Find files that belong to a group not in the /etc/group database.
-atime *n*	Find files that have been accessed within the last *n* days.
-mtime *n*	Find files that have been modified within the last *n* days.

Table 18   Options to the find Command (Continued)

Option	Description
`-ctime` *n*	Find files that have been changed within the last *n* days. Changes can include changes to a file's attributes such as the number of links, its owner, or its group.
`-xdev`	Restrict search to one file system.

See the `find`(1) manual page for a complete list of options.

Finding the Type of a File (file)

Sometimes you need to determine the type of a file. To find the type of a file, type **file** *filename* and press Return. The output of the command makes an educated guess about the type of the file.

For example, if you are trying to execute an ASCII file that does not have execute permissions or to execute an empty file, displaying the file type tells you whether the system recognizes the file as a command.

In the following example, the file is empty.

```
anastasia% file junk1
junk1: empty file
anastasia%
```

In the following example, the file is an ASCII text file.

```
anastasia% file junk2
junk2: ascii text
anastasia%
```

In the following example, the file is a text file with executable permissions, so the `file` command reports that the file contains commands and is text.

```
anastasia% chmod 777 junk3
anastasia% file junk3
junk: commands text
anastasia%
```

NOTE. You can, of course, determine if the command has execute permissions with the `ls -l` *command.*

To show the file type for all files in a directory, type **file *** and press Return. The files are listed in alphabetical order followed by the file type.

```
$ file *
coterie:      directory
course:       ascii text
dead.letter   ascii text
ksyms         English text
people:       directory
personal:     directory
showrev:      ascii text
status:       directory
text:         directory
todo:         ascii text
$
```

Finding Information in Files (grep, egrep)

You can use the grep and egrep commands to search files and command output for specific information.

Searching Files for Text Strings   To search files for a specific text string, type **grep *search-string filename*** and press Return. Lines in the files containing the string are displayed.

In the following example, the passwd file is searched for lines containing csh.

```
oak% grep csh /etc/passwd
ignatz::6693:10:Iggy Ignatz 64607:/home/ignatz:/bin/csh
fred::14072:10:Fred Lux:/home/fred:/bin/csh
oak%
```

You can search more than one file by specifying a series of file names separated by spaces or by using *metacharacters* such as the asterisk (*) or question mark (?) together with (or in place of) the file name.

To print lines that do not contain the specified string, type **grep -v *search-string filename*** and press Return. Lines in the file that do not contain the string are displayed.

Searching Input for Lines with a Given Pattern   You can use the grep command with pipes in combination with many administrative commands. For example, if you want to find all of a user's current processes, pipe the output of the ps command to grep and search for the user name, type **ps -e | grep *name*** and press Return. The listing for the name you specify is displayed. See "Combining Commands (|)" on page 122 for more information.

The following example finds the OpenWindows process.

```
oak% ps -e | grep openwin
PID TTY       TIME COMD
2212 pts/0    0:00 openwin
oak%
```

Looking at Files

You undoubtedly will spend lots of time looking at the content of files. When you need to look at the entire file, use the `more` command. When the information you need is at the end of the file (for example, in a log file), use the `tail` command to display the last lines (10 by default) of the file. When important information is at the beginning of the file, use the `head` command to display the first lines (10 by default) of the file.

Viewing a File (more)

To view a file, type **more** *filename* and press Return. The file is displayed one screen at a time. Press Return to display the next line. Press space to view the next screen.

To search for a specific string in a file you are viewing with `more`, type */search-string* and press Return. The text scrolls to display the place in the file that contains the text of the *search-string* variable and displays the search string and the message `. . . skipping` at the top of the window. If no match is found, the message `Pattern not found` is displayed at the bottom of the window and the text does not scroll.

For example, to find the words **Local aliases** in the `/etc/mail/aliases` file, type **/Local aliases** and press Return.

```
/Local aliases
...skipping

########################
# Local aliases below #
########################
```

NOTE. You must use exact capitalization in the search string for the more *command. If you type* **/local aliases** *in the previous example, the pattern is not found.*

To search for the next occurrence of the search string, type **n**. To quit `more`, type **q**. The shell prompt is redisplayed.

Another way to quit `more`, if Control-C is set as your shell kill character, is to press Control-C. The shell prompt is redisplayed.

To display the shell `intr` (interrupt) character, type **stty -a** and press Return. A list of the `stty` settings is displayed. In the following example, ^c is the shell `intr` character.

```
castle% stty -a
ispeed 88840 baud; ospeed 88824 baud;
rows = 36; columns = 113; ypixels = 478; xpixels = 801;
eucw 1:0:0:0, scrw 1:0:0:0
intr = ^c; quit = <undef>; erase = ^h; kill = ^u;
eof = ^d; eol = <undef>; eol2 = <undef>; swtch = <undef>;
start = ^q; stop = ^s; susp = ^z; dsusp = ^y;
rprnt = ^r; flush = ^o; werase = ^w; lnext = ^v;
-parenb parodd cs8 cstopb hupcl cread -clocal loblk crtscts crtsxoff parext
-ignbrk -brkint -ignpar -parmrk -inpck -istrip -inlcr -igncr icrnl -iuclc
ixon -ixany ixoff -imaxbel
isig icanon -xcase echo echoe echok -echonl -noflsh
-tostop echoctl -echoprt echoke -defecho -flusho -pendin iexten
opost -olcuc onlcr -ocrnl -onocr -onlret -ofill -ofdel
castle%
```

Looking at the End of a File (tail)

To look at the end of a file, type **tail _filename_** and press Return. The last 10 lines of the file are displayed.

The following example shows the tail of the /etc/lp/Systems file. Because the file contains only seven lines, the entire file is displayed.

```
castle% /usr/bin/tail /etc/lp/Systems
#
#ident   "@(#)Systems    1.8     97/06/09 SMI"   /* SVr4.0 1.2    */
# This file previously contained an LP private interface.  It's
# contents are no longer used by the printing system and therefore
# obsolete.  Expect the file to be removed in a subsequent release
# of Solaris, along with the lpsystem(1M) command.
+:x:-:bsd:-:n:10:-:-:Allow all connections
castle%
```

By default, the `head` and `tail` commands display 10 lines. You can change the number of lines displayed by using the -n option. Substitute the number of lines you want to display for the letter n. For example, to display the last 20 lines of a file, type **tail -20 _filename_** and press Return.

NOTE. `tail` *shows a maximum of 4096 bytes (about 400 lines).*

Looking at the Beginning of a File (head)

To look at the beginning of a file, type **head _filename_** and press Return. The first 10 lines of the file are displayed.

The following example shows the head of the /etc/passwd file.

```
paperbark% head /etc/passwd
root:x:0:1:Super-User:/:/sbin/sh
daemon:x:1:1::/:
bin:x:2:2::/usr/bin:
sys:x:3:3::/:
```

```
adm:x:4:4:Admin:/var/adm:
lp:x:71:8:Line Printer Admin:/usr/spool/lp:
uucp:x:5:5:uucp Admin:/usr/lib/uucp:
nuucp:x:9:9:uucp Admin:/var/spool/uucppublic:/usr/lib/uucp/uucico
listen:x:37:4:Network Admin:/usr/net/nls:
nobody:x:60001:60001:Nobody:/:
paperbark%
```

Changing File Ownership or Permissions (chown, chmod, chgrp)

Many user problems can be traced to file ownership or permissions problems. Use the `ls` command to check the permissions and ownership on a file. If you need to change one or both, use the `chown`, `chmod`, and `chgrp` commands.

Changing File Ownership   You must own a file or directory (or have root permission) to be able to change its owner.

The operating system has a configuration option, `{_POSIX_CHOWN_RESTRICTED}`, to restrict ownership changes. When this option is in effect, even the owner of the file cannot change the owner ID of the file. Only superuser can arbitrarily change owner IDs regardless of whether this option is in effect. To set the `{_POSIX_CHOWN_RESTRICTED}` configuration option, include the following line in the `/etc/system` file.

```
set rstchown = 1
```

To disable the `{_POSIX_CHOWN_RESTRICTED}` option, include the following line in `/etc/system`.

```
set rstchown = 0
```

`{_POSIX_CHOWN_RESTRICTED}` is enabled by default. See `system`(4) and `fpathconf`(2).

Use the following steps to change the ownership of a file.

1. Type **ls -l** *filename* and press Return.
   The owner of the file is displayed in the third column.
2. Become superuser if necessary.
3. Type **chown** *new-owner filename* and press Return.
   Ownership is assigned to the new owner you specify.

```
oak% ls -l quest
-rw-r--r--  1 fred    staff    6023 Aug  5 12:06 quest
oak% su
Password:
# chown ignatz quest
# ls -l quest
-rw-r--r--  1 ignatz   staff    6023 Aug  5 12:06 quest
#
```

See Chapter 12, "Recognizing File Access Problems," for more information.

Changing File Permissions   You can change file permissions by using the symbolic values r, w, x, and -. You can also change file permissions by using a set of octal numbers. Table 19 shows the octal values for setting file permissions. You use these numbers in sets of three to set permissions for owner, group, and other. For example, the value 644 sets read/write permissions for owner and read-only permissions for group and other.

Table 19   Octal Values for File Permissions

Value	Description
0	No permissions.
1	Execute-only.
2	Write-only.
3	Write, execute.
4	Read-only.
5	Read, execute.
6	Read, write.
7	Read, write, execute.

1. Type **ls -l** *filename* and press Return. The long listing shows the current permissions for the file.
2. Type **chmod** *nnn* *filename* and press Return. Permissions are changed according to the numbers you specify.

*NOTE. You can change permissions on groups of files or on all files in a directory by using metacharacters such as * and ? in place of file names or in combination with them.*

The following example changes the permissions of a file from 666 (read/write, read/write, read/write) to 644 (read/write, read-only, read-only).

```
oak% ls -l quest
-rw-rw-rw-  1 ignatz    staff    6023 Aug  5 12:06 quest
oak% chmod 644 quest
oak% ls -l
-rw-r--r--  1 ignatz    staff    6023 Aug  5 12:06 quest
oak%
```

Changing File Group Ownership (chgrp)

To change the group ownership of a file, type **chgrp** *gid filename* and press Return. The group ID for the file you specify is changed.

```
$ ls -lg junk
-rw-r--r-- 1 other 0 Oct 31 14:49 junk
$ chgrp 10 junk
$ ls -lg junk
-rw-r--r-- 1 staff 0 Oct 31 14:49 junk
$
```

Group IDs are defined in the nameservice `group` database or the local `/etc/group` file. See Chapter 5, "Administering User Accounts and Groups," for more information about groups.

Setting or Displaying the System Environment

The shell maintains an environment with a set of specifications that it gets from the shell initialization files. Users can also modify the shell environment for a session by issuing commands directly to the shell. The shell receives its information about the environment from environment variables. See "Setting Aliases, Paths, and Environment Variables" on page 116 for more information.

CDE Environment Variables

The Common Desktop Environment (CDE) has its own set of environment variables. Desktop search paths are created at login by the desktop command `dtsearchpath`. The `dtsearchpath` command uses a combination of environment variables and built-in locations to create the search paths.

The environment variables that `dtsearchpath` reads are called *input variables*. These are variables set by the system administrator or end user. The input variables use the naming convention `DTSP*`, which is an abbreviation for desktop search path.

When `dtsearchpath` runs at login, it assembles the values assigned to these variables, adds built-in locations, and creates values for output variables. Each search path has an output variable, as shown in Table 20.

Table 20   CDE Search Path Environment Variables

Search Path	Output Environment Variable	Systemwide Input Variable	Personal Input Variable
Applications	DTAPPSEARCHPATH	DTSPSYSAPPHOSTS	DTSPUSERAPPHOSTS

Table 20   CDE Search Path Environment Variables (Continued)

Search Path	Output Environment Variable	Systemwide Input Variable	Personal Input Variable
Database: actions, data types, and front panel definitions	DTDATABASESEARCHPATH	DTSPSYSDATABASEHOSTS	DTSPUSERDATABASEHOSTS
Icons	XMICONSEARCHPATH, XMICONBMSEARCHPATH	DTSPSYSICON	DTSPUSERICON
Help data	DTHELPSEARCHPATH	DTSPSYSHELP	DTSPUSERHELP

CDE components use the values of the output variables. For example, Application Manager uses the value of the application search path (DTAPPSEARCHPATH) to locate application groups. For more information about CDE, refer to *Solaris Common Desktop Environment: Advanced User's and System Administrator's Guide.*

Tools in the Solaris Management Console

The Solaris Management Console (SMC)—introduced in the Solaris 8 Update 3 (1/01) release—is your access point for system administration tools.

SMC software provides a consistent, easy-to-use interface for managing and administering a Solaris server, the clients of the server, and the applications running on the server. With SMC, you can manage a Solaris server from almost anywhere—from a browser, from any Solaris workstation or server, from an NT server, or as a stand-alone system. You can also plug SMC into other systems' consoles.

By default, SMC manages accounts on the local system. You can create a nameservice domain toolbox to manage accounts in the LDAP, DNS, NIS+, or NIS nameservices. Refer to the *Solaris Management Console Tools* book available from Sun Microsystems Press and Prentice Hall for instructions on how to create a nameservice domain toolbox.

Refer to the *Solaris Management Console Tools* book, published by Sun Microsystems Press and Prentice Hall, for complete information about SMC 2.0 , including how to create or edit an SMC toolbox, create a toolbox that is shared by other toolboxes, or create a toolbox that includes all tools on a number of servers for a particular functionality.

NOTE. This book focuses on basic system administration tasks and refers to the Solaris Management Console Tools *book for detailed instructions on the tools available in SMC 2.0. The upcoming second edition of the* Solaris Management Console Tools *book will include information about the new tools available in the Solaris 9 SMC 2.1 release.*

SMC Tools Available in SMC 2.1

Table 21 describes the tools available in SMC 2.1, available in the Solaris 9 release.

Table 21   Solaris SMC Tools

Category	Tool	Description
System Status		
	System Information	View read-only information about your system's host, hardware, software, memory, and network. New in SMC 2.1.
	Log Viewer	View and manage log files for SMC.
	Processes	View and manage system processes.
System Configuration		
	Users	Create and manage user account information, including user templates, rights, administrative roles, groups, and mailing lists.
	Computer and Networks	View, define, modify, delete, find, sort, and filter computers, networks, and subnetworks. New in SMC 2.1.
	Projects	Manage the Solaris project database (`/etc/project`). New in SMC 2.1.
	Patches	Display the patches installed on your system. New in SMC 2.1.
Services		
	Scheduled Jobs	Schedule jobs that are run at predetermined times (UNIX `cron` jobs).
Storage		
	Mounts and Shares	View and manage mounts, shares, and usage information in the current management domain (single server only).

Table 21   Solaris SMC Tools (Continued)

Category	Tool	Description
	Disks	Display disk information, display partition information, partition disks, copy disk layouts from one disk to a disk of the same size and manufacture, create fdisk partitions, and change the active fdisk partition on an IA computer.
	Enhanced Storage	Create and manage RAID0 volumes, including stripes and concatenation; RAID! volumes, including mirrors; RAID5 volumes; soft partitions; hot spare pools; disksets; and the state configuration database (`metab`). New in SMC 2.1.
Devices and Hardware		
	Serial Ports	Configure and manage serial ports for modems and alphanumeric terminals.
Performance		Monitor system performance on the local system. New in SMC 2.1.

Starting SMC

You can start SMC in any one of the following ways.

- By choosing Solaris Management Console from the Tools menu of the CDE front panel.
- By double-clicking on the SMC icon in CDE Applications Manager or File Manager.
- From a command line by typing **/usr/sadm/bin/smc&** and pressing Return.

NOTE. You can start SMC as a normal user, but some tools or applications may not load unless you log in as root, have Primary Administrator rights, or assume a role during SMC server login.

Figure 1 shows the elements of the default console.

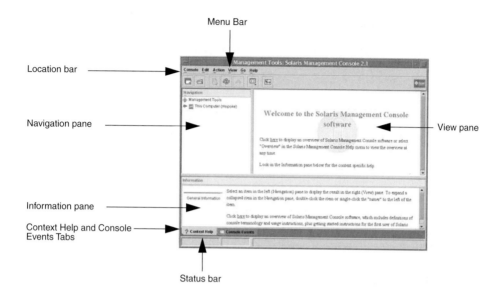

Figure 1   Elements of the Default SMC Console

Refer to the *Solaris Management Console Tools* book by Janice Winsor, published by Sun Microsystems Press and Prentice Hall, for complete information about SMC, including how to create or edit an SMC toolbox, create a toolbox that is shared by other toolboxes, or create a toolbox that includes all tools on a number of servers for a particular functionality.

2

USING BASIC OS
COMMANDS

This chapter explains some basic operating system commands that help you find information about users and the system environment. It also describes several ways to create and edit files, combine commands and redirect output, display manual pages, and locate basic disk information.

Finding User Information

When administering systems, you often need to find out who is using the system and what they are doing. This section describes the commands—`w`, `who`, `finger`, `rusers -l`, `whodo`, `id`—that you can use to find information about users.

Determining Who Is Logged In to a System (w, who, finger, rusers -l, whodo)

You can use any one of the following commands (`w`, `who`, `finger`, `rusers -l`, or `whodo`) to find out who is logged in to a system. Each command gives you different information.

Using the w Command

The `w` command displays a summary of the current activity on the system, including what each user is doing. The header line shows the current time, the length of time the system has been up, the number of users logged in to the system, and the average number of jobs in the run queue over the last 1, 5, and 15 minutes. w is a combination of who, uptime, and ps -a.

The following example shows the output of the w command on the system paperbark.

```
paperbark% w
  3:29pm  up  1:45,  1 user,  load average: 0.00, 0.00, 0.01
User     tty            login@  idle  JCPU   PCPU  what
winsor   console        1:46pm  1:43                /usr/dt/bin/sdt_shell -c
  unseten
winsor   pts/4          1:46pm  1:42                /bin/csh
winsor   pts/5          1:46pm  1:42                /bin/csh
winsor   pts/6          1:46pm  1:42                /bin/csh
winsor   pts/7          1:46pm  1:22                w
paperbark%
```

Using the who Command

The who command displays a list of the users logged in to a system, with the login TTY port and the date and time. When a user is logged in remotely, the remote system name for that user is also displayed. To use the who command, type **who** and press Return.

In the following example, irving is logged in remotely (as shown by the system name in parentheses), and ignatz is logged in locally to the system oak.

```
oak% who
irving pts/1   Oct 31 14:33 (elm)
ignatz console Oct 31 12:22
oak%
```

Using the finger Command

The finger command displays a list of the login names of users logged in to a system, along with the complete name of the user (from the GECOS field of their /etc/password entry), the TTY port, the day of the week, the login time, and the remote system name if the user is logged in remotely. To use the finger command, type **finger** and press Return.

In the following example, user winsor is logged in remotely from castle.

```
oak% rlogin drusilla
drusilla% finger
Login  Name           TTY    Idle When      Where
winsor Janice Winsor pts/0  11   Thu 09:59 castle
drusilla%
```

Using the rusers -l Command

The rusers -l (remote users, login) command displays a list of login names of users who are logged in on remote systems, along with the name of the system a user is logged in to, the TTY port, the month, date, login time, and idle time. If the host is not idle, no time is displayed in the last field. To use the rusers -l command, type **rusers -l** and press Return.

The following example shows six users logged in to the console and two users logged in to TTY ports.

```
cinderella% rusers -l
Sending broadcast for rusersd protocol version 3...
Sending broadcast for rusersd protocol version 2...
jah        caps:console        Mar  3 13:03   22:03
amber      facehole:console    Mar  2 07:40
sebree     ondine:console      Mar  2 10:35      14
tut        cairo:console       Mar  2 10:48
jrt        cairo:ttyp5         Mar  2 16:20   47:54  (gap)
ramseyis mowthelawn:console    Mar  2 16:33      28
ramseyis mowthelawn:ttyp6      Mar  3 14:20   25:14  (:0.0)
(More logins not shown)
cinderella%
```

Using the whodo Command

The whodo command displays the date, time, and system name. For each user logged in, the terminal device name, UID, and login time are shown, followed by a list of active processes associated with the UID. The list includes the terminal device name, PID, CPU minutes and seconds used, and process name.

To find out who is logged in and doing what, type **whodo** and press Return.

The following example shows that user winsor is running a number of CDE applications and Netscape Navigator.

```
paperbark% whodo
Wed May  3 15:34:41 WST 2000paperbark

console       winsor   13:46
     ?          376     0:00 Xsession
   pts/3        422     0:00 sdt_shell
   pts/3        488     0:00 dtfile
   pts/3        485     0:00 dtfile
   pts/3        484     0:00 sh
   pts/3        462     0:00 dtpad
   pts/3        460     0:00 sh
   pts/3        440     0:00 ttsession
   pts/3        441     0:00 dtsession
     ?          448     0:02 dtwm
     ?          452     0:00 sdtperfmeter
     ?          451     0:00 dtterm
   pts/6        472     0:00 csh
   pts/5        469     0:00 csh
   pts/4        466     0:00 csh
   pts/4        536     0:00 ftp
     ?          449     0:00 netscape
     ?          463     0:00 netscape
     ?          461     0:06 .netscape.bin
```

```
     ?              477    0:00  .netscape.bin
   pts/3            424    0:00  csh
     ?              386    0:00  fbconsole
     ?              425    0:00  dsdm

pts/4        winsor   13:46

pts/5        winsor   13:46

pts/6        winsor   13:46

pts/7        winsor   13:46
   pts/7          475    0:00  csh
   pts/7          539    0:00  whodo
paperbark%
```

Finding User UID and GID Settings (id)

Use the id command to display the user ID and group ID number for a user
who is logged in. This information can be helpful for troubleshooting
problems when users cannot access files they think they own or when users
want to find out which group they belong to. To use the id command, have
the user log in, type **id**, and press Return. If the UID, GID, or secondary
GIDs of a user do not match the owner or the group for the troublesome file,
you may need to change the ownership or group on the file or add the user to
the appropriate group.

See "Changing File Ownership or Permissions (chown, chmod, chgrp)" on
page 77 and "Setting Up and Administering Groups" on page 164 for more
information.

The following example shows that the UID for user winsor is 6693 and
the GID is 10. For superuser, the UID is 0 and the GID is 1.

```
mopoke% id
uid=6693(winsor) gid=10(staff)
mopoke% su
Password:
# id
uid=0(root) gid=1(other)
#
```

New!

You can use the id -a option to display the user name, user ID, and all of
the groups to which the user belongs, as shown in the following example.

```
mopoke% id -a
uid=6693(winsor) gid=10(staff) groups=10(staff)
mopoke%
```

Creating and Editing Files (cat, touch, cp, mv, vi)

This section describes how to create and edit files with the cat, touch, cp, mv, Text Editor, and vi commands.

Using the cat Command

Use the cat command to create short files or to append a small amount of text to an existing file. Use the following steps to create files with the cat command.

1. Type **cat > *filename*** and press Return.
2. Type one or more lines of text into the new file.
3. When you've completed the text, press Return to start a new line.
4. Press Control-D on a line that contains no text.

   The text is saved and the shell prompt is redisplayed.

Use the following steps to append text to an existing file.

1. Type **cat >> *filename*** and press Return.
2. Type one or more lines of text into the new file.
3. When you've completed the text, press Return to start a new line.
4. Press Control-D on a line that contains no text.

   The text is saved and the shell prompt is redisplayed.

To view the contents of the file, type **cat *filename*** and press Return. The contents of the file are displayed. If the file is too long to fit in the terminal window, it flies by and shows you the lines at the end of the file that fit in the window or on the screen.

The following example creates a file named kookaburra with the first verse of the kookaburra song, displays the contents of the file, appends the second verse to the file, and displays the contents again.

```
castle% cat > kookaburra
Kookaburra sits in the old gum tree
Merry merry king of the bush is he
Laugh kookaburra, laugh kookaburra
Gay your life must be.
^D
castle% cat kookaburra
Kookaburra sits in the old gum tree
Merry merry king of the bush is he
Laugh kookaburra, laugh kookaburra
Gay your life must be.

castle% cat >> kookaburra
Kookaburra sits in the old gum tree
Eating all the gumdrops he can see
Stop kookaburra, stop kookaburra
Leave some there for me.
```

```
^D
castle% cat kookaburra
Kookaburra sits in the old gum tree
Merry merry king of the bush is he
Laugh kookaburra, laugh kookaburra
Gay your life must be.

Kookaburra sits in the old gum tree
Eating all the gumdrops he can see
Stop kookaburra, stop kookaburra
Leave some there for me.
castle%
```

Using the touch Command

The touch command sets the access and modification times for each file to the current time. If a file does not exist, an empty one is created. You can use the touch command to create an empty file to check the default permissions and ownership or to create a file to which you add text at a later time.

To create an empty file, type **touch *filename*** and press Return. A new, empty file is created. If the file exists, then its modification time is updated to the current date and time.

The following example uses the ls command to determine that there is not a file named junk, creates the file, and uses the ls command to verify that the empty file is created.

```
oak% ls -l junk
junk:  No such file or directory
oak% touch junk
oak% ls -l junk
-rw-r--r--  1 irving      staff 0 Sep 11 15:06 junk
oak%
```

Copying (cp) or Renaming (mv) an Existing File

New!

With the cp command, you can perform the following actions.

- Make copies of individual files and assign new names to them.
- Copy one or more files into a different existing directory, keeping the existing file names.
- Recursively copy an entire directory structure to another directory.
- Copy extended file attributes.

  In the Solaris 9 Operating Environment, the UFS, NFS, and TMPFS file systems are enhanced to include extended file attributes. These file attributes enable application developers to associate specific attributes with a file. For example, a developer of a file management application for a windowing system might choose to associate a display icon with a file.

The options for both `/usr/bin/cp` and `/usr/xpg4/bin/cp` are listed in Table 22.

Table 22   Options for /usr/bin/cp and /usr/xpg4/bin/cp

Option	Description
@	Preserve extended attributes. `cp` tries to copy all of the extended attributes of the source file along with the file data to the destination file. Extended attributes are new in the Solaris 9 release.
-f	If a file descriptor for a destination file cannot be obtained, try to unlink the destination file and proceed.
-i	Interactively prompt for confirmation whenever the copy would overwrite an existing *target*. A y answer means proceed with the copy. Any other answer prevents `cp` from overwriting *target*.
-p	`/usr/bin/cp` only. Duplicate not only the contents of *source-file*, but also preserve ID, permission modes, modification and access time, and ACLs if applicable. Note that the command may fail if you copy ACLs to a file system that does not support them. The command does not fail if unable to preserve modification and access time or permission modes. If unable to preserve owner and group ID, `cp` does not fail and it clears S_ISUID and S_ISGID bits in the *target*. Print a diagnostic message to standard error and return a non-zero exit status if unable to clear these bits. To preserve the owner and group ID, permission modes, and modification and access times, users must have the appropriate file access permissions; this includes being superuser or the same owner ID as the destination file.
-p	`/usr/xpg4/bin/cp` only. Same as -p, above, except the command fails if unable to duplicate the modification and access time or the permission modes. Print a diagnostic message to standard error and return a non-zero exit status.
-r	Recursively copy the directory and all its files, including any subdirectories and their files, to *target*.
-R	Same as -r, except replicate pipes.

To copy an existing file, type **cp** *old-filename new-filename* and press Return. You have made a copy of the file, retaining the original one. Suppose you need to modify the /etc/group file and you want to keep the original copy around in case you make a mistake. Just copy /etc/group to /etc/group.orig, as shown in the following example.

```
# cp /etc/group /etc/group.orig
#
```

To move (and rename) an existing file, type **mv** *old-filename new-filename* and press Return. You have changed the name of the file. Suppose you've downloaded the myapp.tar.gz file and think that it may be corrupt, although you're not completely certain. So, you move it out of the way so that you can download a fresh copy and still retain the original copy with a descriptive name, just in case.

```
oak% mv myapp.tar.gz myapp.tar.gz-possiblycorrupt
oak%
```

Using Text Editor

You can use the CDE Text Editor to create and edit files. To start Text Editor from the CDE front panel, click on the Applications menu and click on Text Editor. To start the CDE Text Editor from the command line, type **/usr/dt/bin/dtpad&** and press Return. A Text Editor window is displayed. Use the commands from the Edit menu or the Cut, Copy, Paste, and Undo keys from the keyboard to make editing changes.

Using vi

The visual editor, vi, is commonly used by system administrators to edit text files. Whole books have been written about using vi. This section provides only a quick-reference table with some of the most commonly used editing commands.

To start vi, type **vi** *filename* and press Return. If the file does not exist, a new file is opened. The new file is created when you save changes made to it. If the file exists, the beginning of the file is displayed.

The three `vi` modes are described in Table 23.

Table 23   vi Modes

Mode	Description
Command	Normal and initial mode. Other modes return to command mode on completion. Use the ESC key to cancel a partial command.
Input	Enter input mode by setting any of the following options: `a A i I o O c C s S R`. You can then type arbitrary text. You usually exit input mode with an ESC character or, abnormally, with an interrupt.
Last line	Read input for `:` `/` `?` or `!`. Terminate by pressing Return. An interrupt cancels termination.

Table 24 shows a few of the many `vi` editing commands.

Table 24   Some Basic vi Commands

Task	Command
How to save/quit a file.	
Quit without saving changes.	`:q!`
Write changes.	`:w`
Write changes and quit.	`:wq`
Write changes and quit.	`ZZ`
How to move around in a file.	
Move cursor one character left.	`h`
Move cursor one character right.	`l`
Move cursor up one line.	`k`
Move cursor down one line.	`j`
Go to end of the file.	`G`
How to add text.	
Insert text (insert mode).	`i` *text* `Esc`
Append text at cursor location.	`a` *text* `Esc`
Append text at end of the line.	`A` *text* `Esc`
How to exit to command mode.	`Esc`

Table 24   Some Basic vi Commands (Continued)

Task	Command
How to make changes to a file.	
Delete line.	dd
Delete character.	x
Delete word.	dw
Open new line above.	O *text* Esc
Open new line below.	o *text* Esc
Yank/copy line.	Y
Put before.	P
Put after.	p

Using Manual Pages

Manual pages are on-line technical references for each Solaris command. Manual pages are grouped into sections, with similar types of commands within the same section. For example, most user commands are in section (1), and system administration commands are in section (1M). Manual pages may be installed on a local system or NFS-mounted from a server. This section tells you how to display manual pages and how to find out the section numbers for an individual command.

Displaying a Manual Page (man)

To display a manual page, type **man *command-name*** and press Return. The manual page is displayed. The following example shows the beginning of the grep(1) manual page.

```
cinderella% man grep

grep(1)     USER COMMANDS     grep(1)

NAME
  grep - search a file for a pattern

SYNOPSIS
     grep   [   -bchilnsvw   ]  limited-regular-expression     [
(Additional lines deleted from this example)
```

Finding Manual Page Sections (man)

New!

The Solaris Operating Environment organizes commands by different sections. A section name consists of a major section name, typically a single digit, optionally followed by a subsection name, typically one or more letters. For example, the command lpr(1B) is in Section (1), User Commands, and belongs to the BSD Compatibility Package section. The major sections are listed in Table 25.

Table 25   The Major Manual Page Sections

Section	Description
1	User commands.
1M	System maintenance commands.
4	Information on file formats.
5	Descriptions of publicly available files and miscellaneous information pages.
6	Computer demonstrations.

Some commands are listed in more than one section. If you type the name of a command that is available in multiple sections, man displays the first manual page the system encounters in the first man section searched. You can find the section number(s) for a manual page with the whatis command. Then you can specify the section number as an argument to the man command so that you display the command from that specified section.

Creating Preformatted Manual Pages (catman)

New!

You can use the catman *n* command to create formatted manual pages, where *n* is the manual page section you want to format. Because catman makes the directories of preformatted manual pages self-contained and independent of the unformatted entries, you can easily distribute these preformatted manual pages among a group of associated systems. Running catman with no arguments reformats every manual page, which can be a lengthy procedure.

You can also use the catman -w option to create just the windex database file that is used by the whatis and apropos commands and the man -f and -k options.

Use the following steps to create or update the windex database file.

1. Become superuser.
2. Type **catman -w** and press Return.

   The windex database is created or updated.

Finding the Section Number for a Manual Page (whatis, man)

New!

Some commands are listed in more than one section. If you type the name of a command that is available in multiple sections, man displays the first manual page the system encounters in the first man section searched. You can find the section number(s) for a manual page with the whatis command. Then you can specify the section number as an argument to the man command so that you display the command from that specified section.

> *NOTE. The* whatis *command works only if you have first used the* catman *command to set up your manual pages. To use the* catman *command to set up manual pages, refer to "Creating Preformatted Manual Pages (catman)" on page 95.*

Use the following steps to find the section number for a manual page.

1. Type **whatis** *command-name* and press Return.

   The first line of the manual page for the command is displayed. Use the section number to display the manual page in the next step.

2. Type **man -s***section-number* *command-name* and press Return.

   The manual page is displayed.

The following example shows the four different chown manual pages and displays the manual page for the chown(2) command.

```
oak% whatis chown
chown     chown (1)     - change owner of file
chown     chown (1b)    - change owner
chown     chown (1m)    - change owner
chown     chown (2)     - change owner and group of a file
oak% man -s2 chown
chown(2)                 SYSTEM CALLS                    chown(2)

NAME
 chown, lchown, fchown - change owner and group of a file

SYNOPSIS
 #include <unistd.h>
 #include <sys/types.h>

 int chown(const char *path, uid_t owner, gid_t group);

 int lchown(const char *path, uid_t owner, gid_t group);

 int fchown(int fildes, uid_towner, gid_t group);
```

```
DESCRIPTION
chown() sets the owner ID and group ID of the file specified by path or
  referenced by the open file descriptor fields to owner and group
  respectively. If owner or group is specified as -1, chown() does not change
  the corresponding ID of the file.
(Additional lines deleted from this example)
```

When the `windex` database is available, you can also use the `man -k` option to display the section number of a command. The following example shows the output of the `man -k chown` command.

```
mopoke% man -k chown
chown            chown (1)      - change file ownership
chown            chown (1b)     - change owner
chown            chown (1m)     - change owner
chown            chown (2)      - change owner and group of a file
fchown           chown (2)      - change owner and group of a file
fchownat         chown (2)      - change owner and group of a file
lchown           chown (2)      - change owner and group of a file
nischown         nischown (1)   - change the owner of a NIS+ object
mopoke%
```

The `apropos` command also searches the `windex` database and does the same thing as the `man -k` command, as shown in the following example.

```
mopoke% apropos chown
chown            chown (1)      - change file ownership
chown            chown (1b)     - change owner
chown            chown (1m)     - change owner
chown            chown (2)      - change owner and group of a file
fchown           chown (2)      - change owner and group of a file
fchownat         chown (2)      - change owner and group of a file
lchown           chown (2)      - change owner and group of a file
nischown         nischown (1)   - change the owner of a NIS+ object
mopoke%
```

Finding Disk Information

Use the `df` and `du` commands described in the following sections to show disk use information and to tell if a file system is local (UFS) or remote (NFS).

You can also use the SMC tools in the Storage category—Mounts and Shares, Disks, and Enhanced Storage—to find and manage disk information. Refer to the *Solaris Management Console Tools* book, published by Sun Microsystems Press and Prentice Hall, for more information about the SMC tools.

Displaying Used Disk Space in a Human-Readable Format (df -h)

Use the -h option of the df command—new in the Solaris 9 Operating Environment—to display disk information in a format that is easier to read, for example, 14K, 234M, 2.7G, or 3.0T. Scaling is done by repetitively dividing by 1024. The following example shows the disk use for the mopoke system.

```
mopoke% df -h
Filesystem           size   used  avail capacity  Mounted on
/dev/dsk/c1t0d0s0    9.6G   2.0G   7.6G    21%     /
/proc                  0K     0K     0K     0%     /proc
mnttab                 0K     0K     0K     0%     /etc/mnttab
fd                     0K     0K     0K     0%     /dev/fd
swap                 533M    40K   533M     1%     /var/run
swap                 534M   344K   533M     1%     /tmp
/dev/dsk/c1t0d0s7    3.9G    11M   3.9G     1%     /export/home
/vol/dev/dsk/c1t1d0/sol_9_doc_1of2
                     356M   356M     0K   100%     /cdrom/sol_9_doc_1of2
/export/home/winsor  3.9G    11M   3.9G     1%     /home/winsor
mopoke%
```

Displaying Used Disk Space in Kilobytes and Percentage of Capacity (df -k)

Use the -k option of the df command to display disk information in the table format used with SunOS 4.x system software. Type **df -k** and press Return. The file system, total kilobytes, used kilobytes, available kilobytes, percentage of capacity used, and mount point for local disk partitions are displayed, as shown in the following example.

```
paperbark% df -k
Filesystem          kbytes    used    avail capacity  Mounted on
/dev/dsk/c0t0d0s0  1388215  920657   412030   70%     /
/proc                    0       0        0    0%     /proc
fd                       0       0        0    0%     /dev/fd
mnttab                   0       0        0    0%     /etc/mnttab
swap                529832       0   529832    0%     /var/run
swap                530136     304   529832    1%     /tmp
/dev/dsk/c0t0d0s7   112783   25289    76216   25%     /export/home
/dev/dsk/c0t1d0s7  2012390       9  1952010    1%     /export/home0
paperbark%
```

Determining Whether File Systems Are Local or NFS Mounted (df)

To find out whether file systems are local or NFS mounted, type **df *filesystem*** and press Return. Disk formatting information (including disk location or mount point) for the file system you specify is displayed.

In the following example, the file system is NFS mounted.

```
oak% df /home/ignatz
bigriver:/export/home/ignatz
     538980  399435   85647    82%    /home/ignatz
oak%
```

In the following example, the file system is on a local disk.

```
# df /
/dev/dsk/c0t0d0s0   30383    11885   15468    43%    /
#
```

Finding All Mounted File Systems of a Specific Type (df -F)

If you want to display all the mounted file systems of one file system type, use the -F option followed by the file system type. The most common file system types are ufs for local file systems and nfs for network file systems. To find all mounted file systems of a specific type, type **df -F** *filesystem-type* and press Return.

In the following example, the mounted NFS file systems are displayed.

```
cinderella% df -F nfs
/net   (cinderella:(pid153)):       0 blocks      -1 files
/usr/dist cinderella:(pid153)):    1276248 blocks  -1 files
/home  (cinderella:(pid153)):       0 blocks      -1 files
/usr/man      (oak:/export/man):   272934 blocks  -1 files
cinderella%
```

In the following example, the mounted UFS (local) file systems are displayed.

```
cinderella% df -F ufs

  (/dev/dsk/c0t0d0s0): 36992   blocks   13558 files
/usr   (/dev/dsk/c0t0d0s6):  274346 blocks   94403 files
/export/home/cinderella (/dev/dsk/c0t3d0s7):379670 blocks      96046 files
cinderella%
```

In the following example, information about the mounted temporary file system is displayed.

```
cinderella% df -F tmpfs
/tmp            (swap       ):   88528 blocks   3156 files
cinderella%
```

NOTE. You cannot use the df *command to display SWAPFS file systems because they are never mounted.*

3

UNDERSTANDING THE FLASH INSTALL AND LIVE UPGRADE FEATURES

The Solaris 9 release provides two new installation configurations.

New!

- Flash installation. With Flash installation, you can create a base configuration and install it on a master system. This base installation includes the Solaris Operating Environment and can install other, third-party, software. You then use the master system to create a Flash archive that you can use to replicate the configuration as an initial installation on clone systems. You can create as many Flash archives as you need to accommodate any number of standard configurations for your site.

- Solaris Live Upgrade. With Solaris Live Upgrade, you create a duplicate boot environment. You can perform JumpStart installs, install and remove patches, and perform regular `suninstall` installations and upgrades on an inactive boot environment. You can also install Flash archives on the inactive boot environment. When you are ready, you activate the duplicate boot environment. At the next reboot, it becomes the active boot environment. If a failure occurs, you can recover your original boot environment with a simple activate and reboot.

As a security enhancement, starting with the Solaris 9 Operating Environment, the base installation package has been divided into smaller packages so that you can install commands, such as `telnet`, as an individual package. This division provides finer granularity and enables system administrators to create a base installation and deselect some packages. With this new arrangement, you can create more secure installations.

NOTE. Refer to Sun's Solaris 9 Installation Guide for instructions on performing installations with `suninstall`, *JumpStart, and WebStart.*

Flash Installation

With Flash installation, you can create a single reference installation of the Solaris Operating Environment on one system, called the master system. You then can replicate that installation as a new installation on any number of systems, called clone systems, that have the same architecture as the master system.

The process of installing clone systems with Flash installation has three parts.

1. Install the master system. Select a system and use any of the Solaris installation methods to install the Solaris Operating Environment and any additional software packages.
2. Create the Flash archive. This archive contains a copy of all of the files on the master system.
3. Install the Flash archive on clone systems. All the files in the archive are copied to that system to create a system that has the same installation configuration as the original master system.

You can use Flash archives with either WebStart or JumpStart to perform initial installations. The Flash archive snapshot contains the Solaris Operating Environment as well as all software, including third-party software, that you want to install on the new systems. You stream the entire archive to the boot disk. Flash installation would make reinstalling a machine much faster.

NOTE. You cannot use the Flash installation to upgrade a system that is running the Solaris Operating Environment. You can use Flash installation only for initial installation.

Designing the Master System Installation

The first step in the Flash installation process is to install the master system with the configuration that you want to replicate on each of the clone systems. You can use any of the Solaris installation methods to install a subset or a complete installation of the Solaris Operating Environment on the master system.

NOTE. The master system and the clone systems must have the same kernel architecture. If you have a site with systems that have multiple architectures, you can create a Flash installation archive for each architecture and use that archive for installation on clone systems with the same architecture. However, under Solaris 7, 8, and 9, all models of the UltraSPARC chip have the same sun4u *kernel architecture.*

Decide what configuration you want to make available to the clone systems. Consider the following elements.

- The software you want to install on the clone systems.
- Peripheral devices that are connected to the master system and the clone systems.
- The architecture of the master system and the clone systems.

After you install the Solaris Operating Environment on the master system, you can delete software that is not needed on the clone systems. You can install Solaris packages or third-party software. Any software you install on the master system is included in the Flash archive and is installed on the clone systems. You can modify configuration files on the master system. For example, you can modify the /etc/inet/inetd.conf file to restrict the daemons that the system runs.

After you install the Flash archive on a clone system, the installation program uses the sys-unconfig(1M) command and the sysidtool(1M) programs to delete and re-create the host-specific network configuration files. These files include /etc/hosts, /etc/defaultrouter, and /etc/defaultdomain.

Be sure to consider what peripheral devices on the clone systems might need drivers that are not needed on the master system. For example, if you install the Entire Software Group on a master system with a cg6 frame buffer, the installation contains support for only the cg6 frame buffer. You can use this archive file to install on clone systems that have either the cg6 frame buffer or no frame buffer. If you use this archive to install a clone system with an Elite 3D frame buffer, the Elite 3D is unusable because the required drivers were not installed.

You can install support for different peripherals in one of the following ways.

- Install the Entire Plus OEM Software Group. This software group contains every package found in the Solaris Operating Environment and thus contains all of the drivers installed with the Solaris release. A Flash archive that is created from a master system with this installation works on any clone system that has peripheral devices that are supported by the installed release of the Solaris Operating Environment.

- Install selected packages that install support only for the peripherals that you know exist on the master system or clone systems.

Refer to the *Solaris 9 Installation Guide* for complete information on designing a master system for use with Flash Installation.

Creating a Flash Archive

After you install the master system, you create the Flash archive. All the files on the master system are copied to the archive along with various pieces of identifying information. You can create a Flash archive while the master system is running in multiuser mode or single-user mode. You can also create a Flash archive after you boot from one of the following:

- Solaris 9 DVD.
- Solaris 9 Software 1 of 2 CD.
- An image of the Solaris 9 Software and the Solaris 9 Language CDs.

Create the archive when the system is in as static a state as possible.

You run the `flarcreate(1M)` command to create the archive. The `flarcreate` command requires the `-n` *name* option and a file name for the archive. The command also has options for the following actions.

- Compressing (`-c`).
- Listing directories and sizes (`-R` *root*, `-S`, `-H`).
- Excluding files and directories (`-x` *exclude*).
- Enabling user-defined sections (`-u` *section*, `-d` *dir*).
- Using with tape archives (`-t`, `-p` *posn*).
- Specifying block size (`-b` *blocksize*).
- Specifying files (`-f` *file_list*, `-F`).
- Identifying archive (`-U` *key-val*, `-i` *date*, `-m` *master*, `-e` *descr*, `-E` *descr_file*, `-a` *author*, `-T` *type*).

Refer to the `flarcreate(1M)` manual page for a more detailed description of these options.

You can create layered Flash archives by creating partial Flash archives that you install in a variety of combinations. For example, you can create one archive that contains the Solaris Operating Environment files, a second archive that contains the files for a Web server, and a third archive that contains the files for an NFS server. You would then install the first and second archives to create a Web server and install the first and third archives on another system to create an NFS server.

You can save the archive on the hard disk of the master system or on a tape. After you save the archive, you copy it to any file system or medium.

You can use the flar(1M) command to administer archives. You can use the flar command to extract information from an archive, split archives into sections, and combine archives from individual sections.

Use the following steps to create a Flash archive.

1. Boot the master system and run it either in single-user mode or in multiuser mode in as inactive a state as possible.

2. If in multiuser mode, become superuser.

3. Type **flarcreate -n *name options path/archivename*** and press Return.

   When the archive creation is successful, flarcreate returns an exit code of 0. If archive creation fails, the command returns a non-zero exit code.

The following example creates an archive for the master system named mopoke, running in multiuser mode, with a name of mopokearchive and an archive name of mopokearchive in the current directory, specifies the name of the master system, and compresses the archive.

```
# flarcreate -n mopokearchive -c -m mopoke mopokearchive
Determining which filesystems will be included in the archive...
Determining the size of the archive...
The archive will be approximately 1.05GB.
Creating the archive...
3979899 blocks
Archive creation complete.
#
```

Choosing a Flash Archive Installation Method

You can use any of the following Solaris installation methods to install Flash archives on clone systems.

With the Solaris WebStart program on the Solaris 9 DVD or Solaris 9 Installation CD, you can install Flash archives that are stored on any of the following media.

- Disc (DVD or CD).
- NFS server.
- HTTP server.

- FTP server.
- Local tape.

With the Solaris `suninstall` program on the Solaris 9 Software 1 of 2 CD, you can install Flash archives that are stored on the following media.

- Local device, including CD.
- NFS server.
- HTTP server.
- FTP server.
- Local tape.
- Local file.

With the custom JumpStart installation program, you can install Flash archives that are stored on any of the following media.

- Local device, including DVD or CD.
- NFS server.
- HTTP server.
- FTP server.
- Local tape.
- Local file.

With Solaris Live Upgrade, you can install Flash archives that are stored on any of the following media.

- Local device, including DVD or CD.
- NFS server.
- HTTP server.
- FTP server.
- Local tape.
- Local file.

See "Solaris Live Upgrade" on page 108 for more information about Solaris Live Upgrade.

Installing a Flash Archive with the Solaris WebStart Program

The following steps describe the process for installing a Flash archive with the Solaris WebStart program.

1. At the OpenBoot PROM, insert the Solaris 9 Installation CD or DVD in the drive and boot from the disc.
2. Specify the language and locale.

3. Specify the configuration information for this system.

4. On the Specify Media panel, select the location of the Flash archive.

   The Solaris WebStart program prompts you to proceed, depending on the media you selected.

5. Type the information required.
   - For DVD or CD, insert the disc containing the Flash archive(s).
   - For Network File System, specify the path to the network file system where the Flash Archive is located. You can also specify the archive file name.
   - For HTTP, specify the URL and proxy information that is needed to access the Flash archive.
   - For FTP, specify the FTP server and the path to the Flash archive. Specify the user and password information that enables you to access the FTP server. Specify any proxy information that is needed to access the FTP server.
   - For local tape, specify the local tape device and the position on the tape where the Flash archive is located.

6. For archives stored on a disc or an NFS server, on the Select Flash Archives pane, select one or more Flash archives to install.

7. On the Flash Archives Summary panel, confirm the selected archives and click Next.

8. On the additional Flash Archives panel, you can select to install layered Flash archives by specifying the medium where another archive is located. If you do not want to install additional archives, select None and click Next to continue the installation.

Installing a Flash Archive with the suninstall Program

The following steps describe the process for installing a Flash archive with the Solaris suninstall program.

1. Insert the Solaris 9 Software 1 of 2 CD or DVD in the drive.
2. Specify the language and install the miniroot.
3. Specify the configuration information for this system.
4. Press F4 to choose Initial Install for a Flash archive installation.

   Press F4 to choose Flash installation.
5. On the Flash Archive Retrieval Method screen, select the type of medium that contains the Flash archive.

The `suninstall` program prompts you to proceed, depending on the medium you selected.

6. Type the information required.

   • For DVD or CD, insert the disc containing the Flash archive(s).

   • For Network file system, specify the path to the network file system where the Flash archive is located. You can also specify the archive file name.

   • For HTTP, specify the URL and proxy information that is needed to access the Flash archive.

   • For FTP, specify the FTP server and the path to the Flash archive. Specify the user and password information that enables you to access the FTP server. Specify any proxy information that is needed to access the FTP server.

   • For local tape, specify the local tape device and the position on the tape where the Flash archive is located.

7. For archives stored on a disc or an NFS server, on the Select Flash Archives pane, select one or more Flash archives to install.

8. On the Flash Archives Summary panel, confirm the selected archives and click Next.

9. On the additional Flash Archives panel, you can select to install layered Flash archives by specifying the medium where another archive is located. If you do not want to install additional archives, select None and click Next to continue the installation.

Refer to the *Solaris 9 Installation Guide* for instructions on custom JumpStart installation.

Solaris Live Upgrade

With Solaris Live Upgrade, you can create separate, inactive boot environments without affecting the currently running system. After you have created the boot environment (BE) and installed it, you activate that BE and reboot. The original BE remains available, and you can revert to it with a simple reboot.

With Solaris Live Upgrade you can do the following tasks.

   • Upgrade a system.

   • Change the disk configuration on the new boot environment to different file system types, sizes, and layouts.

- Maintain numerous boot environments with different images. For example, you can create a boot environment that contains current patches and create a boot environment that contains an Update release.

To use the Solaris Live Upgrade process, you perform the following tasks.

- Create a BE.
- Copy critical file systems to the BE.
- Upgrade the BE.
- Activate the BE.
- Reboot the system.

Describing the Solaris Live Upgrade method is beyond the scope of this book. Refer to the *Solaris 9 Installation Guide* for complete instructions.

Solaris Live Upgrade Commands

The Solaris Live Upgrade feature provides the commands listed in Table 26.

Table 26   Solaris Live Upgrade Commands

Command	Description
live_upgrade(5)	Overview of the Live Upgrade feature.
lu(1M)	FLMI-based interface to Live Upgrade functions.
luactivate(1M)	Activate a boot environment.
lucancel(1M)	Cancel a scheduled Live Upgrade copy or create procedure.
lucompare(1M)	Compare boot environments.
lucreate(1M)	Create a new boot environment.
lucurr(1M)	Display the name of the current active boot environment.
ludelete(1M)	Delete a boot environment.
ludesc(1M)	Display or set boot environment description.
lufslist(1M)	List configuration of a boot environment.
lumake(1M)	Populate a boot environment.
lumount(1M)	Mount all file systems in a boot environment.
lurename(1M)	Rename a boot environment.
lustatus(1M)	Display status of boot environments.
lutab(4)	List boot environments.

Table 26   Solaris Live Upgrade Commands (Continued)

Command	Description
luumount(1M)	Unmount all file systems in a boot environment.
luupgrade(1M)	Install, upgrade, and perform other functions on software on a boot environment.

Creating a Boot Environment

You can create one or more boot environments and copy critical file systems from an active BE to the new BE. You can reorganize the disk if necessary and customize file systems.

You can create a boot environment on an unused partition on an existing hard drive or on a separate hard drive.

Creating a BE can be a bit tricky. Refer to the *Solaris 9 Installation Guide* for complete instructions. This section provides a single example. Describing the complete process for creating all of the possible boot environment configurations is beyond the scope of this book.

Solaris Live Upgrade distinguishes between critical file systems and shareable file systems. Critical file systems required by the Solaris Operating Environment are separate mount points in the vfstab file of the active and inactive boot environments. Examples are root (/), /usr, /var, or /opt. You always copy these file systems from the source to the inactive BE.

Live Upgrade duplicates only file systems that are specific to the operating environment configuration. Live Upgrade considers operating environment file systems critical. When you create a new boot environment, Live Upgrade makes sure that these critical file systems are copied to different slices and that Live Upgrade updates the /etc/vfstab in the new boot environment accordingly. By contrast, shareable file systems are those that need not be duplicated, for example, user files such as those in the /export directory. Thus, when you create a boot environment, the /etc/vfstab file in the new boot environment does not update such shared file systems. Instead, it points to the same file system as the original boot environment.

The sharing of swap is a special circumstance. All swap slices are shared by default, but you can specify a destination directory for swap and copy the swap slice. A swap slice is not required.

Part of creating a new BE involves copying critical file systems to another slice. You may need to prepare the disk before you create the new BE. Check the disk to make sure it is formatted properly.

- Identify slices large enough to hold the file systems to be copied. If these slices do not exist on the disk on which you intend to create the new boot environment, you must create them manually with either the format(1M) or fmthard(1M) command.
- Identify file systems that contain directories that you want to share among boot environments.

NOTE. The slice must not be mounted or listed in the /etc/vfstab file.

You can use the (undocumented) /usr/lib/lu/ludevices command to list available spare partitions. In the following example, partition c1t0d0s4 is available for use as a BE.

```
# /usr/lib/lu/ludevices
/dev/dsk/c1t0d0s4 9216144
#
```

You can use the /usr/lib/lu/ludevices -x 9 option to display complete debugging information for all devices on a system.

Use the following steps to create a boot environment on a free slice on an existing disk.

1. Become superuser.
2. Type **lu** and press Return.
   The Live Upgrade character screen is displayed.
3. Use the arrow keys to highlight the Create menu option and press F3.
   The Live Upgrade Create screen is displayed.
4. Press the F2 function key (CHOICE) to choose an available slice for the BE.
   The slice you chose is displayed in the root (/) Device field.
5. Press F3 to save the changes.
   The slice you specified for the BE you specified is activated and formatting begins. Formatting takes some time. When the process is complete, the Live Upgrade character screen is displayed and shows the message Live Upgrade Create operation completed successfully.

The following example shows the progress message for successfully creating a BE named s9beta on slice c1d0t0s4 on the same disk as the active BE.

```
Updating system configuration files.

Creating configuration for boot environment <s9beta>.
```

```
****************************************************************

Beginning process of creating Boot Environment <s9beta>.
No more user interaction is required until this process is complete.

****************************************************************

Creating file systems on BE <s9beta>.
Creating <ufs> file system on </dev/dsk/c1t0d0s4>.
Mounting file systems for BE <s9beta>.
Calculating required sizes of file systems for BE <s9beta>.
Populating file systems on BE <s9beta>.
Copying file system contents to BE <s9beta>.
Copying of file system / directory </> is in progress...
```

Upgrading a Boot Environment

After you have created a BE, it remains unchanged until you are ready to upgrade it. You can upgrade the BE at any time. The upgrade does not affect any files in the active BE. When you are ready, you activate the new release and reboot the system.

Instead of upgrading a BE, you can install a Flash archive on a BE. The Flash installation feature enables you to create a single reference installation of the Solaris Operating Environment, including third-party software, on a master system. You can then replicate that installation on a number of clone systems. The inactive BE is considered a clone. See "Flash Installation" on page 102 for more information about the Flash installation feature.

Activating a Boot Environment

When the inactive BE is configured and upgraded, you use the following procedure to activate the new boot environment.

1. Become superuser.
2. Type **lu** and press Return.
   The Live Upgrade character screen is displayed.
3. Choose the Activate menu item and press F3.
   The Activate a Boot Environment window is displayed.
4. Type the name of the boot environment you want to activate and press F3.
   The BE you specified is activated.
5. Press F6 to exit the screens, then use the arrow keys to scroll down to the Exit menu item and press Return.
   The Live Upgrade program is terminated.
6. Type init 6 and press Return.
   The system is rebooted, using the newly activated BE.

Alternatively, you can use the luactivate command to activate a BE.

4

UNDERSTANDING
SHELLS

The Solaris 9 Operating Environment provides six shells for use as command interpreters. The three basic shells are the Bourne shell (the default), the C shell, and the Korn shell. In addition, the Solaris 9 Operating Environment includes three freeware shells: the Bourne-Again shell (`bash`), the TC shell (`tcsh`), and the Z shell (`zsh`). One shell is defined as the default shell for each user, but users can start a new shell from the command line. This chapter describes elements that are common to all shells and then provides a section for each shell that describes some of the prevalent shell features.

The root account uses the Bourne shell because it is statically linked and does not require any commands from the `/usr` account to function.

New!

Table 27 lists the basic shell features and shows which shells provide each feature.

Table 27   *Basic Features of Bourne, Bourne-Again, Korn, Z, C, and TC Shells*

Feature	Bourne	bash	Korn	zsh	C	tcsh
Aliases.	Yes	Yes	Yes	Yes	Yes	Yes
Command-line editing.	No	Yes	Yes	Yes	Yes	Yes
Enhanced cd.	No	Yes	Yes	Yes	Yes	Yes
History list.	No	Yes	Yes	Yes	Yes	Yes
Ignore CTRL-D (ignoreeof).	No	Yes	Yes	Yes	Yes	Yes

Table 27   Basic Features of Bourne, Bourne-Again, Korn, Z, C, and TC Shells (Continued)

Feature	Bourne	bash	Korn	zsh	C	tcsh
`.profile` initialization file.	Yes	Yes	Yes	Yes	No	No
`.cshrc` initialization file.	No	No	No	No	Yes	Yes
Supplementary initialization file, for example, *ksh-env* file.	No	Yes	Yes	Yes	No	No
Job control.	Yes	Yes	Yes	Yes	Yes	Yes
Logout file.	No	Yes	No	Yes	Yes	Yes
Protection of files from overwriting (`noclobber`).	No	Yes	Yes	Yes	Yes	Yes
Syntax compatible with Bourne shell.	Yes	Yes	Yes	Yes	No	No

New!

Tasks Common to All Shells

The following sections describe concepts and tasks that can be used with any shell.

Setting a Default Shell

New!

The user's login shell is set in the last field of the user's entry in the Passwd database or /etc/passwd file. Use the SMC System Configuration:Users: User Accounts tool to edit the Passwd database in a networked environment.

Changing Shells from a Command Line (csh, ksh, sh, bash, tcsh)

If you want to use another shell without modifying the Passwd database, you can change shells at a command-line prompt by simply typing the name of the shell you want to use.

To change to the C shell, type **csh** and press Return. The default C shell prompt is the system name followed by a percent sign (%).

```
$ csh
paperbark%
```

To change to the Korn shell, type **ksh** and press Return. The default Korn shell prompt is a dollar sign ($).

```
paperbark% ksh
$
```

To change to the Bourne shell, type **sh** and press Return. The default Bourne shell prompt also is a dollar sign ($).

```
$ sh
$
```

To change to the Bourne-Again shell, type bash and press Return. The default Bourne-Again shell prompt is bash-*version*$, where *version* is the particular bash shell you are using.

New!

```
paperbark% bash
bash-2.03$
```

NOTE. The default prompt can change if you apply subsequent Solaris patches to the shell.

New!

To change to tcsh, type tcsh and press Return. The default tcsh prompt is >.

```
paperbark% tcsh
>
```

To change to the Z shell, type zsh and press Return. With no startup files, the prompt does not change.

Quitting from a Shell (exit)

If you start a new shell from the command line, you can quit it and return to the old shell. To quit from a shell, type **exit** and press Return. If you have started (layered) another shell, you are returned to the original shell prompt.

```
$ exit
oak%
```

New!

Setting Aliases, Paths, and Environment Variables

Environment variables in a shell are inherited by all subsequent shells and any programs you start from them. For shells that have two login files—all but the Bourne shell—you should set all environment variables in the `.login` file.

Aliases and functions are not inherited by subsequent shells. They are redefined for each shell separately. Set aliases and functions in the `.cshrc` file for the C shell, in the `.ksh_env` file for the Korn shell, and in the relevant files for `tcsh`, `bash`, and `zsh` shells.

The following example shows what can go wrong if you don't follow the guidelines about where to set environment variables. Using the C shell as an example, suppose you know your login C shell sources `$HOME/.cshrc` whenever you start a shell—call this Shell1. Now, you add the following command to the `PATH` variable in `$HOME/.cshrc`.

```
setenv PATH ${PATH}:/my/dir
```

If you now start another shell from Shell1, that shell inherits the `PATH` setting from Shell1 (because it's an environment setting), but your `$HOME/.cshrc` file gets sourced again, thus adding `: ...:/my/dir:/my/dir` .to the end of your `PATH`. Not good. This construct can, over time, overflow your `PATH` environment variable, resulting in an administrative nightmare.

However, when you use `$HOME/.login` as the place to set the `PATH` environment variable, your login shell gets the definition of `PATH` and all subsequent shells inherit it.

NOTE. You must export environment variables for the Bourne, Korn, Bourne-Again, and Z shells so that their children can inherit them.

The Solaris Operating Environment provides several default environment variables.

- `PS1` defines the shell prompt for the Bourne and Korn shells. The default prompt for the Bourne and Korn shells is `$`. The default prompt for root in either shell is `#`.

- `HOME` defines the absolute path to the user's home directory. The default value for `HOME` is automatically defined and set to the login directory specified in the `/etc/passwd` file as part of the login process. The shell subsequently uses this information to determine the directory to change to when you type the `cd` command without an argument.

- LOGNAME defines the user's login name. The default value for LOGNAME is automatically defined and set to the login name specified in the /etc/passwd file as part of the login process.

- PATH lists, in order, the directories that the shell searches to find the program to run. When the user executes a command and uses the full path name, the shell finds the command by using that path name. However, when the user specifies only a command name, the shell searches the directories for the command in the order specified by the PATH variable. If the command is found in one of the directories, the shell executes it. If the directory containing the command is not in the search path, the user must then type the complete path name of a command.

  The default PATH is automatically defined and set as specified in .profile (Bourne or Korn shell) or .login (C shell) as part of the login process (see "Setting the Path for Bourne and Korn Shells" and "Setting the Path for Bourne and Korn Shells" on page 119 for details). When identically named commands exist in different locations, the first command found with that name is used. For example, suppose that PATH is defined (in Bourne and Korn shell syntax) as PATH=/bin:/usr/bin:/usr/sbin:$HOME/bin; then suppose a file named sample resides in both /usr/bin and /home/jean/bin. If the user types the command sample without specifying its full path name, the version found in /usr/bin is used.

  A default su path (/sbin:/usr/sbin:/usr/bin:/etc) is set by the system, but most users modify it to add other command directories. Many user problems related to setting up the environment and accessing the right version of a command or a tool can be traced to incorrectly defined paths.

CAUTION. *Including . in the path to search the current directory is a potential security problem. If security is an issue at your site, do not include . as part of a user's path. Never use . as part of the root path.*

- The LANG and LC environment variables specify the locale-specific conversions and conventions for the shell, such as time zones, collation order, and format of dates, time, currency, and numbers. In addition, you can use the stty command in a user-initialization file to set whether the system supports multibyte characters.

  LANG sets all possible conversions and conventions for the given locale. If you have special needs, you can set various aspects of localization separately by using the following LC variables.

  - LC_COLLATE
  - LC_CTYPE
  - LC_MESSAGES

- LC_NUMERIC
- LC_MONETARY
- LC_TIME

Table 28 lists the values for the LANG and LC environment variables.

Table 28   Values for LANG and LC Variables

Value	Locale
DE	German.
FR	French.
ISO_8859_1	English and European.
IT	Italian.
JAPANESE	Japanese.
KOREAN	Korean.
SV	Swedish.
TCHINESE	Taiwanese.

Other environment variables include the following.

- ARCH sets the user's system architecture (for example sun4, i386). You can set this variable in the Bourne or Korn shells with ARCH = `uname -p` or in the C shell with setenv ARCH `uname -p`. No built-in behavior of the shell depends on this variable. However, it is a useful variable for branching within shell scripts.
- CALENDAR sets the path to the Calendar executables.
- CDPATH (or cdpath in the C shell) sets a variable used by the cd command. If the target directory of the cd command is specified as a relative path name, the cd command first looks for the target directory in the current directory (.). If the target is not found, the path names listed in the CDPATH variable are searched consecutively until the target directory is found and the directory change is completed.
- DESKSET sets the path to the DeskSet executables.
- history sets history for the C shell.
- LD_LIBRARY_PATH sets the search path for dynamically linked libraries.
- LPDEST sets the user's default printer.
- MAIL tells the shell where to look for new mail.
- MANPATH sets the hierarchies of the available manual pages.

- MANSECTS sets the available sections of manual pages.

- OPENWINHOME sets the path to the OpenWindows executables.

- prompt defines the shell prompt for the C shell.

- SHELL sets the default shell used by make, vi, and other tools.

- TERM sets the terminal definition. This variable should be reset in /etc/profile or /etc/.login. When the user invokes an editor, the system looks for a file with the same name as the definition of this environment variable. The system searches the directory referenced by TERMINFO to determine the terminal characteristics.

- TERMINFO specifies the path name for an unsupported terminal that has been added to the terminfo file. Use the TERMINFO variable in /etc/profile or /etc/.login.

- TZ sets the time zone.

Users and system administrators can define additional variables for their own use. When you define an environment variable from a shell command, the variable remains in effect while you are working in the shell. When you exit the shell, the environment variable is not retained. Store "permanent" environment variables that are likely to be used during each login session in the .profile or .login file. The syntax for defining environment variables depends on the shell and is described elsewhere in this chapter.

Setting the Path for Bourne and Korn Shells

The path for the Bourne and Korn shells is specified in the user's $HOME/.profile file as shown in the following example.

```
PATH=/usr/bin:/$HOME/bin:.
```

Setting the Path for the C Shell

The path for the C shell is specified in the user's $HOME/.cshrc file (with the set path environment variable) as shown in the following example.

```
set path = (/usr/bin $home/bin .)
```

See the appropriate manual pages for an in-depth description of these commands, and also see Chapter 12, "Recognizing File Access Problems," for more information about troubleshooting problems with paths.

Displaying Environment Variable Settings (env)

Each shell maintains an environment with a set of specifications that it gets from the user's initialization files (`.profile` for the Bourne and Korn shells or `.cshrc` and `.login` for the C shell) or from environment variables set interactively from a shell. These environment variables can specify information such as the user's home directory, login name, default printer, location for e-mail messages, and path for accessing the OpenWindows environment.

To display a list of the current environment variable settings, type **env** and press Return.

The following example shows all the environment variables for a system running CDE.

```
paperbark% env
MANPATH=/usr/dt/man:/usr/man:/usr/openwin/share/man
DTDATABASESEARCHPATH=/export/home/winsor/.dt/types,/etc/dt/appconfig/types/%L,
   /etc/dt/appconfig/types/C,/usr/dt/appconfig/types/%L,/usr/dt/appconfig/types
   /C
DTXSERVERLOCATION=local
LANG=C
HELPPATH=/usr/openwin/lib/locale:/usr/openwin/lib/help
DTSOURCEPROFILE=true
PATH=/usr/openwin/bin:/usr/dt/bin:/export/home/opt/SUNWadm/bin:/bin:/usr/bin:/
   usr/sbin:/usr/ucb:/etc:/usr/proc/bin:/usr/ccs/bin:/opt/hpnp/bin:/opt/NSCPcom
   :/usr/local/games:.
AB_CARDCATALOG=/usr/dt/share/answerbooks/C/ab_cardcatalog
DTUSERSESSION=winsor-paperbark-0
XMICONBMSEARCHPATH=/export/home/winsor/.dt/icons/%B%M.bm:/export/home/winsor/.
   dt/icons/%B%M.pm:/export/home/winsor/.dt/icons/%B:/etc/dt/appconfig/icons/%L
   /%B%M.bm:/etc/dt/appconfig/icons/%L/%B%M.pm:/etc/dt/appconfig/icons/%L/%B:/e
   tc/dt/appconfig/icons/C/%B%M.bm:/etc/dt/appconfig/icons/C/%B%M.pm:/etc/dt/ap
   pconfig/icons/C/%B:/usr/dt/appconfig/icons/%L/%B%M.bm:/usr/dt/appconfig/icon
   s/%L/%B%M.pm:/usr/dt/appconfig/icons/%L/%B:/usr/dt/appconfig/icons/C/%B%M.bm
   :/usr/dt/appconfig/icons/C/%B%M.pm:/usr/dt/appconfig/icons/C/%B
SESSION_SVR=paperbark
OPENWINHOME=/usr/openwin
EDITOR=/usr/dt/bin/dtpad
LOGNAME=winsor
DTSCREENSAVERLIST=StartDtscreenSwarm StartDtscreenQix        StartDtscreenFlame
   StartDtscreenHop StartDtscreenImage StartDtscreenLife      StartDtscreenRotor
   StartDtscreenPyro StartDtscreenWorm StartDtscreenBlank
MAIL=/var/mail/winsor
USER=winsor
DISPLAY=:0.0
SHELL=/bin/csh
DTAPPSEARCHPATH=/export/home/winsor/.dt/appmanager:/etc/dt/appconfig/appmanage
   r/%L:/etc/dt/appconfig/appmanager/C:/usr/dt/appconfig/appmanager/%L:/usr/dt/
   appconfig/appmanager/C
HOME=/export/home/winsor
XFILESEARCHPATH=/usr/openwin/lib/locale/%L/%T/%N%S:/usr/openwin/lib/%T/%N%S
XMICONSEARCHPATH=/export/home/winsor/.dt/icons/%B%M.pm:/export/home/winsor/.dt
   /icons/%B%M.bm:/export/home/winsor/.dt/icons/%B:/etc/dt/appconfig/icons/%L/%
   B%M.pm:/etc/dt/appconfig/icons/%L/%B%M.bm:/etc/dt/appconfig/icons/%L/%B:/etc
   /dt/appconfig/icons/C/%B%M.pm:/etc/dt/appconfig/icons/C/%B%M.bm:/etc/dt/appc
   onfig/icons/C/%B:/usr/dt/appconfig/icons/%L/%B%M.pm:/usr/dt/appconfig/icons/
   %L/%B%M.bm:/usr/dt/appconfig/icons/%L/%B:/usr/dt/appconfig/icons/C/%B%M.pm:/
   usr/dt/appconfig/icons/C/%B%M.bm:/usr/dt/appconfig/icons/C/%B
TERM=dtterm
dtstart_sessionlogfile=/dev/null
TZ=Australia/West
```

```
DTHELPSEARCHPATH=/export/home/winsor/.dt/help/winsor-paperbark-0/%H:/export/ho
  me/winsor/.dt/help/winsor-paperbark-0/%H.sdl:/export/home/winsor/.dt/help/wi
  nsor-paperbark-0/%H.hv:/export/home/winsor/.dt/help/%H:/export/home/winsor/.
  dt/help/%H.sdl:/export/home/winsor/.dt/help/%H.hv:/etc/dt/appconfig/help/%L/
  %H:/etc/dt/appconfig/help/%L/%H.sdl:/etc/dt/appconfig/help/%L/%H.hv:/usr/dt/
  appconfig/help/%L/%H:/usr/dt/appconfig/help/%L/%H.sdl:/usr/dt/appconfig/help
  /%L/%H.hv:/usr/dt/appconfig/help/C/%H:/usr/dt/appconfig/help/C/%H.sdl:/usr/d
  t/appconfig/help/C/%H.hv
XMBINDDIR=/usr/dt/lib/bindings
WINDOWID=96469001
TERMINAL_EMULATOR=dtterm
PWD=/export/home/winsor
paperbark%
```

Clearing a Shell Window (clear)

You can clear the contents of a shell window and redisplay the prompt at the top of the window. To clear the contents of a shell window, type **clear** and press Return.

```
oak% ls -l /home/ignatz/quest
-rw-r--r--   1 ignatz    staff         24 Jul 16 15:07 quest
oak% clear
```

The window is cleared and the prompt is redisplayed at the top.

Setting the Shell Backspace Key (stty erase)

If you want to change the erase key from Delete to Backspace, type **stty erase**, then press Control and Shift together, and then type **H** and press Return. The Backspace key is set as the erase key. The following example changes the erase key for the C shell.

```
oak% stty erase ^H
oak%
```

Typing Several Commands on the Same Command Line (;)

You can type more than one command on a single command line by typing a semicolon (;) between the commands.

For example, you can change to a directory and list the commands by typing **cd /usr/bin;ls** and pressing Return. The following example sets an environment variable for the Bourne shell and then exports the variable.

```
$ PATH=/usr/bin:$HOME/bin:.;export PATH
$
```

Redirecting Output (<>)

Unless you indicate otherwise, commands normally display their results on the screen. You can, however, redirect the output of a command by using the redirect symbols < and >. For example, to save the output to a file instead of displaying it on the screen, use the > redirect symbol to tell the shell to put the contents into a file. In the following example, the output of the date command is redirected to a new file called date.file.

```
$ date > date.file
$
```

The following example shows the contents of date.file.

```
paperbark% more date.file
Wed May  3 15:59:50 WST 2000
paperbark%
```

You can also redirect input in the other direction. For example, to mail the contents of a file to user ignatz@oak, type **mail ignatz@oak < report.file** and press Return. The file called report.file is sent by e-mail to ignatz@oak.

Combining Commands (|)

You can use the pipe (|) operator to connect two or more commands, using the output from one command as the input to the next one. This section provides two examples of the many ways you can combine commands in a pipeline.

To print the cat(1) manual page, type **man cat | lp** and press Return. The manual page is not displayed on the screen. Instead, the output is sent to the lp command, which prints it on the default printer.

You can search the process list for a particular command by piping the output of ps -e to the grep command. The output is displayed on the screen. The following example displays process information for OpenWindows.

```
cinderella% ps -e | grep openwin
   260 ?         0:00 openwin
cinderella%
```

If you want to print the information, you can add an additional pipe command (| lp) to the end of the sequence and send it to the printer, as shown in the following example.

```
anastasia% ps -e | grep openwin | lp
request id is castle-51 (request id is castle-51 (standard input)
anastasia%
```

The Bourne Shell

The default shell for the Solaris Operating Environment is the Bourne shell, developed by Steve Bourne when he was at AT&T Bell Laboratories. The Bourne shell is a small shell for general-purpose use. It also provides a full-scale scripting language that is used to develop shell scripts to capture frequently performed commands and procedures. Describing how to write shell scripts is beyond the scope of this book.

An excellent shell programming reference is *UNIX Shell Programming,* *New!* Revised Edition, by Stephen G. Kochan and Patrick H. Wood, Hayden Books.

Reviewing the Bourne Shell Initialization File

The Bourne shell, when invoked as a login shell, first reads the *New!* /etc/profile file and then reads the $HOME.profile file in the user's home directory to set the user's environment. When the user logs in or starts a Bourne shell from the command line, the .profile file is read. Use this file to set the user's path and any environment variables.

Defining Bourne Shell Environment Variables

The syntax for defining an environment variable is the same for both the Bourne and Korn shells; type *VARIABLE=value;*export *VARIABLE* and press Return.

```
$ PS1=oak$;export PS1
$
```

Using Functions to Simulate Aliases for the Bourne Shell

In the Bourne shell, you can use functions to define aliases in the .profile file. The syntax for creating an alias function is shown below.

```
alias-name() {
     command-sequence
}
```

For example, if you frequently use the `ftp` command to send batches of files and don't want to be prompted for each file, you can create an alias for the `ftp -i` command to turn off interactive prompting. When you add the following line to your `.profile` file, `ftp` is started with interactive prompting turned off.

```
ftp() {
     ftp -i
}
```

New!

After you have made changes to a `.profile` file, the changes are not recognized unless you source the `.profile` file by typing `. .profile` or you log out and log in again. When you source the `.profile` file in a shell, the changes are recognized only in the current shell or any other shells or programs invoked from that shell.

The C Shell

The C shell, written by Bill Joy when he was at UC Berkeley, is popular with many users of Berkeley UNIX. The C shell is completely different from the Bourne and Korn shells and has its own syntax. The most important advantages of the C shell are command history, command editing, and aliases. *Command history* stores a record of the most recent commands that you have used. You can display these commands and reuse them as originally issued. *Command editing* enables you to change a command by editing it. *Aliases* let you type short names for frequently used commands. You can also combine sequences of frequently used commands and provide an alias for the sequence.

Reviewing C Shell Initialization Files

The C shell uses two initialization files in the user's home directory to set the user's environment: `.login` and `.cshrc` (C shell run control).

When you log in, the `.login` file is read, and then the `.cshrc` file. When you start the C shell from a command line, only the `.cshrc` file is read.

Defining C Shell Environment Variables

To define an environment variable for the C shell, type
setenv *VARIABLE value* and press Return.

```
oak% setenv DISPLAY rogue:0
oak%
```

Creating Aliases for the C Shell

Define any aliases for the user in the .cshrc file. The syntax for creating an alias is **alias** *alias-name command-sequence*. For example, if you frequently use the ftp command to send batches of files and don't want to be prompted for each file, you can create an alias for the ftp -i command to turn off interactive prompting. When you add the following line to your .cshrc file, ftp is started with interactive prompting turned off.

```
alias ftp "ftp -i"
```

The following example shows aliases from a .cshrc file. Note that if the command contains spaces, you enclose the entire command in quotes. Both double and single quotes are used in the following examples.

NOTE. Double quotes enable variables to be interpolated and single quotes don't.

```
alias a alias
a h history
a c clear
a lf ls -F
a ll "ls -l | more"
a la ls -a
a s "source .cshrc"
a f 'find ~ -name core -print'
a copytotape "tar cvf /dev/rmt/0 *"
a ftp "ftp -i"
```

After you have made changes to a .cshrc file, the changes are not recognized unless you source the .cshrc file by typing source .cshrc or until you log out and log in again. When you source the .cshrc file in a shell, the changes are recognized only in the current shell and any other shells and programs invoked from that shell.

Setting the History Size for the C Shell

The default is for the C shell to save only the most recent command in its history list. You can change the number of commands the shell saves. To set history for the C shell, on a command line type **set history=**n and press Return. history is set to the number of lines you specify.

```
oak% set history=10
oak%
```

You can set history temporarily for a shell window or set it "permanently" so that the same history setting is available at each login session. Enter the command as a line in your .cshrc file and type **source .cshrc**.

Using history for the C Shell

To display the history for the C shell, on a command line type **history** and press Return. The last n commands that you had set for the history are displayed.

```
oak% history
     26   pwd
     27   kermit
     28   cd Howto
     29   tar xvf /dev/rmt/0
     30   ls -l howto*
     31   cd
     32   cd Config/Art
     33   ls -l
     34   tar cvf /dev/rmt/0
     35   history
oak%
```

To repeat the previous command in a C shell, type ! ! and press Return. The previous command is executed again.

```
oak% history
     26   pwd
     27   kermit
     28   cd Howto
     29   tar xvf /dev/rmt/0
     30   ls -l howto*
     31   cd
     32   cd Config/Art
     33   ls -l
     34   tar xvf /dev/rmt/0
     35   history
oak% !!
history
     27   kermit
     28   cd Howto
     29   tar xvf /dev/rmt/0
     30   ls -l howto*
     31   cd
     32   cd Config/Art
     33   ls -l
     34   tar xvf /dev/rmt/0
     35   history
     36   history
oak%
```

To repeat the last word of the previous command in a C shell, type **!$** and press Return. The last word from the previous command is used as part of the command-line argument.

For example, you might list the complete path name of a file and then use the path name as the argument to edit the file with vi or to print it.

```
oak% ls -l /home/ignatz/quest
-rw-r--r--   1 ignatz    staff          24 Jul 16 15:07 quest
oak% lp !$
lp /home/ignatz/quest
oak%
```

You can use the !$ command anywhere within the command line. In the following example, the file /home/ignatz/quest is copied to the /tmp directory.

```
oak% ls -l /home/ignatz/quest
-rw-r--r--   1 ignatz    staff          24 Jul 16 15:07 quest
oak% cp !$ /tmp
cp /home/ignatz/quest /tmp
oak%
```

To repeat a numbered command in a C shell, type **!n** and press Return. The number in the shell prompt is *n*. The command is executed again.

```
oak% history
29  tar xvf /dev/rmt/0
30  ls -l howto*
31  cd
32  cd Config/Art
33  ls -l
34  tar xvf /dev/rmt/0
35  ls -l
36  cd
37  lp howto*
38  history
oak% !32
cd Config/Art
oak%
```

Incorporating a New Command for the C Shell (rehash)

The C shell keeps an internal record of the location of all executable files that are found in the directories named in the the path variable. This internal record is called a hash table. When you add a new command to any of the directories in your path, the C shell cannot see it until you use the rehash command to refresh the hash table. Any new commands are then incorporated into your command search path.

```
oak% newcommand
newcommand: Command not found
oak% rehash
oak% newcommand
Command output
oak%
```

Editing C Shell History Commands

You can edit commands retrieved from the history list by using the
s/*oldstring*/*newstring*/ form to substitute the retrieved string in the
command. In the following example, an incorrectly typed command from the
history list is corrected.

```
oak% history
    31  cd
    32  ls
    33  cd /home/frame3.1
    34  ls
    35  cd ..
    36  tar cvf /dev/rmt/0 frame3.1
    37  lp questionnaire
    38  lpstat -t
    39  echo $PaTH
    40  history
oak% !39:s/a/A/
echo $PATH
.:/home/winsor:/usr/openwin/bin:/usr/deskset/bin:/home/
  winsor/bin:/bin:/home/bin:/etc:/usr/etc:/usr/bin:/home/ frame3.1/bin
oak%
```

New!   An excellent C shell programming reference is *Using csh and tcsh*, by Paul
DuBois, O'Reilly & Associates, 1995.

The Korn Shell

The Korn shell, developed by David Korn of AT&T Bell Laboratories, is a
superset of the Bourne shell. That is, the Korn shell uses the same syntax as
the Bourne shell, but the Korn shell has more built-in functions that can be
defined directly from the shell. The Korn shell provides a more sophisticated
form of command editing than does the C shell. The Korn shell also provides
a command history and aliases.

The Korn shell provides a complete command and scripting language. The
following sections introduce some of the most basic features of the Korn shell.

Reviewing Korn Shell Initialization Files

The Korn shell uses two initialization files in the user's home directory to set the user's environment: .profile and *.ksh-env*, a file denoted by the ENV environment variable. You might want to name the file .kshrc because its function is similar to that of the C shell .cshrc file.

When the user logs in, the .profile file is read and then the *.ksh-env* file. The *.ksh-env* file lets you configure the Korn shell session to your needs. Put environment variable settings into the $HOME/.profile file, and put all aliases, functions, and set -o commands in the *.ksh-env* file.

You must set the ENV environment variable to point to the *.ksh-env* file. The syntax for setting environment variables in the Korn shell is the same as for the Bourne shell: *VARIABLE=value*;export *VARIABLE*. As in the Bourne shell, you must export the variable to make it inheritable by subsequent shells and programs invoked by the exporting shell. The following example sets the environment variable for a .kshrc file.

```
$ ENV=$HOME/.kshrc;export ENV
$
```

You must set this environment variable in the .profile file; otherwise, the .kshrc file is not found when you log in. The ENV variable has no default setting. Unless you set it, the feature is not used. The *.ksh-env* file is read each time you start the Korn shell from a command line.

Using Korn Shell Options

The Korn shell has a number of options that specify the user's environment and control execution of commands. To display the current option settings, type **set -o** and press Return. In the following example, the default options for the Korn shell for the Solaris Operating Environment are displayed.

```
$ set -o
Current option settings
allexport        off
bgnice           on
emacs            off
errexit          off
gmacs            off
ignoreeof        off
interactive      on
keyword          off
markdirs         off
monitor          on
noexec           off
noclobber        off
noglob           off
nolog            off
nounset          off
privileged       off
restricted       off
```

```
trackall        off
verbose         off
vi              off
viraw           off
xtrace          off
$
```

The default options are described in Table 29. Customarily, you set these options in the *.ksh-env* file.

Table 29   Korn Shell Options

Option	Default	Description
allexport	off	Automatically export variables when defined.
bgnice	on	Execute all background jobs at a lower priority.
emacs	off	Set emacs/gmacs as the in-line editor.
errexit	off	If a command returns the value False, the shell executes the ERR trap (if set) and immediately exits.
gmacs	off	Set gmacs as the in-line editor.
ignoreeof	off	When the interactive option is also set, the shell does not exit at end-of-file. Type **exit** to quit the shell.
interactive	on	The shell automatically turns the interactive option on so that shell prompts are displayed.
keyword	off	The shell puts each word with the syntax of a variable assignment in the variable assignment list.
markdirs	off	Display a / following the names of all directories resulting from path-name expansion.
monitor	on	Enable job control.
noclobber	off	Do not overwrite an existing file when the redirect operator (>) is used.
noexec	off	Read commands but do not execute them. You can use this option to debug shell script syntax errors.
noglob	off	Disable file-name expansion.
nolog	off	Do not store function definitions in the history file.

Table 29   *Korn Shell Options (Continued)*

Option	Default	Description
nounset	off	Display an error message when the shell tries to expand a variable that is not set.
privileged	off	When this option is off, the effective UID and GID of the user are ignored and the real UID and GID are used. When this option is on, the shell uses the effective UID and GID of the user.
restricted	off	Set a restricted shell.
trackall	off	Make command-tracked aliases when they are first encountered.
verbose	off	Display the input as it is read.
vi	off	Set vi as the in-line editor.
viraw	off	Specify character-at-a-time input from vi.
xtrace	off	Display commands and arguments as they are executed.

New!

To enable an option, type **set -o** *option-name* and press Return. To disable an option, type **set +o** *option-name* and press Return.

For example, entering this line in the user's *.ksh-env* file sets the in-line editor to vi.

```
set -o vi
```

The following example turns off vi as the in-line editor.

```
set +o vi
```

You can also set these options from a command line, using the same syntax.

Creating Korn Shell Aliases

The syntax for creating aliases for the Korn shell is alias *name=value*. The following example creates an alias for the alias command.

```
$ alias a=alias
$
```

The following example uses the a alias created in the last example to alias the history command to the letter h.

```
$ a h=history
$
```

The Korn shell comes with a default set of predefined aliases. To display the list, type **alias** and press Return.

```
$ alias
autoload=typeset -fu
false=let 0
functions=typeset -f
hash=alias -t -
history=fc -l
integer=typeset -i
nohup=nohup
r=fc -e -
stop=kill -STOP
suspend=kill -STOP $$
true=:
type=whence -v
$
```

The default aliases are described in Table 30.

Table 30   Korn Shell Preset Aliases

Alias	Value	Definition
autoload	typeset -fu	Allow function definitions to be deferred until the first time they are invoked. At that time, they are autoloaded on-the-fly.
		For example, autoload sum; *other shell statements;* sum 3 7 autoloads the sum function, then does other work. Finally, the command runs the sum function with the arguments 3 and 7. At this point, the shell searches all directories specified in the FPATH environment variable for a file named sum. If found, this file—which should contain the definition for the sum function—is sourced. Only then is the sum function called.

New!

Table 30 *Korn Shell Preset Aliases (Continued)*

Alias	Value	Definition	
command	command='command'	Used within a function to invoke a built-in shell command or an external program that happens to have the same name as the function so that you don't call the function recursively.	New!
functions	typeset -f	List all currently defined functions.	
history	fc -l	List the last 16 commands that were run in this shell.	
integer	typeset -i	Declare integer variable. For example, integer i=7.	
local	typeset	Allow the definition of a shell variable in a function that is local to that function. Without this alias, any shell you define in a function is global to the entire script.	New!

		Consider the following example.
		
		`function printdate {`
		`   local x=$(date)`
		`   echo ${x}`
		`}`
		
		Inside the function printdate, the local variable x is defined and is assigned the output of the date command. The contents of x are then printed. Note that x is not defined once the printdate function returns.	

nohup	nohup	When used on a program invoked from the shell, this alias prevents the program from receiving the hang-up (HUP) signal. This action prevents the program from being terminated if you log out, as it normally would be.	
r	'fc -e -'	Reexecute the previous command.	

Table 30   *Korn Shell Preset Aliases (Continued)*

Alias	Value	Definition
stop	kill -STOP	Send the STOP signal to the process with the PID you give as an argument. This alias stops the process until you use the bg or fg commands to allow the process to continue.
suspend	kill -STOP $$	Suspend the current shell by sending it the STOP signal. You do this only if you were running a shell, then invoked another shell from within it, and want to temporarily return to the original shell by suspending the second one.

Editing Commands with the Korn Shell In-line Editor

You can use the Korn shell in-line editor to edit the current command before you execute it. You can choose one of three in-line editors: emacs, gmacs, or vi. You specify the in-line editor by using the set -o *editor* option or by setting either the EDITOR or VISUAL environment variable. This section describes how to use the vi in-line editor to edit commands.

The vi in-line editor is a modified subset of the vi program; it lacks some of the features of vi. The vi in-line editor is automatically in insert mode. You can type commands and execute them by pressing Return without using the vi in-line editor. If you want to edit a command, press Escape to enter command mode. You can move along the command line with the standard cursor movement commands and use standard vi editing commands to edit the contents of the line. When the command is edited, press Return to execute it or press Escape to return to input mode.

If you want to edit the command line in a vi file, type **v** to open a vi file containing the contents of the command line. When you leave vi, the command is executed. Refer to Table 24 on page 93 for a quick-reference to common vi commands.

Setting the Size of the Korn Shell's History

The Korn shell stores history commands in a file specified by the HISTFILE variable. If the variable is not set, the files are stored in

$HOME/.sh_history. You can specify the number of commands stored by using the HISTSIZE variable. If the variable is not set, the most recent 128 commands are saved. When the history list contains the maximum number of commands, then as new commands are entered, the oldest commands become unavailable.

To set a different history size, type **HISTSIZE=*n*;export HISTSIZE** and press Return. History is set to the number of lines you specify.

The following example sets the history size to 200.

```
$ HISTSIZE=200;export HISTSIZE
$
```

You can set the history temporarily for a shell window or set it "permanently" by entering the command as a line in the .profile file.

Displaying Korn Shell History Commands

You can use two commands to show the commands from the history list: fc and history. Because history is aliased to fc -l as one of the default aliases, you can use the commands interchangeably. If you do not specify a range with either the history or fc -l command, the last 16 commands are displayed.

To display the last 16 commands in the history list, type **history** and press Return. The last 16 commands in the history list are displayed.

```
$ history
   16  pwd
   17  ps -el
   18  ps -el | grep openwin
   19  cd
   20  more questionnaire
   21  su
   22  lp /etc/passwd
   23  lpstat -t
   24  man ksh
   25  du
   26  maker &
   27  tip -2400 5551212
   28  alias h=history
   29  find / -name ksh -print
   30  df -k
   31  history
$
```

An alternative way to display the same information is to type **fc -l** and press Return.

The history and fc commands take additional arguments that let you specify a range, display the last *n* number of commands, and display the commands in reverse order. See the ksh(1) manual page for more information.

Using Korn Shell History Commands

To use a command from the history list, type **r** **n** to reuse a command by number. The following example reuses command 27.

```
$ r 27
tip -2400 5551212
(Connection messages are displayed)
```

To repeat the last command in the history list, type **r** and press Return.

Editing Korn Shell History Commands

You can display individual history commands and edit them by using the fc command with the following syntax.

```
fc [-e editor] [-r] [range]
```

The following syntax also works.

```
fc -e - [old=new] [command]
```

You use the -e option to specify an editor. If no editor is specified, the FCEDIT environment variable value is used. If no value is set, the default editor is /bin/ed. The -r option reverses the order of the commands, displaying the most recent commands at the top of the list. If you specify no range, the last command is edited.

For example, to use vi to edit the last command in a history list, type **fc -e vi** and press Return. A vi file is created containing the last entry from the history list. When you edit the command and save the changes, the command is executed.

New!

An excellent Korn shell programming reference is *The New Korn Shell Command and Programming Language*, Second Edition, by Morris I. Bolsky and David G. Korn, Prentice Hall, 1995.

The Bourne-Again Shell

The Bourne-Again shell, `bash`, is a Bourne-shell-compatible language interpreter that executes commands read from the standard input or from a file. `bash` incorporates useful features from the Korn and C shells. `bash` is a conformant implementation of the IEEE POSIX Shell and Tools specification (IEEE Working Group 1003.2).

Reviewing Bourne-Again Shell Initialization Files

`bash`, when invoked as an interactive login shell or as a non-interactive shell with the `--login` option, first reads and executes commands from the `/etc/profile` file if that file exists. After reading `/etc/profile`, `bash` looks for `~/.bash_profile`, `~/.bash-login`, and `~/.profile`, in that order. It reads and executes commands from the first file that exists and is readable. To prevent the shell from reading these files, you can invoke `bash` with the `--noprofile` option.

When a login shell exits, `bash` reads and executes commands from the `~/.bash_logout` file if it exists.

When you start an interactive shell that is not a login shell, `bash` reads and executes commands from `~/.bashrc` if it exists. You can inhibit this behavior by using the `--norc` option when you start the interactive shell. Alternatively, you can force `bash` to read and execute commands from another file by specifying the `--rcfile` *file* option.

When you start `bash` interactively, for example, to run a shell script, `bash` looks for the `BASH_ENV` environment variable, expands its value, and uses the expanded value as the name of a file to read and execute. `bash` behaves as if you executed the following command, but the value of the `PATH` variable is not used in the search for the file name.

```
if [ -n "$BASH_ENV" }; then . "$BASH_ENV"; fi
```

Refer to the `bash`(1) manual page for complete information.

An excellent `bash` shell programming reference is *Learning the Bash Shell*, by Cameron Newham and Bill Rosenblatt, O'Reilly & Associates, 1998.

New!

The TC Shell

The `tcsh` shell is an enhanced and completely compatible variation of the Berkeley UNIX C shell, `csh(1)`. You can use `tcsh` as an interactive login shell and a shell script command processor. It includes a command-line editor, programmable word completion, spelling correction, a history mechanism, job control, and a C-like syntax.

Reviewing TC Shell Initialization Files

`tcsh`, when invoked as an interactive login shell, executes commands from the `/etc/csh.cshrc` and `/etc/csh.login` files. It then executes commands from files in the user's home directory, in the following order.

- `~/.tshrc`
- `~/.cshrc` (if `/.tcshrc` is not found)
- `~/.history` (or the value of the `histfile` shell variable)
- `~/.login`
- `~/.cshdirs` (or the value of the `dirsfile` shell variable)

Depending on how the shell is compiled, it may read `/etc/csh.login` before `/etc/csh.cshrc`, and `~/.login` before `~/.tcshrc` or `~/.cshrc` and `~/.history`.

When you start an interactive shell that is not a login shell, only `/etc/csh.cshrc` and `~/.tcshrc` or `~/.cshrc` are read on startup.

Refer to the `tcsh(1)` manual page for complete information.

New! *NOTE. The Solaris Operating Environment does not provide default* `csh.cshrc` *or* `csh.login` *files.*

New! An excellent `tcsh` shell programming reference is *Using csh and tcsh*, by Paul DuBois, O'Reilly & Associates, 1995.

The Z Shell

The Z shell (`zsh`) is a UNIX command interpreter that you can use as an interactive login shell and as a shell script command processor. The Z shell most closely resembles the Korn shell with enhancements. The Z shell provides command-line editing, built-in spelling correction, programmable command completions, shell functions (with autoloading), a history mechanism, and a host of other features.

Reviewing Z Shell Initialization Files

The Z shell first reads files from the /etc/zshenv file. If the RCS option is not set in /etc/zshenv, all other initialization files are skipped. Otherwise, commands are read from $ZDOTDIR/.zshenv. If ZDOTDIR is not set, HOME is used instead. If the first character of argument zero passed to the shell is - or if you use the -l option, then the shell is assumed to be a login shell, and commands are read from /etc/zprofile and then $ZDOTDIR/.zprofile. Then, if the shell is interactive, commands are read from /etc/zshrc and then $ZDOTDIR/.zshrc. Finally, if the shell is a login shell, /etc/zlogin and $ZDOTDIR/.zlogin are read.

Refer to the zsh(1) manual page for complete information.

5

ADMINISTERING USER ACCOUNTS AND GROUPS

This chapter provides background information about how to set up and administer user accounts and groups. Starting with the Solaris 8 Update 3 (1/01) release, the SMC System Configuration/Users tools replace Admintool and AdminSuite.

New!

> *NOTE. The Solaris Operating Environment provides the following SVR4 useradd commands:* `useradd, userdel, usermod, groupadd,` `groupmod,` *and* `groupdel.` *Because these commands are only minimally network-aware, they are not described in this chapter. If you want to use these commands to administer user accounts on stand-alone systems, refer to the appropriate manual pages.*

Role-based access control (RBAC) is provided starting with the Solaris 8 release. See Chapter 6, "Administering Rights and Roles," for information on how to grant users selected superuser permissions. The `useradd, userdel,` and `usermod` commands have been modified to enable you to create, modify, and delete role accounts on a local system.

Tools for Adding and Administering User Accounts

Table 31 lists the recommended tools for adding and administering user accounts on systems with a graphics monitor running an X Window System such as CDE or OpenWindows.

Table 31   Recommended Tools for Administering User Accounts

Environment	Recommended Tool	Availability/ Documentation
Remote or local systems in a networked, nameservice (NIS, NIS+, LDAP, or DNS) environment.	SMC System Configuration/Users tools.	Available starting with the Solaris 8 Update 3 (1/01) release.
Local system.	SMC System Configuration/Users tools.	Provided with the Solaris Operating Environment. Documentation available in *Solaris Management Console Tools*, available from Sun Microsystems Press and Prentice Hall.
Command line.	Terminal window (CDE Environment) or shell tool or command tool (OpenWindows environment).	Provided with the Solaris Operating Environment. See Table 32 for a list of available commands. Refer to the appropriate manual pages.

New!

New!

By default, SMC manages accounts on the local system. You can create a nameservice domain toolbox to manage accounts in the LDAP, DNS, NIS+, or NIS name services. Refer to the *Solaris Management Console Tools* book available from Sun Microsystems Press and Prentice Hall for instructions on how to create a nameservice domain toolbox. Chapter 2, "Working with the Solaris Management Console (Tasks)," in the *Sun System Administration Guide: Basic Administration* also contains information about how to create a nameservice domain toolbox.

You can add and administer user accounts from the command line if you choose not to use the SMC System Configuration/Users tools. Table 32 lists the Solaris commands you can use to administer user accounts.

Table 32   Solaris Commands Used to Administer User Accounts

Task	Name Service	Commands
Add a user account.	NIS +	nistbladm nisclient
	NIS	make
	None	useradd
Modify a user account.	NIS+	nistbladm
	NIS	make
	None	usermod
Delete a user account.	NIS+	nistbladm nisclient
	NIS	make
	None	userdel
Set up user account defaults.	NIS+	not available
	NIS	make
	None	useradd -D
Disable a user account.	NIS+	nistbladm
	NIS	passwd -r nis -l make
	None	passwd -r files -l
Change a user's password.	NIS+	passwd -r nisplus
	NIS	passwd -r nis
	None	passwd -r files
Sort user accounts.	NIS+	niscat sort
	NIS	ypcat sort

*Table 32   Solaris Commands Used to Administer User
            Accounts (Continued)*

Task	Name Service	Commands
	None	awk sort
Find a user account.	NIS+	nismatch
	NIS	ypmatch
	None	grep
Add a group.	NIS+	nistbladm
	NIS	groupadd make
	None	groupadd
Modify users in a group.	NIS+	nistbladm
	NIS	groupmod make
	None	groupmod
Delete a group.	NIS+	nistbladm
	NIS	groupdel make
	None	groupdel

You may find it useful to create a form from the following checklist to ensure that you have all the needed information about a user account before you create it.

- User name.
- UID.
- Primary group.
- Secondary groups.
- Comment.
- Default shell.
- Password status and aging.
- Home directory server name.
- Home directory path name.
- Mounting method.

- Permissions on home directory.
- Mail server.
- Department name.
- Department administrator.
- Manager.
- Employee name.
- Employee title.
- Employee status.
- Employee number.
- Start date.
- Mail aliases to add account to.
- Desktop system name.

Adding User Accounts

Before you add users to the network, the users' systems must be installed and configured. When appropriate, NIS+, LDAP, or NIS software should be installed and running on the network.

Adding users so that they can log in and start working has two parts: setting up the user account and providing the user with a working environment.

When you set up a user account, you perform the following tasks.

- Edit the `/etc/passwd` file.
- Define the user's group(s).
- Create a home directory.
- Define the user's environment.
- Create a password.

The next sections provide background information. Refer to the *Solaris Management Console Tools* book for detailed instructions on how to create and manage user accounts in a networked environment.

Editing the /etc/passwd File

You must be root or have the appropriate rights before you can edit the local `/etc/passwd` file.

You need the following information for each user you plan to add.

- Login name.
- User ID (UID).
- Primary group ID (GID).
- Secondary groups.
- Identifying information (name, office, extension, home phone).
- Home directory.
- Login shell.

New!

User ID Number

A UID is always associated with each user name and is used by systems to identify the owners of files and directories and to identify the user at login. If you create user accounts for a single individual on more than one system, always use the same user name and UID. In that way, the user can easily move and copy files between systems without ownership problems.

A UID must be a whole number less than or equal to 2147483647. The maximum UID was increased from 60000 to 2147483647 starting with the Solaris 2.5.1 release.

UIDs are required for both regular user accounts and special system accounts. Table 33 lists the UIDs that are reserved for user accounts and system accounts.

Table 33   Reserved UIDs

UIDs	Login Accounts	Description
0	`root`	Root account.
1	`daemon`	Daemon account.
2	`bin`	Pseudouser `bin` account.
3-99	`sys`, `uucp` `logins`, `who`, `tty`, and `ttytype`	System accounts.
100-60000	Regular users	General-purpose accounts.
60001	`nobody`	Unauthenticated users.
60002	`noaccess`	Compatibility with previous Solaris and SVR4 releases.
60003-2147483647	Regular users	General-purpose accounts.

CAUTION. Be careful when using UIDs in the 60000 to 2147483647 range. These numbers do not have full functionality and are incompatible with many Solaris subsystems. See Table 34 for more information.

Even though UIDs 0 through 99 are reserved for use by system accounts, you can add a user with one of these UIDs. You should not, however, use these UIDs for regular user accounts. Use the numbers 0 through 99 to assign system accounts, uucp logins, and pseudouser logins.

Large User IDs and Group IDs

Previous Solaris Operating Environments used 32-bit data types to contain UIDs and GIDs. UIDs and GIDs were constrained to a maximum useful value of 60000. The limit on UID and GID values has been raised to the maximum value of a signed integer, or 2147483647 starting with the Solaris 2.5.1 release. Table 34 lists the interoperability issues with the Solaris Operating Environment products and commands.

Table 34   Interoperability Issues for UIDs and GIDs over 60000

Category	Product/Command	Issues/Cautions
NFS Interoperability.	SunOS 4.x NFS software.	SunOS 4.x NFS server and client code truncates large UIDs and GIDs to 16 bits. This truncation can create security problems if SunOS 4.x systems are used in an environment where large UIDs and GIDs are being used. SunOS 4.x and compatible systems require a patch.
Nameservice Interoperability.	NIS nameservice. File-based nameservice.	Users with UIDs above 60000 can log in and use the su command on systems running the Solaris 2.5 Operating Environment and compatible versions; however, their UIDs and GIDs are set to 60001 (nobody).
	NIS+ nameservice.	Users with UIDs above 60000 are denied access on systems running the Solaris 2.5 Operating Environment, compatible versions, and the NIS+ name service.

Table 35 summarizes the limitations of using large UIDs and GIDs.

Table 35   Limitations of Using UIDs and GIDs over 60000

UID/GID Number	Limitation
60003 or greater.	A UID and GID of nobody are assigned to users who log in to systems running the Solaris 2.5 Operating Environment and compatible releases and the NIS or files nameservice.
65536 or greater.	Solaris 2.5 Operating Environment and compatible release systems running the NFS version 2 software truncate UIDs in this category to 16 bits, creating possible security problems.
	Using the cpio command with the default archive format to copy files displays an error message for each file, and the UID and GID are set to nobody in the archive.
	SPARC-based systems: Systems running the SunOS 4.0 Operating Environment and compatible applications display EOVERFLOW messages from some system calls, and the UID and GID are set to nobody.
	IA-based systems: SVR3-compatible applications on an IA system are likely to display EOVERFLOW messages from system calls.
	IA-based systems: If users create a file or directory on a mounted System V file system, the System V file system returns an EOVERFLOW error.
100000 or greater.	The ps -l command displays a maximum five-digit UID, so the printed column is not aligned when it includes a UID or GID greater than 99999.
2622144 or greater.	Using the cpio command with -H odc format or the pax -x cpio command to copy files returns an error message for each file, and the UIDs and GIDs are set to nobody in the archive.
10000000 or greater.	The ar command sets UIDs and GIDs to nobody in the archive.
2097152 or greater.	UIDs and GIDs are set to nobody when the tar command, the cpio -H ustar command, or the pax -x tar command is used.

Creating a Home Directory

The *home directory* is that portion of a file system that is allocated to an individual user for storing private files. The amount of space you allocate for a home directory may vary, depending on the kinds of files the users create and the type of work they do. You should probably allocate at least 15 Mbytes of disk space for each user's home directory.

A user's home directory can be either on the local system or on a remote file server. In either case, by convention the home directory is created as /export/home/*login-name*. Note that this convention is new with the Solaris Operating Environment. The server name is no longer included as part of the user's home directory path. On a large server that supports a number of users' home directories, there may be a number of directories under /export—such as home1, home2, home3, and so on—with directories for different users under them. Regardless of where their home directory is located, users access their home directory through a mount point named /home/*login-name*.

Always refer to the home directory as $HOME, not as /home/*login-name*. In addition, use relative paths to create any symbolic links in a user's home directory (for example, ../../../x/y/x) so that the links are valid no matter where the home directory is mounted.

This section describes the default procedure for the Solaris Operating Environment; the procedure assumes that the user's system is on a network and that the automounter is used to make the home directory accessible. Whether the home directory originates on a server or on the local system, you need to make it accessible to other systems by using the share command to export the file system so that the user can access the home directory from other systems on the network.

In addition, you must define how the home directory is mounted. Use one of the following ways.

- Add an entry to the NIS+ Auto_home database, NIS auto.home map, or local /etc/auto_home files so that the home directory is automatically mounted. This method is preferred.
- Add an entry in the /etc/vfstab file on the user's system to NFS-mount the home directory.

To support automatic mounting of home directories, the Solaris Operating Environment includes the following entry in the /etc/auto_master file.

```
/home          auto_home        -nobrowse
```

This entry tells the automounter to mount the directories specified in the auto_home database onto the /home mount point on the local system. The entries in auto_home use the following format.

```
login-name      system-name:/export/home/login-name
```

When a user logs in with *login-name*, the automounter mounts the specified directory (/export/home/*login-name*) from the specified system (*system-name*) onto the /home/*login-name* mount point on the system to which the user is logged in.

This method works even when the home directory is stored on the same system to which the user has logged in. But more importantly, the user can log in to any other system and have his or her home directory mounted on /home/*login-name* on that system.

NOTE. When the automounter is used to mount home directories, you are not permitted to create any directories under the /home mount point on the user's system. The system recognizes the special status of /home when the automounter is active.

To create a home directory, you must already have created the user's account. You need the following information.

- User's login name and UID.
- The name of the system on which to create the home directory. The home directory server and the user's system can be on any network segment.

  Use the df command to check the servers to make sure there is enough space for a new home directory.

- The name of the directory under which you will create the user's account.

  By convention, the home directory is named /export/home. However, on a large file server you may have multiple directories—/export/home1, /export/home2, and so on. Under each directory, different subdirectories are created for different users (for example, /export/home/*login-namea*, /export/home/*login-nameb* ... /export/home1/*login-namey* ... /export/home2/*login-namez*, and so forth).

All the following steps apply regardless of whether the home directory is created on the local system or on a remote file server.

1. Become superuser on the system on which you want to create the home directory.

2. Type **cd /export/*home-root*** and press Return.

home-root is the name of the directory under which you want to create the user's home directory. The following example changes to the directory /export/home1.

```
# cd /export/home1
```

3. Type **mkdir *login-name*** and press Return.

login-name is the login name of the user. You have created a directory that matches the login name of the user. The following example creates a directory for a user with a login name of ignatz.

```
# mkdir ignatz
```

4. Type **chown *login-name* *login-name*** and press Return.

The user now owns the home directory. The following example changes the ownership for user ignatz.

```
# chown ignatz ignatz
```

5. Type **chgrp *primary-GID* *login-name*** and press Return.

The user is assigned to the primary group you specified for the user account. The following example changes the primary group for user ignatz to the staff group.

```
# chgrp staff ignatz
#
```

6. Type **chmod 755 /export/*home-root*/*login-name*** and press Return.

The user's home directory permissions are set to rwx for owner, r-x for group, and r-x for other. The following example changes home directory permissions for user ignatz.

```
# chmod 755 /export/home1/ignatz
#
```

The following steps describe how to share a home directory from a Solaris server.

1. Type **share** and press Return to find out whether the home directory has already been shared.

   If the home directory is listed, information that looks like the following example is displayed.

```
oak% su
Password:
# share
-               /export/home1      rw      " "
#
```

   If the home directory root is not listed, perform the following steps to set it up so that it can be shared by other systems. You perform these steps once for each /export/*home-root* directory. By convention, these directories are named /export/home, /export/home1, /export/home2, and so on.

2. Edit the file /etc/dfs/dfstab and add the following line.

```
share -F nfs /export/home-root
```

3. Type **shareall -F nfs** and press Return.

   All the share commands in the /etc/dfs/dfstab file are executed so you do not need to reboot the system. If you reboot the system, the shareall command is automatically run.

4. Type **ps -ef | grep mountd** and press Return.

   If the daemon mountd is running, the procedure is complete. The following example shows that mountd is not running. If mountd is not running, follow the next step.

```
# ps -ef | grep mountd
    root     221     218  16  18:07:25 pts/1   0:00 grep mountd
#
```

5. Type **/etc/init.d/nfs.server start** and press Return.

   The daemons required for sharing file directories are started.

   NOTE. If your network is not running NIS, NIS+, or LDAP, you need to add the home directory server's Internet Protocol (IP) address and system name to the /etc/hosts *file on the user's system.*

   After you have created the user's home directory, you must make it available. You make the home directory available by adding it to the appropriate NIS, NIS+, or LDAP database or by adding an entry to the /etc/vfstab file on the user's system for NFS mounting.

NFS-Mounting the Home Directory

If the directory (disk space) for a user's home directory is located on another system and the automounter is not being used to make that space available, use the following steps to NFS-mount the home directory.

1. Become superuser on the user's system.
2. Edit the `/etc/vfstab` file and create an entry for the user's home directory.

   For example, to create an entry for user `ignatz` with a home directory on server `oak`, you would add the following line to the file.

```
oak:/export/home1/ignatz - /home/ignatz nfs - yes rw,intr
```

3. To create the mount point on the user's system, type **mkdir /home/*login-name*** and press Return.

NOTE. The home directory does not have the same name on the user's system as it does on the server. For example, `/export/home/ignatz` on the server is mounted as `/home/ignatz` on the user's system.

4. Type **chown *login-name* /home/*login-name*** and press Return.

   The user now owns the home directory.
5. Type **chgrp *primary-GID* /home/*login-name*** and press Return.

   The user's primary group has permission to access the user's home directory.
6. Type **mountall** and press Return.

   All entries in the current `vfstab` file (whose `mount at boot` fields are set to `yes`) are mounted.
7. To verify that all entries are mounted, type **mount** and press Return.

   The file systems that are mounted are displayed.

Defining the User's Environment

To completely set up the user account, you must also perform the following tasks.

- Define default initialization files.
- Set up a mail account.
- Set up a printer.

Defining Initialization Files

When a user logs in, the `login` program sets a number of variables, such as HOME, LOGNAME, and TZ. Then, the user's shell is launched and runs a file called the *system profile (initialization file)* to set systemwide defaults such as PATH, message of the day, and `umask`. Finally, the user profile initialization file (or files) that sets variables specific to the user is run. For example, the user profile can modify the PATH to include applications run by only that user. Each shell has its own initialization file (or files), as shown in Table 36.

Table 36   Shell User Initialization Files

Shell	Initialization File	Purpose
C	`$HOME/.login`	Define user's environment at login.
	`$HOME/.cshrc`	Define user's environment for all C shells invoked after login shell.
Bourne	`$HOME/.profile`	Define user's environment at login.
Korn	`$HOME/.profile`	Define user's environment at login.
	`$HOME/ksh-env`	Define user's environment at login in the file specified by the *ksh-env* environment variable.

The Solaris Operating Environment provides default user initialization files for each shell in the `/etc/skel` directory, as shown in Table 37.

Table 37   Default Home Directory Initialization Files

Shell	File Name
C	`/etc/skel/local.login`
C	`/etc/skel/local.cshrc`
Bourne or Korn	`/etc/skel/local.profile`

The default `/etc/skel/local.login` file is shown below.

```
# @(#)local.login 1.5     98/10/03 SMI
stty -istrip
# setenv TERM `tset -Q -`

#
# if possible, start the windows system.  Give user a chance to bail out
#
if ( "`tty`" == "/dev/console" ) then

    if ( "$TERM" == "sun" || "$TERM" == "sun-color" || "$TERM" == "AT386" )
  then

            if ( ${?OPENWINHOME} == 0 ) then
```

```
              setenv OPENWINHOME /usr/openwin
        endif

        echo ""
        echo -n "Starting OpenWindows in 5 seconds (type Control-C to
  interrupt)"
        sleep 5
        echo ""
        $OPENWINHOME/bin/openwin
        clear              # get rid of annoying cursor rectangle
        logout             # logout after leaving windows system

     endif

endif
```

The default `/etc/skel/local.cshrc` file is shown below.

```
# @(#)cshrc 1.11 89/11/29 SMI
umask 022
set path=(/bin /usr/bin /usr/ucb /etc .)
if ( $?prompt ) then
        set history=32
endif
```

The default `/etc/skel/local.profile` file is shown below.

```
# @(#)local.profile 1.8    99/03/26 SMI
stty istrip
PATH=/usr/bin:/usr/ucb:/etc:.
export PATH

#
# If possible, start the windows system
#
if [ "`tty`" = "/dev/console" ] ; then
    if [ "$TERM" = "sun" -o "$TERM" = "sun-color" -o "$TERM" = "AT386" ]
    then

        if [ ${OPENWINHOME:-""} = "" ] ; then
            OPENWINHOME=/usr/openwin
            export OPENWINHOME
        fi

        echo ""
        echo "Starting OpenWindows in 5 seconds (type Control-C to
  interrupt)"
        sleep 5
        echo ""
        $OPENWINHOME/bin/openwin

        clear              # get rid of annoying cursor rectangle
        exit               # logout after leaving windows system

     fi
fi
```

As you can see, these files define a minimal environment. To minimize the need to edit the customization files for each user, you can customize the files in `/etc/skel` to set as many systemwide default variables as you want.

Creating Site Initialization Files

It is important that both the administrator and the user are able to customize the user initialization files. You can create site initialization files by locating the initialization files centrally and distributing them globally. With site initialization files, you can continue to introduce new functionality to the user's work environment and also enable the user to customize individual user initialization files.

You create a site initialization file and add a reference to it in the user's initialization file. When you reference a site initialization file in a user initialization file, all updates to the site initialization file are automatically reflected when the user logs in to the system or when a user starts a new shell.

You can do any customization in a site initialization file that you can do in a user initialization file. Site initialization files typically reside on a server or a set of servers and appear as the first statement in a user initialization file. Each site initialization file must be the same type of shell script as the user initialization file that references it. Thus, you have site initialization files for each shell used at your site.

To reference a site initialization file for a C shell user initialization file, put a line similar to the following example at the beginning of the user initialization file.

```
source /home/site-files/site-init-files
```

To reference a site initialization file in a Bourne or Korn shell user initialization file, put a line similar to the following example at the beginning of the user initialization file.

```
. /home/site-files/site-init-files
```

Example of a Site Initialization File   The following example shows a C shell site initialization file named `site.login` in which a user can choose a particular version of an application.

```
# @(#)site.login
main:
echo "Application Environment Selection"
echo ""
echo "1. Application, Version 1"
echo "2. Application, Version 2"
echo ""
echo -n "Type 1 or 2 and press Return to set your
application environment: "
set choice = $<
if ( $choice !~ [1-2] ) then
goto main
endif
```

```
switch ($choice)
case "1":
setenv APPHOME /opt/app-v.1
breaksw
case "2":
setenv APPHOME /opt/app-v.2
endsw
```

You would reference the site.login site initialization file located on a server named server2 in a user's .cshrc file (C shell users only) with the following line. The automounter must be running on the user's system.

```
source /home/site-init-files/site.login
```

Avoiding Local System References in Site Initialization Files Do not add specific references to the local system in the user's initialization file. Instructions in a user initialization file should be valid regardless of the system to which the user logs in.

To make a user's home directory available anywhere on the network, always refer to the home directory with the variable $HOME. For example, use $HOME/bin instead of /home/*login-name*/bin. $HOME automounts the user's home directory when the user logs in to another system.

To access files on a local disk, create an indirect map that mounts only this file system, for example /home/site-init-files or /site/init-files. Such directories can be mounted automatically on any system to which the user logs in, assuming the system is running the automounter.

Setting Up User Initialization Files

To set up user initialization files, you must already have created the user's home directory and know which shell (C, Bourne, or Korn) is set in the user's account entry in the Passwd database. Use the following steps to set up the user's initialization files.

1. Become superuser on the system with the user's home directory.
2. Type **cd /home/*login-name*** and press Return.

    Focus is in the user's home directory. The following example changes to user ignatz's directory, which is in /export/home.

```
# cd /home/ignatz
#
```

3. Type **cp /etc/skel/local.*** . and press Return.

    You have copied all of the default user initialization files to the user's home directory.

4. Type **chmod 744 local.*** and press Return.

   Permissions are set for the initialization files.

5. Type **chown *login-name* *** and press Return.

   The user now owns the initialization files.

```
# chown ignatz *
#
```

6. Type **chgrp *primary-GID* local.*** and press Return.

   The files are assigned to the primary group (for example, staff) you specified in the Passwd database for the user account.

```
# chgrp staff local.*
#
```

7. Rename the shell initialization files. If the user's shell is the C shell, type **mv local.login .login; mv local.cshrc .cshrc** and press Return. If the user's shell is the Korn or Bourne shell, type **mv local.profile .profile** and press Return.

8. Type **rm local.*** and press Return.

   You have removed the unused shell initialization files.

9. On the user's system, log in as the user.

10. Assign the user an interim password.

    See "Creating a Password" on page 162 for information on how to create passwords.

11. Check to make sure the user's environment is set up correctly.

12. Edit the user's initialization file (or files) and make changes as needed.

Use the following steps to edit the user's initialization file (or files).

1. Set the user's default path to include any additional directories or mount points for the user's windowing environment and applications.

   For the Bourne, Bourne Again, or Korn shell, type
   PATH=*/dirname1:/dirname2:/dirname3...:.*;export PATH.
   For example, enter a line such as the following in the user's
   $HOME/.profile file.

```
PATH=/usr/openwin/bin:/usr/dt/bin:/usr/bin:/$HOME/bin:/lib:/usr/lib:.; export
   PATH
```

2. To check that the PATH environment variable is set correctly, type **echo $PATH** and press Return.

```
paperbark% echo $PATH
/usr/openwin/bin:/usr/dt/bin:/usr/bin:/export/home/winsor/bin:/lib:/usr/lib:.
paperbark%
```

3. Add or change the settings of environment variables. For the C shell, type **setenv *VARIABLE value*** (or **set *variable=value*** for the path and term variables).

NOTE. Set environment variables in the .login *file for the C and TC shells and* .profile *for the Bourne, Bourne Again, and Korn shells.*

New!

The following example sets the history to the last 100 commands.

```
setenv HISTORY 100
```

For the Bourne or Korn shell, type ***VARIABLE=value*; export *VARIABLE*.**

The following example sets the user's default mail directory.

```
MAIL=/var/mail/ignatz;export MAIL
```

4. Check the umask setting. If you need to change it, type **umask *nnn*** and press Return. You can either include or omit leading zeros.

For example, to set file permissions to 644, type **umask 022** and press Return. Table 38 shows the file permissions that are created for each of the octal values of umask.

Table 38   Permissions for umask Values

Octal Value	File Permissions
0	rwx
1	rw-
2	r-x
3	r--
4	-wx
5	-w-
6	--x
7	--- (none)

The LANG variable and LC environment variables determine the locale-specific conversions and conventions the shell uses. These conversions and conventions include time zones, collation orders, and formats of dates, time, currency, and numbers. If necessary, set these variables in the user's initialization file. LANG sets all possible conversions and conventions for a given locale. If you have special needs, you can set various aspects of localization separately by using the LC variables LC_COLLATE, LC_CTYPE, LC_MESSAGES, and LC_NUMERIC. Table 39 shows the values for several locales.

Table 39   Values for LANG and LC Variables

Value	Locale
de	German
fr	French
iso_8895_1	English and European
it	Italian
japanese	Japanese
korean	Korean
sv	Swedish
tchinese	Taiwanese

If the system needs to support multibyte characters (for example, Japanese), add the following command to the system initialization file (/etc/profile or /etc/.login).

```
stty cs8 defeucw
```

The preceding command sets character size to the maximum (cs8) and sets the width of multibyte characters to the default values for the locale specified by LC_CTYPE.

When the initialization files are complete, log out of the user's account.

Setting Up a User's Mail Account

Each user has a mailbox either on a local system or on a mail server and a mail alias in the /etc/mail/aliases file or in an NIS, NIS+, or LDAP nameservice database that points to the location of the mailbox. Use the following steps to set up a mail client with a mailbox on a mail server.

1. Become superuser on the mail client's system.
2. Create a /var/mail mount point on the mail client's system.

3. Create a direct automounter map or edit the /etc/vfstab file and add an entry for the /var/mail directory on the mail server, mounting it on the local /var/mail directory. Use the actimeo=0 option, as shown in the following example; otherwise, locking of the mailbox files fails.

```
server:/var/mail - /var/mail nfs - no rw,hard,actimeo=0
```

The client's mailbox is automatically mounted any time the system is rebooted.

4. Type **mount -a** to mount the mailbox.

The client's mailbox is mounted.

NOTE. The sendmail *program automatically creates mailboxes in the* /var/mail *directory the first time a message is delivered. You do not need to create individual mailboxes for your mail clients.*

If you are using NIS+, use the following steps to set up mail aliases for the user.

1. Compile a list of each of your mail clients, the locations of their mailboxes, and the names of the mail server systems.

2. Become superuser on any system.

3. For each alias, type **aliasadm -a *alias expanded-alias* [*options comments*]** and press Return.

The alias is added to the NIS+ aliases table. The following example adds an alias for user iggy.ignatz.

```
# aliasadm -a iggy iggy.ignatz "Iggy Ignatz"
#
```

4. Type **aliasadm -m *alias*** and press Return.

The entry you created is displayed.

5. Check the entry to be sure it is correct.

Alternatively, when you have created a nameservice domain toolbox for SMC, you can use SMC/System Configuration/Users/Mailing Lists to edit network mail aliases.

Setting Up a User's Printer

After adding users to a system, make sure they have access to a printer. See Chapter 11, "Administering Printing," for information on how to set up printing services.

Creating a Password

Passwords are an important part of system security. Each user account should be assigned a password of 6 to 10 characters as a combination of letters and numbers.

New!

You can assign and manage passwords with the SMC Users tool. By default, SMC manages accounts on the local system. You can create a nameservice domain toolbox to manage accounts in the LDAP, DNS, NIS+, or NIS nameservices. Refer to the *Solaris Management Console Tools* book available from Sun Microsystems Press and Prentice Hall for instructions on how to create a nameservice domain toolbox.

New!

Table 40 lists the commands that you use to manage passwords in the passwd and shadow databases in nameservice domains.

Table 40   Nameservice Commands for Managing Passwords

Nameservice	Commands
files	passwd [-r files] *username*
NIS	passwd -r nis *username* (replacement for yppasswd(1).)
NIS+	passwd -r nisplus *username* (replacement for nispasswd(1).)
LDAP	passwd -r ldap *username*

In the Solaris Operating Environment, the encrypted password and associated password aging information are stored in the nameservice password or shadow database or in the local /etc/shadow file. Permissions for the /etc/shadow file are -r--------. Only root can read the /etc/shadow file, and only the passwd command can write to the file.

The following example shows the contents of an /etc/shadow file.

```
root:4ZfnV.kupl.SA:11081::::::
daemon:NP:6445::::::
bin:NP:6445::::::
sys:NP:6445::::::
adm:NP:6445::::::
lp:NP:6445::::::
uucp:NP:6445::::::
nuucp:NP:6445::::::
listen:*LK*:::::::
nobody:NP:6445::::::
noaccess:NP:6445::::::
nobody4:NP:6445::::::
winsor:OVHZsESoDAEwk:11081::::::
ray:::::::::
des:::::::::
rob::11080::::::
ppp:*LK*:::::::
ignatz:::::::::
```

Users can create or change their own passwords at any time. You must be root to create the initial password for any other user. In addition, to create a nameservice password, you must have the appropriate privileges and you must have established the necessary networkwide credentials.

Use the following steps to create a local password.

1. Become superuser on the local system.
2. Type **passwd** *login-name* and press Return.

    The prompt New password: is displayed.
3. Type the new password and press Return.

    The prompt Re-enter new password: is displayed.
4. Retype the password and press Return.

    The password is assigned, as shown in the following example, and added to the /etc/shadow file.

```
oak% su
# passwd smallberries
New password:
Re-enter new password:
#
```

NOTE. You can also use passwd *to define, change, and view password attributes, such as password aging. You can use password aging for the file, NIS+, and LDAP nameservices, but not for NIS. See the* passwd(1) *manual page for more information.*

Changing a local password is similar to adding a new password. When prompted to do so, type the old password, and then type the new password two times, as prompted.

To create or change passwords in NIS, NIS+, and LDAP nameservice environments, use the passwd -r (repository) option to specify an nis, nisplus, or ldap repository.

New!

Disabling User Accounts

Occasionally, you may need to temporarily or permanently disable a login account. You should have good reason for taking such action. For example, the user may be on leave of absence or you may have strong evidence that the account is being misused or security is being violated.

The easiest way to disable a login account is to lock the account. You can lock an account in SMC from the General tab of the user properties for the user account. Refer to the *Solaris Management Console Tools* book for instructions.

On a local system, you can control access to a user's account by requiring password aging, by setting an expiration date for the login account, or by requiring that a user access the account at regular intervals. Another way that you can disable a login is to temporarily change the password.

Setting Up and Administering Groups

New!

The *group database* (NIS maps, NIS+ tables, LDAP Directory Information Tree (DIT) entries, or local /etc/group file) stores information about user groups, traditionally called *UNIX groups*. A *user group* is a collection of users who can share files and other system resources. For example, a set of users who are working on the same project could be formed into a user group.

Each group has a group ID (GID) that identifies it internally to the system. A group should have a name and a list of user names. User groups can be defined in two ways.

- Implicitly, by the GID for the user's primary group, which is defined in the user account. Whenever a new GID appears in the relevant field of a nameservice database, a new group is defined.
- Explicitly, by name, GID, and user list.

NOTE. It's best to explicitly define all groups so that every group has a name.

All users belong to at least one group—their primary group—which is indicated by the Group field of their user account. Although it is not required by the operating system, you should add the user to the member list of the group you've designated as his or her primary group. Optionally, users can belong to up to 16 secondary groups. To belong to a secondary group, the user must be added to the group's member list.

The groups command shows the groups to which a user belongs. In the following example, the user belongs to the staff group.

New!

```
mopoke% groups
staff
mopoke%
```

You can use the `id -a` command to display more information about a user
account, including the group name and GID, as shown in the following
example.

```
mopoke% id -a
uid=1001(winsor) gid=10(staff) groups=10(staff)
mopoke%
```

For any user, only one group at a time can be considered the primary
group. However, users can temporarily change the primary group (with the
`newgrp` command) to any other group they belong to.

Some applications look at the user's primary group only. For example,
ownership of files created and accounting data recorded reflect only the
primary group. Other applications may take into account a user's
membership across groups. For example, when using Admintool (which has
been replaced by the SMC tools) a user had to be a member of the `sysadmin`
group to make changes to a database, but it didn't matter if `sysadmin` was
the current primary group or a secondary group.

User groups are probably best known as the groups referred to by the
read-write-execute permissions for the user, group, and other on files and
directories. These permissions are a cornerstone of security. You cannot access
others' files (if they do not allow world access) unless your primary or a
secondary group has permission to access the files. For example, a group
called `techwrite` could be created for technical writers, and a central
directory of document files could be set up with write permission for the
`techwrite` group. That way, only writers would be able to change the files.

User groups can be local to a workstation or used across a network. Across
the network, user groups allow a set of users on the network to access a set of
files on a workstation or file server without making those files available to
everyone.

*NOTE. NIS+ supports another, unrelated, kind of group, called an
NIS+ group, which assigns access rights to NIS+ objects. These
groups have nothing to do with using NIS+ to maintain a database of
user groups.*

You can use the SMC System Configuration/Users/Groups tool to create
and administer groups. By default, SMC manages accounts on the local
system. You can create a nameservice domain toolbox to manage accounts in
the LDAP, DNS, NIS+, or NIS nameservices. Refer to the *Solaris
Management Console Tools* book for instructions.

Setting Up Fields in the Group Database

The `Group` database (NIS maps, NIS+ tables, LDAP DIT entries, or local `/etc/group` file) has the following fields.

- Group Name.
- Group ID.
- User (Member) List.

An additional Group Password field is rarely used. The Group Password field is a relic of earlier versions of UNIX. It is usually left empty or filled with an asterisk. If a group has a password, the `newgrp` command prompts users to enter it. However, there is no command to set the password.

Setting Up a Group Name Field

The Group Name field contains the name assigned to the group. For example, members of the chemistry department in a university may be called `chem`. Group names can have a maximum of nine characters.

Setting Up a Group ID Field

The Group ID field contains the group's numerical ID. It must be unique from all other group IDs on a system and should be unique across the entire organization. You can assign GIDs as a whole number between 100 and 60000. Numbers 60001 and 60002 are assigned to `nobody` and `noaccess`, respectively, and numbers under 100 are reserved for system default group accounts.

New!

Starting with the Solaris 2.5.1 release, you can also assign GID numbers between 6003 and 2147483647. If you use GID numbers in this range, refer to Table 34 on page 147 and Table 35 on page 148 for information about interoperability issues and limitations on large GID numbers.

When you use the SMC Users tool to add user accounts, the default group is `staff`. You can choose another primary group from the menu. For security reasons, do not set the primary group as root with a GID of 0.

Setting Up a User (Member) List Field

The User List field contains a list of the users in the group. User names are separated by commas. These names must be the official login names defined in the password nameservice database or the local `/etc/passwd` file if no nameservice is used. As already noted, each user can belong to a maximum of 17 groups.

Identifying Default UNIX User Groups

By default, all Solaris workstations and servers have the following groups.

```
root::0:root
other::1:
bin::2:root,bin,daemon
sys::3:root,bin,sys,adm
adm::4:root,adm,daemon
uucp::5:root,uucp
mail::6:root
tty::7:root,tty,adm
lp::8:root,lp,adm
nuucp::9:root,nuucp
staff::10:
daemon::12:root,daemon
sysadmin::14:
nobody::60001:
noaccess::60002:
nogroup::65534
```

> *NOTE. The* `sysadmin` *group with a GID of 14 is part of the default set of groups.*

Creating New Groups

As a system administrator, you frequently may create new group accounts. You must create a group and assign it a GID before you can assign users to it.

Use SMC to create and maintain local groups. You must have root access or the appropriate rights to be able to administer the `/etc/group` file. By default, SMC manages accounts on the local system. You can create a nameservice domain toolbox to manage group accounts in the LDAP, DNS, NIS+, or NIS nameservices. Refer to the *Solaris Management Console Tools* book for instructions.

You need the following information to create a new group.

- Login names of users who will belong to the group.
- Group name.
- GID.

Modifying Groups

Membership in group accounts can change frequently as new employees are hired and other employees change job responsibilities. Consequently, you will modify existing group accounts to add or remove users. If you choose to have a user belong to secondary groups, you must modify those groups to add the user to the user lists. When adding groups, you may make a mistake. The ability to modify or delete groups helps you correct such mistakes.

If a group account is no longer needed, you can delete user accounts from it.

Deleting User Accounts

Use the following checklist for deleting a user account.

- Delete the user's entry from the NIS+ `Passwd` database, NIS map, or `/etc/passwd` files.
- Remove the user's name from entries in the NIS+ `Group` database, NIS map, or `/etc/group` files. If a group is no longer needed, you can delete user accounts from it.
- Remove the user from any printer access or deny lists.
- Decide whether to delete or archive all of the user's files and do so.
- Delete the user's mail file.
- Remove the user from any aliases.

Using Solaris User Registration

Solaris User Registration is a tool for gathering information about new Solaris releases, upgrade offers, and promotions. This tool automatically starts when a user first logs in to the desktop. The Solaris User Registration tool enables a user to register now or later. If you do not choose to register either now or later, click on the Never button to prevent display of the Solaris User Registration tool at each log in. The registration process provides Sun with the user's Solaris version, survey type, platform, hardware, and locale.

NOTE. Solaris User Registration is not started when a user is logged in as root.

If the user chooses to register, a copy of the completed form is stored in `$HOME/.solregis/uprops`. If the user chooses to never register, he can always start User Registration in one of the following ways.

- By typing **solregis&** at any command-line prompt.
- By clicking on the Registration icon in the Application Manager's desktop tools folder in the CDE environment.

For more information, refer to the `solregis(1)` manual page.

Accessing Solaris Solve/BigAdmin

When users complete the Solaris User Registration process, they can access Solaris Solve, an exclusive Web site that offers valuable Solaris product information and solutions in one convenient location. Beginning on April 16, 2001, users of the Solaris Solve Web site are automatically redirected to the BigAdmin System Administrator's Portal. BigAdmin provides a quick and easy way for users to get the most recent information on what is happening with the latest Solaris release. BigAdmin also provides a preview of additional Sun contract and service opportunities.

> *NOTE. Solaris Solve (redirected to BigAdmin) and SunSolve are separate Web sites.*

To complete the Solaris User Registration form and access BigAdmin, users can follow the steps below.

1. Fill in the electronic Solaris User Registration profile.
2. Submit the profile by e-mail or print the profile to fax or mail.
3. Access the BigAdmin site at `http://www.sun.com/bigadmin/`.

Error Conditions

Table 41 suggests ways to resolve user problems with registration.

Table 41   Registration Errors

Problem	Solution
Registration form failed to initialize: Web page window is displayed, requesting that user see the system administrator to resolve the problem.	Check for missing registration files.
Form could not be e-mailed: Dialog box is displayed requesting that user see the system administrator to resolve the problem.	Check whether e-mail is configured correctly. Also ensure that CDE is available on the user system because it must be present before the completed registration form can be e-mailed. Alternatively, users can print the form and fax or mail it.

Table 41   Registration Errors (Continued)

Problem	Solution
Form could not be printed: Dialog box is displayed requesting that the user see the system administrator to resolve the problem.	Check whether the printer is configured correctly. Alternatively, user can e-mail form.
Form could not be saved: Dialog box is displayed, verifying that registration succeeded; however, the registration information cannot be recalled when updating registration.	Check user's home directory. Required action depends on the system configuration.

Restarting Solaris User Registration

Use the following steps to restart the Solaris User Registration process.

1. Type **cd $HOME/.solregis** and press Return.
   Focus is in the .solregis directory.

2. Type **rm uprops** and press Return.
   You have removed the uprops file that contains the previous registration information.

3. Type **/usr/dt/bin/solregis&** and press Return.
   The Solaris User Registration form is redisplayed.

4. Fill in the form and click on the appropriate button at the bottom of the window to either register by e-mail or print a copy to fax or mail.

Disabling User Registration

If system administrators register for your organization, you may want to disable individual user registration as part of setting up user accounts. You can disable User Registration either before or after installing Solaris software. Before Solaris software is installed, you can disable User Registration in the following ways.

- Deselect the SUNWsregu package (interactive installation).
- Modify a custom JumpStart profile to not install the SUNWsregu package.

- Create and run a finish script that creates a file named `solregis` that contains the line: `DISABLE=1` in the `/etc/default` directory on one or more systems.

After Solaris software is installed, you can disable User Registration in the following ways.

- Use the `pkgrm` command to remove the `SUNWsregu` package.
- Create a `solregis` file that contains the line `DISABLE=1` in the `/etc/default` directory.

6

ADMINISTERING RIGHTS AND ROLES

Starting with the Solaris 8 Operating Environment, role-based access control (RBAC) provides a flexible way to package certain superuser privileges for assignment to user accounts. You no longer need to give users all superuser privileges to enable them to perform a set of tasks that require superuser privileges.

With traditional security models, superuser has full superuser privileges and other users do not have enough power to fix their own problems. With role-based access control (RBAC), you now have an alternative to the traditional all-or-nothing security model.

With RBAC, you can divide superuser capabilities into several packages and assign them separately to individuals sharing administrative responsibilities. When you separate superuser privileges with RBAC, users can have a variable degree of access, and you can control delegation of privileged operations to other users.

RBAC includes the following features.

- Right—A right used to grant access to a restricted function.

- Role—A special type of user account that can be used to perform a set of administrative tasks.

New! Using SMC to Grant Access Rights to Users

The SMC 2.1 System Configuration/User Accounts tool enables you to assign a subset of superuser rights to individual user accounts. You can grant or deny individual rights, enable all rights, or disable all rights. When rights are granted, users have superuser access to the commands and tools associated with the set of rights that you grant.

The rights you can grant a user account are listed in Table 42.

Table 42   Available Rights

Right	Description
All	Automatically assigned to each user. It grants the right for a user or role to use any command when working in an administrator's shell such as Administrator's Korn or Administrator's C shells. The All right should always be the last right in the list. If All is first, no other rights are consulted when command attributes are looked up.
Audit Control	Grants the right to manage the audit subsystem but not the right to read audit files.
Audit Review	Grants the right to read the audit trail but not to manage the audit subsystem.
Basic Solaris User	Assigned to every user who logs in to SMC. Provides read permissions to users of applications and enables users to add `cron` jobs to their own `crontab` files. The Basic Solaris User right always includes the All right.
Cron Management	Grants the right to manage the `cron` table and daemon.
Device Management	Grants the right to allocate and deallocate devices and to correct error conditions relating to those devices.
Device Security	Grants the right to manage and configure devices and volume manager.
DHCP Management	Grants the right to manage the DHCP service.
File System Management	Grants the right to manage file system mounts and shares.
File System Security	Grants the right to manage file system security attributes.

Table 42   Available Rights (Continued)

Right	Description
FTP Management	Grants the right to configure the FTP server.
iPlanet Directory Management	Grants the rights to manage iPlanet directory servers.
Log Management	Grants the right to manage log files.
Mail Management	Grants the right to configure `sendmail`, modify mailing lists, and check mail queues.
Maintenance and Repair	Grants the right to use commands needed to maintain or repair a system.
Media Backup	Grants the right to back up files but not the right to restore them.
Media Restore	Grants the right to restore backed-up files but not the right to perform system backup.
Message Queue Management	Grants the right to manage message queues.
Name Service Management	Grants the right to control the daemons used by a nameservice.
Name Service Security	Grants the right to manage all nameservice properties and table data.
Network Management	Grants the right to manage the host and network configuration.
Network Security	Grants the right to manage network and host security with authorizations for modifying trusted network databases.
Object Access Management	Grants the right to file ownership and permissions.
Operator	Contains Printer Management, Media Backup, and All rights. Operator rights also include Process Management, Rights Delegation, and Software Installation rights.
Primary Administrator	Assigns all the rights of the root user and is responsible for assigning rights to users, assigning users to roles, creating new roles, and changing the rights associated with administrative roles. The Primary Administrator can designate other users as a Primary Administrator. The Primary Administrator can also grant Rights Delegation, which gives other

Table 42   Available Rights (Continued)

Right	Description
	administrators the limited ability to grant to others only rights the delegators already have or rights to roles to which the delegators are already assigned.
Printer Management	Grants the right to manage printer devices, daemons, and spooling.
Process Management	Grants the right to manage current processes and daemons.
Project Management	Grants the right to perform project management.
Rights Delegation	Grants the user or role limited ability to assign to other users or roles those rights and roles already assigned to the user with the Rights Delegation right.
Software Installation	Grants the right to add and remove application software.
System Administrator	Contains Audit Review, Cron Management, Device Management, File System Management, Mail Management, Maintenance and Repair, Media Backup, Media Restore, Name Service Management, Network Management, Object Access Management, Printer Management, Process Management, Software Installation, User Management, and All rights.
User Management	Grants the right to create and modify user accounts—except for its own user account. It does not grant the right to modify user passwords.
User Security	Grants the right to create and modify user passwords.

New! Using SMC to Administer Role Accounts

A role is an account with all the attributes of a user account, including a user name, user ID (UID), password, and home directory. A role also has a specific set of administrative rights. Instead of a login shell, a role has a role shell (for example, Administrator's Bourne instead of Bourne shell). The root account is a role with all rights, whereas other roles may have more limited rights.

When a user is associated with a role, that user first logs in as usual with the individual's user name and password. The user can then use the su *rolename* command with the role password to assume the rights of the specific role. User accounts can have both individual rights and role membership.

Use the SMC Administrative Roles tool to create role accounts and to administer the user account memberships in each role. Refer to the *Solaris Management Console Tools* book for instructions on creating and administering role accounts.

The RBAC Databases

Four RBAC databases provide users access to privileged operations.

- /etc/user_attr (extended user attributes database)—Associates users and roles with authorizations and execution profiles.
- /etc/security/auth_attr (authorization attributes database)—Defines authorizations and their attributes and identifies the associated help file.
- /etc/security/prof_attr (execution profile attributes database)—Defines profiles, lists the profile's assigned authorizations, and identifies the associated help file.
- /etc/security/exec_attr (profile execution attributes database)—Defines the privileged operations assigned to a profile.

The user_attr database is the only database that is required. Use of the other databases depends on which security features are implemented.

You can directly assign authorizations and profiles to users in the user_attr database. You can also assign the user to a role to give the user access to any privileged operations associated with that role.

Profiles are defined in the prof_attr database and can include authorizations defined in auth_attr and commands with attributes defined for that profile in exec_attr.

The pfexec(1) command executes commands with the attributes specified by the user profiles in the exec_attr(4) database. Commands that are assigned to profiles are run in special shells called *profile shells*.

- pfsh corresponds to the Bourne shell (sh).
- pfcsh corresponds to the C shell (csh).
- pfksh corresponds to the Korn (ksh) shell.

See the pfexec(1) manual page for more information.

Commands for Managing Role-Based Access Control

Direct editing of the databases is not recommended. Instead, use the SMC tools to manage role-based access control. You can also use the commands listed in Table 43 to manage role-based access control.

Table 43   Commands for Managing Role-Based Access Control

Command	Description
auths(1)	Display authorizations for a user.
makedbm(1M)	Make a dbm file.
ncsd(1M)	Nameservice cache daemon. This daemon is useful for caching the user_attr, prof_attr, and exec_attr databases.
pam_roles(5)	Role account management module for PAM. Checks for the authorization to assume a role.
pfexec(1) pfsh(1) pfcsh(1) pfksh(1)	Profile shells, used to execute commands with attributes specified in the exec_attr database.
policy.conf(4)	Configuration file for security policy. Lists granted authorizations.
profiles(1)	Display profiles for a specified user.
roles(1)	Display roles granted to a user.
roleadd(1M)	Add a role account on the system.
roledel(1M)	Delete a role's account from the system.
rolemod(1M)	Modify a role's account information on the system.
useradd(1M)	Add a user account on the system. The -P option assigns a policy, the -R option assigns a role, the -A option assigns an authorization.
userdel(1M)	Delete a user's login from the system.
usermod(1M)	Modify a user's account information on the system. The -P option modifies a policy, the -R option modifies a role, and the -A option modifies an authorization.

7

Administering File Systems

A file system is a structure of directories used to locate and store files. The term *file system* is used in several different ways.

- To describe the entire file tree from the root directory downward.
- To describe a particular type of file system: disk based, network based, or virtual.
- To describe the data structure of a disk slice or other media storage device.
- To describe a portion of a file tree structure that is attached to a mount point on the main file tree so that a portion is accessible.

Usually, you can tell from context which meaning is intended.

The Solaris system software uses the *virtual file system (VFS)* architecture, which provides a standard interface for different file system types. The *kernel* handles basic operations—such as reading, writing, and listing files—without requiring the user or program to know about the underlying file system type.

The file system administrative commands provide a common interface that enables you to maintain file systems of different types. These commands have two components: a generic component and a component specific to each type of file system. The generic commands apply to most types of file systems; the specific commands apply to only one type of file system.

Administering the Solaris file system is one of your most important system administration tasks. The file system story is a complex one, and understanding it can help you more effectively administer file systems. This chapter describes the following topics.

- The types of file systems.
- The default Solaris file system.
- The virtual file system table (`/etc/vfstab`).
- The file system administrative commands.
- Making local and remote files available to users.
- Backing up and restoring file systems.

New! What's New in File Systems in the Solaris 9 Release

The Solaris 9 release provides the following new file system features.

- The UFS, NFS, and TMPFS file systems are enhanced to include extended file attributes. Application developers can use extended file attributes to associate specific attributes with a file. Extended file attributes are represented as files within a hidden attribute directory associated with the target file. You can use the `runat(1)` command to add attributes and execute shell commands in the hidden attribute directory. Many Solaris file system commands now have an `-@` option that you can use to query, copy, or find file attributes.

- You can use the new `fssnap(1M)` command to create a read-only snapshot of a UFS file system. You can use this temporary image as a stable and unchanging device interface to back up a file system. See "Creating a Snapshot of a UFS File System" on page 218 for information on how to use the `fssnap` command.

- Direct I/O performance—used by database applications to access unbuffered file system data—now permits concurrent read and write access to regular UFS files. In previous releases, an operation that updated file data locked out other read or write access until the update operation was completed. Consider enabling direct I/O if you are already using UFS to store database tables. You can enable direct I/O with your database administrative procedures. If you cannot enable direct I/O through your database product, you can use the `mount -forcedirectio` option to enable direct I/O for each file system. Alternatively, use the `directio(3C)` library call to enable direct I/O. See `mount_ufs(1M)` or `directio(3C)` for more information.

- When you create file systems, `mkfs` command performance is often 10 times faster than in previous Solaris releases. The biggest performance improvements occur when creating file systems on systems with high-capacity or high-speed disks.
- The `labelit`(1M) command provides new options for use with Universal Disk Format (UDF) file systems. You can use new options to identify the author name (`-o lvinfo1`), organization (`-o lvinfo2`), and contact information (`-o lvinfo3`) for a UDF volume. In previous releases, no mechanism was available to update this information. The maximum length of each option is 35 bytes. See `labelit_udfs`(1M) for more information.

What's New in File Systems in the Solaris 8 Release

The Solaris 8 release provides the following new file system features.

- The TMPFS file system provides a `/var/run` repository for temporary system files. See "The Temporary File System (TMPFS)" on page 184 for more information.
- The `/etc/mnttab` file is no longer a text-based file. Instead, it is an MNTFS file system that provides read-only information directly from the kernel about mounted file systems for the local system. See "The /etc/mnttab File System (MNTFS)" on page 187 for more information.
- The UDF file system, the industry-standard format for storing information on optical media technology called Digital Versatile Disc or Digital Video Disc (DVD), is included in this release. See "Disk-Based File Systems" on page 182 for more information.
- The `-F xmemfs` option to the `mount` command is new in the Solaris 8 release. XMEMFS is an IA-platform extended-memory file system that provides file system semantics to manage and access large amounts of physical memory that can exceed 4 Gbytes in size. See "Understanding Mounting and Unmounting" on page 200 for more information.

Types of File Systems

The Solaris Operating Environment supports three types of file systems.

- Disk based.
- Network based.
- Virtual (previously called pseudo).

Disk-Based File Systems

Disk-based file systems are stored on physical media such as hard disks, CD-ROMs, diskettes, and DVD discs. Disk-based file systems can be written in different formats. The following list describes the available formats.

- UFS—UNIX file system (based on the BSD Fat Fast File system that was provided in the 4.3 Tahoe release). The default disk-based file system in Solaris system software is UFS. Before you can create a file system on a disk, the disk must be formatted and divided into slices (partitions).

- S5FS—IA UNIX file system (based on the BSD Fat Fast File system that was provided in the 4.3 Tahoe release). The default disk-based file system in Solaris IA system software is S5FS.

- HSFS—High Sierra and ISO 9660 file system. High Sierra is the first CD-ROM file system; ISO 9660 is the official standard. The HSFS file system is used on CD-ROM and is a read-only file system. The Solaris HSFS supports Rock Ridge extensions to ISO 9660, which provide all UFS file system semantics and file types except for writability and hard links.

- PCFS—The PC file system allows read/write access to data and programs on DOS-formatted diskettes written for DOS-based personal computers.

- UDFS—Universal Disk Format file system, new in the Solaris 8 release, is the industry-standard format for storing information on the optical media technology called DVD (Digital Versatile Disc or Digital Video Disc). See "Using DVD-ROM Devices" on page 256 for more information.

  UDFS support is provided in the following new packages.

  - SUNWudfr—32-bit kernel component.
  - SUNWudfrx—64-bit kernel component.
  - SUNWudf—/usr component.

  The Solaris UDF file system provides the following features.

- Access to industry-standard CD-ROM and DVD-ROM media when they contain a UDF file system.
- Flexibility in exchanging information across platforms and operating systems.
- A mechanism for implementing, according to the DVD video specification based on the UDF format, new applications that offer broadcast-quality video, high-quality sound, and interactivity.

This UDF release does not contain the following features.

- Support for write-once media, CD-RW, and DVD-RAM, with either the sequential disk-at-once and incremental recording.
- UFS components such as quotas, ACLs, transaction logging, file system locking, and file system threads. These components are not part of the UDF 1.50 specification.

The System V (S5) file system traditionally provided with System V releases is not included in the Solaris Operating Environment because of significant limitations, such as a maximum of 64,000 files in a file system, a restriction of 14 characters for file names, and lack of a quota facility.

Each type of disk-based file system is customarily associated with a particular media device.

- UFS and S5FS with hard disk and any other media (CD-ROM, DVD, diskette).
- HSFS with CD-ROM.
- PCFS with diskette.
- UDF with DVD.

These associations are not, however, restrictive. For example, CD-ROMs and diskettes can have UFS file systems installed on them.

Network-Based File Systems

Network-based file systems are file systems that are accessed over the network. Typically, network-based file systems are file systems that reside on one system and are accessed by other systems across the network. The available network-based file system is the NFS network, or distributed file system.

With NFS you can administer distributed resources (files or directories) by sharing them (exporting them from a server) and mounting them on individual systems. See "Making File Systems Available" on page 199 for more information.

Virtual File Systems

Virtual file systems (previously called pseudo file systems) are virtual or memory-based file systems that provide access to special kernel information and facilities. Most virtual file systems do not use file system disk space. Some virtual file systems, such as the temporary file system, may, however, use the swap space on a physical disk. Cache file systems use a file system on the disk to contain the cache.

The Cache File System (CacheFS)

You can use the Cache file system to improve performance of remote file systems or slow devices such as CD-ROM drives. When a file system is cached, the data read from the remote file system or CD-ROM is stored in a cache on the local system. See "Cache File Systems" on page 223 for more information.

The Temporary File System (TMPFS)

The TMPFS file system uses local memory for disk reads and writes. Access to files in a TMPFS file system is typically much faster than access to files in a UFS file system. Files in the TMPFS file system are not permanent. They cease to exist when the file system is unmounted and when the system is shut down. When the system is rebooted, the entire file system is recreated.

TMPFS is the default file system type for the /tmp directory in the Solaris Operating Environment. You can copy or move files into or out of the /tmp directory, just as you would in a UFS /tmp file system.

TMPFS file systems can improve system performance by saving the cost of reading and writing temporary files to a local disk or across the network. For example, temporary files are created when you compile a program. The operating system generates a lot of disk or network input and output activity while manipulating these files. Using TMPFS file systems to hold these temporary files can significantly speed up their creation, manipulation, and deletion.

The TMPFS file system uses swap space as a temporary storage area. If a system with a TMPFS file system does not have adequate swap space, two problems can occur.

- The TMPFS file system can run out of space, just as a regular file system can fill up.
- Because TMPFS allocates swap space to save file data (if necessary), some programs may not be able to execute because there is not enough swap space.

See Chapter 9, "Administering Systems," for information about increasing swap space.

The Loopback File System (LOFS)

The LOFS file system lets you create a new virtual file system. You can access files through an alternative path name. For example, you can create a loopback mount of / onto /tmp/newroot. The entire file system hierarchy looks like it is duplicated under /tmp/newroot, including any file systems that were mounted from NFS servers. All files are accessible either with a path name starting from / or with a path name starting from /tmp/newroot until a different file system is mounted in /tmp/newroot or any of its subdirectories. See "Making File Systems Available" on page 199 for more information about mounting and unmounting file systems.

The Process File System (PROCFS)

The PROCFS file system maps all processing information into a file system so _New!_ that you can use the file system programming paradigm to manipulate and debug processes and perform accounting and other activities.

The PROC file system resides in memory. It contains a list of active processes, by number, in the /proc directory. Information in the /proc directory is used by commands such as ps. Debuggers and other development tools can also access the address space of the processes by using file system calls. The following example shows a listing of the contents of the /proc directory.

```
paperbark% ls -l /proc
total 128
dr-x--x--x   5 root      root          736 May 11 08:45 0
dr-x--x--x   5 root      root          736 May 11 08:45 1
dr-x--x--x   5 root      root          736 May 11 08:46 108
dr-x--x--x   5 root      root          736 May 11 08:46 125
dr-x--x--x   5 root      root          736 May 11 08:46 155
dr-x--x--x   5 root      root          736 May 11 08:46 161
dr-x--x--x   5 daemon    daemon        736 May 11 08:46 165
dr-x--x--x   5 root      root          736 May 11 08:46 168
dr-x--x--x   5 root      root          736 May 11 08:46 179
dr-x--x--x   5 root      root          736 May 11 08:46 185
dr-x--x--x   5 root      root          736 May 11 08:46 195
dr-x--x--x   5 root      root          736 May 11 08:45 2
dr-x--x--x   5 root      root          736 May 11 08:46 200
dr-x--x--x   5 root      root          736 May 11 08:46 213
dr-x--x--x   5 root      root          736 May 11 08:46 222
dr-x--x--x   5 root      root          736 May 11 08:46 225
dr-x--x--x   5 root      root          736 May 11 08:46 227
dr-x--x--x   5 daemon    other         736 May 11 08:46 241
dr-x--x--x   5 daemon    other         736 May 11 08:46 242
dr-x--x--x   5 root      root          736 May 11 08:46 275
dr-x--x--x   5 root      root          736 May 11 08:45 3
dr-x--x--x   5 root      root          736 May 11 08:46 304
dr-x--x--x   5 root      root          736 May 11 08:46 317
dr-x--x--x   5 root      root          736 May 11 08:46 323
dr-x--x--x   5 root      root          736 May 11 08:46 324
dr-x--x--x   5 root      root          736 May 11 08:46 333
dr-x--x--x   5 root      root          736 May 11 08:46 336
dr-x--x--x   5 root      root          736 May 11 08:46 337
dr-x--x--x   5 root      staff         736 May 11 08:46 340
dr-x--x--x   5 root      root          736 May 11 08:46 346
dr-x--x--x   5 root      root          736 May 11 08:46 349
dr-x--x--x   5 root      root          736 May 11 08:46 350
dr-x--x--x   5 root      root          736 May 11 08:46 357
dr-x--x--x   5 root      root          736 May 11 08:47 370
```

```
dr-x--x--x   5 winsor    staff          736 May 11 08:47 375
dr-x--x--x   5 winsor    staff          736 May 11 08:47 385
dr-x--x--x   5 winsor    staff          736 May 11 08:47 389
dr-x--x--x   5 winsor    staff          736 May 11 08:47 421
dr-x--x--x   5 winsor    staff          736 May 11 08:47 422
dr-x--x--x   5 winsor    staff          736 May 11 08:47 424
dr-x--x--x   5 winsor    staff          736 May 11 08:47 439
dr-x--x--x   5 root      root           736 May 11 08:45 44
dr-x--x--x   5 winsor    staff          736 May 11 08:47 440
dr-x--x--x   5 root      root           736 May 11 08:47 441
dr-x--x--x   5 winsor    staff          736 May 11 08:47 447
dr-x--x--x   5 winsor    staff          736 May 11 08:47 449
dr-x--x--x   5 winsor    staff          736 May 11 08:47 450
dr-x--x--x   5 winsor    staff          736 May 11 08:47 451
dr-x--x--x   5 winsor    staff          736 May 11 08:47 452
dr-x--x--x   5 winsor    staff          736 May 11 08:47 453
dr-x--x--x   5 winsor    staff          736 May 11 08:47 455
dr-x--x--x   5 root      root           736 May 11 08:45 46
dr-x--x--x   5 winsor    staff          736 May 11 08:48 461
dr-x--x--x   5 winsor    staff          736 May 11 08:48 462
dr-x--x--x   5 winsor    staff          736 May 11 08:48 463
dr-x--x--x   5 winsor    staff          736 May 11 08:48 464
dr-x--x--x   5 winsor    staff          736 May 11 08:48 466
dr-x--x--x   5 root      root           736 May 11 08:48 468
dr-x--x--x   5 winsor    staff          736 May 11 08:48 470
dr-x--x--x   5 winsor    staff          736 May 11 08:48 473
dr-x--x--x   5 winsor    staff          736 May 11 08:48 476
dr-x--x--x   5 winsor    staff          736 May 11 08:48 483
dr-x--x--x   5 winsor    staff          736 May 11 08:48 486
dr-x--x--x   5 winsor    staff          736 May 11 09:36 521
paperbark%
```

*NOTE. /*proc *files do not use disk space, so there is little reason to delete files from this directory.*

The /proc directory does not require any system administration.

Starting with the Solaris 2.6 release, the flat /proc file system is restructured into a directory hierarchy that contains additional subdirectories for state information and control functions. It also provides a watchpoint facility that remaps read/write permissions on the individual pages of the address space of a process. This facility has no restrictions and is multithread (MT) safe.

The new /proc file structure provides complete binary compatibility with the old /proc interface except that the new watchpoint facility cannot be used with the old interface. Debugging tools have been modified to use the new /proc watchpoint facility, which means the entire watchpoint process is faster.

The following restrictions no longer apply to setting watchpoints with the dbx debugging tool.

- Setting watchpoints on local variables on the stack because of SPARC register windows.
- Setting watchpoints on multithreaded processes.

For more information, refer to the proc(4), core(4), and adb(4) manual pages.

The /etc/mnttab File System (MNTFS)

The system modifies the /etc/mnttab (mount table) whenever you mount or unmount a file system. In previous Solaris releases, the /etc/mnttab mount table was a text-based file that stored information about mounted file systems. This file could get out of sync with the state of mounted file systems.

In the Solaris 8 release, /etc/mnttab is an MNTFS file system that provides read-only information directly from the kernel about mounted file systems for the local system.

Because of this structural difference, the following mnttab behavior is changed.

- Programs or scripts cannot write to /etc/mnttab.
- The mount -m option for faking mnttab entries no longer works.

MNTFS requires no administration. See mnttab(4) for more information.

You can display the contents of the /etc/mnttab file with the cat or more commands, but you cannot edit it. The following example shows an /etc/mnttab file. You can use the grep command to search for specific entries in the /etc/mnttab file.

```
paperbark% more /etc/mnttab
/dev/dsk/c0t0d0s0          /        ufs
  rw,intr,largefiles,onerror=panic,suid,de
v=800000          958013089
/proc    /proc    proc     dev=2d80000      958013088
fd       /dev/fd  fd       rw,suid,dev=2e40000      958013090
mnttab   /etc/mnttab      mntfs    dev=2f40000      958013092
swap     /var/run         tmpfs    dev=1    958013092
swap     /tmp     tmpfs    dev=2    958013094
/dev/dsk/c0t0d0s7          /export/home     ufs
  rw,intr,largefiles,onerror=panic
,suid,dev=800007          958013094
/dev/dsk/c0t1d0s7          /export/home0    ufs
  rw,intr,largefiles,onerror=panic
,suid,dev=80000f          958013094
-hosts   /net     autofs   indirect,nosuid,ignore,nobrowse,dev=3000001
  95801311
8
auto_home         /home    autofs   indirect,ignore,nobrowse,dev=3000002
  95801311
8
-xfn     /xfn     autofs   indirect,ignore,dev=3000003      958013118
paperbark:vold(pid228)    /vol     nfs      ignore,dev=2fc0001       958013123
paperbark%
```

Additional Virtual File Systems

The following additional types of virtual file systems are listed for your information. They do not require administration.

- FIFOS (first-in first-out)—Named pipe files that give processes common access to data.

- FDFS (file descriptors)—Provides explicit names for opening files using file descriptors.
- NAMEFS—Used mostly by STREAMS for dynamic mounts of file descriptors on top of files.
- SPECFS (special)—Provides access to special character and block devices.
- SWAPFS—Slice or file system used by the kernel when you create additional swap space with the `swap` command. When you put the swap file in a file system, you first create a special file with the `mkfile` command.

The Default Solaris File System

The Solaris file system is hierarchical, starting with the root directory (/) and continuing downward through a number of directories. The Solaris Operating Environment installs a default set of directories and uses a set of conventions to group similar types of files together. Table 44 describes the default Solaris file system and shows the type of each file system.

Table 44   The Default Solaris File System

Directory	File System Type	Description
/	ufs	The top of the hierarchical file tree. The root directory contains the directories and files critical for system operation, such as the kernel (`/kernel/unix`), the device drivers, and the programs used to start (boot) the system. It also contains the mount point directories to which local and remote file systems can be attached to the file tree.
/etc/mnttab	mntfs	Read-only information provided directly from the kernel about mounted file systems for the local system. New in the Solaris 8 Operating Environment.

Table 44   *The Default Solaris File System (Continued)*

Directory	File System Type	Description
/usr	ufs	System files and directories that can be shared with other users. Files that run only on certain types of systems are in the /usr directory (for example, SPARC executables). Files (such as manual pages) that can be used on all types of systems are in /usr/share. Sun's current recommendation is that you make /usr part of the root file system.
/export/home or /home	ufs, NFS	The mount point for the users' home directories, which store users' work files. By default, /home is an automounted file system. On stand-alone systems, /export/home is a UFS file system on a local disk slice.
/var	ufs	System files and directories that are likely to change or grow over the life of the local system. These include system logs, vi and ex backup files, uucp files, and mail and calendar files. Sun's current recommendation is that you make /var part of the root file system. Because /var is the most likely directory to fill up with with log files, the Solaris 9 Operating Environment provides a log management command that you can use to rotate, compress, age, and eventually remove log files before they fill up this file system. See logadm(1M) and logadm.conf(4) for more information.
/opt	ufs	Mount point for optional, third-party software. Sun's current recommendation is that you make /opt part of the root file system unless it is too large to fit on the boot disk.
/tmp	tmpfs	Temporary files, cleared each time the system is booted or unmounted.

Table 44   The Default Solaris File System (Continued)

Directory	File System Type	Description
/var/run	tmpfs	A file system for storing temporary files that are not needed after the system is booted.
/proc	procfs	A list of active system processes, by number.

New!

The root (/) and /usr file systems are both needed to run a system. Some of the most basic commands from the /usr file system (such as mount) are included in the root file system so that they are available when the system boots or is in single-user mode. If you make /usr part of the / file system, both partitions are always available.

The Virtual File System Table (/etc/vfstab)

Each system has a virtual file system table, /etc/vfstab, that lists all the disk slices and file systems available to the system. The file system table also specifies the mount point and options for each file system. The /etc/vfstab file replaces /etc/fstab and functions in a similar manner. The default file system configuration table (the /etc/vfstab file) depends on the selections made for each system when system software was installed. You should edit the /etc/vfstab file for each system to automatically mount local UFS file systems, essential NFS file systems, and any other appropriate file systems.

This section describes the contents of the /etc/vfstab file and provides information on how to edit and use the file. The file system table is an ASCII file. Comment lines begin with #. The following example shows an /etc/vfstab file for a system with two slices.

```
castle% more /etc/vfstab
#device          device          mount          FS      fsck    mount     mount
#to mount        to fsck         point          type    pass    at boot   options
#
#/dev/dsk/c1d0s2 /dev/rdsk/c1d0s2 /usr           ufs     1       yes       -
fd          -       /dev/fd fd       -       no      -
/proc       -       /proc   proc     -       no      -
/dev/dsk/c0t3d0s1          -       -       swap     -       no      -
/dev/dsk/c0t3d0s0          /dev/rdsk/c0t3d0s0      /       ufs     1       no        -
swap        -       /tmp    tmpfs    -       yes     -
castle%
```

Refer to "Disk-Naming Conventions" on page 296 for information on disk device naming conventions.

Note that for / and /usr, the mount at boot field value is specified as no because these file systems are mounted as part of the boot sequence before the mountall command is run. If the mount at boot field value is specified as yes, the mountall program redundantly (and unnecessarily) tries to mount these already mounted file systems.

The file system table has seven fields, each separated by a Tab, as described in Table 45.

Table 45   Fields in the /etc/vfstab File

Field	Description
device to mount	The device to mount can be one of the following.
	The slice for local UFS file systems (for example, /dev/dsk/c0t0d0s0).
	The resource name for remote file systems (for example, myserver:/export/home for an NFS file system).
	The name of the slice on which to swap (for example, /dev/dsk/c0t3d0s1).
	The /proc directory and proc file system type.
	A block special device that denotes a particular slice on a CD-ROM. This slice has an HSFS file system or some other CD-ROM-compatible file system written to it.
	/dev/diskette as PCFS or UFS file system type. This field is also used to specify swap file systems.
device to fsck	The raw (character) special device that corresponds to the file system identified by the device to fsck field (for example, /dev/rdsk/c0t0d0s0). This field determines the raw interface that is used by fsck. Use a dash (-) when either there is no file system written on the slice or the entry denotes an NFS-mounted file system.
mount point	The mount point directory (for example, /usr for /dev/dsk/c0t0d0s6).
FS type	The type of file system identified by the device to fsck field.

Table 45   Fields in the /etc/vfstab File (Continued)

Field	Description
fsck pass	The pass number used by fsck to decide whether to check a file system. When the field contains a dash (–), the file system is not checked. When the field contains a value of 1 or more, the file systems are checked sequentially; non-ufs file systems with a zero fsck pass are checked. For ufs file systems only, when the field contains a zero (0), the file system is not checked. When fsck is run on multiple ufs file systems that have fsck pass values greater than 1 and the preen option (-o p) is used, fsck automatically checks the file systems on different disks in parallel to maximize efficiency. Otherwise, the value of the pass number has no effect.
mount at boot	Indicate yes or no for whether the file system should be automatically mounted by mountall when the system is booted.
mount options	A list of comma-separated options (with no spaces) that are used in mounting the file system. Use a dash (–) to show no options. See the mount_*file-system-type*(1M) manual page for a list of the available options.

*   In the Solaris Operating Environment, fsck pass does not explicitly specify the order in which file systems are checked as it did with SunOS 4.x system software.

> *NOTE. You must have an entry in each field in the* /etc/vfstab *file. If there is no value for the field, be sure to enter a dash (–).*

NFS Client Failover

NFS client *failover*, introduced in the Solaris 2.6 release, provides a high level of availability of read-only file systems by enabling a client to automatically mount the file system from another server if the first server becomes unavailable.

The file system can become unavailable if the server crashes, if the server is overloaded, or if a network faults. The failover in these conditions can occur at any time without disrupting the processes running on the client.

Failover file systems must be mounted read-only. The file systems must be identical for failover to succeed. You cannot use file systems mounted by CacheFS with failover because extra information stored for each CacheFS file system cannot be updated during failover.

When using client failover, you specify additional hosts from which to mount a file system in case the first host cannot be reached. You can specify alternative failover servers in the /etc/vfstab file, through the automounter, or from the command line.

The following example shows an /etc/vfstab client failover entry.

```
paperbark,castle:/export/share/local  -  /usr/local  nfs  -  no  ro
```

NOTE. You cannot mix servers running different versions of the NFS protocol by using a command line or in an /etc/vfstab entry. You can mix servers supporting NFS V2 and V3 protocols only with the automounter. In this case, client failover uses the best subset of version 2 or version 3 servers.

The following example uses the mount command with client failover.

```
# mount -F nfs -o ro paperbark,castle:/export/share/man /usr/man
#
```

Creation of an Entry in the File System Table

Use the following steps to create an entry in the file system table.

1. Become superuser.
2. Edit the /etc/vfstab file, using an editor such as vi.
3. Add the entry, separating each field with white space (a space or a Tab). If a field has no entry, enter a dash (-).
4. Save the changes.
5. Check to be sure the mount point directory is present. If it's not, create the mount point by changing to the directory in which you want to create it, typing **mkdir *directory-name***, and pressing Return.
6. Type **mount *mount-point*** and press Return.

   The entry is mounted.

The following example mounts the disk slice /dev/dsk/c0t3d0s7, which contains a UFS file system, as a ufs file system attached to the mount point directory /files1 with the default mount options (read/write). It specifies the raw character device /dev/rdsk/c0t3d0s7 as the device to check with fsck. The fsck pass value of 2 means that the file system is checked, but not sequentially.

#device	device	mount	FS	fsck	mount	mount
#to mount	to fsck	point	type	pass	at boot	options

```
#
/dev/dsk/c0t3d0s7 /dev/rdsk/c0t3d0s7 /files1  ufs   2     yes      -
```

The following example mounts the directory /export/man from the system oak as an nfs file system on mount point /usr/man. You do not specify a device to fsck or a fsck pass for NFS file systems. In the following example, mount options are ro (read-only) and soft. For greater reliability, for read/write NFS file systems, specify the hard mount option (rw,hard).

```
#device          device         mount        FS      fsck     mount     mount
#to mount        to fsck        point        type    pass     at boot   options
oak:/export/man  -              /usr/man     nfs     -        yes       ro,soft
```

The following example mounts a CD-ROM drive on a mount point named /hsfiles. CD-ROM files typically are read-only, so you specify ro for the mount options. Specify no for mount at boot because you are most likely to mount and unmount a CD-ROM from the command line or by using volume management. Because hsfs is read-only, specify no device to fsck and no fsck pass number.

```
#device          device         mount        FS      fsck     mount     mount
#to mount        to fsck        point        type    pass     at boot   options
/dev/dsk/c0t6d0s2 -             /hsfiles     hsfs    -        no        ro
```

The following example mounts the diskette drive on a mount point named /pcfiles. Specify no for mount at boot because you are most likely to mount and unmount a diskette from the command line or by using volume management. Specify no to fsck or fsck pass because the pcfs file system does not support fsck.

```
#device          device         mount        FS      fsck     mount     mount
#to mount        to fsck        point        type    pass     at boot   options
/dev/diskette    -              /pcfiles     pcfs    -        no        rw
```

The following example mounts the root file system on a loopback mount point named /mnt/newroot. Specify yes for mount at boot, no device to fsck, and no fsck pass number. Loopback file systems must always be mounted after the file systems used to make up the loopback file system. Be sure that the loopback entry is the last entry in the /etc/vfstab file so that it follows the entries that depend on it.

```
#device          device         mount        FS      fsck     mount     mount
#to mount        to fsck        point        type    pass     at boot   options
/                -              /tmp/newroot lofs    -        yes       -
```

File System Administrative Commands

This section lists the file system administrative commands and describes the syntax.

Most file system administrative commands have a generic and a file system-specific component. Use the generic commands, which use the file system-specific component. Table 46 lists the generic file system administrative commands, which are located in the /usr/sbin directory. Most of these commands also have file system-specific counterparts.

Table 46   Generic File System Administrative Commands

Command	Description
clri(1M)	Clear inodes.
df(1M)	Report the number of free disk blocks and files.
ff(1M)	List file names and statistics for a file system.
fsck(1M)	Check the integrity of a file system and repair any damage found.
fsdb(1M)	File-system debugger.
fstyp(1M)	Determine the file system type.
labelit(1M)	List or provide labels for file systems when copied to tape (for use by the volcopy command only).
mkfs(1M)	Make a new file system.
mount(1M)	Mount file systems and remote resources.
mountall(1M)	Mount all file systems specified in a file system table.
ncheck(1M)	Generate a list of path names with their i-numbers.
umount(1M)	Unmount file systems and remote resources.
umountall(1M)	Unmount all file systems specified in a file system table.
volcopy(1M)	Make an image copy of a file system.

CAUTION. Do not use the file-system–specific commands directly. If you specify an operation on a file system that does not support it, the generic command displays the error message command: Operation not applicable for FSType type.

Syntax of Generic Commands

Most of the generic file system commands use the following syntax.

```
command [-F FStype] [-V][generic-options][-o specific-options]
   [special|mount-point] [operands]
```

The options and arguments to the generic commands are shown in Table 47.

Table 47   *Generic File System Command Syntax*

Option	Description
-F *FStype*	Specify the type of file system. If you do not use this option, the command looks for an entry that matches the special, raw device, or mount point field in the /etc/vfstab file. Otherwise, the default is taken from the file /etc/default/fs for local file systems and from the file /etc/dfs/fstypes for remote file systems.
-V	Echo the completed command line. The echoed line may include additional information derived from /etc/vfstab. Use this option to verify and validate the command line. It does not execute the command.
generic-options	
	Options common to different types of file systems.
-o *specific-options*	
	A list of options specific to the type of file system. The list must have the following format: -o followed by a space, followed by a series of *keyword* [=*value*] pairs separated by commas with no intervening spaces.
special	*mount-point*	
	Identify the file system. Name either the *mount-point* or the *special* device file for the slice holding the file system. For some commands, the *special* file must be the raw (character) device, and for other commands it must be the block device. See Chapter 8, "Administering Devices," for more information about disk device names. In some cases, this argument is used as a key to search the /etc/vfstab file for a matching entry from which to obtain other information. In most cases, this argument is required and must come immediately after *specific-options*. However, it is not required when

Table 47   *Generic File System Command Syntax (Continued)*

Option	Description
	you want a command to act on all the file systems (optionally limited by type) listed in the /etc/vfstab file.
operands	Arguments specific to a type of file system. See the specific manual page of the command (for example, mkfs_ufs) for a detailed description.

Manual Pages for Generic and Specific Commands

Both the generic and specific commands have manual pages. The specific manual page is a continuation of the generic manual page. To look at a specific manual page, append an underscore and the file system type abbreviation to the generic command name. For example, to see the specific manual page for mounting an HSFS file system, type **man mount_hsfs** and press Return. LOFS, PCFS, and PROCFS do not have specific manual pages for the mount command.

How File System Commands Determine File System Type

The generic file system commands determine the file system type with the following sequence.

1. From -F if supplied.
2. By matching a special device with an entry in /etc/vfstab (if *special* is supplied). For example, fsck first looks for a match against the fsck device field; if no match is found, it then checks against the *special* device field.
3. By using the default specified in /etc/default/fs for local file systems and in /etc/dfs/fstypes for remote file systems.

Types of File Systems

If you want to determine the type of a file system, you can obtain the information from the same files that the generic commands use.

- The FS type field in the file system table (/etc/vfstab).
- The /etc/default/fs file for local file systems.

- The `/etc/dfs/fstypes` file for remote file systems.
- The `fstyp(1M)` command.

To find a file system's type in the `/etc/vfstab` file, type **grep *mount-point* /etc/vfstab** and press Return. Information for the mount point is displayed, as shown in the following example.

```
drusilla% grep /tmp /etc/vfstab
swap            -               /tmp         tmpfs    -       yes     -
drusilla%
```

If `vfstab` does not have an entry for a file system, use one of the following procedures to determine the file system's type.

To identify a mounted file system's type, type **grep *mount-point* /etc/mnttab** and press Return. Information on the mount point is displayed, as shown in the following example.

```
drusilla% grep /home /etc/mnttab
drusilla:(pid129)   /home nfs   ro,ignore,map=/etc/auto_home,indirect,dev=21c0004
    693606637
bigriver:/export/home/bigriver   /tmp_mnt/home/bigriver  nfs      rw,dev=21c0005
    695409833
drusilla%
```

NOTE. Starting with the Solaris 8 release, the `/etc/mnttab` *file is no longer a text file, but you can still use the* `grep` *command to search it for specific entries.*

Or, type **mount** and press Return. A list of the mounted file systems is displayed, as shown in the following example.

```
drusilla% mount
/ on /dev/dsk/c0t3d0s0 read/write on Tue Dec 24 12:29:22 1999
/usr on /dev/dsk/c0t1d0s6 read/write on Tue Dec 24 12:29:22 1999
/proc on /proc read/write on Tue Dec 24 12:29:22 1999
/usr/man on swsvr4-50:/export/svr4/man read/write/remote on Mon Dec 30 12:49:11
    1999
/usr/openwin on swsvr4-50:/export/svr4/openwinV3 read/write/remote on Mon Dec 30
    13:50:54 1999
/tmp on swap o on Wed Jan  8 13:38:45 1992
/mnt on swsvr4-50:/export/svr4 read/write/remote on Fri Jan 10 15:51:23 1992
/tmp_mnt/home on bigriver:/export/home read/write/remote on Tue Jan 14   09:23:53
    1992
drusilla%
```

Or, use the following steps.

1. Type **devnm *mount-point*** and press Return.
   The raw device name is displayed.
2. Become superuser.

3. Type **fstyp /dev/rdsk/c*n*t*n*d*n*s*n** and press Return.

    The type of the file system is displayed, as shown in the following example.

```
drusilla% devnm /usr
/dev/dsk/c0t1d0s6 /usr
drusilla% su
Password:
# fstyp /dev/rdsk/c0t3d0s0
ufs
#
```

Making File Systems Available

When you have created a file system, you need to make it available; you do this by mounting it. A mounted file system is attached to the system directory tree at the specified mount point and becomes available to the system. The root file system is always mounted. Any other file system can be connected or disconnected from the root file system.

You can mount a local file system in the following ways.

- By creating an entry in the /etc/vfstab (virtual file system table) file. The /etc/vfstab file contains a list of file systems that are automatically mounted when the system is booted in multiuser state. See "The Virtual File System Table (/etc/vfstab)" on page 190 for a description of the /etc/vfstab file.
- From a command line by using the mount command.

File systems on disk slices must always be mounted on the server system and shared (exported) before other systems can access them. See "Sharing Files from a Server" on page 207 for information about sharing file systems. When file systems are shared from a server, a client can mount them as NFS file systems in any of the following three ways.

- By adding an entry to the /etc/vfstab file so that the file system is automatically mounted when the system is booted in multiuser state.
- By using the automount program to automatically mount or unmount the file system when a user changes into (mount) or out of (umount) the automounting directory.
- By using the mount command at a command line.

Understanding Mounting and Unmounting

File systems can be attached to the hierarchy of directories available on a system. This process is called *mounting*. To manually mount a file system, you need the following things.

- To be superuser.
- A mount point on the local system. The mount point is a directory to which the mounted file system is attached.
- The resource name of the file system to be mounted (for example, /usr).

As a general rule, local disk slices should always be included in the /etc/vfstab file. Any software from servers, such as CDE, OpenWindows, or manual pages, and home directories from a server can either be included in the /etc/vfstab file or be automounted, depending on the policy at your site.

When you mount a file system, any files or directories that might be present in the mount point directory are unavailable as long as the file system is mounted. These files are not permanently affected by the mounting process and become available again when the file system is unmounted. However, mount directories typically are empty because you usually do not want to obscure existing files.

Using Mount and Unmount File System Commands

Table 48 lists the commands in the /usr/sbin directory that you use to mount and unmount file systems.

Table 48   Commands for Mounting and Unmounting File Systems

Command	Description
mount(1M)	Mount file systems and remote resources.
mountall(1M)	Mount all file systems specified in a file system table.
umount(1M)	Unmount file systems and remote resources.
umountall(1M)	Unmount all file systems specified in a file system table.

The mount command does not mount a read/write file system that has inconsistencies. If you receive an error message from the mount or mountall command, you may need to check the file system.

The umount command does not unmount a file system that is busy. A file system is considered busy if a user is in a directory in the file system or if a program has a file open in that file system.

Table 49 describes the general mount options that you can specify with the
-o option of the `mount` command. If you specify multiple options, separate
them with commas (no spaces). For example, -o ro,nosuid.

Table 49   *Commands for Mounting and Unmounting File
Systems*

Option	File System	Description
rw | ro	CacheFS, NFS, PCFS, UFS, S5FS, UDFS	Specify read/write or read-only. If you do not specify this option, the default is read/write.
nosuid	HSFS, NFS, UFS, UDFS	Prevent setuid execution and prevent devices on the file system from being opened. The default is to enable setuid execution and enable devices to be opened.
remount	NFS, UFS, S5FS, UDFS	Remount a file system with different options.
f	None	Forcibly unmount a file system. Without this option, umount does not allow a file system to be unmounted if a file on that file system is busy. This option can result in data loss for open files; programs that access files after the file system has been unmounted get an error (IEO).
m	UFS, S5FS	Mount the file system without making an entry in /etc/mnttab.
logging | nologging		
	UFS	Enable or disable UFS logging. See "UFS Logging" on page 202 for more information.
bg | fg	NFS	If the first attempt fails, retry in the background (bg) or in the foreground (fg). The default is fg.
soft | hard		
	NFS	Specify the procedure if the server does not respond. soft indicates that an error is returned. hard indicates that the retry request is continued until the server responds. The default is hard.

New!

*Table 49   Commands for Mounting and Unmounting File
              Systems (Continued)*

Option	File System	Description
`intr	nointr`		
	NFS	Specify whether keyboard interrupts can be used to kill a process hung while waiting for a response on hard-mounted file systems. The default is `intr` (interrupts allowed).
`retry=n`	NFS	Retry the mount operations when it fails.
`largefiles`		
	NFS	A file system mounted using this option may contain files larger than 2 Gbytes, but it is not a requirement. This option is the default.
`nolargefiles`		
	NFS	Disable the `-largefiles` mount option to provide backward compatibility with previous file system behavior and enforcing the 2-Gbyte maximum file size limit.
`index filename`		
	NFS URL	Automatically load a file matching `filename` if it is found in a directory referenced by an NFS URL.
`public`	NFS URL	Reset the `public` file handle to the current directory to enable you to access an NFS URL even if the file system cannot be mounted in the usual way.
`size=sz`	XMEMFS	Specify the size of the XMEMFS file system. This option is required.
`largebsize`	XMEMFS	Specify the large memory page size as the file system block size.

UFS Logging

UFS logging, new starting with the Solaris 7 Operating Environment, is the process of storing transactions (the changes that make up a complete UFS operation) in a log file before the transactions are applied to the UFS file system. Once a transaction is stored, the file system can apply the transactions to the file system later, if needed, during a recovery.

UFS logging is not enabled by default. To enable UFS logging, specify the -o logging option with the mount command when mounting a file system.

If you specify logging, then logging is enabled while the file system is mounted. This option prevents file systems from becoming inconsistent, thereby eliminating the need to run fsck. And, because you can bypass fsck, logging reduces the time required to reboot a system after a crash or after an unclean halt. The default behavior is nologging.

The log is allocated from free blocks on the file system and sized at approximately 1 Mbyte per 1 Gbyte of file system up to a maximum of 64 Mbytes. You can enable logging on any UFS file system, including root (/). The log created by UFS logging is continually flushed as it fills up. The log is totally flushed when the file system is unmounted when the lockfs -f command is run.

The fsdb command has been updated with new debugging options to support UFS logging.

Finding the Mounted File Systems

To display a list of mounted file systems, type **mount** and press Return. All the file systems currently mounted are displayed, as shown in the following example.

```
oak% mount
/ on /dev/dsk/c0t0d0s0 read/write/setuid on Wed Oct 23 10:08:50 1999

/usr on /dev/dsk/c0t0d0s6 read/write/setuid on Wed Oct 23 10:08:50 1999

/proc on /proc read/write/setuid on Wed Oct 23 10:08:50 1999

/tmp on swap on Wed Oct 23 10:08:52 1999

/usr/openwin on cheers:/export/openwin hard/remote on Wed Oct 23
10:11:08 1999

/home on blowup:(pid136) read only/intr/map=auto.home/indirect on Wed Oct 23
   10:11:10 1999

/vol on blowup:(pid136) read only/intr/map=auto.vol/indirect on Wed Oct 23
   10:11:10 1999

/nse on blowup:(pid136) read only/intr/map=/etc/auto.nse /indirect on Wed Oct
   23 10:11:10 1999
oak%
```

Mounting All File Systems in the /etc/vfstab File

Use the following steps to mount all file systems in the `/etc/vfstab` file.

1. Become superuser.
2. Type **mountall** and press Return.

   All the file systems in the local `/etc/vfstab` file are mounted, as shown in the following example.

```
oak% su
Password:
# mountall
oak#
```

Mounting All File Systems of a Specific Type

Use the following steps to mount all file systems of a specific type that are in the `/etc/vfstab` file. The most common file system types are `ufs` for local disk slices and `nfs` for network file systems. See "Types of File Systems" on page 197 for a complete list of file system types.

1. Become superuser.
2. Type **mountall -F** *filesystem-type* and press Return.

   All the file systems of the type you specify that are in the local `/etc/vfstab` file are mounted.

The following example mounts all NFS file systems.

```
oak% su
Password:
# mountall -F nfs
#
```

Starting with the Solaris 2.6 release, the `-largefiles` mount option is used as the default for mounting UFS file systems. If you want to prevent users from mounting file systems that contain files larger than 2 Gbytes, you must explicitly use the `nolargefiles` mount option to disable the default behavior.

Mounting a Single File System (mount)

Use the following steps to mount a single file system that has an entry in the `/etc/vfstab` file.

1. Become superuser.
2. Type **mount** *mount-point* and press Return.

   The file system is mounted, as shown in the following example.

```
oak% su
Password:
# mount /opt
#
```

Remounting a UFS File System Without Large Files (mount)

After you mount a file system with the default `largefiles` option to `mount` and large files have been created, you cannot remount the file system with the `nolargefiles` option until you remove any large files and run `fsck` to reset the state to `nolargefiles`.

The `nolargefiles` option to `mount` provides total compatibility with previous file system behavior and enforces the 2-Gbyte maximum file size limit.

Use the following steps to remount a UFS file system without large files.

1. Become superuser.
2. Type **cd** */filesystem* and press Return.
3. Type **find . -xdev -size +2147485647c -exec ls -l {} \;** and press Return.
4. Remove any large files listed as the result of the **find** command.
5. Type **umount** */filesystem* and press Return.
6. Type **fsck /dev/rdsk/***device-name* and press Return.
7. Type **mount -o nolargefiles /dev/rdsk/***device-name* and press Return.

   The file system is mounted.

In the following example, the directory `/files1` is searched for large files, unmounted, `fsck` is run, and the directory is mounted again with the `nolargefiles` option.

```
oak% su
Password:
# cd /files1
# find . -xdev -size +2000000 -exec ls -l {} \;
# umount /files1
# fsck /dev/rdsk/c0t3dos7 /files1
# mount -o nolargefiles /dev/dsk/c0t3d0s7 /files1
#
```

Unmounting All Remote File Systems (umountall -F nfs)

Follow these steps to unmount all remote file systems.

1. Become superuser.
2. Type **umountall -F nfs** and press Return.

    All the remote file systems in the local/etc/vfstab file are
    unmounted, as shown in the following example.

```
oak% su
Password:
# umountall -F nfs
#
```

> CAUTION. *If you unmount all file systems (by using* umountall
> *without any arguments), the system may be unusable and you may
> need to reboot it.*

Unmounting Individual File Systems (umount)

You cannot unmount a directory that is being used. If you want to unmount a
directory that is being used, all users must close any open files and change
out of the directory.

1. Become superuser.
2. If necessary, have users change out of the directory you want to
    unmount.
3. Type **umount *mount-point*** and press Return.

    The file system you specify is unmounted.

In the following example, the mount command is used first to find the
mount point for the file system to be unmounted.

```
oak% mount
/ on /dev/dsk/c0t0d0s0 read/write/setuid on Wed Oct 23 10:08:50 1999

/usr on /dev/dsk/c0t0d0s6 read/write/setuid on Wed Oct 23 10:08:50 1999

/proc on /proc read/write/setuid on Wed Oct 23 10:08:50 1999

/tmp on swap on Wed Oct 23 10:08:52 1999

/usr/openwin on cheers:/export/openwin hard/remote on Wed Oct 23
10:11:08 1999

/home on blowup:(pid136) read only/intr/map=auto.home/indirect on Wed Oct 23
    10:11:10 1999

/vol on blowup:(pid136) read only/intr/map=auto.vol/indirect on Wed Oct 23 10:11:10
    1999

/nse on blowup:(pid136) read only/intr/map=/etc/auto.nse /indirect on Wed Oct 23
10:11:10 1999
[41]oak% su
Password:
```

```
# cd /
# umount /home
#
```

Automounting Directories

You can mount file systems shared through NFS by using a method called *automounting*. The AutoFS subsystem runs in the background and mounts and unmounts remote directories as they are needed. Whenever a user on a client system running the automounter accesses a remote file or directory available through the automounter, the automounter mounts the file system on the user's system. The remote file system remains mounted as long as the user remains in the directory and has one or more files open. If the remote file system is not accessed for a certain period of time, it is automatically unmounted. The automounter mounts and unmounts file systems as required without any intervention on the part of the user other than changing into or out of a directory.

You can mount some file hierarchies with the automounter, and you can change others by using the /etc/vfstab file and the mount command. A diskless machine *must* have entries for / (root), /usr, and /usr/kvm in the /etc/vfstab file.

The automounter works with the file systems specified in maps. These maps can be maintained as NIS, NIS+, or local files. The automounter maps can specify several remote locations for a particular file system. This way, if one of the servers is down, the automounter can try to mount from another machine.

You can specify which servers are preferred for each resource in the maps by assigning each server a weighting factor. The automounter starts automatically when a system enters run level 3. You can also start it from a command line. (Describing how to set up and administer the automounter is beyond the scope of this book.) By default, the Solaris Operating Environment automounts /home.

Sharing Files from a Server

NFS is a distributed file system that can be used to share files or directories from one system to other systems across a network. Computers that are running different operating systems can also share files. For example, systems running DOS can share files with systems running UNIX.

NFS makes the actual physical location of the file system irrelevant to the user. You can use NFS to enable users to see all the relevant files, regardless of location. Instead of placing copies of commonly used files on every system,

NFS enables you to place one copy on one system's disk and let all other systems access it across the network. Under NFS, remote file systems are virtually indistinguishable from local ones.

A system becomes an NFS server if it has file systems to share or export over the network. A server keeps a list of currently exported file systems and their access restrictions (such as read/write or read-only).

You may want to share resources, such as files, directories, or devices from one system on the network (typically, a server) with other systems. For example, you might want to share third-party applications or source files with users on other systems.

When you share a resource, you make it available for mounting by remote systems. You can share a resource in the following ways.

- Using the `share` or `shareall` command. For the `shareall` command to run, the `/etc/dfs/dfstab` file must already exist. The `share` command can be run without the `dfstab` file.

- Adding an entry to the `/etc/dfs/dfstab` (distributed file system table) file.

The default `/etc/dfs/dfstab` file shows the syntax and an example of entries.

```
paperbark% more /etc/dfs/dfstab

#       Place share(1M) commands here for automatic execution
#       on entering init state 3.
#
#       Issue the command '/etc/init.d/nfs.server start' to run the NFS
#       daemon processes and the share commands, after adding the very
#       first entry to this file.
#
#       share [-F fstype] [ -o options] [-d "<text>"] <pathname> [resource]
#       .e.g,
#       share  -F nfs  -o rw=engineering  -d "home dirs"  /export/home2

paperbark%
```

Checking the Data Consistency of a File System (fsck)

The UFS file system relies on an internal set of tables to keep track of *inodes*—structures the kernel uses to maintain information about each file—and used and available blocks. When these internal tables are not properly synchronized with data on a disk, inconsistencies result and file systems need to be repaired.

File systems can be damaged or become inconsistent because of abrupt termination of the operating system in the following ways.

- Power failure.
- The system halted by either the `halt` or `uadmin` command.
- The system turned off without proper shutdown procedure.
- A software error in the kernel.

File system corruption, though serious, is not common. When a system is booted, a file system consistency check is done automatically. Most of the time, this file system check repairs problems it encounters.

Check file systems with the `fsck` (file system check) command. The `fsck` command puts files and directories that are allocated but unreferenced in the `lost+found` directory in that file system. The inode number of each file is assigned to the name of the recovered file. If the `lost+found` directory does not exist, `fsck` creates it. If there is not enough space in the `lost+found` directory, `fsck` increases its size.

You may need to interactively check file systems in the following cases.

- When you cannot mount them.
- When they develop problems while in use.

NOTE. When an in-use file system develops inconsistencies, strange error messages may be displayed in the console window or the system may crash. Before using `fsck`, *you may want to refer to the* `fsck(1M)` *manual page for more information.*

Finding Out Whether a File System Needs Checking

Use the following steps to determine whether a file system needs to be checked.

1. Become superuser.
2. Unmount the file system if it is mounted.
3. Type **fsck -m /dev/rdsk/c*n*t*n*d*n*s*n*** and press Return.

The state flag in the superblock of the file system you specify is checked to determine whether the file system is clean or requires checking.

If you omit the device argument in the `fsck` command, all the UFS file systems listed in `/etc/vfstab` with a `fsck` pass value greater than 0 are checked. In the following example, the first file system needs to be checked; the second file system does not.

```
paperbark% su
Password:
# umount /dev/rdsk/c0t0d0s6
# fsck -m /dev/rdsk/c0t0d0s6
** /dev/rdsk/c0t0d0s6
ufs fsck: sanity check: /dev/rdsk/c0t0d0s6 needs checking
# umount /dev/rdsk/c0t0d0s7
# fsck -m /dev/rdsk/c0t0d0s7
** /dev/rdsk/c0t0d0s7
ufs fsck: sanity check: /dev/rdsk/c0t0d0s7 okay
#
```

Checking File Systems Interactively

Use the following steps to check all file systems interactively.

1. Become superuser.
2. Unmount the file system.
3. Type **fsck** and press Return.

   All file systems in the /etc/vfstab file with entries in the fsck pass field greater than 0 are checked. You can also specify the mount point directory or /dev/rdsk/c*nt*n*d*n*s*n as arguments to fsck. Any inconsistency messages are displayed.

In the following example, /dev/rdsk/c0t0d0s6 is checked and the incorrect block count is corrected.

```
paperbark% su
Password:
# umount /dev/rdsk/c0t0d0s6
# fsck /dev/rdsk/c0t0d0s6
checkfilesys: /dev/rdsk/c0t0d0s6
** Phase 1 - Check Block and Sizes
INCORRECT BLOCK COUNT I=2529 (6 should be 2)
CORRECT? y

** Phase 2 - Check Pathnames
** Phase 3 - Check Connectivity
** Phase 4 - Check Reference Counts
** Phase 5 - Cylinder Groups
Dynamic 4.3 FFFS
929 files, 8928 used, 2851 free (75 frags, 347 blocks, 0.6% fragmentation)
/dev/rdsk/c0t0d0s6 FILE SYSTEM STATE SET TO OKAY

***** FILE SYSTEM WAS MODIFIED *****
```

Backing Up and Restoring File Systems

Backing up files means making copies of them, usually on removable media, as a safeguard in case the originals get lost or damaged. Backup tapes are convenient for restoring accidentally deleted files, but they are essential in case of serious hardware failures or other disasters.

Backing up files is one of the most crucial system administration functions. You must plan and carry out a procedure for regularly scheduled backups of your file systems for three major reasons.

- To ensure file system integrity against a possible system crash.
- To protect user files against accidental deletion.
- To act as an important safeguard before reinstalling or upgrading a system.

When you back up file systems as scheduled, you have the assurance that you can restore any files to a reasonably recent state. In addition, you may want to back up file systems to transport them from one system to another or to *archive* them—saving files on a transportable medium—so that you can remove or alter the files that remain on the system.

When you plan a backup schedule, you need to consider the following factors.

- Which command to use to back up the file systems.
- What medium to use.
- What backup schedule to use.
- Which file systems to back up.
- Which files are critical to users on this system.
- Where the files are located—are they in a single file system?
- How often these files change.
- How quickly you would need to restore these files in the event of damage or loss.
- How often the relevant file systems can be unmounted so that they are available for backup.

Outlining possible backup strategies is beyond the scope of this book. See the ufsdump(1M) manual page for a suggested dump schedule. The discussions that follow describe how to use the ufsdump command to make backups and how to retrieve files with the ufsrestore command.

Table 50 lists the commands that you can use to back up and restore individual files and file systems.

Table 50 Commands for Backing Up and Restoring Files and File Systems

Task	Command
Back up complete or individual file systems to a local or remote tape device.	`ufsdump`
Restore complete or individual file systems to a local disk.	`ufsrestore`

Specifying Tape Characteristics

The `ufsdump` command uses a set of defaults when you do not specify any tape characteristics. Note that you can specify the options in any order as long as the arguments that follow match the order of the options.

Specifying a Backup Level

New!

You can specify a numerical argument to `ufsdump` from 0 to 9 to designate the level of the backup to be performed. A level 0 dump backs up all of the files in the file systems you specify. All files that have been modified since the last `ufsdump` at a lower dump level are copied to the dump file destination. For example, if a level 2 dump was done on Monday, followed by a level 4 dump on Tuesday, a subsequent level 3 dump on Wednesday would contain all files modified or added since the level 2 (Monday) backup.

Backing Up a File System with Cartridge Tapes (ufsdump)

To do a full backup on a file system, be sure all users are logged out. Then bring the system to single-user mode. (See "Tape Device–Naming Conventions" on page 241 if you need information about tape device names.)

You can dump or restore files from a remote drive by adding *remote-host:* to the front of the tape device name with the following syntax.

```
remote-host:/dev/rmt/unit
```

For example, the device name for a remote tape drive /dev/rmt/0, on the system oak, would be oak:/dev/rmt/0.

Use the following steps to do a level 0 (full) backup of a file system.

1. Type **telinit s** and press Return.

   The system is brought to single-user mode, which ensures that no users can change the file systems you are backing up.

2. Insert a tape cartridge in the QIC-150 tape drive.

3. Type **ufsdump 0cuf /dev/rmt/*unit* c*nt*x*dns* *[[0-7]*** and press Return.

   The 0 option specifies a level 0 (complete) dump. The c option specifies cartridge tape. The u option updates the dump record. The f option followed by the device name specifies the device file. Type the raw disk slice for the file system you want to back up, for example, c0t0d0s7 for /files1.

   The following example does a level 0 dump of the c0t0d0s7 slice.

```
oak% su
Password:
# telinit s
# ufsdump 0cuf /dev/rmt/0 c0t0d0s7
  DUMP: Date of this level 0 dump: Wed Mar 11 10:16:53 1992
  DUMP: Date of last level 0 dump: the epoch
  DUMP: Dumping /dev/rdsk/c0t3d0s7 (/export/home) to /dev/rmt/0
  DUMP: mapping (Pass I) [regular files]
  DUMP: mapping (Pass II) [directories]
  DUMP: estimated 956 blocks (478KB)
  DUMP: Writing 63 Kilobyte records
  DUMP: dumping (Pass III) [directories]
  DUMP: dumping (Pass IV) [regular files]
  DUMP: level 0 dump on Wed Mar 11 10:16:53 1992
  DUMP: 956 blocks (478KB) on 1 volume
  DUMP: DUMP IS DONE
#
```

4. If the dump requires more than one tape, the ufsdump command tells you when to change to a new tape.

5. Label the tape with the command, file system, and date so that you can easily find the backup tape if you need to restore files.

Performing Incremental Backups

You can specify different backup levels with the ufsdump command, making it possible to back up only those files that were changed since a previous backup at a lower level. Use the following steps to back up incremental changes since the last complete dump.

1. Bring the system to single-user mode.

2. Become superuser.

3. Put a tape into the tape drive.

4. All on one line, type **ufsdump [*1-9*]ucf /dev/rmt/*unit* /dev/rdsk/c*nt*n*d*n*s*n** and press Return. Type the level of the backup at the beginning of the ufsdump arguments. For example, for a level 9 backup, type **9ucf** as the first argument.

5. Remove the tape from the tape drive and label it. If you put multiple backups on the same tape, be sure you add each incremental backup to the label of the tape.

Restoring a Backed-Up File System (ufsrestore)

The ufsrestore command copies files from backups created by the ufsdump command into the current working directory. You can use ufsrestore to reload an entire file system hierarchy from a level 0 dump and incremental dumps that follow it or to restore one or more single files from any dump tape. Files are restored with their original owner, last modification time, and mode (permissions).

Before you start to restore files or file systems, you need the following information.

- Which tapes you need.
- The raw device name for the file systems you want to restore.
- The device name (local or remote) for the tape drive.

Determining Which Tapes to Use

Before you can begin restoring file systems or files, you must determine which backup tapes you need. When restoring an entire file system, you always need the most recent level 0 backup tape. You also need the most recent incremental backup tapes made at each of the higher levels. Refer to the backup plan that you are using to determine the levels and number of tapes you need. For example, if you make level 0 and level 9 backups, you need the most recent level 0 and level 9 backup tapes.

Use the following steps to determine which tapes to use to restore individual files or file systems.

1. Ask the user the date when the file or file system was lost or the approximate date of the files to be recovered.

2. Refer to your backup plan to find the date of the last backup that would have the file or file system on it.

   Note that you do not necessarily use the most recently backed up version of the file. To retrieve the most recent version of a file, work backward through the incremental backups from highest to lowest level and most recent to least recent.

3. If you have on-line archive files created by the `ufsdump -a` option, type **ufsrestore ta** *archive-name* **/***path***/***filename (s)* and press Return. Be sure to use the complete path for the *filename*(s).

   A list of the files and the media they are stored on is displayed.

4. Retrieve the media containing the backups.

   Be aware of the storage organization of backup media at your site so that you can locate media that are months or years old.

5. Insert media in the drive and type **ufsrestore tf** *device-name* **/***path***/***filename*(s) and press Return. Be sure to use the complete path for the *filename*(s).

   If a file is in the backup, its name and inode number are listed. Otherwise, a message says it is not on the volume.

6. If you have multiple dump files on the same tape, you can use the `-s` *n* option to position the tape at the dump you want to use.

   For example, type **ufsrestore xfs /dev/rmt0 5** and press Return to position the tape at the fifth dump and restore it.

Restoring a Full Backup

Use the following steps to restore a full backup of a file system on a cartridge tape.

CAUTION. This procedure completely destroys any data already in the file system by overwriting any files or directories under the directory to which you tell `ufsrestore` *to restore.*

1. Become superuser.
2. Type **telinit s** and press Return.

   The system is brought to single-user mode, which ensures that no one is using the file system you are restoring.

3. Type **umount** *mount-point* and press Return.

   The mount point you specify (for example, `/files1`) is unmounted.

4. Type **newfs /dev/rdsk/***cxtxdxsx* and press Return.

   The raw device file for the disk slice (for example, `/dev/rdsk/c0t0d0s7` for the `/home` slice) is wiped clean and the file system is rebuilt.

5. Type **mount /dev/dsk/c*n*t*n*d*n*s*n*** and press Return.

   The file system, specified as the block file device (for example, /dev/dsk/c0t0d0s7 for /files1), is remounted at the mount point you specify.

6. Type **cd *mount-point*** and press Return.

   Focus is in the directory you want to restore.

7. Insert the tape cartridge in the QIC-150 tape drive.

8. Type **ufsrestore rvf /dev/rmt/0h** and press Return.

   The h option extracts the actual directory instead of the files that it references. This option prevents hierarchical restoration of complete subtrees from the tape. The file system is restored.

   In the following example, the /files1 slice c0t0d0s7 is restored.

```
oak% su
Password:
# telinit s
# umount /files1
# newfs /dev/rdsk/c0t0d0s7
# mount /dev/dsk/c0t0d0s7 /files1
# cd /files1
# ufsrestore rvf /dev/rmt/0h
#
```

Restoring Files Interactively

When restoring individual files and directories, it is a good idea to restore them to a temporary directory such as /var/tmp. After you verify them, you can move the files to their proper locations. You can restore individual files and directories to their original locations. If you do so, be sure you are not overwriting newer files with older versions from the backup tape.

Use the following steps to restore files interactively.

1. Become superuser.

2. Write-protect the tape for safety.

3. Put the backup tape in the tape drive.

4. Type **cd /var/tmp** and press Return.

   If you want to restore the files to a different directory, substitute the directory name for /var/tmp in this step.

5. Type **ufsrestore if /dev/rmt/*unit*** and press Return.

   Some informational messages and the restore> prompt are displayed.

6. Create a list of files to be restored.

   • To list the contents of a directory, type **ls** and press Return.

- To change directories, type **cd *directory-name*** and press Return.

- To add a directory or file name to the list of files to be restored, type **add *filename*** and press Return.

- To remove a directory or file name from the list of files to be restored, type **delete *filename*** and press Return.

- To keep the mode of the current directory unchanged, type **setmodes** and press Return. Then type **n** and press Return.

7. When the list is complete, type **extract** and press Return. Then, ufsrestore asks you which volume number to use.

8. Type the volume number and press Return. If you have only one volume, type **1** and press Return.

   The files and directories in the list are extracted and restored to the current working directory.

9. Type **quit** and press Return.

   The shell prompt is displayed.

10. Use the ls -l command to list the restored files and directories.

    A list of files and directories is displayed.

11. Check the list to be sure all the files and directories you specified in the list have been restored.

12. Use the mv command to move the files to the proper directories.

The following example restores the files backup.examples and junk from the pubs directory.

```
# cd /var/tmp
# ufsrestore if /dev/rmt/0
ufsrestore > ls
.:
 lost+found/    pubs/

ufsrestore > cd pubs
ufsrestore > ls
./pubs:
.Xauthority           .login            .profile          backup.examples%
.Xdefaults            .mtdeletelog      .wastebasket/     core
.cshrc                .openwin-init     Junk/             dead.letter
.desksetdefaults      .openwin-init.BAK backup.examples   junk
ufsrestore > add backup.examples
ufsrestore > add junk
ufsrestore > setmodes
set owner/mode for '.'? [yn] n
ufsrestore > extract
You have not read any volumes yet.
Unless you know which volume your file(s) are on you should start
with the last volume and work towards the first.
Specify next volume #: 1
set owner/mode for '.'? [yn] n
ufsrestore > quit
# ls -l
total 6
drwxrwxrwt   3 sys       sys           512 Mar 11 10:36 ./
```

```
drwxrwxr-x  18 root     sys          512 Mar 10 16:43 ../
drwxr-xr-x   2 pubs     staff        512 Mar 11 10:11 pubs/
# pwd
/var/tmp
# cd pubs
# ls
./                   ../              backup.examples    junk
#
```

Restoring a Single File from a Backup Tape (ufsrestore)

Use the following steps to restore a single file from a backup tape.

1. Become superuser.
2. Put the backup tape in the tape drive.
3. Type **cd /var/tmp** and press Return.

    If you want to restore the files to a different directory, substitute the directory name for /var/tmp in this step.

4. Type **ufsrestore xf /dev/rmt/*unit* /*pathto/filename*** and press Return.

    The x option tells ufsrestore to copy specific files or directories in the */pathto/filename* argument. The message set owner/mode for '.'? [yn] is displayed.

5. Type **n** and press Return.

    Directory modes remain unchanged.

6. Type the volume number where files are located and press Return. If there is only one volume, type **1** and press Return.

    The file is restored to the current working directory.

7. Type **ls -l *filename*** and press Return.

    A listing for the file is displayed.

8. Use the mv command to move the file to the proper directory.

New! Creating a Snapshot of a UFS File System

You can use the fssnap(1M) command, new in the Solaris 9 release, to create a read-only snapshot of a file system. You can use the snapshot to back up file systems while the file system is mounted.

When you run the fssnap command, it creates a *virtual device* and a *backing-store* file. You can use any of the existing Solaris backup commands to back up the virtual device, which looks and acts like a real device. The backing-store is a bitmapped file that contains copies of presnapshot data that has been modified since the snapshot was taken.

With UFS snapshots, you can keep the file system mounted and the system in multiuser mode while performing system backups. In previous releases, you were advised to bring the system to single-user mode to keep the file system inactive while using the `ufsdump` command to back up file systems.

UFS snapshots are similar to the Instant Image process. Instant Image allocates space equal to the size of the entire file system being captured. The UFS snapshot backing-store file occupies only as much disk space as needed and you can place a maximum size on the backing-store file.

NOTE. Although you can use UFS snapshots to make copies of large file systems, it is better suited for smaller systems. Instant Image is better suited for enterprise-level systems.

When you first create the UFS snapshot, users of the file system might notice a slight pause. The length of the pause increases with the size of the file system being captured. While the snapshot is active, users of the file system may notice a slight performance impact when writing to the file system but will notice no impact when the file system is read.

Syntax and Options of the fssnap Command

The syntax of the `fssnap` command is shown below.

```
/usr/sbin/fssnap [-F FSType] [-V] -o special_options [mount-point | special ]
/usr/sbin/fssnap -d [-F FSType] [-V] -o special_options [mount-point | special ]
/usr/sbin/fssnap -i [-F FSType] [-V] -o special_options [mount-point | special]
```

The options to the `fssnap` command are described in Table 51.

Table 51   Options to the fssnap Command

Option	Description
-d	Delete the snapshot associated with the given file system.
-F *FSType*	Specify the file system type to be used. You can specify the *FSType* here, or `fssnap` determines it by matching the block special device with an entry in the `/etc/vfstab` table or by consulting `/etc/default/fs`.
-i	Display the state of any given *FSType* snapshot. If you specify no *mount-point* or *device*, `fssnap` displays a list of all snapshots on the system. When you specify a *mount-point* or *device*, `fssnap` provides detailed information for the specified file system snapshot by default. The format and meaning of this information is file system dependent. See the *FSType*-specific `fssnap` manual page for details.

Table 51 *Options to the fssnap Command (Continued)*

Option	Description	
-o *special_options*		
	See the *FSType*-specific manual page for fssnap. The UFS *special_options* are listed below	
	backing-store=*path*	
		Use *path* as the backing-store file. *path* must not reside on the file system that is being captured in a snapshot. *path* must exist and must be either a directory or a regular file. If *path* is a directory, then a temporary file is created and held open. That device is then used as-is. You can abbreviate this option as bf=*path* or bs=*path*.
	unlink	Unlink the backing-store file after the snapshot is created. This option specifies that the backing-store file does not need to be removed manually when the snapshot is deleted. This behavior might make administration more difficult because the file is not visible in the file system. If you do not specify this option, manually remove the backing-store files after the snapshot is deleted.
	chunksize=*n* [k,m,g]	
		Use *n* to specify the granularity of the data that is sent to the backing-store. Specify chunksize in k for kilobytes, m for megabytes, or g for gigabytes. By default, chunk size is four times the block size of the file system (typically 32k).
	maxsize=*n*[k,m,g]	
		Do not allow the size of the backing-store file to exceed *n*, where *n* is the specified unit. The snapshot is deleted automatically when the backing-store file exceeds maxsize. Specify maxsize in k for kilobytes, m for megabytes, or g for gigabytes.

Table 51   Options to the fssnap Command (Continued)

Option	Description	
	`raw`	Display to standard output the name of the raw device instead of the block device when a snapshot is created. The block device is printed by default (when you do not specify `raw`). This option makes it easier to embed `fssnap` commands in the command line for commands that require the raw device instead. Both devices are always created. This option affects only the output.
`-V`	Echo the complete command line, but do not execute the command.	

Creating a UFS Snapshot

When you use the `fssnap` command to create a UFS snapshot, observe how much disk space is consumed by the backing-store file. Make sure the backing-store file has enough space to grow, or limit its size with the `-o maxsize=`n `[k,m,g]` option.

Use the following steps to create a UFS snapshot.

1. Become superuser or assume an equivalent role.
2. Type **df -h** and press Return.

   Check the output to make sure that the file system has enough disk space for the backing-store file.
3. Type **ls** */backing-store-file* and press Return.

   Check to make sure that a backing-store file of the same name and location does not already exist.
4. Type **fssnap -F ufs -o bs=***/backing-store-file* */file-system* and press Return.

   The backing-store file must reside on a different file system from the file system for which you are making a snapshot.
5. Type **/usr/lib/fs/ufs/fssnap -i** */file-system* and press Return.

   Verify that the snapshot has been created.

The following example creates a snapshot of the root file system with a `/home/winsor/rootbackup` backing-store file.

```
mopoke% df -h
Filesystem          size  used  avail capacity  Mounted on
/dev/dsk/c1t0d0s0   4.3G  1.1G  3.2G    26%     /
```

```
/proc                    0K      0K      0K      0%    /proc
mnttab                   0K      0K      0K      0%    /etc/mnttab
fd                       0K      0K      0K      0%    /dev/fd
swap                   545M     40K    545M      1%    /var/run
swap                   546M    304K    545M      1%    /tmp
/dev/dsk/c1t0d0s7      4.9G    1.1G    3.8G     22%    /export/home
/export/home/winsor   4.9G    1.1G    3.8G     22%    /home/winsor
mopoke% su
Password:
# fssnap -F ufs -o bs=/home/winsor/rootbackup
  /
/dev/fssnap/0
# fssnap -i
    0    /
# /usr/lib/fs/ufs/fssnap -i /
Snapshot number               : 0
Block Device                  : /dev/fssnap/0
Raw Device                    : /dev/rfssnap/0
Mount point                   : /
Device state                  : idle
Backing store path            : /home/winsor/rootbackup
Backing store size            : 1536 KB
Maximum backing store size    : Unlimited
Snapshot create time          : Mon Sep 30 15:36:11 2002
Copy-on-write granularity     : 32 KB
#
```

Deleting a UFS Snapshot

You can delete a snapshot either by rebooting the system or by using the fssnap -d command and specifying the path of the file system that contains the UFS snapshot.

Use the following steps to delete a UFS snapshot with the fssnap -d command.

1. Become superuser or assume an equivalent role.
2. Type **fssnap -i** and press Return.

   A list of available snapshots is displayed.
3. Type **fssnap -d /_file-system_** and press Return.

   The snapshot is deleted.
4. (Optional.) If you did not use the -o unlink option when you created the snapshot, you need to delete the backing-store file manually by typing **rm /file-system/_backing-store-file_** and pressing Return.

The following example shows how to delete a snapshot and assumes that the unlink option was not used.

```
# fssnap -i
    0    /
# fssnap -d /
Deleted snapshot 0.
# ls /home/winsor/rootbackup
rootbackup
# rm /home/winsor/rootbackup
#
```

Backing Up a UFS Snapshot

You can create a full or incremental backup of a UFS snapshot and use the standard Solaris `ufsdump` command to back up a UFS snapshot. Simply specify the raw device name of the snapshot, for example, `/dev/rfssnap/1`, as the final argument to the `ufsdump` command.

Restoring Data from a UFS Snapshot Backup

Any backup you create from a virtual device is simply a backup of the state of the original file system when you took the snapshot. When you restore from the backup, restore with the `ufsrestore` command as if you had taken the backup directly from the original file system.

Cache File Systems

You can use CacheFS to improve NFS server performance and scalability by reducing server and network load. CacheFS is designed as a layered file system that enables the system to cache one file system on another. In an NFS environment, CacheFS enables you to have more NFS clients for each NFS server because each client can cache NFS information, thus reducing the load on the NFS server. CacheFS improves performance for clients on slow links such as Point-to-Point Protocol (PPP).

Understanding CacheFS

With CacheFS you can enable a client system to cache a file system from a server. Initial access to the file system may seem slow, but subsequent uses of the same file by the user are faster. Typically, you would cache an NFS or HSFS file system. You create cache file systems individually on each client system that needs improved NFS performance.

NOTE. CacheFS does not support caching of the root (/) and /usr file systems.

1. On the client system, use the `cfsadmin`(1M) command to create a cache so that file systems you specify to be mounted in the cache can be accessed by the user locally instead of across the network. To prevent conflicts within the CacheFS software, after you have created the cache you should not perform any operations within the cache directory on the client system.
2. On the client, create a mount point at which the file system from the server—called the *back file system*—is mounted.

3. Note the name of the server and path to the back file system you want to cache. The format is *server*: *back-filesystem*.

4. Mount a file system in a cache by using the `mount` command on the client, adding an entry to the client's /etc/vfstab file, or using the automounter to automount the file system.

After you have completed the setup of the CacheFS, files are dynamically placed in the cache as the user accesses them.

NOTE. You can mount only file systems that are shared from the server in question. Refer to the `share(1M)` *manual page for more information or see "Sharing Files from a Server" on page 207.*

Creating a Cache

Use the following steps on a client system to create a cache.

1. Decide what name you want to use for the cache directory.

2. On the client system, become superuser.

3. Type **cfsadmin -c *cache-directory*** and press Return.

In the following example, a cache directory named cachefile is created in the /local directory.

```
oak% su
# cfsadmin -c /local/cachedir
#
```

Specifying a File System to Be Mounted in the Cache

You can specify file systems to be mounted through the cache so that users can locally access files in the cache file system you create. You can specify the file systems to be cached in three ways.

- Using the mount(1M) command on the client system. When you use the mount command, the files must be mounted from the command line every time the system is rebooted.

- Editing the /etc/vfstab file on the client system. When you add an entry to the /etc/vfstab file, the specified files are available for caching even when the system is rebooted.

- Using the automounter. When you modify automounter maps, the specified files are available for caching even when the system is rebooted.

Creating a Mount Point

Regardless of the mechanism you choose to mount the file system, you need to create a mount point on the client system where CacheFS mounts the files. The mounted files are then cached in the cache directory that you created.

Type **mkdir** *mount-point* and press Return. In the following example, a mount point named /cachemount is created.

```
# mkdir /cachemount
#
```

Specifying a File System (mount) You provide the following parameters for the mount command.

- The file system type of the back file system on the server: **backfstype=*fstype***. The value for *fstype* can be either nfs or hsfs.
- The name of the cache directory on the client system: **cachedir=*cache-directory***.
- The name of the back file system on the server: ***server*:*back-filesystem***.
- The mount point on the client system: ***mount-point***.

Use the following steps to mount a cache file system from a command line.

1. On the client system, become superuser.
2. All on one line, type **mount -F cachefs -o backfstype=*fstype*,cachedir=*cache-directory* [,*options*] *back-file-system mount-point*** and press Return.
3. Type **cachefsstat** *mount-point* and press Return.

   The output from this command verifies that the cache you created was mounted.

The following example creates a cache directory named /local/cachedir, creates a mount point named /usr/local, and mounts the NFS file system castle:/export/local as a cached file system named /usr/local in the cache named /local/cachedir.

```
paperbark% su
Password:
# mkdir /usr/local
# mkdir /local
# cfsadmin -c /local/cachedir
# mount -F cachefs -o backfstype=nfs,cachedir=/local/cachedir castle:/export/local
  /usr/local
# cachefsstat /usr/local

    /usr/local
```

```
              cache hit rate:   100% (0 hits, 0 misses)
         consistency checks:      0 (0 pass, 0 fail)
                   modifies:      0
         garbage collection:      0
#
```

If the file system was not mounted in the cache, an error message similar to the following is displayed.

```
# cachefsstat /local
cachefsstat: /local not a cachefs mountpoint
#
```

Specifying a File System (/etc/vfstab File)   When you add a cache file system to the /etc/vfstab file on the client system, the back file system remains available to users as a cached file system.

When you have created the cache directory and the mount point, use the following steps to mount a cache file system from the /etc/vfstab file.

1. On the client system, become superuser.
2. Using an editor, add the following line to the /etc/vfstab file.

```
/dev/dsk/device-name  /dev/rdsk/device-name /mount-point cachefs 2 yes  -
```

3. Type **mount *mount-point*** and press Return or reboot the system to mount the file system.

New!

The following example mounts the /export /local directory from the remote system castle with the back file system /local/cachedir on the cache directory /usr/local.

```
castle:/export/local /local/cachedir  /usr/local  7   yes
   local-access,bg,nosuid,demandconst,backfstype=nfs,cachedir=/usr/local
```

Specifying a File System (Automounter Map)   You add a cache file system to the auto_direct automounter map by specifying the -fstype=cachefs option to mount. Note that you also specify the CacheFS mount options (for example, backfstype and cachedir). Refer to the automount(1M) manual page for more information about automount maps or to the *Solaris Advanced System Administrator's Guide,* available from Sun Microsystems Press.

Use the following steps to specify a cache file system in the automounter map.

1. Become superuser.
2. Using an editor, add the following line to the auto_direct map.

```
/mount-point -fstype=cachefs,cachedir=/directory, backfstype=nfs
   server:/file-system
```

3. Using an editor, add /- to the auto_master map.

   The /- entry is a pointer to check the auto_direct map.
4. Reboot the system.
5. Type cd *files-system* and press Return.
6. Type ls *files-system* and press Return.

   Review the output of the ls command to verify that the entry was made correctly.

Maintaining Caches

After you set up cache file systems, you can perform the following maintenance tasks on them.

- Modify file systems in the cache by unmounting, deleting, re-creating, and remounting the cache.
- Display cache information.
- Check cache consistency.
- Delete a file system from the cache.
- Check cached file system integrity.

If you are using the /etc/vfstab file to mount file systems, you modify the cache by editing the file system options in the /etc/vfstab file. If you are using the automounter, you modify the cache by editing the file system options in the automounter maps.

Table 52 lists the commands that you can use to perform cache maintenance. Refer to the appropriate manual page for more details.

Table 52   Commands for Maintaining Cache File Systems

Command	Description
cfsadmin	Display information about cached file systems, delete a cached file system from a specified cache, and specify consistency checking on demand. See the cfsadmin(1M) manual page for more information.

Table 52   Commands for Maintaining Cache File Systems (Continued)

Command	Description
cachefspack	Create packing lists that specify individual files and directories that you want packed in the cache. A packing list contains files or directories to be packed in the cache. If a directory is in the packing list, all its subdirectories and files are also packed. See the cachefspack(1M) manual page for more information.
cachefslog	Specify the location of a CacheFS log file. This command also displays where statistics are currently being logged and enables you to halt logging. See the cachefslog(1M) manual page for more information.
cachefswssize	Interpret the log file to give a recommended cache size. See the cachefswssize(1M) manual page for more information.
cachefsstat	Display statistical information about a specific file system or all cached file systems. The information provided in the output of this command is taken directly from the cache. See the cachefsstat(1M) manual page for more information.
fsck -F cachefs {-m} {-o noclean} *cache-directory*	
	Check the integrity of cached file systems and automatically correct problems without requiring user interaction. See the fsck_cachefs(1M) manual page for more information.

8

ADMINISTERING DEVICES

Device management in the Solaris Operating Environment continues to evolve. This chapter introduces what's new in device management in the Solaris 9 release.

This chapter explains disk device names and commands used for administering disks, describes how to use DVD devices, how to use tapes and diskettes to copy files, and how to use volume management to access diskettes and CD-ROMs. This chapter also introduces the Service Access Facility (SAF)—which you must use to administer terminals and modems with the Solaris Operating Environment—provides steps for setting up port monitors for print servers and print clients, and provides steps for adding a bidirectional modem to a system.

See Chapter 7, "Administering File Systems," for information about how to back up and restore complete file systems. See Chapter 11, "Administering Printing," for information about administering printers.

What's New in Device Management in the Solaris 9 Release

New!

This section describes device management features new in the Solaris 9 release.

RCM Scripting

The new Reconfiguration Coordination Manager (RCM) script enables you to write your own scripts to shut down your applications or to cleanly release the devices from your applications during dynamic reconfiguration.

An RCM script is an executable shell script (Perl, `sh`, `csh`, or `ksh`) or binary program that the RCM daemon runs. Perl is the recommended scripting language. An RCM script requires the RCM commands listed in Table 53.

Table 53   RCM Commands Required in an RCM Script

Command	Description
`scriptinfo`	Gather script information.
`register`	Register interest in resources.
`resourceinfo`	Gather resource information.

You can also use the RCM commands listed in Table 54 in RCM scripts, but these commands are optional.

Table 54   Optional RCL Commands for an RCM Script

Command	Description
`queryremove`	Query whether the resource can be released.
`preremove`	Release the resource.
`postremove`	Provide post-resource-removal notification.
`undoremove`	Undo the actions done in `preremove`.

Refer to the "Reconfiguration Coordination Manager (RCM) Script Overview" section in the Sun *System Administration Guide: Basic Administration* and the `rcmscript`(4) and `cfgadm`(1M) manual pages for more information about writing and administering RCM scripts.

Dynamic Reconfiguration Error Messages

The error messages of the dynamic reconfiguration software have been enhanced to improve the troubleshooting of dynamic reconfiguration problems.

New Device Allocation Commands

The Solaris 9 Operating Environment provides a device allocation method that fulfills the Trusted Computer System Evaluation Criteria (TCSEC) object-reuse requirement for computing systems at level C2 and above.

See "Allocating Devices" on page 232 for more information.

Automatically Configuring Devices

The Solaris kernel is configured automatically. A kernel module is a software component that performs a specific task on the system. An example of a loadable kernel module is a device driver that is loaded when the device is accessed.

At boot time, the OpenBoot PROM determines what devices are attached to the system and creates an internal device tree, which it hands off to the kernel. The kernel then configures itself dynamically, loading needed modules into memory. Device drivers are loaded when devices such as disk and tape devices are accessed for the first time. This process is called *autoconfiguration* because all kernel modules are loaded automatically as they are needed.

With autoconfiguration, main memory is used more efficiently because modules are loaded as they are needed. Also, you do not need to reconfigure the kernel when new devices are added to the system.

You can customize the way kernel modules are loaded by modifying the /etc/system file. See system(4) for more information.

Improved Device Configuration (defvsadm)

In previous Solaris releases, the drvconfig command handled device configuration to manage the physical device entries in the /devices directory. Five link generators—devlinks, disks, tapes, ports, and audlinks—managed the logical links in the /dev directory. These commands were not aware of hot-pluggable devices nor were they flexible enough for devices with multiple instances. For compatibility, in the Solaris 8 release, these commands are symbolic links to the new devfsadm command.

In the Solaris 8 release, the devfsadm command manages the special device files in the /dev and /devices directories. By default, devfsadm tries to load every driver in the system and attach to all possible device instances. It then creates the device files in the /devices directory and the logical links in the /dev directory. In addition, devfsadm also maintains the path_to_inst(4) database.

devfsadmd, the devfsadm daemon, handles both processing the reconfiguration boot and updating the /dev and /devices directories in response to dynamic reconfiguration events. This daemon is started from the /etc/rcS.d/S50devfsadm script when a system is booted.

Because devfsadmd automatically detects device configuration changes generated by any reconfiguration event, you do not need to run devfsadm interactively.

Display of Device Configuration Information

Use the commands in Table 55 to display system and device configuration information.

Table 55   Device Configuration Commands

prtconf(1M)	Display system configuration information, including total amount of memory and the device configuration as described by the device hierarchy of the system.
sysdef(1M)	Display device configuration information, including system hardware, pseudodevices, loadable modules, and selected kernel parameters.
dmesg(1M)	Display system diagnostic messages as well as a list of devices attached to the system since the last reboot.

See Chapter 9, "Administering Systems," for examples of these commands.

New! Allocating Devices

The Solaris 9 Operating Environment provides a device allocation method that fulfills the Trusted Computer System Evaluation Criteria (TCSEC) object-reuse requirement for computing systems at level C2 and above.

The device allocation mechanism prevents simultaneous access to a device, prevents one user from reading media being written to the device by another user, and prevents one user from accessing any information from the device or driver internal storage after another user is finished with the device.

For example, several users often share a single tape drive that may not be located at an individual user's location. If the tape drive is located remotely, some time can elapse between the time the user loads a tape in the drive and the time the user invokes a command to access the tape in the drive. Because other users could access the drive while the tape is unattended, another user could access or overwrite the data on the tape. With the device allocation mechanism, you can ensure that one user at a time has access to a specific tape device.

Use the commands described in Table 56 to manage device allocation.

Table 56   *Device Allocation Commands*

Command	Description
`allocate(1)`	
	Allocate ownership of devices.
`deallocate(1)`	
	Deallocate ownership of devices.
`dminfo(1M)`	Report information about a device entry in a device maps file.
`list_devices(1)`	
	List the allocatable devices in the system according to specified qualifications.

NOTE. The device allocation commands are available only if the Basic Security Module (BSM) has been enabled.

Enabling BSM

The basic security module (BSM) is the Sun Microsystem implementation of C2 security. It provides an auditing capability with self-contained audit records that contain all the relevant information about an event. For example, an audit record describing a file event contains the absolute path name and a time stamp and date stamp of the opening or closing of the file.

Use the `bsmconv` command as root to enable BSM.

NOTE. The `bsmconv` command adds a line to `/etc/system` that disables the ability to abort the system with the Stop-A keyboard sequence. If you want to retain that ability, you must comment out the following line in the `/etc/system` file after you run the `bsmconv` command.

```
set abort_enable = 0
```

Use the following procedure to enable BSM.

1. Become superuser.

2. Type **telinit 1** and press Return to bring the system to single-user mode.

3. Type **/etc/security/bsmconv** and press Return to begin the process of enabling BSM.

4. Type **y** and press Return to enable BSM.

5. Type **telinit 6** and press Return to reboot the system as a multiuser BSM system.

The following example uses the bsmconv command to enable the basic security model and uses the telinit 6 command to reboot the system.

```
# /etc/security/bsmconv
This script is used to enable the Basic Security Module (BSM).
Shall we continue with the conversion now? [y/n] y
bsmconv: INFO: checking startup file.
bsmconv: INFO: move aside /etc/rc2.d/S92volmgt.
bsmconv: INFO: turning on audit module.
bsmconv: INFO: initializing device allocation files.

The Basic Security Module is ready.
If there were any errors, please fix them now.
Configure BSM by editing files located in /etc/security.
Reboot this system now to come up with BSM enabled.
# telinit 6
```

Disabling BSM

If you no longer require BSM, you can disable it with the bsmconv command. Use the following steps to disable BSM and remove the BSM entry from the /etc/system file.

1. Become superuser.

2. Type **telinit 1** and press Return to bring the system to single-user mode.

3. Type **/etc/security/bsmunconv** and press Return to begin the process of disabling BSM.

4. Type **y** and press Return to disable BSM.

5. Type **telinit 6** and press Return to reboot the system without BSM.

The following example uses the bsmunconv command to disable the basic security model.

```
# /etc/security/bsmunconv
This script is used to disable the Basic Security Module (BSM).
Shall we continue the reversion to a non-BSM system now? [y/n] y
bsmunconv: INFO: moving aside /etc/security/audit_startup.
bsmunconv: INFO: restore /etc/rc2.d/S92volmgt.
bsmunconv: INFO: removing c2audit:audit_load from /etc/system.
```

```
The Basic Security Module has been disabled.
Reboot this system now to come up without BSM.
# telinit 6
```

Listing Device Information

You can access information about allocatable devices with the list_devices command.

Table 57 lists the options to the list_devices command.

Table 57   *Options to the list_devices Command*

-l [*device*]	
	List the path name(s) of the device special files associated with the device that are allocatable to the current process. If *device* is given, list only the files associated with the specified device.
-n [*device*]	
	List the path name(s) of device special files associated with the device that are allocatable to the current process but are not currently allocated. If you specify *device*, list_devices lists only the files associated with that device.
-s	Silent. Suppress any diagnostic output.
-u [*device*]	
	List the path name(s) of device special files associated with the device that are allocated to the owner of the current process. If you specify *device*, list_devices lists only the files associated with that device.
-U *uid*	Use the user ID *uid* instead of the real user ID of the current process when performing the list_devices operation. Only a user with the solaris.devices.revoke authorization can use this option.

The following example shows the long listing for the list_devices command.

```
mopoke% list_devices -l
device: audio type: audio files: /dev/audio /dev/audioctl /dev/sound/0
 /dev/sound/0ctl
device: fd0 type: fd files: /dev/diskette /dev/rdiskette /dev/fd0a /dev/rfd0a
 /dev/fd0 /dev/fd0b /dev/rfd0b /dev/fd0c /dev/rfd0c /dev/rfd0
```

```
device: sr0 type: sr files: /dev/sr0 /dev/rsr0 /dev/dsk/c1t1d0s0 /dev/dsk/c1t1d0s1
 /dev/dsk/c1t1d0s2 /dev/dsk/c1t1d0s3 /dev/dsk/c1t1d0s4 /dev/dsk/c1t1d0s5
 /dev/dsk/c1t1d0s6 /dev/dsk/c1t1d0s7 /dev/rdsk/c1t1d0s0 /dev/rdsk/c1t1d0s1
 /dev/rdsk/c1t1d0s2 /dev/rdsk/c1t1d0s3 /dev/rdsk/c1t1d0s4 /dev/rdsk/c1t1d0s5
 /dev/rdsk/c1t1d0s6 /dev/rdsk/c1t1d0s7
mopoke%
```

The /etc/security/device_maps file contains access information about each physical device. Each device is represented by a one-line entry.

The default device_maps file is shown below.

```
mopoke% more /etc/security/device_maps
audio:\
        audio:\
        /dev/audio /dev/audioctl /dev/sound/0 /dev/sound/0ctl:\

fd0:\
        fd:\
        /dev/diskette /dev/rdiskette /dev/fd0a /dev/rfd0a /dev/fd0 /dev/fd0b /de
v/rfd0b /dev/fd0c /dev/rfd0c /dev/rfd0:\

sr0:\
        sr:\
        /dev/sr0 /dev/rsr0 /dev/dsk/c1t1d0s0 /dev/dsk/c1t1d0s1 /dev/dsk/c1t1d0s2
 /dev/dsk/c1t1d0s3 /dev/dsk/c1t1d0s4 /dev/dsk/c1t1d0s5 /dev/dsk/c1t1d0s6 /dev/ds
k/c1t1d0s7 /dev/rdsk/c1t1d0s0 /dev/rdsk/c1t1d0s1 /dev/rdsk/c1t1d0s2 /dev/rdsk/c1
t1d0s3 /dev/rdsk/c1t1d0s4 /dev/rdsk/c1t1d0s5 /dev/rdsk/c1t1d0s6 /dev/rdsk/c1t1d0
s7:\

mopoke%
```

You can use the dminfo command to report information about a device entry in the /etc/security/device_maps file.

Table 58 lists the options to the dminfo command.

Table 58   Options to the dminfo Command

Option	Description
-a	Succeed if any of the requested entries are found. If used with -v, print all entries that match the requested case(s).
-d *dev-path*	Search by *dev-path*. Search device_maps(4) for a device special path name in the *device_list* field matching the *dev-path* argument. You cannot use this option with -n, -t, or -u.
-f *pathname*	Use a device_maps file with *pathname* instead of /etc/security/device_maps.
-n *dev-name*	Search by *dev-name*. Search device_maps(4) for a *device_name* field matching *dev-name*. You cannot use this option with -d, -t, or -u.

Table 58   Options to the dminfo Command (Continued)

Option	Description
-t *dev-type*	Search by *dev-type*. Search device_maps(4) for a *device_type* field matching the given *dev-type*. You cannot use this option with -d, -n, or -u.
-u *dm-entry*	Update the device_maps(4) file. You can use this option to add entries to the device_maps(4) file. The *dm-entry* must be a complete device_maps(4) file entry. The *dm-entry* has fields, as in the device_maps file. Use the colon (:) as a field separator and white space as the device_list subfield separators. If any fields are missing or if the entry would be a duplicate, *dm-entry* is not made. Only superuser or a user with the appropriate rights can update the default device_maps file.
-v	Print the requested entry or entries, one line per entry, on the standard output. If you specify no entries, all are printed.

The following example uses the verbose option to display all device_maps entries.

```
mopoke% dminfo -v
audio:audio:/dev/audio /dev/audioctl /dev/sound/0 /dev/sound/0ctl:
fd0:fd:/dev/diskette /dev/rdiskette /dev/fd0a /dev/rfd0a /dev/fd0 /dev/fd0b
 /dev/rfd0b /dev/fd0c /dev/rfd0c /dev/rfd0:
sr0:sr:/dev/sr0 /dev/rsr0 /dev/dsk/c1t1d0s0 /dev/dsk/c1t1d0s1 /dev/dsk/c1t1d0s2
 /dev/dsk/c1t1d0s3 /dev/dsk/c1t1d0s4 /dev/dsk/c1t1d0s5 /dev/dsk/c1t1d0s6
 /dev/dsk/c1t1d0s7 /dev/rdsk/c1t1d0s0 /dev/rdsk/c1t1d0s1 /dev/rdsk/c1t1d0s2
 /dev/rdsk/c1t1d0s3 /dev/rdsk/c1t1d0s4 /dev/rdsk/c1t1d0s5 /dev/rdsk/c1t1d0s6
 /dev/rdsk/c1t1d0s7:
mopoke%
```

Allocating a Device

Use the allocate command to allocate a device.

Table 59 lists the options to the allocate command.

Table 59   Options to the allocate Command

-F *device*	
	Reallocate a device allocated to another user. This option is often used with -U to reallocate a specific device to a specific user. Only a user with the solaris.devices.revoke authorization is permitted to use this option.

Table 59   Options to the allocate Command (Continued)

	Use the *device* argument to specify the device to be manipulated, for example, st0 for a streaming tape device. You can display a list of available devices with the -l option to the list_devices(1) command, also new in the Solaris 9 Operating Environment. The default allocate operation allocates the device special files associated with *device* to the UID of the current process.
	When you specify the -F option, the device-cleaning program is executed when allocation is performed. This cleaning program is found in /etc/security/lib. The name of this program is found in the device_allocate(4) entry for the device in the *dev-exec* field.
-g *dev-type*	
	Allocate a nonallocated device with a device type matching *dev-type*.
	Use the *dev-type* argument to specify the type of device. You can determine the type of device from the output of the list_devices -l command.
-s	Suppress any diagnostic output.
-U *uname*	Use the user ID *uname* instead of the user ID of the current process when performing the allocate operation. Only a user with the solaris.devices.revoke authorization is permitted to use this option.

The following example allocates a tape drive.

```
mopoke% allocate st0
mopoke%
```

The following example allocates audio files by type.;

```
mopoke% allocate -g audio files
mopoke%
```

Deallocating a Device

Use the deallocate command to deallocate a device allocated to the evoking user.

Table 60 lists the options to the `deallocate` command.

Table 60   Options to the deallocate Command

Option	Description
device	Deallocate the device associated with the device special file specified by *device*.
	device can be a device defined in `device_allocate`(4) or one of the device special files associated with the device. The command resets the ownership and the permission on all device special files associated with *device*, disabling the user's access to that device. An authorized user can use this option to remove access to the device by another user. The required authorization is `solaris.devices.allocate`.
-F *device*	Force deallocation of the device associated with the file specified by *device*. Only a user with the `solaris.devices.revoke` authorization is permitted to use this option.
-I	Force deallocation of all allocatable devices. Only a user with the `solaris.devices.revoke` authorization is permitted to use this option. Use this option only at system initialization.
-s	Silent. Suppress any diagnostic output.

The following example deallocates the `st0` device.

```
mopoke% deallocate st0
mopoke%
```

Using SCSI and PCI Hot-Plugging

Hot-plugging is the capability to physically add, remove, or replace system components while a system is running. *Dynamic reconfiguration*, available on certain SPARC servers, enables a service provider to remove and replace hot-pluggable system I/O boards in a running system, thereby eliminating the time lost in rebooting. Also, if a replacement board is not immediately available, the system administrator can use dynamic reconfiguration to shut down a failing board while the system continues to operate.

With the Solaris 8 release, you can use the `cfgadm` command to hot-plug SCSI devices on SPARC- and IA-based platforms and PCI adapter cards on

IA-based systems. The `cfgadm` command enables you to perform the following tasks.

- Display system component status.
- Test system components.
- Change component configurations.
- Display configuration help messages.

With the `cfgadm` command you can reconfigure system components while the system is running. The `cfgadm` command guides you through the steps needed to add, remove, or replace system components. See `cfgadm`(1M) for more information.

NOTE. Not all SCSI and PCI controllers support hot-plugging with the `cfgadm` *command.*

Specifying Device Names

You need to know how to specify device names when using commands to manage disks, file systems, and other devices. In most cases, you use logical device names to represent devices connected to the system. Both logical and physical device names are represented on the system by logical and physical device files.

When a system is booted for the first time, the kernel creates a device hierarchy to represent all of the devices connected to the system. The kernel uses the device hierarchy information to associate drivers with their appropriate devices and provides a set of pointers to the drivers that perform specific operations.

You reference devices in the following three ways in the Solaris Operating Environment.

- Physical device name—The full device path name in the device information hierarchy. You find physical device files in the `/devices` directory.
- Instance name—The abbreviation name the kernel uses for every possible device on the system. For example, `sd0` and `sd1` represent the instance names of two disk devices. Instance names are mapped in the `/etc/path_to_inst` file.
- Logical device name—You use logical device names with most file system commands to refer to devices. Logical device files in the `/dev` directory are symbolically linked to physical device files in the `/devices` directory.

See "Tape Device–Naming Conventions" below for information on tape device-naming conventions. See "Disk-Naming Conventions" on page 296 for information on disk-naming conventions.

Using Tapes

This section describes tape device-naming conventions, useful commands for streaming tape cartridges, and ways to use the tar, cpio, and pax commands to archive and retrieve files from tapes.

You can use the tar, cpio, and pax commands to copy files and file systems to tape. The command you choose depends on how much flexibility and precision you require for the copy.

Use tar to copy files and directory subtrees to a single tape. Note that the Solaris tar command can archive special files (block and character devices, fifos), but the SunOS 4.x tar command cannot extract them. The cpio command provides better portability between different versions of the UNIX operating system.

Use cpio to copy arbitrary sets of files, special files, or file systems that require multiple tape volumes, or to copy files from Solaris systems to SunOS 4.x systems. The cpio command packs data onto tape more efficiently than does tar and skips over any bad spots in a tape when restoring. The cpio command also provides options for writing files with different header formats (tar, ustar, crc, odc, bar) for portability between systems of different types.

Use pax to copy files, special files, or file systems that require multiple tape volumes or when you want to copy files to and from POSIX-compliant systems.

Because tar, cpio, and pax use the raw tape device, you do not need to format or make a file system on tapes before you use them. The tape drive and device name you use depend on the hardware and configuration for each system.

Tape Device–Naming Conventions

Tape device-naming conventions use a logical—not a physical—device name. Logical tape device files are located in the /dev/rmt subdirectory as symbolic links to the /devices directory. In general, you specify a tape drive device as shown in Figure 2.

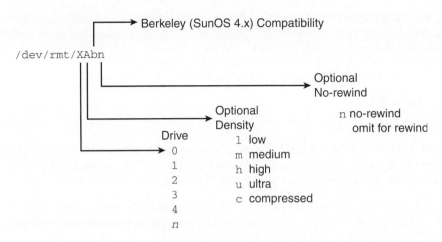

Figure 2   Tape Drive Device Names

Device 0 is the first tape device connected to the system (/dev/rmt/0). The tape device could be a QIC-11, QIC-24, QIC-150, 4mm, 8mm, AIT, DTL, or DAT drive.

Specifying the Drive Number by the Default Density

Normally, you specify a tape drive by its *logical device name*, which is a number from 0 to n. If you do not specify a density, the drive writes at its "preferred" density, which is usually the highest density the tape supports.

You can attach a maximum of seven SCSI tape drives to a narrow SCSI controller. You can attach a maximum of 15 drives to a wide SCSI controller.

To specify the first drive, use the following device name.

```
/dev/rmt/0
```

To specify the second drive, use the following device name.

```
/dev/rmt/1
```

NOTE. Most device names start their numbering sequence with zero (0). Consequently, when you talk about the first disk or target, its number is 0, not 1.

Specifying Different Densities for a Tape Drive

You may want to transport a tape to a system whose tape drive supports only a certain density. In that case, specify a device name that writes at the desired density. Use the following naming convention.

```
/dev/rmt/XA
```

To determine the different densities that are supported for a drive, look at the /dev/rmt subdirectory, which includes the set of tape device files that support different output densities for each tape.

The unit and density characters are shown in Table 61. For example, to specify a raw magnetic tape device on the first (0) drive with medium density, use the following device name.

```
/dev/rmt/0m
```

Table 61   Unit and Density Characters in Tape Device Names

Device Name	= /dev/rmt/XA
X	Tape drive number (digit) from 0 to n, regardless of controller type.
A	Density (character), depending on controller and drive type.
null	Default, preferred (highest) density.
l	Low.
m	Medium.
h	High.
u	Ultra.
c	Compressed.

Specifying the No-Rewind Option

After the command is executed, the tape is automatically rewound unless you specify the no-rewind option as part of the device name. You would specify no-rewind when you intend to continue writing to the tape at the place just after you completed writing the last time.

To specify no rewinding, type **n** at the end of the device name.

For example, to specify a raw magnetic tape device on the first (0) drive with medium density and no rewind, use the following device name.

```
/dev/rmt/0mn
```

Understanding Device Abbreviations for Different Tape Controllers and Media

New!

You can have both SCSI and non-SCSI tape drives on the same system. A narrow SCSI controller can have a maximum of seven SCSI tape drives, and a wide SCSI controller can have a maximum of 15 tape drives. For each drive number (X), the density character depends on the controller and drive type, as described in the following paragraphs.

For ½-inch, rack-mounted tape drives with either a Tapemaster or Xylogics 472 controller, substitute the density from Table 62 for the A variable in the device name (`/dev/rmt/XA`).

Table 62   Designating Density for Rack-Mounted, ½-Inch Tape Drives

Character	Density
null	Default "preferred" (highest) density (usually 6250 bpi uncompressed).
l	800 bpi.
m	1600 bpi.
h	6250 bpi.
u	6250 bpi compressed.

If you omit the density character, the tape is usually written at its highest density, not compressed.

New!

Each SCSI tape drive vendor encodes the vendor and tape drive model into their drives. When the OpenBoot PROM or Solaris Operating Environment probes the SCSI bus, each SCSI device returns its SCSI information that contains the vendor and drive model data. Solaris matches the returned value against each entry in the `/kernel/drv/st.conf` file and turns on the proper SCSI transport and tape drive features such as compression and data density.

Using SCSI ¼-Inch Cartridge and ½-Inch Front-Loaded Reel Drives

For SCSI ¼-inch cartridge and ½-inch front-loaded reel drives—a set of legacy drives—substitute the density from Table 63 for the *A* variable in the device name (`/dev/rmt/XA`).

Table 63   Designating Format or Density for SCSI Tape Drives

Character	Density, ¼-Inch Cartridge	Density, ½-Inch Front-Loaded Reel-to-Reel
`null`	Default, preferred (highest) density.	Default, preferred (highest) density.
`l`	QIC-11 format.	800 bpi.
`m`	QIC-24 format.	1600 bpi.
`h`	QIC-150.	6250 bpi.
`u`	Reserved.	Reserved.

For ¼-inch cartridges, density is specified by the format in which the data is written: the QIC format. The QIC-11 and QIC-24 formats write approximately 1000 bpi on each track. The density for QIC-150 is somewhat higher. The preferred density for a 60-Mbyte ¼-inch cartridge drive is QIC-24 and for a 150-Mbyte ¼-inch cartridge drive, it is QIC-150.

A 150-Mbyte drive can write only QIC-150; it cannot be switched to write QIC-24 or QIC-11. Format selection is useful only for drives that can write both QIC-24 and QIC-11.

Specifying Helical Scan Drives

Helical scan drives (for example, Exabyte 8mm or Wang/DAT 4mm) are a special case of SCSI drives. They write only at the preferred density. Consequently, you always specify them by using only the drive number, for example, `/dev/rmt/0`. You can also specify the no-rewind option.

Using DLT and AIT Tape Drives

New!

DLT (Digital Linear Tape) 1/2-inch cartridge tapes have a 35- to 70-Gbyte capacity and a standard SCSI-2 interface that can connect to a wide range of host adapters, including Fast-Wide SCSI. The DLT7000 supports most data management software packages, including Solstice Backup and VERITAS NetBackup.

AIT (Advanced Intelligent Tape) is another standard SCSI tape device with an intelligent chip inside each tape cartridge.

When you add a DLT or AIT drive to a Solaris system, check for an appropriate entry in the `/kernel/drv/st.conf` file. It is likely that no relevant entry exists for a new tape drive. Contact the vendor of the drive for the syntax of the line to insert into the `/kernel/drv/st.conf` file. Once you insert the line in the file and reboot the system, Solaris can take full advantage of all features of the new tape drive.

Useful Commands for Streaming Tapes

The following sections contain a few commands for use with streaming tapes.

Rewinding a Magnetic Tape

To rewind a magnetic tape, type **mt -f /dev/rmt/n rewind** and press Return. The tape in the tape drive you specify by the device number n is rewound.

The following example rewinds the tape in drive `/dev/rmt/1`.

```
oak% mt -f /dev/rmt/1 rewind
oak%
```

Showing the Status of a Magnetic Tape Drive

To show the status of a magnetic tape drive, type
mt -f /dev/rmt/n status and press Return. Status for the tape drive you specify is displayed.

The following example shows that no tape is in drive `/dev/rmt/1`.

```
oak% mt -f /dev/rmt/1 status
/dev/rmt/1: no tape loaded or drive offline
oak%
```

The following example shows the status for the tape in drive `/dev/rmt/1`.

```
oak% mt -f /dev/rmt/1 status
Archive QIC-150 tape drive:
    sense key(0x6)= unit attention   residual= 0    retries= 0
    file no= 0    block no= 0
oak%
```

The tar Command

Use the `tar` command to copy files and directory subtrees to a single tape. The advantages of the `tar` command are that it is available on most UNIX operating systems and that public domain versions are readily available. The disadvantages of the `tar` command are that `tar` is not aware of file system boundaries, full path-name length cannot exceed 255 characters, `tar` does not copy empty directories or special files such as device files, and it cannot be used to create multiple tape volumes.

> *NOTE. The* `/usr/sfw/bin/gtar` *GNU tar command now ships with the Solaris 9 Operating Environment and has none of the limitations of the* `tar` *command.*

New!

The following sections describe how to use the `tar` command to copy files to a tape, list the files, append the files, and retrieve the files.

Copying Files to a Tape (tar)

Use the following steps to copy files to a tape.

1. Change to the directory that contains the file you want to copy.
2. Insert a write-enabled tape into the tape drive.

> *CAUTION. Copying files to a tape with the* c *option to* `tar` *destroys any files already on the tape. If you want to preserve the files already on the tape, use the* r *option described in "Appending Files to a Tape (tar)" on page 248.*

> *Using absolute path names can be dangerous because you can overwrite the original files, and you cannot choose to restore files to a different location.*

3. Type **tar cvf /dev/rmt/***n* **filename filename filename ...** and press Return.

   The c (create) option copies the files you specify, the v (verbose) option displays information about the files as they are copied, and the f (files) option followed by the tape device name specifies where the `tar` files are to be written. The file names you specify are copied to the tape, overwriting any existing files on the tape.

> *NOTE. You can use metacharacters (? and *) as part of the file names you specify. For example, to copy all documents with a* `.doc` *suffix, type* ***.doc** *as the file-name argument. If you specify a directory name as the file name, the directory and all its subdirectories are recursively copied to the tape.*

4. Remove the tape from the drive and write the names of the files on the tape label.

The following example copies two files to a tape in tape drive 0.

```
oak% cd /home/winsor
oak% ls evaluation*
evaluation.doc    evaluation.doc.backup
oak% tar cvf /dev/rmt/0 evaluation*
a evaluation.doc 86 blocks
a evaluation.doc.backup 84 blocks
oak%
```

Listing the Files on a Tape (tar)

Use the following steps to list the files on a tape.

1. Insert a tape into the tape drive.
2. Type **tar tvf /dev/rmt/*n*** and press Return.

    The t (table) option lists the files you specify, the v (verbose) option displays complete information about the files as they are listed in a form similar to the ls -1 command, and the f (files) option followed by the tape device name specifies the device where the tar files are located.

In the following example, the table of contents for the tape in drive 0 contains two files.

```
oak% tar tvf /dev/rmt/0
rw-rw-rw-6693/10   44032 Apr 23 14:54 2000 evaluation.doc
rw-rw-rw-6693/10   43008 Apr 23 14:47 2000 evaluation.doc.backup
oak%
```

Reading from left to right, the first column shows the permissions for the file; the second column shows the UID and GID file ownership; the third column shows the number of characters (bytes) in the file; the fourth, fifth, sixth, and seventh columns contain the month, day, time, and year the file was last modified, and the final column contains the name of the file.

Appending Files to a Tape (tar)

Use the following steps to append files without overwriting files already on the tape.

1. Change to the directory that contains the file you want to copy.
2. Insert a tape that is not write-protected into the tape drive.
3. Type **tar rvf /dev/rmt/*n* *filename filename filename* ...** and press Return.

    The file names you specify are appended to the files already on the tape in the drive you specify.

NOTE. You can use metacharacters (? and *) as part of the file names you specify. For example, to copy all documents with a .doc *suffix, type* ***.doc** *as the file-name argument.*

4. Remove the tape from the drive and write the names of the files on the tape label.

The following example appends one file to the files already on the tape in drive 0.

```
oak% cd /home/winsor
oak% tar cvf /dev/rmt/0 junk
a junk 1 blocks
oak% tar rvf /dev/rmt/0 evaluation.doc
rw-rw-rw-6693/10  44032 Apr 23 14:54 2000 evaluation.doc
rw-rw-rw-6693/10     18 Dec 10 11:36 2000 junk
oak%
```

You can put more than one tar archive on a tape if you use the n (no-rewind) option as part of the tape device name. For example, type **tar cvf /dev/rmt/*rn filename*.** The tape is not rewound after the files are copied, and the next time you use the tape, the files are written after the end of the previous set of files. See "Specifying the No-Rewind Option" on page 243 for more information.

Retrieving Files and Directories from a Tape (tar)

Use the following steps to retrieve files from a tape.

1. Change to the directory into which you want to put the files.
2. Insert the tape into the tape drive.
3. Type **tar xvf /dev/rmt/*n*** and press Return.

   All the files on the tape in the drive you specify are copied to the current directory.

The following example copies all files from the tape in drive 0.

```
oak% cd /home/winsor/Evaluations
oak% tar xvf /dev/rmt/0
x evaluation.doc, 44032 bytes, 86 tape blocks
x evaluation.doc.backup, 43008 bytes, 84 tape blocks
oak%
```

To retrieve individual files from a tape, type **tar xvf /dev/rmt/*n filename filename filename*.**.. and press Return. The file names you specify are extracted from the tape and placed in the current working directory. The following example copies the evaluation.doc file from the tape in drive 0.

```
oak% cd /home/winsor/Evaluations
oak% tar xvf /dev/rmt/0 evaluation.doc
x evaluation.doc, 44032 bytes, 86 tape blocks
oak%
```

Use the following steps to retrieve directories and subdirectories recursively from a tape.

1. Change to the parent directory into which you want to copy the files.

    If the directory already exists, be sure you are in the parent directory and that it is okay to overwrite the contents of the directory before you copy the files from the tape. For example, to restore the contents of a directory named Book that is in /home/winsor/Book, you would change to /home/winsor and type **tar xvf /dev/rmt/ _n_ Book** and press Return. If you are in the directory /home/winsor/Book, the files are restored as /home/winsor/Book/Book.

2. Type **tar xvf /dev/rmt/ _n_ _directory-name_** and press Return.

    The directory and all its subdirectories are recursively copied from the tape.

NOTE. The names of the files extracted from the tape exactly match the names of the files stored on the archive. If you have any doubts about the names or paths of the files, first list the files on the tape. See "Listing the Files on a Tape (tar)" on page 248 for instructions and the tar(1) manual page for more information.

The cpio Command

The cpio command copies files, special files (files used to represent peripheral devices attached to a system), and file systems that require multiple tape volumes, and provides compatibility for copying files from Solaris systems to SunOS 4.x systems. Advantages of using the cpio command are that it packs data onto tape more efficiently than does the tar command, skips over any bad spots in a tape when restoring files, provides options for writing files with different header formats (tar, ustar, crc, odc, bar) for portability between different system types, and creates multiple tape volumes.

When you use the cpio command to create an archive, the command takes a list of files or path names from standard input and writes to standard output. You redirect the output to a file, a directory, or a device. The following sections describe how to use the cpio command to copy files to a cartridge tape, list the files, retrieve all files, and retrieve a subset of the files from a cartridge tape.

Copying All Files in a Directory to a Tape (cpio)

Use the following steps to copy all files in a directory to a tape.

1. Insert a write-enabled tape into the tape drive.
2. Type **ls | cpio -oc > /dev/rmt/n** and press Return.

   The o option copies the files. The c option writes header information in ASCII character form for portability. All the files in the directory are copied to the tape in the drive you specify, overwriting any existing files on the tape, and the total number of blocks copied is displayed.
3. Remove the tape from the drive and write the names of the files on the tape label.

In the following example, all the files in the directory /home/winsor/TOI are copied to the tape in tape drive 0.

```
oak% cd /home/winsor/TOI
oak% ls | cpio -oc > /dev/rmt/0
31 blocks
oak%
```

Listing the Files on a Tape (cpio)

Use the following steps to list files on a tape.

1. Insert a tape into the tape drive.
2. Type **cpio -civt < /dev/rmt/n** and press Return. The -c option reads header information in ASCII character format for portability. The i option reads in the contents of the tape. The v option displays the output in a format similar to the output from the ls -l command. The t option lists the table of contents for the files on the tape in the tape drive you specify.

   NOTE. Listing the table of contents takes as long as it does to read the archive file because the cpio *command must process the entire archive.*

In the following example, the table of contents for the tape in drive 0 contains four files.

```
oak% cpio -civt < /dev/rmt/0
100666 winsor   3895  Feb 24 15:13:02 2000  Boot.chapter
100666 winsor   3895  Feb 24 15:13:23 2000  Directory.chapter
100666 winsor   6491  Feb 24 15:13:52 2000  Install.chapter
```

```
100666 winsor   1299  Feb 24 15:14:00 2000  Intro.chapter
31 blocks
oak%
```

The first column shows permissions in octal format; the second column shows the owner of the file; the third column displays the number of characters (bytes) in the file; the fourth, fifth, sixth, and seventh columns show the month, date, time, and year the file was last modified; and the final column shows the name of the file.

Retrieving All Files from a Tape (cpio)

If the archive was created with relative path names, the input files are built as a directory within the current directory. If, however, the archive was created with absolute path names, the same absolute paths are used to re-create the file.

> CAUTION. *Using absolute path names can be dangerous because you can overwrite the original files and you cannot choose to restore files to a different location.*

Use the following steps to retrieve all files from a tape.

1. Change to the directory into which you want to put the files.
2. Insert the tape into the tape drive.
3. Type **cpio -icv < /dev/rmt/*n*** and press Return.

   All the files on the tape in the drive you specify are copied to the current directory.

The following example copies all files from the tape in drive 0.

```
oak% cpio -icv < /dev/rmt/0
Boot.chapter
Directory.chapter
Install.chapter
Intro.chapter
31 blocks
oak%
```

Retrieving a Subset of Files from a Tape (cpio)

You can retrieve a subset of the files from the archive by specifying a pattern to match and using shell wildcard characters enclosed in quotation marks after the options.

1. Change to the directory into which you want to put the files.
2. Insert the tape into the tape drive.
3. Type **cpio -icv "**∗*file*"** < /dev/rmt/*n*** and press Return.

All the files that match the pattern "*file" are copied to the current directory. You can specify multiple patterns, but each must be enclosed in quotation marks.

The following example copies all files that end in the suffix chapter from the tape in drive 0.

```
oak% cd /home/winsor/Book
oak% cpio -icv "*chapter" < /dev/rmt/0
Boot.chapter
Directory.chapter
Install.chapter
Intro.chapter
31 blocks
oak%
```

See the cpio(1) manual page for more information.

The pax Command

Starting with the Solaris 2.5 release, the pax command, which stands for *portable archive interchange,* is provided. The pax command provides better portability than do the tar or cpio commands for POSIX-compliant systems. Use the pax command to copy files, special files, or file systems that require multiple tape volumes or when you want to copy files to and from POSIX-compliant systems. Disadvantages of the pax command are that it is not aware of file system boundaries and that the full path-name length cannot exceed 255 characters.

Copying All Files in a Directory to a Tape (pax)

Use the following steps to use the pax command to copy all the files in the current directory to a tape.

1. Change to the directory that contains the files you want to copy.
2. Insert a write-enabled tape into the tape drive.
3. Type **pax -w -f /dev/rmt/*n* .** and press Return.

    The -w option writes the current directory contents to tape. The -f option identifies the tape drive. The dot (**.**) at the end of the command specifies the current directory. The pax command does not list the files as they are copied.
4. Type **pax -l -f /dev/rmt/*n*** and press Return.

    The -l option lists the files on the tape to verify that the files are copied.
5. Remove the tape from the drive and write the names of the files on the tape label.

The following example copies all files from the tape in drive 0.

```
castle% pax -w -f /dev/rmt/0 .
castle% pax -l -f /dev/rmt/0
.
./addusr-1.rs
./addusr-2.rs
./at-addmn.rs
./at-base.rs
./at-menu.rs
castle%
```

See the pax(1) manual page for more information.

NOTE. When you use the pax *command to copy files to a single-volume tape, you can also list and retrieve files from that tape with the* tar *command.*

Retrieving All Files on a Tape (pax)

Use the following steps to use the pax command to copy all the files on a tape into the current directory.

1. Change to the directory into which you want to copy the files.
2. Insert a write-enabled tape into the tape drive.
3. Type **pax -r -f /dev/rmt/*n* .** and press Return.

   The -r option reads the contents of the tape to the current directory. The -f option identifies the tape drive. The dot (.) at the end of the command specifies the current directory. The pax command does not list the files as they are copied.
4. Type **ls -l** and press Return.

   The ls -l command lists the files in the current directory and shows their permissions to verify that the files are copied.
5. Remove the tape from the drive and write the names of the files on the tape label.

The following example copies all files from the tape in drive 0.

```
castle% pax -r -f /dev/rmt/0 .
castle% ls -l
-rw-rw-rw-  1 winsor   staff       245660 Sep 12 11:52 addusr-1.rs
-rw-rw-rw-  1 winsor   staff       245660 Sep 12 10:31 addusr-2.rs
-rw-rw-rw-  1 winsor   staff       181315 Sep 12 10:29 at-addmn.rs
-rw-rw-rw-  1 winsor   staff       181309 Sep 12 10:27 at-base.rs
-rw-rw-rw-  1 winsor   staff       181315 Sep 12 10:28 at-menu.rs
castle%
```

Accessing Removable Media Devices

When volume management is running, you can access CD-ROM, DVD-ROM, Iomega Zip, and Iomega Jaz devices by simply inserting the medium into the appropriate drive. After the medium is mounted, a File Manager window showing the contents of the medium is displayed.

You must manually mount diskettes before you can access them. See "Diskettes and Volume Management" on page 276 for information on how to access diskettes with volume management.

Removable Media Manager

You can use CDE Removable Media Manager to format, protect, and view data on removable media devices such as diskettes, CD-ROM, DVD-ROM, Iomega Zip, and Iomega Jaz devices.

NOTE. Removable Media Manager was introduced in the Solaris 8 6/00 release.

When you start Removable Media Manager, it displays all media currently loaded into the drives. If none of the drives contain any media, nothing is displayed in the Removable Media Manager window. The different forms of devices are represented by icons and are unlimited. For example, if a system has three drives loaded with diskettes, three diskette icons are displayed, and the icon view is updated each time you insert or eject a device. Each class of media is represented by a different icon.

Starting Removable Media Manager

You can open the Removable Media Manager in any of the following ways.

- From the File Manager File menu, choose Removable Media Manager.
- From the Front Panel Files subpanel, click on the Removable Media Manager icon.
- From the Workspace menu Folders menu, choose Removable Media Manager.

Figure 3 shows the Removable Media Manager window with one CD-ROM device and one diskette.

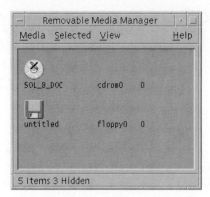

Figure 3   Removable Media Manager Window

A device is displayed with a nickname (cdrom0), an optional volume name (SOL_8_DOC), and an optional partition or slice number (0). You can view additional information about a device and set properties. You can select one or more devices and perform operations on them, such as formatting and slicing devices, creating Solaris slices, and write-protecting a device either with or without a password.

Supported Media Devices

Removable Media Manager supports the following devices.

- Diskette.
- CD-ROM.
- DVD-ROM.
- Iomega Zip drive.
- Iomega Jaz drive.
- Rmdisk (generic call that includes Syquest devices).

The following sections provide information about the supported media classes.

Using DVD-ROM Devices

The Solaris 8 Operating Environment includes support for the Universal Disk Format (UDFS) file system, which is the industry-standard format for storing information on the optical media technology called DVD (Digital Versatile Disc or Digital Video Disc).

UDFS is provided as dynamically loadable 32-bit and 64-bit modules, with system administration commands that you can use to create, mount, and check the file system on both SPARC and IA platforms. The Solaris UDFS works with supported ATAPI and SCSI DVD drives, CD-ROM devices, and disk and diskette drives. In addition, the Solaris UDFS is fully compliant with the UDF 1.50 specification. See "Disk-Based File Systems" on page 182 for more information.

Hardware and Software Requirements

The UDF file system requires the following components.

- The Solaris 7 11/99 or Solaris 8 Operating Environment.
- Supported SPARC or Intel platforms.
- Supported CD-ROM or DVD-ROM device.

UDF Compatibility Issues

This first Solaris UDF file system implementation provides support for industry-standard read-write UDF version 1.50 and fully internationalized file system commands.

Connecting a DVD-ROM Device

Use the following steps to connect a DVD-ROM device.

1. Become superuser.
2. Type **touch /reconfigure** and press Return.
    The /reconfigure file is created.
3. Type **telinit 0** and press Return to shut down the system and turn off power.
4. Connect the DVD-ROM device.
5. Turn on power to the system.

Accessing Files on a DVD-ROM Device

Use the following steps to access files on a DVD-ROM device.

NOTE. If a system has both a CD-ROM and a DVD-ROM device, the CD-ROM might be named /cdrom/cdrom0 *and the DVD-ROM might be named* /cdrom/cdrom1. *If the system has only a DVD-ROM device, try using* /cdrom/cdrom0.

1. Type **ls /cdrom** and press Return.

   The contents of the /cdrom directory are displayed.

2. Type **ls /cdrom/cdrom1** (or **ls /cdrom/cdrom0** if the system has no CD-ROM device) and press Return.

   The following example displays the contents of a DVD-ROM device.

```
$ ls /cdrom/cdrom1
Copyright  install.sh  product.gz
$
```

Automatic display with the CDE file manager is not yet implemented. You can use all other CDE file manager functions, such as drag and drop for copying and imagetool features.

Displaying UDF File System Parameters

Use the -F udfs and -m options of the mkfs command to display UDF file system parameters.

1. Become superuser.

2. Type **mkfs -F udfs -m /dev/rdsk/*device-name*** and press Return.

   See mkfs_udfs(1M) for more information.

Creating a UDF File System

Use the -F udfs option of the mkfs command to create a UDF file system.

1. Become superuser.

2. Type **mkfs -F udfs /dev/rdsk/*device-name*** and press Return.

   See mkfs_udfs(1M) for more information.

3. Verify the UDF file system is created by mounting it.

   See "Mounting a UDF File System" on page 259 for more information.

Determining Whether a File System Is a UDF File System

Use the fstyp command to determine whether a file system is a UDF file system.

1. Become superuser.

2. Type **fstyp -v /dev/rdsk/*device-name*** and press Return.

Checking a UDF File System

Use the `-F udfs` option of the `fsck` command to check the integrity of a UDF file system.

1. Become superuser.
2. Type **fsck -F udfs /dev/rdsk/*device-name*** and press Return.

   See `fsck_udfs`(1M) for more information.

Mounting a UDF File System

Use the `-F udfs` option of the `mount` command to mount UDF file systems.

1. Become superuser.
2. Type **mount -F udfs /dev/rdsk/*device-name* /*mountpoint*** and press Return.
3. Type **ls /*mountpoint*** and press Return to verify that the UDF file system is mounted.

   See `mount_udfs`(1M) for more information.

Unmounting a UDF File System

Use the `umount` command to unmount UDF file systems.

1. Become superuser.
2. Type **umount /dev/rdsk/*device-name*** and press Return.

Labeling a Device with a UDF File System and Volume Name

Use the `-F udfs` option of the `labelit` command to create a file system and volume name for a UDF file system.

1. Become superuser.
2. Type **labelit -F udfs /dev/rdsk/*device-name* *fsname* *volume*** and press Return.

   See `labelit_udfs`(1M) for more information.

New! Using Jaz or Zip Drives

You can connect Iomega USB Jaz or Zip drives to systems that have a USB port. Remember to use the `boot -r` command to reconfigure devices so that the system recognizes the Jaz or Zip drive.

> *NOTE. If the system has the Solaris 8 10/00 or Solaris 8 01/01 release installed, Jaz or Zip drives do not work. At the time of this writing, no workaround exists. These problems are fixed in the Solaris 8 04/01 and following releases.*

See "Formatting a UFS Diskette (rmformat)" on page 289 for instructions on how to use the `rmformat` command to format Jaz or Zip disks. You can also use Removable Media Manager to format Jaz or Zip disks. The procedure is similar to formatting diskettes. See "Using Removable Media Manager to Format Diskettes" on page 282 for more information.

To access information on a Jaz or Zip drive, insert a disk into the drive. The file systems on the drive are mounted, and a File Manager window opens showing the contents, as shown in Figure 4.

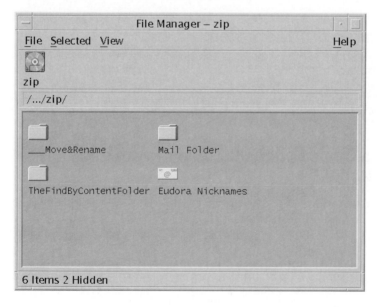

Figure 4   File Manager Window with Mounted Zip Disk File Systems

You can also access the file systems on a Zip or Jaz drive from the command line with the following steps.

1. Type **ls /rmdisk** and press Return.

    The default /rmdisk mount point is used for any removable media disk devices. The contents of the /rmdisk drive are displayed.

2. Type **cd /rmdisk/zip** or **cd /rmdisk/jaz** and press Return.

    The file systems on the Zip or Jaz drive are displayed. The following example shows the contents of a Zip disk.

```
mopoke% ls /rmdisk
zip   zip0
mopoke% cd /rmdisk/zip
mopoke% ls
___Move&Rename          Mail Folder
Eudora Nicknames        TheFindByContentFolder
mopoke%
```

You can also use the Removable Media Manager to format, protect, and view data on removable media devices.

Creating an Alternative fdisk Partition

You can create an fdisk partition and a PCFS file system on removable media such as diskettes, Zip, or Jaz disks on a SPARC-based system to facilitate data transfers to IA-based systems.

Use the following steps to format removable media for a PCFS file system and create an alternative fdisk partition.

NOTE. If you want to create a PCFS file system without an fdisk *partition, skip step 4.*

1. Type **rmformat -F quick** *device-name* and press Return.
2. When prompted, type **y** and press Return.

    The disk is formatted.

3. Become superuser.
4. Type **fdisk** *device-name* and press Return.
5. Type **mkfs -F pcfs** *device-name* and press Return.
6. When prompted, type **y** and press Return.

    A new FAT file system is created in the specified partition.

The following example creates an alternative fdisk partition on /dev/rdsk/c0t4d0s2:c.

```
paperbark% rmformat -F quick /dev/rdsk/c0t4d0s2:c
Formatting will erase all the data on disk.
Do you want to continue? (y/n) y
paperbark% su
Password:
# fdisk /dev/rdsk/c0t4d0s2:c
```

```
# mkfs -F pcfs /dev/rdsk/c0t4d0s2:c
Construct a new FAT file system on /dev/rdsk/c0t4d0s2:c (y/n)? y
#
```

[New!] Writing CD Discs

You can use the cdrw command to create data and audio CDs. You can also use this command to extract audio tracks from an audio CD. The cdrw command works with any MMC-compliant CD-R or CD-RW drive.

The cdrw command was initially provided starting with the Solaris 8 Update 2 (10/00) release on the separate Software Supplement CD for the Solaris 8 Operating Environment. Starting with the Solaris 9 release, the cdrw command is included in the Solaris 9 release and is available when you install the SUNWcdrw package.

Table 64 lists the options to the cdrw command.

Table 64   Options to the cdrw Command

Option	Description
-a	Create an audio disc. You must specify at least one audio-file name. Because a CD cannot have more than 99 audio tracks, you can specify no more than 99 audio files. The maximum audio data that can be written to the CD by default is 74 minutes unless you specify the -C option.
-b all | session	
	Blank a CD-RW disc. You must specify the type of erasing by specifying the all or session argument.
-c	Copy a CD. If you specify no other argument, the default CD writing device is assumed to be the source device as well. In this case, the copying operation reads the source CD into a temporary directory and prompts you to put a blank CD into the drive for copying to proceed.
-C	Use the CD stated capacity. Without this option, cdrw uses a default value for writable discs, which is 74 minutes for an audio CD or 681,984,000 bytes for a data CD.
-d	Specify CD writing device.
-h	Help. Print usage message.

Table 64   *Options to the cdrw Command (Continued)*

Option	Description
-i	Specify an image file for creating data CDs. The file size should be less than what can be written on a CD-R or CD-RW disc, which is 681,984,000 bytes by default or the CD stated capacity when you use the -C option. Also, it is better to have the file locally available instead of having it on an NFS-mounted file system because the CD writing process expects data to be available continuously without interruptions.
-l	List all the CD writers found in the system.
-m	Use an alternative temporary directory instead of the system default temporary directory for storing track data while copying a CD. You might use an alternative temporary directory because the amount of data on a CD can be huge (as much as 800 Mbytes for an 80-minute audio CD) and the system default temporary directory might not have that much space.
-M	Report CD status. cdrw reports whether the disc is blank; if not, cdrw reports the table of contents, the last session's start address, and the next writable address if the disc is open.
-O	Keep the disc open. cdrw closes the session, but it keeps the disc open so that another session can be added later to create a multisession disc.
-p	Set the CD writing speed. For example, -p 4 sets the speed to 4X. If you do not specify this option, cdrw uses the default speed of the CD writer. If you specify this option, cdrw tries to set the drive write speed to this value, but the speed actually used by the drive is not guaranteed.
-s	Specify the source device for copying to the CD.
-S	Operate in simulation mode. In this mode, cdrw does everything with the drive laser turned off, so nothing is written to the CD. You can use this option to verify that the system can provide data at a rate good enough for CD writing.
-T	Specify the audio format to use extracting audio files or reading audio files for audio CD creation. The audio type can be sun, wav, cda, or aur.
-v	Use verbose mode.

Table 64   Options to the cdrw Command (Continued)

Option	Description
-x	Extract audio data from an audio track.

Creating Data CDs

To create a data CD, you first prepare the data with the mkisofs(1M)
command to convert the file and file format into the High Sierra format used
on CDs. When creating data CDs, cdrw uses the track-at-once mode of
writing. Use the -i option to specify a file that contains the data to write on
CD media. If you do not specify a file, cdrw reads data from standard input.

The following example creates a data CD.

```
example% cdrw -i /local/iso_image
```

The following example creates a CD from the directory tree /home/foo.

```
example% mkisofs -r /home/foo 2>/dev/null | cdrw -i -p 1
```

Creating Audio CDs

Use the -a option to create an audio CD. You can specify single or multiple
audio files. All of the audio files should be in the supported audio formats.

The currently approved formats are listed in Table 65.

Table 65   Supported Audio Formats for the cdrw Command

Format	Description
sun	Sun .au files with data in Red Book CDDA form.
wav	RIFF (.wav) files with data in Red Book CDDA form.
cda	.cda files with raw CD audio data (that is, 16-bit PCM stereo at 44.1 kHz sample rate in little-endian byte order).
aur	.aur files with raw CD data in big-endian byte order.

The following example extracts an audio track number 1 to
/home/foo/song1.wav.

```
example% cdrw -x -T wav 1 /home/foo/song1.wav
```

The following example creates an audio CD from wav files on disc.

```
example% cdrw -a song1.wav song2.wav song3.wav song4.wav
```

See the cdrw(1) manual page for more information about this command.

Volume Management

Starting with the Solaris 2.2 system software, volume management automates mounting of CD-ROMs and diskettes; users no longer need to have superuser permissions to mount a CD-ROM or a diskette.

CAUTION. The Solaris 2.0 and 2.1 procedures for mounting CD-ROMs and diskettes do not work for Solaris 2.2 and later releases. Volume management controls the /dev/dsk/c0t6d0s2 *path to a CD-ROM drive and the* /dev/diskette *path to the diskette drive. If you try to access a CD-ROM or diskette and specify these paths, an error message is displayed.*

Volume management provides users with a standard interface for dealing with diskettes and CD-ROMs. Volume management provides three major benefits.

- Automatically mounting diskettes and CDs simplifies their use.
- Users can access diskettes and CDs without having to become superuser.
- Users on the network can gain automatic access to diskettes and CDs mounted on remote systems.

Mounting devices manually requires the following steps.

1. Insert medium.
2. Become superuser.
3. Determine the location of the medium device.
4. Create a mount point.
5. Make sure the current working directory is in the mount point directory.
6. Mount the device using the proper mount options.
7. Exit the superuser account.
8. Work with files on the medium.
9. Become superuser.
10. Unmount the medium device.

11. Eject medium.

12. Exit the superuser account.

Using volume management requires the following steps.

1. Insert medium.

2. For diskettes, use the `volcheck` command.

3. Work with files on the medium.

4. Eject medium.

Volume Management Files

Volume management consists of the `/usr/sbin/vold` volume management daemon, the `/etc/vold.conf` configuration file used by the `vold` daemon to determine which devices to manage, the `/etc/rmmount.conf` file used to configure removable media mounts, and actions in `/usr/lib/rmmount`. The volume daemon logs messages in the `/var/adm/vold.log` file.

The default `/etc/vold.conf` file is shown below.

New!

```
# ident      "@(#)vold.conf    1.26     00/07/17 SMI"
#
# Volume Daemon Configuration file
#

# Database to use (must be first)
db db_mem.so

# Labels supported
label cdrom label_cdrom.so cdrom
label dos label_dos.so floppy rmdisk pcmem
label sun label_sun.so floppy rmdisk pcmem

# Devices to use
use cdrom drive /dev/rdsk/c*s2 dev_cdrom.so cdrom%d
use floppy drive /dev/rdiskette[0-9] dev_floppy.so floppy%d
use pcmem drive /dev/rdsk/c*s2 dev_pcmem.so pcmem%d forceload=true
use rmdisk drive /dev/rdsk/c*s2 dev_rmdisk.so rmdisk%d

# Actions
eject dev/diskette[0-9]/* user=root /usr/sbin/rmmount
eject dev/dsk/* user=root /usr/sbin/rmmount
insert dev/diskette[0-9]/* user=root /usr/sbin/rmmount
insert dev/dsk/* user=root /usr/sbin/rmmount
notify rdsk/* group=tty user=root /usr/lib/vold/volmissing -p
remount dev/diskette[0-9]/* user=root /usr/sbin/rmmount
remount dev/dsk/* user=root /usr/sbin/rmmount

# List of file system types unsafe to eject
unsafe ufs hsfs pcfs udfs
```

If a system has additional diskette drives, volume management automatically creates two subdirectories in /vol/dev for each additional drive—one to provide access to the file systems and the other to provide access to the raw device. For a second diskette drive, volume management creates directories named diskette1 and rdiskette1. For a third diskette drive, it creates directories named diskette2 and rdiskette2 (and so on for additional drives).

The syntax for a Devices to use entry is shown below.

```
use device type special shared-object symname options
```

Volume management does not automatically mount DVD devices.

Table 66 describes each of the fields for the Devices to use syntax.

Table 66   *Device Control Syntax Descriptions*

Field	Supported Default Values	Description
device	cdrom, floppy	The removable medium device.
type	drive	The type of device—multiple or single media support.
special	/dev/rdsk/c0t6 /dev/rdiskette	Path name of the device to be used in the /dev directory.
shared-object	/usr/lib/vold/*shared-object*-name	Location of the code that manages the device.
symname	cdrom0, floppy0	The symbolic name that refers to this device. The *symname* is placed in the device directory: either /cdrom or /floppy).
options	user=nobody group=nobody mode=0666	The user, group, and mode permissions for the inserted media.

The /etc/rmmount.conf file is shown below.

New!

```
# ident      "@(#)rmmount.conf      1.12      00/08/29 SMI"
#
# Removable Media Mounter configuration file.
#

# File system identification
ident udfs ident_udfs.so cdrom floppy rmdisk
ident hsfs ident_hsfs.so cdrom
ident ufs ident_ufs.so cdrom floppy rmdisk pcmem
ident pcfs ident_pcfs.so floppy rmdisk pcmem

# Actions
action cdrom action_filemgr.so
action floppy action_filemgr.so
action rmdisk action_filemgr.so

# Mount
mount * hsfs udfs ufs -o nosuid
```

The files in the /usr/lib/vold directory are listed below.

New!

New!

```
castle% ls -1 /usr/lib/vold
db_mem.so.1
db_nis.so.1
dev_cdrom.so.1
dev_cdtest.so.1
dev_floppy.so.1
dev_pcmem.so.1
dev_rmdisk.so.1
dev_test.so.1
eject_popup
label_cdrom.so.1
label_dos.so.1
label_sun.so.1
label_test.so.1
volcancel
volmissing
volmissing_popup
volstat
castle%
```

The files in the /usr/lib/rmmount directory are listed below.

New!

```
oak% ls -1 /usr/lib/rmmount
action dvdvideo.so.1
action_filemgr.so.1
action_workman.so.1
oak%
```

If you encounter problems with volume management, check the /var/adm/vold.log file for information. An example of this file is shown below.

```
oak% more /var/adm/vold.log
Tue Jun  1 17:34:24 1999 warning: dev_use: couldn't find a driver for drive
  cdrom at /dev/dsk/c0t6
Tue Jun  1 17:39:12 1999 warning: dev_use: couldn't find a driver for drive
  cdrom at /dev/dsk/c0t6
Tue Jun  1 18:24:24 1999 warning: dev_use: couldn't find a driver for drive
  cdrom at /dev/dsk/c0t6
```

```
Wed Jun 23 15:08:47 1999 warning: check device 36.2: device not managed
Wed Jun 23 15:09:58 1999 warning: check device 36.2: device not managed
Wed Jun 23 15:11:08 1999 warning: check device 36.2: device not managed
Thu Jul 15 13:51:23 1999 warning: check device 36.2: device not managed
Thu Jul 15 13:52:53 1999 warning: check device 36.2: device not managed
Thu Jul 15 14:04:37 1999 warning: check device 36.2: device not managed
Thu Jul 15 14:05:52 1999 warning: check device 36.2: device not managed
Thu Jul 15 14:06:16 1999 warning: check device 36.2: device not managed
Wed Jul 21 16:33:33 1999 fatal: svc_tli_create: Cannot create server handle
Thu Jul 22 16:32:28 1999 warning: cdrom: /dev/rdsk/c0t6d0s2; Device busy
castle%
```

If you want to display debugging messages from the volume management daemon, you can start the daemon by typing **/usr/sbin/vold -v -L 10**. With these flags set, the volume management daemon logs quite a bit of information in /var/adm/vold.log.

Another way to gather debugging information is to run the rmmount command with the debug flag. To do so, edit /etc/vold.conf and change the lines with /usr/sbin/rmmount in them to include the -D flag, as shown in the following example.

```
insert dev/diskette[0-9]/* user=root /usr/sbin/rmmount -D
```

Volume Management Mount Points

Volume management automatically mounts CD-ROM and DVD-ROM file systems on the /cdrom mount point when you insert the media into the drive.

New!

Volume management automatically mounts Jaz and Zip file systems on /rmdisk/jaz or /rmdisk/zip mount points.

New!

When you insert a diskette in the diskette drive, you must ask the system to check the diskette drive. You can check for a diskette in any one of the following ways.

- From the command line, type **volcheck** and press Return.
- From the CDE front panel, click on the Folders menu and then click on Open Floppy.
- From the CDE File Manager File menu, choose Open Floppy.
- From the OpenWindows File Manager File menu, choose Check for Floppy.

When you use any of these methods, the files are mounted on the /floppy mount point. Table 67 describes the mount points and how volume management uses them.

Table 67   *Volume Management Mount Points*

Medium/Mount Point	State of Medium
Diskette	
/floppy/floppy0	Symbolic link to mounted diskette in local diskette drive.
/floppy/*floppy-name*	Mounted named diskette.
/floppy/unnamed_floppy	Mounted unnamed diskette.
CD-ROM	
/cdrom/cdrom0	Symbolic link to mounted CD-ROM in local CD-ROM drive.
/cdrom/*CD-ROM-name*	Mounted named CD-ROM.
/cdrom/*CD-ROM-name/partition*	Mounted named CD-ROM broken up into more than one partition, each of which has a file system written on it. The file system on the mentioned partition is currently mounted.
/cdrom/unnamed_cdrom	Mounted unnamed CD-ROM.
Jaz and Zip Disks	
/rmdisk/zip and /rmdisk/zip0	Mounted Zip disk.
/rmdisk/jaz and /rmdisk/jaz0	Mounted Jaz disk.

New!

If the medium does not contain a file system, volume management provides block and character devices in the /vol file system, as shown in Table 68.

Table 68   *CD-ROM and Diskette Device Locations When No File System Is Present*

Medium/Device Location	State of Medium
Diskette	
/vol/dev/diskette0/unnamed_floppy	Formatted unnamed diskette—block device access.

Table 68   CD-ROM and Diskette Device Locations When No File System Is Present (Continued)

Medium/Device Location	State of Medium
`/vol/dev/rdiskette0/unnamed_floppy`	Formatted unnamed diskette—raw device access.
`/vol/dev/diskette0/unlabeled`	Unlabeled diskette—block diskette device access.
CD-ROM	
`/vol/dev/dsk/c0t6d0/unnamed_cdrom`	CD-ROM—block device access.
`/vol/dev/rdsk/c0t6d0/unnamed_cdrom`	CD-ROM—raw device access.

Limitation on UFS Formats with Volume Management for CDs

UFS formats are not portable between architectures, so you must use them on the architecture for which they were formatted. For example, a UFS CD formatted for a SPARC platform cannot be recognized by an IA platform. Likewise, an IA UFS CD cannot be mounted by volume management on a SPARC platform. The same limitation applies to diskettes.

Most CDs are formatted according to the ISO 9660 standard (High Sierra File System—HSFS), which imposes no limitations on volume management.

CD-ROMs and Volume Management

The following sections describe how to access files from local and remote CD-ROM drives.

Mounting a Local CD-ROM

Use the following procedure to mount a CD-ROM from a local drive.

1. Push the button on the front of the CD-ROM drive to open the tray.
2. Place the CD-ROM into the tray so that the CD label is visible.

   Volume management creates a subdirectory on the `/cdrom` mount point, using the label written on the CD-ROM, or creates an unlabeled subdirectory if the CD-ROM doesn't have a label. Then volume management mounts the file system on the CD on that subdirectory. If File Manager is running, a window displays the contents of the CD-ROM, as shown in Figure 5.

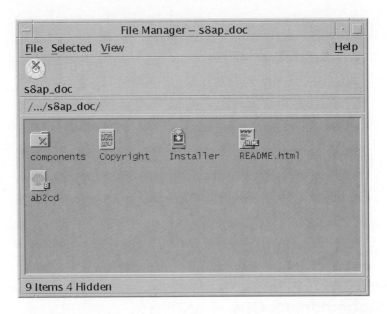

Figure 5   The CDE File Manager CD-ROM Window

3. To access files on the CD-ROM from a command line, type
   cd /cdrom/cdrom0 and press Return.

4. Type **ls -L** and press Return.

   The list of files in the /cdrom/cdrom0 directory is displayed. Use the
   -L option because some of the files on the CD may be symbolic links.

You can use the File Manager CD-ROM window and the command line
interchangeably. For example, you can eject a CD-ROM either from a
command line by typing **eject cdrom** or by choosing Eject from the File
menu in the File Manager CD-ROM window.

New!

Sharing Local Media Drives with NFS

You can configure a system to share its media drives to make any medium
in those drives available to other systems. Once the media drives are
shared, other systems can access the medium they contain simply by
mounting them.

Use the following steps to make available local media devices.

1. Become superuser.

2. Type **ps -ef | grep nfsd** and press Return.

   Review the output to determine whether the NFS daemon (nfsd) is
   running. If nfsd is running, skip to Step 7.

3. Type **mkdir** */dummy-dir* and press Return.

   You have created a dummy directory for nfsd to share. You can use any directory name. This directory will not contain any files. Its sole purpose is to wake up the NFS daemon so that it notices the shared media drive.

4. Add the following entry to the /etc/dfs/dfstab file.

   share -F nfs -o ro [-d *comment***]** */dummy-dir*

   When you start the NFS daemon, it sees this entry, wakes up, and notices the shared media drive. The -d *comment* is optional.

5. Type **/etc/init.d/nfs.server start** and press Return.

   NFS services are restarted.

6. Type **ps -ef | grep nfsd** and press Return.

   Review the output to verify that the NFS daemon (nfsd) is running.

7. Type **eject** *medium* and press Return.

   You have ejected any medium currently in the drive.

8. Type **chmod 644 /etc/rmmount.conf** and press Return.

   You have assigned root write permissions to the /etc/rmmount.conf file.

9. Add the following lines to the /etc/rmmount.conf file.

   # File System Sharing
   share *media**

   These lines share any medium loaded into your system's CD-ROM drive. You can, however, limit sharing to a particular CD or series of CDs, as described in share(1M).

10. Type **chmod 444 /etc/rmmount.conf** and press Return.

    You have removed write permissions from the /etc/rmmount.conf file and returned the file to its default permissions.

11. Load the medium.

    Any medium loaded into this system's drive is available to other systems. Remember to wait until the light on the drive stops blinking before you verify this task.

12. Type **share** and press Return.

    Review the output and verify that the medium is shared.

The following example makes a local CD available to other systems on the network when the nfsd daemon is not running.

```
# ps -ef | grep nfsd
#
# mkdir /dummy
# vi /etc/dfs/dfstab
(Add the following line:).
```

```
share -F nfs -o ro /dummy
# eject /cdrom/cdrom0
# chmod 644 /etc/rmmount.conf
# vi /etc/rmmount.conf
```
(Add the following line to the FIle System Sharing section)
```
share cdrom*
# chmod 444 /etc/rmmount.conf
# /etc/init.d/nfs.server start
# ps -ef | grep nfsd
   root   577      1  0 10:51:55 ?        0:00 /usr/lib/nfs/nfsd
# share
-                   /dummy   ro    " "
#
```

The following example uses the ps command to verify that the mountd daemon is not already running, and if you are superuser, it runs the S15nfs.server script to stop NFS services and restart them.

```
oak% ps -ef | grep mountd
   root   4571   4473  5 12:53:51 pts/3    0:00 grep mountd
oak% su
Password:
# /etc/rc3.d/S15nfs.server stop
# /etc/rc3.d/S15nfs.server start
#
```

How to Access an NFS-Shared CD-ROM File System   You can use the /mnt directory as the mount point for the CD-ROM files, or you can create another directory.

> *NOTE. Do not use the /cdrom mount point to mount NFS file systems. Volume management may interfere with accessing files on the volume management /cdrom mount point.*

When the CD-ROM is in the remote drive and the files are shared by NFS, use the following steps to access the shared files on a local system.

1. On the local system, become superuser.

2. All on one line, type **mount -F nfs -o ro nfs-server:/cdrom/cdrom0 /mount-point** and press Return.

    The files from the remote system directory /cdrom/cdrom0 are mounted on the /mount-point directory. The cdrom0 subdirectory is symbolically linked to the actual name of the CD-ROM that has a name assigned by the application vendor.

The following example mounts the files from the remote system `castle` on the /mnt mount point.

```
oak% su
Password:
# mount -F nfs -o ro castle:/cdrom/cdrom0 /mnt
# cd /mnt
# ls
SUNWssser   SUNWsssra   SUNWsssrb   SUNWsssrc   SUNWsssrd   SUNWssstr
#
```

How to Unmount an NFS-Shared CD-ROM File System   When you are through using the CD-ROM files, use the following steps to unmount the remote CD-ROM file system.

1. On the local system, become superuser.
2. Type **cd** and press Return.
3. Type **umount /*mount-point*** and press Return.

   The files from the remote system directory /cdrom/cdrom0 are unmounted.

How to Find Out If an NFS-Mounted CD-ROM File System Is Still in Use
If a `Device busy` error message is displayed when you try to unmount a CD-ROM, you can use the `fuser` command to find out who is currently accessing the CD.

1. Become superuser.
2. Type **fuser -u /cdrom/cdrom0** and press Return.

   The process ID and user name of those currently accessing the CD are displayed.
3. Type **fuser -u -k /cdrom/cdrom0** and press Return.

   The processes accessing the CD are killed.
4. Type **eject cdrom** and press Return, or choose Eject from the File menu in the CD File Manager window.

In the following example, user `winsor` is accessing the CD.

```
paperbark% eject cdrom
/vol/dev/rdsk/c0t6d0/s8ap_doc: Device busy
paperbark% su
Password:
# fuser -u /cdrom/cdrom0
/cdrom/cdrom0:        467c(winsor)
# fuser -u -k /cdrom/cdrom0
# eject cdrom
# exit
paperbark%
```

Diskettes and Volume Management

When you insert a diskette into the diskette drive, to prevent excessive reads, volume management does not mount the diskette automatically. Excessive reads can quickly wear out the diskette drive. You must use the `volcheck` command that checks for the presence of a diskette in the diskette drive.

Limitation on UFS Formats with Volume Management for Diskettes

UFS formats are not portable between architectures, so you must use them on the architecture for which they were formatted. For example, a UFS diskette formatted for a SPARC platform cannot be recognized by an IA platform. Likewise, an IA UFS diskette cannot be mounted by volume management on a SPARC platform. The same limitation applies to CDs.

UFS incompatibility can occur more often with diskettes than with CDs because formats often can be established by the user. Be aware that if you format a UFS diskette on one architecture, you won't be able to use it on a different architecture.

Command-Line Diskette Formatting (rmformat)

New!

The `rmformat` command, introduced in the Solaris 8 release, was buggy. The bugs in `rmformat` are fixed in the Solaris 9 release, and `rmformat` is preferred command for formatting removable media.

Use the following steps to format a diskette from a command line with the `rmformat` command.

> NOTE. *If the diskette does not have a file system written on it, the* `volcheck` *command accesses the device. However, if the diskette already has a file system on it, you cannot use the* `volcheck` *command to mount the file system on the diskette.* `rmformat` *requires an unmounted diskette for formatting.*

1. Insert a diskette into the diskette drive.
2. Type **rmformat -F quick floppy0** and press Return to format and partition the diskette.

    Use **fdformat -d** to format an MS-DOS file system. `rmformat` does not provide an MS-DOS formatting option.
3. When prompted, type **y** and press Return to begin formatting the diskette.

    When formatting is complete, the prompt is redisplayed. The `rmformat` command automatically creates a new file system on the diskette.

The following example formats a diskette on a system running volume management.

```
mopoke% rmformat -F quick floppy0
Formatting will erase all the data on the disk.
Do you want to continue? (y/n) y
mopoke%
```

Command-Line Diskette Formatting (fdformat)

NOTE. Starting with the Solaris 8 release, fdformat *has been superseded by the* rmformat(1) *command, which provides most* fdformat *functionality.*

New!

Use the following steps to format a diskette from a command line with the fdformat command.

1. Insert a diskette into the diskette drive.
2. Type **volcheck** and press Return.

   The system has access to the unformatted diskette.
3. Type **fdformat** and press Return to format the diskette so that you can later write a UFS file system on it, or **fdformat -d** to format a diskette and immediately write an MS-DOS file system to it.
4. When prompted, press Return to begin formatting the diskette.
5. For UFS file systems, you must also make a new file system on the diskette. To do so, become superuser and type
   newfs /vol/dev/rdiskette0/unnamed_floppy, and press Return.

Use the following steps to access files on a formatted diskette.

1. Insert a formatted diskette in the diskette drive.
2. Type **volcheck** and press Return.

   If there is a formatted diskette in the drive, volume management mounts it on a subdirectory of the /floppy mount point. If no diskette is in the drive, no error message is displayed. The volcheck command redisplays the prompt. When the diskette is mounted on the /floppy subdirectory mount point, you can access files on it either from the command line or from the File Manager Floppy window, described in "CDE File Manager Access" on page 281.
3. Type **cd /floppy** and press Return.
4. Type **ls** and press Return.

   The name of the diskette is displayed.
5. Type **cd *diskette-name*** and press Return.

6. Type **ls** and press Return.

   The names of the files on the diskette are displayed. You can copy files to and from the diskette with the cp command.

In the following example, the diskette is not mounted, so the only directory in /floppy is ms-dos_5. After volcheck mounts the diskette, the directory with the name of the diskette is displayed. The diskette in this example contains only a lost+found directory.

```
oak% cd /floppy
oak% ls
ms-dos_5
oak% volcheck
oak% ls
ms-dos_5          unnamed_floppy
oak% cd unnamed_floppy
oak% ls
lost+found
oak% cp /home/winsor/Appx/appxA.doc .
oak% ls
appxA.doc lost+found
oak%
```

Determining If a Diskette Is Still in Use

You cannot unmount a file system whose current working directory is in use. If you get the message Device busy, a process has its current working directory on the diskette. You can use the fuser command to find out who is currently accessing the diskette.

1. Become superuser.

2. Type **fuser -u /floppy/floppy0** and press Return.

   The process ID and user name of those currently accessing the diskette are displayed.

3. Type **fuser -u -k /floppy/floppy0** and press Return.

   The processes accessing the diskette are killed.

4. Type **eject floppy0** and press Return.

NOTE. On a SPARC platform, the diskette is physically ejected from its drive. On an IA platform, you have to eject the diskette by hand. If you are running on an IA platform, look for a message on screen that says you can now eject the diskette. If the diskette jams, eject it manually by inserting a straightened paper clip about an inch into the small hole in the front of the drive.

Ejecting a Diskette

Use the following steps to eject the diskette.

1. Type **cd** and press Return.

    You have changed out of the /floppy directory.
2. Type **eject** and press Return.

    After a few seconds, the diskette is ejected from the drive.

Accessing the CDE Front Panel

If you are running CDE, you can use the Folders menu on the front panel to display the contents of a diskette. Use the following steps to open a diskette from the front panel.

1. Insert a formatted or unformatted diskette into the diskette drive.
2. From the front panel, open the Folders menu, shown in Figure 6, and click on Open Floppy.

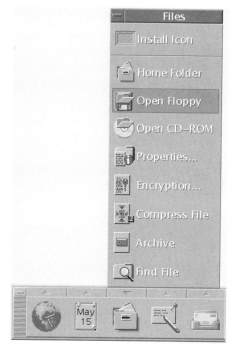

Figure 6   *Front Panel Files Menu*

3. If the diskette is unformatted, the Format Floppy window is displayed, as shown in Figure 7.

```
┌─────────────────────────────────────────────┐
│ ─            Format Floppy                  ◿│
│                                              │
│   Are you sure you want to format this floppy?│
│                                              │
│   Warning: Formatting will destroy any information│
│   on the floppy and is not undoable.         │
│                                              │
│       Format:        UNIX          ⊐         │
│                                              │
│   Disk Name: I                               │
│                                              │
├─────────────────────────────────────────────┤
│    │Format│  Cancel   Cancel & Eject  Help   │
└─────────────────────────────────────────────┘
```

Figure 7   *Format Floppy Window*

4. Choose the format, type a diskette name in the text field if you want to assign one, and click the Format button.

    The diskette is formatted and a new file system is created. When the diskette is formatted and contains the file system, the File Manager Floppy window displays the contents of the diskette. The floppy is mounted to a subdirectory of the /floppy directory and a File Manager window opens.

    If the diskette is already formatted, after the light on the front panel stops flashing (about 5 to 10 seconds), the floppy is mounted to a subdirectory of the /floppy directory and a File Manager window opens. Figure 8 shows an example of the File Manager floppy window for a formatted diskette.

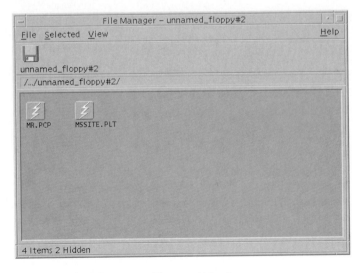

Figure 8   *The CDE File Manager Floppy Window*

CDE File Manager Access

If you are running CDE File Manager, you can use it to format a diskette, display the contents, and copy files to and from the diskette. Use the following steps to open a diskette from the CDE File Manager.

1. Insert a formatted or unformatted diskette into the diskette drive.
2. From the File Manager File menu, shown in Figure 9, choose Open Floppy.

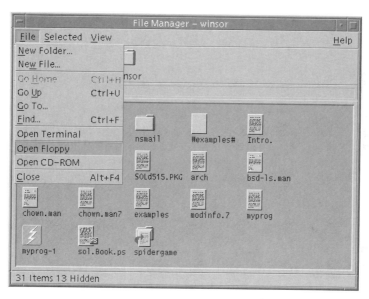

Figure 9   The CDE File Manager Menu

If the disk is unformatted, the Format Floppy window is displayed. If the disk is formatted, the File Manager window display shows the contents of the diskette.

3. From the File Manager File menu you can also eject, format, and rename the diskette, as shown by the menu items in Figure 10.

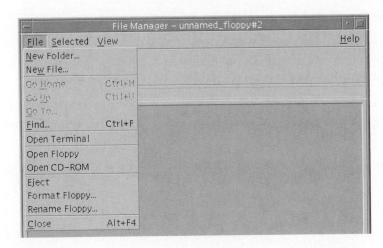

Figure 10   The CDE File Manager Floppy Menu

Using Removable Media Manager to Format Diskettes

New!

You can use the Removable Media Manager graphical user interface to create the following formats and file systems on a diskette.

- PCFS (DOS).
- UFS (UNIX).
- UDFS.
- NEC DOS.

You can format an unformatted diskette or reformat a formatted diskette.

CAUTION. Reformatting a diskette destroys any existing data on the diskette.

Use the following steps to format a diskette with Removable Media Manager.

1. Insert the diskette you want to format in the diskette drive.
2. Choose Open Floppy from the CDE Front Panel Files menu, or, in a Terminal window, type `volcheck` and press Return.

   The command checks the diskette drive and mounts a formatted diskette if found. If volume management finds an unformatted diskette in the drive, the diskette is not mounted. Instead, it is made visible as a raw device to the Removable Media Manager, as indicated by the (`...unformatted`) message and a dash (-) instead of the normal number used to indicate which instance of the diskette is mounted.

3. From the CDE Front Panel Files menu, choose Removable Media
   Manager.

   The Removable Media Manager window opens and displays any
   mounted media on the system. In the example shown in Figure 11, an
   unformatted diskette is the only available medium.

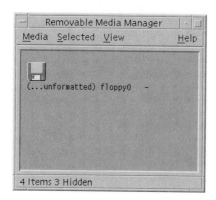

Figure 11   Removable Media Manager Window

4. Click on the diskette icon.

   The diskette is highlighted to show that you selected it.

5. From the Selected menu, choose Format.

   The Media Format window is displayed, as shown in Figure 12.

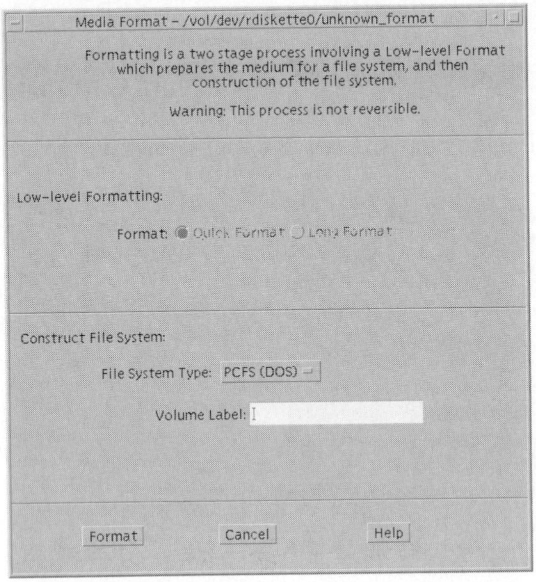

Figure 12   *Removable Media Manager Media Format Window*

6. Choose the file system type from the File System Type menu.

7. (Optional) Type a label in the Volume Label field if you want to assign a name to the device.

8. Click on the Format button.

   The diskette icon is removed from the Removable Media Manager window, and the Format button in the Format window is dimmed. No other status information is displayed while the diskette is formatting. When the diskette is formatted, a notice is displayed, as shown in Figure 13.

Figure 13   *Notice of Successful Formatting*

The icon in the Removable Media Manager window is updated to show the new format and volume name (if assigned), as shown in Figure 14.

Figure 14   Removable Media Manager Window

Using the tar and cpio Commands with Diskettes

If a diskette contains a raw `tar` or `cpio` datastream, volume management does not mount it. You cannot access files on the diskette from the old `/dev/rdiskette` device name.

You can access raw `tar` and `cpio` datastreams on a diskette by using the symbolic link to the character device for the media that is in floppy drive 0 with the following device name.

```
/vol/dev/aliases/floppy0
```

Use the following steps to create a `tar` archive that contains a single file.

1. Insert a formatted diskette into the diskette drive.
2. Type **volcheck** and press Return.
3. Type **tar cvf /vol/dev/aliases/floppy0** *filename* and press Return.

    The files are copied to the diskette.
4. Type **eject** and press Return.

    After a few seconds, the diskette is ejected.

Use the following steps to copy all `tar` files from a diskette.

1. Insert a formatted diskette into the diskette drive.
2. Change to the directory into which you want to put the files.
3. Type **volcheck** and press Return.

    Volume manager creates the proper device files under `/vol/dev` so that you can access the raw device.

4. Type **tar xvf /vol/dev/aliases/floppy0** and press Return.

   The files are extracted from the raw `tar` datastream on the diskette.

5. Type **eject** and press Return.

   After a few seconds, the diskette is ejected.

Alternatively, with Solaris 2.2 (and later) systems, you can access `tar` or `cpio` files by using the following device name syntax.

```
/vol/dev/rfd0/media-name
```

The most common *media-name* is `unlabeled`.

With Solaris 2.3, the device name syntax is changed. You access `tar` or `cpio` files with the following device name syntax.

```
/vol/dev/rdiskette0/media-name
```

The most frequent *media-name* for media without a file system is `unlabeled`.

For example, to put files into a `tar` archive that is sent as a raw datastream to the raw diskette device, type
tar cvf /vol/dev/rdiskette0/unlabeled *filename* and press Return. To read a raw `tar` archive datastream from the raw diskette device and extract the files it contains, type
tar xvf /vol/dev/rdiskette0/unlabeled and press Return.

Volume Management Troubleshooting

From time to time, you may encounter problems with mounting diskettes (or, less frequently, a CD-ROM). If you encounter a problem, first check to find out whether volume management knows about the diskette. The best way to check is to look in `/vol/dev/rdiskette0` to see if something is there. If the diskette device files don't exist, you may have forgotten to run the `volcheck` command or you may have a hardware problem. If references to `/vol` hang, the `/usr/sbin/vold` daemon has probably died, and you should restart it by typing **/etc/init.d/volmgt start** and pressing Return.

If you find a name in `/vol/dev/rdiskette0` and nothing is mounted in `/floppy/`*media-name,* it is likely that the data on the medium is not a recognized file system. It may be a `tar`, `cpio`, or Macintosh file system. You can access these media through the block or character devices found in `/vol/dev/rdiskette0` or `/vol/dev/diskette0` and use your own tools to interpret the data on them.

Volume Management and workman

Many people use the workman program to play music from their CD-ROM
drive. workman is not a Sun product, but it is in wide use. To use workman
with volume management, add the line shown in bold to the
/etc/rmmount.conf file. Be sure the line comes before the cdrom
action_filemgr line.

```
# ident      "@(#)rmmount.conf     1.12      00/08/29 SMI"
#
# Removable Media Mounter configuration file.
#

# File system identification
ident udfs ident_udfs.so cdrom floppy rmdisk
ident hsfs ident_hsfs.so cdrom
ident ufs ident_ufs.so cdrom floppy rmdisk pcmem
ident pcfs ident_pcfs.so floppy rmdisk pcmem

# Actions
action cdrom action_workman.so pathname
action cdrom action_filemgr.so
action floppy action_filemgr.so
action rmdisk action_filemgr.so

# Mount
mount * hsfs udfs ufs -o nosuid
```

A *pathname* is the name of the path by which users access the workman
program—for example, /usr/dist/exe/workman.

When you have made this change, audio CD-ROMs are automatically
detected and the workman program is started when an audio CD-ROM is
inserted into the CD-ROM drive.

NOTE. When you set up workman *in the way described here, you
should not try to start* workman *from the application because volume
management may become confused. In addition, with Solaris 2.2 (and
later) volume management, if you are using* workman, *you must eject
the CD-ROM from the* workman *application. If you eject the CD-ROM
from another window,* workman *hangs. This problem is fixed in
Solaris 2.3 and later system software.*

Disabling Volume Management

You may want to disable volume management for some users. To do so, use
the following steps.

1. Become superuser.
2. Remove or rename the /etc/rc2.d/S92volmgt script.
3. Type **/etc/init.d/volmgt stop** and press Return.

You can disable part of volume management and leave other parts functional. You may, for example, want to automatically mount CD-ROMs but use the Solaris 2.0 method for accessing files on a diskette. You can do so by commenting out the lines for diskettes in the /etc/vold.conf file, as shown below.

```
# ident      "@(#)vold.conf    1.26    00/07/17 SMI"
#
# Volume Daemon Configuration file
#

# Database to use (must be first)
db db_mem.so

# Labels supported
label cdrom label_cdrom.so cdrom
label dos label_dos.so floppy rmdisk pcmem
label sun label_sun.so floppy rmdisk pcmem

# Devices to use
use cdrom drive /dev/rdsk/c*s2 dev_cdrom.so cdrom%d
# use floppy drive /dev/rdiskette[0-9] dev_floppy.so floppy%d
use pcmem drive /dev/rdsk/c*s2 dev_pcmem.so pcmem%d forceload=true
use rmdisk drive /dev/rdsk/c*s2 dev_rmdisk.so rmdisk%d

# Actions
eject dev/diskette[0-9]/* user=root /usr/sbin/rmmount
eject dev/dsk/* user=root /usr/sbin/rmmount
insert dev/diskette[0-9]/* user=root /usr/sbin/rmmount
insert dev/dsk/* user=root /usr/sbin/rmmount
notify rdsk/* group=tty user=root /usr/lib/vold/volmissing -p
remount dev/diskette[0-9]/* user=root /usr/sbin/rmmount
remount dev/dsk/* user=root /usr/sbin/rmmount

# List of file system types unsafe to eject
unsafe ufs hsfs pcfs udfs
```

Using Diskettes Without Volume Management

Use double-sided (DS), high-density (HD) 3.5-inch diskettes. Before you can copy UFS files or file systems to diskette, you must format the diskette. Use the tar command to copy UFS files to a single formatted diskette. Use cpio if you need to copy UFS files to multiple formatted diskettes. The cpio command recognizes end of media and prompts you to insert the next volume.

You also can make a DOS file system on a diskette. To use a DOS-formatted diskette, you mount the diskette as a PCFS file system and use basic OS commands such as cp and mv to archive and retrieve files from the diskette.

Diskette Device Names

The device name for the diskette drive in the Solaris Operating Environment is /dev/diskette. The raw device file for a diskette is /dev/rdiskette.

Diskettes for UFS File Systems

The following sections describe how to format diskettes for use with UFS file systems and how to copy files with the `tar` and `cpio` commands. They also describe how to retrieve files that were created with the SunOS 4.x `bar` command.

Formatting a UFS Diskette (rmformat)

New!

The `rmformat` command, introduced in the Solaris 8 release, was buggy. The bugs to `rmformat` are fixed in the Solaris 9 release, and `rmformat` is the preferred command for formatting removable media.

Use the following steps to format a diskette by using the `rmformat` command from a command line.

NOTE. Do not use the `volcheck` *command to mount the diskette.* `rmformat` *requires an unmounted diskette for formatting.*

1. Insert a diskette into the diskette drive.
2. Type **rmformat -F quick /dev/rdiskette** and press Return to format the diskette.
3. When prompted, type **y** and press Return to begin formatting the diskette.
   When formatting is complete, the prompt is redisplayed.

The following example formats a diskette on a system not running volume management.

```
mopoke% rmformat -F quick /dev/rdiskette
Formatting will erase all the data on the disk.
Do you want to continue? (y/n) y
mopoke%
```

Formatting a UFS Diskette (fdformat)

NOTE. Starting with the Solaris 8 release, `fdformat` *has been superseded by the* `rmformat(1)` *command, which provides most* `fdformat` *functionality.*

New!

Use the following steps to format a diskette for use with Solaris UFS file systems.

1. Check the diskette to make sure that it is not write-protected.
2. Put the diskette in the drive.

CAUTION. Reformatting destroys any files already on the diskette.

3. Type **fdformat** and press Return.

The message `Press return to start formatting floppy` is displayed.

4. Press Return.

    While the diskette is being formatted, a series of dots (. . .) is displayed. When formatting is complete, the prompt is redisplayed.

```
oak%
Press return to start formatting floppy.
..................................................................
oak%
```

Removing a Diskette from the Drive

Use the `eject` command to remove a diskette from the disk drive. You can also use the `eject` command to remove a CD-ROM disc from a CD-ROM drive. The default for the `eject` command is `/dev/diskette` when you type it with no arguments. To remove a diskette from the diskette drive, type **eject** and press Return. The diskette is ejected.

NOTE. If the drive jams, you can eject a diskette manually by inserting a straightened wire paper clip into the pinhole under the diskette slot.

To eject a CD-ROM disc from a CD-ROM drive, type **eject cdrom** and press Return.

Copying UFS Files to a Single Formatted Diskette

This section provides steps for using the `tar` command to copy raw files to a single formatted diskette. Note that the `tar` command does not require the raw device name, `/dev/rdiskette`. You can use either the `/dev/rdiskette` or `/dev/diskette` device name. The examples in this book use the raw device name.

Use the following steps to copy UFS files to a single formatted diskette.

1. Change to the directory that contains the file(s) you want to copy.
2. Insert a write-enabled formatted diskette into the drive.

CAUTION. Copying files to a formatted diskette with the c *option destroys any files already on the diskette. If you want to preserve the files already on the diskette, use the* r *option described in "Appending Files to a Formatted Diskette (tar)" on page 291.*

3. Type **tar cvf /dev/rdiskette** *filename filename filename...* and press Return.

    The file names you specify are copied to the diskette, overwriting any existing files on the diskette.

*NOTE. You can use metacharacters (? and *) as part of the file names you specify. For example, to copy all documents with a* .doc *suffix, type* ***.doc** *as the file-name argument.*

4. Type **eject** and press Return to remove the diskette from the drive.
   The diskette is ejected from the drive.

5. Write the names of the files on the diskette label.

The following example copies two files to a diskette.

```
oak% cd /home/winsor
oak% ls evaluation*
evaluation.doc    evaluation.doc.backup
oak% tar cvf /dev/rdiskette evaluation*
a evaluation.doc 86 blocks
a evaluation.doc.backup 84 blocks
oak% eject
oak%
```

Listing the Files on a Diskette (tar)

Use the following steps to list files that were copied with the tar command.

1. Insert a diskette into the drive.

2. Type **tar tvf /dev/rdiskette** and press Return.
   The t option lists the table of contents for the files on the diskette.

In the following example, the table of contents for the diskette contains two files.

```
oak% tar tvf /dev/rdiskette
rw-rw-rw-6693/10   44032 Apr 23 14:54 2000 evaluation.doc
rw-rw-rw-6693/10   43008 Apr 23 14:47 2000 evaluation.doc.backup
oak%
```

See the tar(1) manual page for more information.

If you need a multiple-volume interchange command, use cpio. The tar command is only a single-volume command.

Appending Files to a Formatted Diskette (tar)

When you copy tar files to a formatted diskette, any files already on the diskette are overwritten. If you want to add other files but keep the files already on the diskette, use the following steps.

1. Change to the directory that contains the file you want to copy.

2. Insert a write-enabled formatted diskette into the drive.

3. Type **tar rvf /dev/rdiskette** *filename filename filename...* and press Return.

The file names you specify are appended to the files already on the diskette.

*NOTE. You can use metacharacters (? and *) as part of the file names you specify. For example, to copy all documents with a* .doc *suffix, type* ***.doc** *as the file-name argument.*

4. Type **eject** and press Return to remove the diskette from the drive.

The diskette is ejected from the drive.

5. Write the names of the additional files on the diskette label.

The following example appends one file to the files already on the diskette.

```
oak% cd /home/winsor
oak% tar rvf /dev/rdiskette junk
a junk 1 blocks
oak% tar tvf /dev/rdiskette
rw-rw-rw-6693/10   44032 Apr 23 14:54 2000 evaluation.doc
rw-rw-rw-6693/10   43008 Apr 23 14:47 2000 evaluation.doc.backup
rw-rw-rw-6693/10      18 Dec 10 11:36 2000 junk
oak% eject
oak%
```

Retrieving Files from a Diskette (tar)

Use the following steps to retrieve all files from a diskette.

1. Change to the directory into which you want to put the files.
2. Insert the diskette into the drive.
3. Type **tar xvf /dev/rdiskette** and press Return.

All the files on the diskette are copied to the current directory.

4. Type **eject** and press Return to remove the diskette from the drive.

The diskette is ejected from the drive.

The following example copies all files from the diskette.

```
oak% cd /home/winsor/Evaluations
oak% tar xvf /dev/rdiskette
x evaluation.doc, 44032 bytes, 86 tape blocks
x evaluation.doc.backup, 43008 bytes, 84 tape blocks
oak% eject
oak%
```

To retrieve individual files from a diskette, type
tar xvf /dev/rdiskette *filename filename filename...* and press Return. The file names you specify are extracted from the diskette and placed

in the current working directory. The following example copies all files with the prefix `evaluation` from the diskette.

```
oak% cd /home/winsor/Evaluations
oak% tar xvf /dev/rdiskette
x evaluation.doc, 44032 bytes, 86 tape blocks
x evaluation.doc.backup, 43008 bytes, 84 tape blocks
oak% eject
oak%
```

Retrieving bar Files from Diskettes (cpio)

The SunOS 4.x `bar` command is not provided with the Solaris Operating Environment. You can retrieve files from diskettes that were archived with the SunOS 4.x `bar` command by using the `-H bar` option to `cpio`.

> *NOTE. You can use the* `-H bar` *option with* `-i` *to retrieve files only. You cannot create files with the* `bar` *header option. It is good practice to list the contents of an archive before extracting them.*

Use the following steps to retrieve `bar` files from a diskette.

1. Change to the directory into which you want to put the files.
2. Insert the diskette that contains `bar` files into the drive.
3. Type **cpio -ivH bar < /dev/diskette** and press Return.
   All the files on the diskette are copied to the current directory.
4. Type **eject** and press Return to remove the diskette from the drive.

Multiple Diskettes for Archiving Files (cpio)

If you are copying large files or file systems onto diskettes, you want to be prompted to replace a full diskette with another formatted diskette. The `cpio` command provides this capability. The `cpio` options you use are the same as you would use to copy files to tape, except you would specify `/dev/rdiskette` as the device instead of the tape device name. See "The cpio Command" on page 250 for information on how to use `cpio`.

Making a UFS File System on a Diskette (newfs /dev/rdiskette)

If you want to mount a formatted UFS diskette, you must first create a file system on it.

1. Format the diskette.
2. Become superuser.
3. Type **newfs /dev/rdiskette** and press Return.

A UFS file system is created on the formatted diskette, as shown in the following example.

```
oak% fdformat
Press return to start formatting floppy.
.............................................................................
oak% su
Password:
# newfs /dev/rdiskette
#
```

Diskettes for PCFS (DOS) File Systems

You can format diskettes with the PCFS file system for use with DOS systems. The following sections describe how to format a DOS diskette and how to mount the diskette for use with the Solaris Operating Environment. See "Types of File Systems" on page 182 for a description of the PCFS file system.

Formatting a Diskette with a PCFS (DOS) File System

New!

NOTE. Starting with the Solaris 8 release, fdformat *has been superseded by the* rmformat(1) *command, which provides most* fdformat *functionality. However, the* rmformat *command does not provide an option for formatting PCFS file systems.*

Use the following steps to format a diskette with the PCFS file system.

1. Put a diskette in the drive.

CAUTION. Reformatting destroys any files already on the diskette.

2. Type **fdformat -d** and press Return.

   The message Press return to start formatting floppy is displayed.

3. Press Return.

   While the diskette is being formatted, a series of dots (. . .) is displayed. When formatting is complete, the prompt is redisplayed, as shown in the following example.

```
oak% fdformat -d
Press return to start formatting floppy.
.............................................................................
oak%
```

Mounting a PCFS Diskette

You can mount a PCFS diskette that was formatted with the fdformat -d command, or a DOS diskette that was formatted on a DOS system. When you mount a PCFS file system, you can create, read, write, and delete files in the file system with Solaris file commands, subject to DOS naming conventions. See the pcfs(7) manual page for more information about the format and features of the PCFS file system.

Use the following steps to mount a PCFS file system from a diskette.

1. Insert the PCFS diskette in the drive.
2. Become superuser.
3. Type **mount -F pcfs /dev/diskette *mount-point*** and press Return.

    The file system is mounted on the *mount-point* you specify.

You can mount a PCFS file system with different mount options (for example, -o rw). See the mount_pcfs(1M) manual page for a description of the options that can be included in the list.

If you use PCFS diskettes frequently, you may want to add the following entry to your /etc/vfstab file.

```
/dev/diskette    -    /pcfs    pcfs    -    no    rw
```

Create a directory named /pcfs to use as the mount point for the diskette. With the mount point and the entry in the /etc/vfstab file, you can mount a PCFS diskette by becoming superuser and typing **mount /pcfs** and pressing Return. Once the diskette is mounted, you can use any of the Solaris file commands such as cp or mv to copy files to and from the diskette.

Unmounting a PCFS Diskette

When you are done with the PCFS diskette, you must unmount it before you can eject it. To unmount the diskette, first make sure the current working directory is not in the mount point directory or any of its subdirectories. Then, type **umount *mount-point*** and press Return. To eject the diskette, type **eject** and press Return.

Administering Disks

The following sections describe the Solaris disk-naming conventions, commands for finding disk information (du, prtvtoc), and ways to repair or replace a bad disk.

Disk-Naming Conventions

Solaris disks have both block and raw (character) device files. The device name is the same, regardless of whether the command requires the block or raw device file.

Each type of device file has its own subdirectory in /dev: /dev/dsk (the block interface) or /dev/rdsk (the raw interface).

Some commands, such as mount, use the block interface device name from the /dev/dsk directory to specify the disk device. Other commands, such as newfs, require the raw interface device name from the /dev/rdsk directory to specify the disk device.

New! Raw device interfaces transfer only small amounts of data at a time. To use a raw device, you specify the device in the /dev/rdsk subdirectory. The r in rdisk stands for raw.

New! Block device interfaces include a buffer from which large blocks of data are read at one time. When a command requires the block device interface, you specify the /dev/dsk subdirectory.

The device name you use to identify a specific disk with either type of interface depends on the controller type: bus-oriented (SCSI) or direct. You refer to a disk device by specifying the subdirectory to which it is symbolically linked (either /dev/dsk or /dev/rdsk) followed by a string identifying the particular controller, disk, and slice.

```
/dev/[r]dsk/cwtxdysz
```

c*w* is the controller number, t*x* is the target number, d*y* is the drive number, and s*z* is the slice identifier. For SCSI drives, the drive number is the equivalent of the Logical Unit Number (LUN) of the drive.

Table 69 shows which interface to use for a few frequently used disk and file system commands.

Table 69   Device Interface Type for Some Frequently Used Commands

Command	Interface Type	Example
df (1M)	Block	df /dev/dsk/c0t1d0s0
fsck	Raw	fsck -p /dev/rdsk/c0t0d0s0
mount (1M)	Block	mount /dev/dsk/c1t0d0s7 /export/home
newfs (1M)	Raw	newfs /dev/rdsk/c0t0d1s1
prtvtoc (1M)	Raw	prtvtoc /dev/rdsk/c0t0d0s2

Using Disks with Bus Controllers

Figure 15 shows the device-naming convention for SPARC disks with bus controllers.

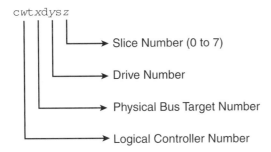

Figure 15   Naming Conventions for SPARC Disks with Bus Controllers

Figure 16 shows naming conventions for IA disks with SCSI controllers.

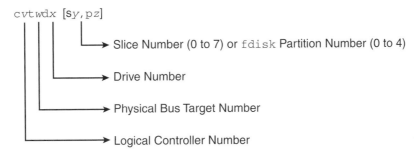

Figure 16   Naming Conventions for IA Disks with Bus Controllers

Each file system on a disk is assigned to a *slice*—a group of cylinders set aside for use by that file system. To specify a slice (partition) on a disk with a bus controller (either SCSI or IPI), use a device name with these conventions: `/dev/dsk/cWtXdYsZ` (the block interface) or `/dev/rdsk/cWtXdYsZ` (the raw interface).

> *NOTE. Solaris disk device names use the term* slice *(and the letter* s *in the device name) to refer to the slice number.* Slice *is simply another name for a disk partition.*

Use the following guidelines to determine the values for the device file name.

- If you have only one controller on your system, *W* is always 0.
- For SCSI controllers, *X* is the target address set by the switch on the back of or inside the unit.

- Y is the Logical Unit Number (LUN) of the drive attached to the target. If the disk has an embedded controller, Y is always 0.
- Z is the slice (partition) number, with a value ranging from 0 to 7. Slice 2 is known as the backup slice and should never be used directly. Table 70 shows conventional assignments of slice (partition) numbers for the disk on which root is found.

Table 70   *Conventional Assignments of Slices for Boot Disk*

Slice	File System	Use
0	root	Operating system.
1	swap	Virtual memory space.
2	–	Entire disk.
3-5		Available for use according to your administrative policy.
6	/usr	Executable programs, program libraries, and documentation.

Table 71 shows some examples of raw device names for disks with bus-oriented controllers.

Table 71   *Examples of Device Names for Disks with Bus-Oriented Controllers*

Device Name	Description
/dev/rdsk/c0t0d0s0	Raw interface to the first slice (root) on the first LUN (disk) at the first SCSI target address on the first controller.
/dev/rdsk/c0t0d0s2	Raw interface to the third LUN (which represents the whole disk) on the first disk at the first SCSI target address on the first controller.
/dev/rdsk/c0t1d0s6	Raw interface to seventh (/usr) slice on the first LUN (disk) at the second SCSI target address on the first controller.

NOTE. In releases before the Solaris 7 Operating Environment, SCSI support on the Intel platform was handled by the cmdk *driver. Starting with the Solaris 7 release, this support is handled by the* sd *driver. This driver is similar to the SCSI disk driver on Solaris SPARC platforms, which is also named* sd.

There is no change in the administration of these devices. You will see references to sd *instead of* cmdk *in the output of the* prtconf, sysdef, dmesg, *and* format *commands.*

Features and functionality are a superset of the features supplied by cmdk, *so applications that use logical disk names in* /dev/dsk *are not affected by the driver change. IA systems with IDE devices still use the* cmdk *driver.*

Using Disks with Direct Controllers

Disks with direct controllers do not have a target entry as part of the device name. To specify a slice (partition) on a disk with a direct controller, use a device name with the following conventions: /dev/dsk/c*X*d*Y*s*Z* (the block interface) or /dev/rdsk/c*X*d*Y*s*Z* (the raw interface).

Figure 17 shows the naming convention for SPARC-based disks with direct controllers. If you have only one controller on your system, *X* is always 0. Slice 2 is a guide to the size of the entire disk.

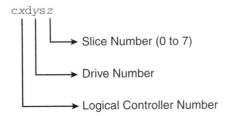

Figure 17   Naming Conventions for SPARC-Based Disks with Direct Controllers

Figure 18 shows the naming convention for IA-based disks with direct controllers.

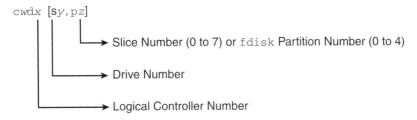

Figure 18   Naming Conventions for IA-Based Disks with Direct Controllers

Use slice 2 (s2) to specify the entire Solaris fdisk partition.

Setting Up Disk Slices

Files are stored within file systems. Each disk slice is treated as a separate disk drive both by the operating system and by the system administrator. When setting up slices, be aware of the following constraints.

- Any disk slice can have a file system written on it.
- No file system can span multiple slices.

You set up slices differently on SPARC and IA platforms, as described in Table 72.

Table 72   Slice Differences on Platforms

SPARC Platform	IA Platform
Entire disk is used for Solaris environment.	Disk is divided into `fdisk` partitions, one per operating environment.
Disk is divided into eight slices, numbered 0–7.	The Solaris `fdisk` partition is divided into 10 slices, numbered 0–9.

SPARC Disk Slices

New!

For SPARC-based systems, Sun recommends that you define only three disk slices, root (/), swap, and the backup slice (slice 2). Table 73 describes additional slice conventions that you can use if you choose.

Table 73   SPARC Disk Slice Conventions

Slice	File System	Client/ Server	Description
0	`root`	Both	Hold files and directories that make up the operating system.
1	`swap`	Both	Provide virtual memory or swap space.
2		Both	By convention, refer to the entire disk. The entire disk is defined automatically by the `format` command and the Solaris installation programs. Do not change the size of this slice.

Table 73   SPARC Disk Slice Conventions (Continued)

Slice	File System	Client/ Server	Description
5	/opt	Both	Hold applications software added to a system. If a slice is not allocated for this file system during installation, the /opt directory is merged into the slice that contains the root (/) file system.
6	/usr	Both	Hold operating system commands—also known as executables—designed to be run by users. This slice also holds documentation, system programs such as init and syslogd, and library routines. If a slice is not allocated for this file system during installation, the /usr directory is merged into the slice that contains the root (/) file system.

NOTE. There is no longer a conventional use for slices 3 and 4.   **New!**

IA Disk Slices

On IA-based systems, you divide disks into fdisk partitions. Each fdisk partition is a section of the disk reserved for a particular operating environment. For a Solaris fdisk partition, you can define 10 slices, numbered from 0 through 9 and assign each to a conventional use. The uses for slices 0–2 and 5–7 are the same as on Solaris systems, described in Table 73. Table 74 describes slices 8 and 9.

Table 74   IA Conventions for Slices 8 and 9

Slice	File System	Client/ Server	Description
8	—	Both	Contain the boot slice information at the beginning of the Solaris partition that enables Solaris to boot from the hard disk.
9	—	Both	Provide an area reserved for alternative disk blocks. Slice 9 is known as the alternative sector slice.

Determining Which Slices to Use

When you set up file systems for a disk, you choose not only the size of each
slice but also which slices to use. Your decisions depend on the configuration
of the system and the software you want to install on the disk. System types
are defined by how they access the root (/) and /usr file systems, including
the swap area. For example, stand-alone and server systems mount these file
systems from a local disk; other clients mount the file system remotely.

In previous releases, you could set up the following five system
configurations.

- Servers.
- Diskless clients.
- Stand-alone systems.
- Dataless clients.
- Solstice AutoClient systems.

With the Solaris 8 release, the system configurations are simplified to
servers, stand-alone systems, and JavaStations. The JavaStation is a client
designed for zero administration. It optimizes Java technology and takes full
advantage of the network to deliver everything from Java applications and
services to complete, integrated system and network management. You do no
local administration for a JavaStation. The server handles booting,
administration, and data storage.

Table 75 summarizes the three system types.

Table 75   System Configurations and Slice Requirements

System Type	Local File Systems	Local Swap	Remote File Systems	Network Use
Server	root (/)	Yes	None	High
	/usr			
	/home			
	/opt			
	/export/home			
	/export/root			
Stand-alone	root (/)	Yes	None	Low
	/usr			
	/export/home			
JavaStation	None	No	/home	High

Disks and SMC

New!

SMC provides two tools in the Storage category, described in Table 76, that you can use to display and format disks.

Table 76   SMC Disks Tools in the Storage Category

Tool	Description
Disks	Display disk information, display partition information, partition disks, copy disk layouts from one disk to a disk of the same size and manufacturer, create `fdisk` partitions, and change the active `fdisk` partition on an IA computer.
Enhanced Storage	Create and manage RAID0 volumes, including stripes and concatenation; RAID1 volumes, including mirrors; RAID5 volumes; soft partitions; hot spare pools; disksets; and the state configuration database (the `metadb`). New in SMC 2.1.

Disk Use Check (du)

To find the number of 512-byte disk blocks used per file or directory, type **du** and press Return. When directories contain subdirectories, the subdirectories and their contents are included in the block count, as shown in the following example.

```
oak% du
2913    ./3.0templates
639     ./Art
347     ./Howto
1998    ./Clipart
607     ./Newtemplates
38      ./Modemstuff
2004    ./Config/Art
6593    ./Config
13280   .
oak%
```

The output is displayed in 512-byte blocks. To convert to megabytes, divide by 2048. In the preceding example, 13280/2048 = 6.48 Mbytes.

Starting with the Solaris 9 release, the du command has an -h option that *New!* you can use to display the output in a user-friendly format, as shown in the following example.

```
mopoke% du -h
   2K    ./.dt/sessionlogs
   1K    ./.dt/types/fp_dynamic
   2K    ./.dt/types
   1K    ./.dt/icons
```

```
   1K    ./.dt/appmanager
  19K    ./.dt/help/winsor-mopoke-0
  20K    ./.dt/help
  11K    ./.dt/sessions/current
  17K    ./.dt/sessions
   1K    ./.dt/tmp
   1K    ./.dt/Trash
   1K    ./.dt/Desktop
   1K    ./.dt/palettes
   2K    ./.dt/.Printers
  56K    ./.dt
   1K    ./.java/.userPrefs
   2K    ./.java
   2K    ./.solregis
  17K    ./.netscape/cache
   1K    ./.netscape/archive
   1K    ./.netscape/xover-cache/host-news
   2K    ./.netscape/xover-cache
 331K    ./.netscape
   1K    ./nsmail
 1.1G    .
mopoke%
```

Disk Information Check (prtvtoc)

Use the prtvtoc (print volume table of contents) command to display
information about disk partitioning. If you use the standard slice-naming
conventions, specifying slice 2 displays the contents of the entire disk.

   Use the following steps to display information about disk partitioning.

   1. Become superuser.
   2. Type **prtvtoc /dev/rdsk/*cntndnsn*** and press Return.

       Information for the disk you specify is displayed, as shown in the
       following example.

```
paperbark% su
Password:
# prtvtoc /dev/rdsk/c0t0d0s2
* /dev/rdsk/c0t0d0s2 partition map
*
* Dimensions:
*     512 bytes/sector
*      80 sectors/track
*      19 tracks/cylinder
*    1520 sectors/cylinder
*    3500 cylinders
*    2733 accessible cylinders
*
* Flags:
*   1: unmountable
*  10: read-only
*
*                          First     Sector    Last
* Partition  Tag  Flags    Sector    Count     Sector   Mount Directory
         0    2    00       1048800   2865200   3913999  /
         1    3    01             0   1048800   1048799
         2    5    00             0   4154160   4154159
         7    8    00       3914000    240160   4154159  /export/home
```

Bad-Disk Repair

The following sections describe the steps for repairing a bad disk or reinstalling a new one.

Try Archiving the Files

If you can access the drive, do a ufsdump of all the file systems on the disk. See "Backing Up and Restoring File Systems" on page 211 for information on how to use the ufsdump command.

Try Copying Data from the Disk

If you cannot run ufsdump on the disk, find another disk of the same type, connect it to the system, and use either the dd or volcopy commands to copy the data from the bad disk. See the dd(1M) and volcopy(1M) manual pages for complete information on how to use these commands.

The dd command makes a literal (block) copy of a complete UFS file system to another file system or to a tape. By default, the dd command copies its standard input to its standard output.

NOTE. Do not use the dd command with variable-length tape drives.

You can specify a device name in place of the standard input, the standard output, or both. The following example copies contents of a diskette to a file in the /tmp directory.

```
oak% dd < /floppy/floppy0 > /tmp/output.file
2400+0 records in
2400+0 records out
oak%
```

The dd command reports on the number of blocks it reads and writes. The number after the + is a count of the partial blocks that were copied.

The dd command syntax is different from most other commands. You specify options as *keyword=value* pairs, where *keyword* is the option you want to set and *value* is the argument for that option. For example, you can replace the standard input and output with the following syntax.

```
dd if=input-file of=output-file
```

The following example uses the *keyword=value* pairs instead of the redirect symbols in the previous example.

```
oak% dd if=/floppy/floppy0 of=/tmp/output.file
```

Use the following steps to clone a disk with the dd command.

1. Make sure the source and destination disks have the same geometry.
2. Become superuser.
3. On the system with the master disk, type **touch /reconfigure** and press Return.

   The /reconfigure file is required on the system with the master disk so that it recognizes the clone disk once it is rebooted.
4. Type **init 0** and press Return to shut down the system.
5. Attach the clone disk to the system and turn on the system.
6. At the ok prompt, type **boot** and press Return.
7. All on one line, type **dd if=/dev/dsk/*device-name* of=/dev/dsk/*device-name* bs=*blocksize*** and press Return.

   The input file, if, is the master disk device. The output file, of, is the clone disk device.
8. Type **fsck /dev/rdsk/*device-name*** and press Return to check the new file system.
9. Type **mount /dev/rdsk/*device-name* /mnt** and press Return to mount the clone disk's root file system.
10. Edit the /etc/vfstab file on the clone disk to reference the correct device names.
11. Type **umount /mnt** and press Return to unmount the clone disk's root file system.
12. Type **init 0** and press Return to shut down the system.
13. Type **boot disk*n* -s** and press Return to boot the clone disk in single-user mode.

    The OpenBoot PROM creates certain well-known disk aliases for disks it expects to be attached to a system. And, the system administrator may have created additional disk aliases when attaching extra disks to a system. Use the appropriate alias for the cloned disk as the disk*n* argument.
14. Type **sys-unconfig** and press Return to unconfigure the clone disk.

    The system is shut down after the disk is unconfigured.
15. Type **boot disk*n*** and press Return to boot the clone disk.
16. Provide the relevant system information such as host name, time zone, and so on.

17. Log in as root to verify the system information once the system has booted, as shown in the following example.

```
oak% su
Password
# dd < /floppy/floppy0 > /tmp/output.file
# boot
(Boot messages)
# dd if=/dev/dsk/c0t0d0s2 of=/dev/dsk/c0t2d0s2 bs=100k
# fsck /dev/rdsk/c0t2d0s2
# mount /dev/dsk/c0t2d0s2 /mnt
# cd /mnt/etc
# vi vfstab
(Modify entries for the new disk)
# cd /
# umount /mnt
# init 0
(Shutdown messages)
# boot disk2 -s
(Boot messages)
# sys-unconfig
# boot disk2
```

Try Repairing Any Bad Blocks

If the disk has bad blocks, you may be able to repair them with the format command. See the format(1M) manual page for more information.

Try Reformatting the Disk

If the disk is bad, reformatting it may fix the problem. Use the format command to reformat a disk. See the format(1M) manual page for more information.

CAUTION. Remember that formatting the disk destroys all data.

Replacing the Bad Disk

If reformatting and repairing bad blocks do not work, replace the disk. See the disk installation manual for more information.

Adding Defect List, Format, Partition, and Label Disk (format)

Use the following steps to put a defect list on a new disk and to format, partition, and label it.

CAUTION. You must format the disk after you add the defect list. Any data on the disk is destroyed by formatting. If the disk is not new, be sure the data is backed up before you proceed. See "Backing Up and Restoring File Systems" on page 211 for complete information on how to back up and restore file systems.

1. Become superuser.
2. Type **format** and press Return.

3. A list of available disks is displayed, as shown in the following example.

```
paperbark% su
# format
Searching for disks...done


AVAILABLE DISK SELECTIONS:
       0. c0t0d0 <SUN2.1G cyl 2733 alt 2 hd 19 sec 80>
          /sbus@1f,0/SUNW,fas@e,8800000/sd@0,0
       1. c0t1d0 <SUN2.1G cyl 2733 alt 2 hd 19 sec 80>
          /sbus@1f,0/SUNW,fas@e,8800000/sd@1,0
Specify disk (enter its number):
```

4. Type the number of the new disk from the list that is displayed.

   The Format menu and the format> prompt are displayed.

5. Type **defect** and press Return.

6. Type **primary** and press Return.

   The original defect list is added to the disk, as shown in the following example.

```
defect> primary
Extracting primary defect list . . . Extraction complete.
Current Defect List updated, \
total of 30 defects.
```

7. Type **quit** and press Return.

   The format> prompt is displayed.

8. Type **format** and press Return.

   The disk begins formatting. Formatting takes about 10 minutes for a 107-Mbyte disk, longer for bigger disks.

9. When the format> prompt is redisplayed, type **partition** and press Return.

10. Re-create the partitions to match the partitions on the defective disk.

11. Type **label** and press Return.

    The disk is labeled.

12. Type **quit** and press Return.

    The Format menu and format> prompt are redisplayed.

13. Type **quit** and press Return.

    The shell prompt is redisplayed, as shown in the following example.

```
oak% su
Password:
# format
Searching for disks...done
```

```
AVAILABLE DISK SELECTIONS:
        0. sd0 at esp0 slave 24
           sd0: <SUN0207 cyl 1254 alt 2 hd 9 sec 36>
        1. sd2 at esp0 slave 16
           sd2: <SUN0207 cyl 1254 alt 2 hd 9 sec 36>
Specify disk (enter its number): 1
selecting c0t0d0
[disk formatted]
FORMAT MENU:
        disk       - select a disk
        type       - select (define) a disk type
        partition  - select (define) a partition table
        current    - describe the current disk
        format     - format and analyze the disk
        repair     - repair a defective sector
        label      - write label to the disk
        analyze    - surface analysis
        defect     - defect list management
        backup     - search for backup labels
        verify     - read and display labels
        save       - save new disk/partition definitions
        inquiry    - show vendor, product and revision
        volname    - set 8-character volume name
        quit
format > defect
defect > primary
Extracting primary defect list . . . Extraction complete.
Current Defect List updated, total of 30 defects.
defect > quit
format > format
format> partition
PARTITION MENU:
        0          - change '0' partition
        1          - change '1' partition
        2          - change '2' partition
        3          - change '3' partition
        4          - change '4' partition
        5          - change '5' partition
        6          - change '6' partition
        7          - change '7' partition
        select - select a predefined table
        modify - modify a predefined partition table
        name   - name the current table
        print  - display the current table
        label  - write partition map and label to the disk
        quit
partition> <partition the disk>
partition> label
partition> quit
format > quit
#
```

Remaking the File Systems (newfs)

A disk must be formatted, partitioned, and labeled before you can create UFS file systems on it. If you are re-creating an existing UFS file system, unmount the file system before performing the following steps.

1. Become superuser.
2. Type **newfs /dev/rdsk/cntndnsn** and press Return.

   You are asked if you want to proceed.

   CAUTION. Be sure you have specified the correct device name for the partition before performing the next step. If you specify the wrong partition, you will erase its contents when the new file system is created.

3. Type **y** to confirm.

   The newfs command uses optimized default values to create the file system.

   The following example creates a file system on /dev/rdsk/c0t3d0s7.

```
oak% su
Password:
# newfs /dev/rdsk/c0t3d0s7
newfs: construct a new file system /dev/rdsk/c0t3d0s7 (y/n)? y
/dev/rdsk/c0t3d0s7:      163944 sectors in 506 cylinders of 9 tracks, 36
  sectors
          83.9MB in 32 cyl groups (16 c/g, 2.65MB/g, 1216 i/g)
super-block backups (for fsck -b #) at:
 32, 5264, 10496, 15728, 20960, 26192, 31424, 36656, 41888,
 47120, 52352, 57584, 62816, 68048, 73280, 78512, 82976, 88208,
 93440, 98672, 103904, 109136, 114368, 119600, 124832, 130064, 135296,
 140528, 145760, 150992, 156224, 161456,
#
```

Mounting the File System on a Temporary Mount Point (mount)

Type **mount /dev/dsk/***cntndnsn* **/mnt** and press Return. The file system is mounted on the /mnt temporary mount point. To mount the disk, specify the block device directory (/dev/dsk), not the raw device directory.

Restoring Files to the File System (ufsrestore)

Restore the contents of the latest full backup, and then restore subsequent incremental backups from lowest to highest level (ufsrestore), by using the following steps.

1. As superuser, type **cd /mnt** and press Return.

   You have changed to the mount point directory.

2. Write-protect the tapes for safety.

3. Insert the first volume of the level 0 tape into the tape drive.

4. Type **ufsrestore rvf /dev/rmt/***unit* and press Return.

   If this is a multivolume restore, when prompted, remove the first tape and insert the last tape in the tape drive. Follow instructions about the order of the rest of the tapes. The level 0 tape is restored.

5. Remove the tape and load the next-lowest-level tape in the drive.

   Always restore tapes starting with 0 and continuing until you reach the highest level.

6. Type **ufsrestore rvf /dev/rmt/***unit* and press Return.

   The next-level tape is restored.

7. Repeat steps 5 and 6 for each additional tape.

8. Type **ls** and press Return.

9. A list of files in the directory is displayed. Check the listing to verify that all the files are restored.

10. Type **rm restoresymtable** and press Return.

   The restoresymtable created by ufsrestore is removed.

Unmounting the File System from Its Temporary Mount Point (umount)

Use the following steps to unmount the file system from its temporary mount point.

1. As superuser, type **cd /** and press Return.

2. Type **umount /mnt** and press Return.

   The file system is unmounted from the temporary mount point.

Checking the File System for Inconsistencies (fsck)

Type **fsck /dev/rdsk/cxtxdxsn** and press Return. The file system is checked for consistency.

Performing a Level 0 Backup of the Restored File System (ufsdump)

You always should do an immediate backup of a newly created file system because ufsrestore repositions the files and changes the inode allocation.

   Use the following steps to perform a level 0 backup of the restored file system.

1. Remove the last tape and insert a new write-enabled tape in the tape drive.

2. Type **ufsdump 0uf /dev/rmt/*unit* /dev/rdsk/cxtxdxsn** and press Return.

Mounting the File System at Its Permanent Mount Point (mount)

Type **mount /dev/dsk/cxtxdxsn** and press Return. The restored file system is mounted and available for use.

Understanding the Service Access Facility

The Solaris Operating Environment uses the *Service Access Facility (SAF)* to register and monitor port activity for modems, terminals, and printers. SAF is new with the Solaris Operating Environment. SAF controls the resources that let users perform the following tasks.

- Log in (either locally or remotely).
- Access printers across the network.
- Access files across the network.

SAF is a complex hierarchy of background processes and administrative commands. Explaining SAF in depth is beyond the scope of this book. The following sections provide a brief introduction to the elements of SAF. For complete information about SAF, see *Solaris Advanced System Administrator's Guide*, available from Sun Microsystems Press.

New!

SMC Tools for SAF

You can use the SMC Devices and Hardware/Serial Ports tool to administer SAF for alphanumeric terminals and modems on a local system. See the *Solaris Management Console Tools* book published by Sun Microsystems Press and Prentice Hall for detailed instructions on how to use the Serial Ports tool.

Port Monitors and Service Access

A *port monitor* is a program that continuously watches for requests to log in or requests to access printers or files. When a port monitor detects a request, it sets the parameters that are needed to establish communication between the operating system and the device that is requesting service. The port monitor then transfers control to other processes that provide the services needed.

The Solaris Operating Environment provides two types of port monitors: listen and ttymon. The *listen port monitor* controls access to network services, fielding remote print and file system requests. The *ttymon port monitor* controls access to login services. You need to set up a ttymon port monitor (using SAF) to process login requests from modems and alphanumeric terminals.

NOTE. The ttymon *port monitor replaces the SunOS 4.x* getty *port monitor. A single* ttymon *can replace multiple* gettys.

SAF Control of Port Monitors and Services

You use three SAF commands to administer modems and alphanumeric terminals: sacadm, pmadm, and ttyadm.

The sacadm command adds and removes port monitors. This command is your main link with the Service Access Controller (SAC) and its administrative file (/etc/saf/_sactab).

The pmadm command adds or removes a service and associates a service with a particular port monitor.

The ttyadm command formats information for inclusion in various SAF administrative files. A ttyadm command often is embedded within a sacadm or pmadm command to provide some of the data needed by those commands.

Table 77 lists the commands associated with specific SAF functions. See the manual pages for more information about each command.

Table 77   SAF Functions and Associated Commands

Function	Command	Description
Overall administration	sacadm	Command for adding and removing port monitors.
Service Access Controller	sac	SAF's master program.
Port monitors	ttymon	Monitor serial port login requests.
	listen	Monitor requests for network services.
Port monitor service administrator	pmadm	Command for controlling port monitors' services.
Services	logins; remote procedure calls; other	Services to which SAF provides access.

Setting Up Printer Port Monitors

If you use the Printer Manager (available starting with SunOS 5.1), you do not need to configure SAF to set up printer port monitors. The Printer Manager automatically sets up the port monitors as part of the printer configuration process.

See "Solaris Print Manager" on page 389 for information on how to add printers.

Setting Up a Bidirectional Modem

To set up a bidirectional modem, you need information for these variables.

- *port-name*—The port to which the modem is connected (typically, ttya or ttyb).
- *svctag*—The name of the port monitor service (for Sun systems, zsmon).
- *port-device-name*—The name of the device for the port (typically /dev/cua/a or /dev/cua/b).
- *short-port-device-name*—The name, without the complete path, for the port.
- *modem-label*—The entry in the /etc/ttydefs file that is used to set the proper baud rate and line discipline.
- *modem-type*—The type of the modem from the /etc/uucp/Dialers file. For example, the type for a Hayes modem is hayes.

Use the following steps to connect a modem.

1. Halt the system.
2. Make sure hardware carrier detect is disabled.

   At the OpenBoot PROM prompt, type
   setenv ttyb-ignore-cd=false and press Return.
3. Reboot the system.
4. Connect the modem and make sure any modem switches are set to allow bidirectional use.
5. Use the SMC Devices and Hardware/Serial Ports tool to configure a serial port for a modem.

   See the *Solaris Management Console Tools* book for detailed instructions.

Using a Modem

To connect through the modem, type **tip** *-baudrate phonenumber* and press Return. When the software on the connecting system is configured properly, the remote system dials the modem phone number and the modem answers automatically.

The following example uses the information phone number, which is not a dial-in modem number.

```
oak% tip -9600 5551212
dialing ... connected
<Login messages>
```

9

ADMINISTERING SYSTEMS

This chapter describes commands that are specific to individual systems. It also shows how to configure additional swap space and how to create a local mail alias.

> *NOTE. Starting with the Solaris 9 release, you can use the following SMC tools. The System Configuration category provides Projects, Computers and Networks, and Patches tools. The System Performance tool enables you to monitor system performance on a local system.*

Displaying System-Specific Information

Use the commands in this section to find system-specific information such as the host ID number, hardware type, processor type, OS release level, system configuration, length of time the system has been up, and system date and time. The following sections also describe how to set the system date and time and change the time zone for a system.

Determining the Host ID Number (sysdef -h, hostid)

To find a system's host ID number, type **sysdef -h** and press Return. The host ID for the system is displayed.

```
mopoke% sysdef -h
*
* Hostid
*
  8304b666
mopoke%
```

New!

You can also display the host ID number with the `hostid` command.

```
mopoke% hostid
8304b666
mopoke%
```

Determining the Hardware Type (uname -m)

To find the hardware type of a system, type **uname -m** and press Return. The hardware type (architecture) for the system is displayed.

```
oak% uname -m
sun4u
oak%
```

New!

NOTE. The Solaris 9 uname *manual page discourages use of the* -m *option. Instead, Sun recommends the* -p *option. See below for an example of the output of the* -p *option.*

Determining the Processor Type (uname -p)

To find the processor type for a system, type **uname -p** and press Return. The processor type for the system is displayed.

```
mopoke% uname -p
sparc
mopoke%
```

Determining the OS Release (uname -r)

To find the OS release level for a system, type **uname -r** and press Return. The OS (kernel) release is displayed.

```
oak% uname -r
5.8
oak%
```

Displaying System Configuration Information (prtconf)

To display the configuration information for a system, type **prtconf** and press Return. The system configuration information is displayed.

```
mopoke% prtconf
System Configuration:  Sun Microsystems  sun4u
Memory size: 128 Megabytes
System Peripherals (Software Nodes):

SUNW,Sun-Blade-100
    packages (driver not attached)
        SUNW,builtin-drivers (driver not attached)
        deblocker (driver not attached)
        disk-label (driver not attached)
        terminal-emulator (driver not attached)
        obp-tftp (driver not attached)
        dropins (driver not attached)
        kbd-translator (driver not attached)
        ufs-file-system (driver not attached)
    chosen (driver not attached)
    openprom (driver not attached)
        client-services (driver not attached)
    options, instance #0
    aliases (driver not attached)
    memory (driver not attached)
    virtual-memory (driver not attached)
    pci, instance #0
        ebus, instance #1
            flashprom (driver not attached)
            eeprom (driver not attached)
            idprom (driver not attached)
        isa, instance #0
            dma, instance #0
                floppy, instance #0
                parallel (driver not attached)
            power, instance #0
            serial, instance #0
            serial, instance #1
        network, instance #0
        firewire, instance #0
        usb, instance #0
            storage, instance #1
                disk, instance #2
            keyboard, instance #2
            mouse, instance #1
        pmu, instance #0
            i2c, instance #0
                temperature, instance #0
                card-reader (driver not attached)
                dimm (driver not attached)
            ppm, instance #1
            beep, instance #1
            fan-control, instance #1
        sound (driver not attached)
        ide, instance #0
            disk (driver not attached)
            cdrom (driver not attached)
            dad, instance #0
            sd, instance #0
        SUNW,m64B, instance #0
        pci (driver not attached)
    SUNW,UltraSPARC-IIe, instance #0
    os-io (driver not attached)
    pseudo, instance #0
mopoke%
```

New!

An alternative way to display system configuration information and show the state of tunable parameters is to type **sysdef** and press Return. System configuration information is displayed. The complete output shown in the following example shows the level of detail you can access about a system's configuration.

New!

```
mopoke% sysdef
*
* Hostid
*
  8304b666
*
* sun4u Configuration
*
*
* Devices
*
packages (driver not attached)
        SUNW,builtin-drivers (driver not attached)
        deblocker (driver not attached)
        disk-label (driver not attached)
        terminal-emulator (driver not attached)
        obp-tftp (driver not attached)
        dropins (driver not attached)
        kbd-translator (driver not attached)
        ufs-file-system (driver not attached)
chosen (driver not attached)
openprom (driver not attached)
        client-services (driver not attached)
options, instance #0
aliases (driver not attached)
memory (driver not attached)
virtual-memory (driver not attached)
pci, instance #0
        ebus, instance #1
                flashprom (driver not attached)
                eeprom (driver not attached)
                idprom (driver not attached)
        isa, instance #0
                dma, instance #0
                        floppy, instance #0
                        parallel (driver not attached)
                power, instance #0
                serial, instance #0
                serial, instance #1
        network, instance #0
        firewire, instance #0
        usb, instance #0
                storage, instance #1
                        disk, instance #2
                keyboard, instance #2
                mouse, instance #1
        pmu, instance #0
                i2c, instance #0
                        temperature, instance #0
                        card-reader (driver not attached)
                        dimm (driver not attached)
                ppm, instance #1
                beep, instance #1
                fan-control, instance #1
        sound (driver not attached)
        ide, instance #0
                disk (driver not attached)
                cdrom (driver not attached)
                dad, instance #0
                sd, instance #0
        SUNW,m64B, instance #0
        pci (driver not attached)
SUNW,UltraSPARC-IIe, instance #0
os-io (driver not attached)
pseudo, instance #0
        clone, instance #0
```

```
        ip, instance #0
        ip6, instance #0
        tcp, instance #0
        tcp6, instance #0
        udp, instance #0
        udp6, instance #0
        icmp, instance #0
        icmp6, instance #0
        sad, instance #0
        conskbd, instance #0
        wc, instance #0
        consms, instance #0
        iwscn, instance #0
        ptsl, instance #0
        rts, instance #0
        tl, instance #0
        keysock, instance #0
        spdsock, instance #0
        sysmsg, instance #0
        cn, instance #0
        mm, instance #0
        kstat, instance #0
        pm, instance #0
        atmmb, instance #0
        q93b, instance #0
        laner, instance #0
        skip_key, instance #0
        screen_skip, instance #0
        log, instance #0
        vol, instance #0
        sy, instance #0
        random, instance #0
        ptm, instance #0
        pts, instance #0
        devinfo, instance #0
        ksyms, instance #0
*
* Loadable Objects
*
* Loadable Object Path = /platform/SUNW,Sun-Blade-100/kernel
*
drv/sparcv9/grppm
drv/sparcv9/pmubus
drv/sparcv9/grfans
drv/sparcv9/grbeep
misc/sparcv9/platmod
*
* Loadable Object Path = /platform/sun4u/kernel
*
tod/todstarfire
tod/todmostek
tod/sparcv9/todmostek
tod/sparcv9/todsg
tod/sparcv9/todstarcat
tod/sparcv9/todstarfire
tod/sparcv9/todds1287
tod/sparcv9/todm5819
genunix
unix
cpu/SUNW,UltraSPARC-III
cpu/SUNW,UltraSPARC-III+
cpu/SUNW,UltraSPARC-II
cpu/SUNW,UltraSPARC-IIi
cpu/SUNW,UltraSPARC-IIe
cpu/SUNW,UltraSPARC
cpu/sparcv9/SUNW,UltraSPARC-II
cpu/sparcv9/SUNW,UltraSPARC-IIi
cpu/sparcv9/SUNW,UltraSPARC-III+
cpu/sparcv9/SUNW,UltraSPARC-IIe
cpu/sparcv9/SUNW,UltraSPARC-III
cpu/sparcv9/SUNW,UltraSPARC
dacf/consconfig_dacf
dacf/sparcv9/consconfig_dacf
drv/dma
drv/ebus
drv/fd
```

```
drv/ledma
drv/pci_pci
drv/pcipsy
drv/power
drv/rootnex
drv/sbbc
drv/sbus
drv/sbusmem
drv/simba
drv/stc
drv/su
drv/trapstat
drv/zs
drv/zsh
drv/sf
drv/i2c
drv/db21554
drv/m64
drv/gfxp
drv/afb
drv/ce
drv/cgsix
drv/tod
drv/bwtwo
drv/cgthree
drv/ffb
drv/gfb
drv/ifb
drv/igs
drv/cpc
        hard link:   sys/cpc
drv/i2cadc
drv/i2cgpio
drv/Neide
drv/atata
drv/ata
drv/disk_ata
drv/cmdk
drv/eide
drv/i8042
drv/kb_ps2
drv/kdmouse
drv/consbus
drv/echip
drv/gchip
drv/scman
drv/lom
drv/lomp
drv/sparcv9/ifb
drv/sparcv9/dma
drv/sparcv9/ebus
drv/sparcv9/fd
drv/sparcv9/gpio_87317
drv/sparcv9/isadma
drv/sparcv9/ledma
drv/sparcv9/lm75
drv/sparcv9/ltc1427
drv/sparcv9/max1617
drv/sparcv9/mc-us3
drv/sparcv9/pcf8574
drv/sparcv9/pcf8584
drv/sparcv9/pcf8591
drv/sparcv9/pci_pci
drv/sparcv9/pcipsy
drv/sparcv9/pcisch
drv/sparcv9/pmc
drv/sparcv9/power
drv/sparcv9/sbbc
drv/sparcv9/sbus
drv/sparcv9/sbusmem
drv/sparcv9/schppm
drv/sparcv9/seeprom
drv/sparcv9/simba
drv/sparcv9/smbus
drv/sparcv9/smbus_ara
drv/sparcv9/ssc050
```

```
drv/sparcv9/ssc100
drv/sparcv9/stc
drv/sparcv9/su
drv/sparcv9/tda8444
drv/sparcv9/trapstat
drv/sparcv9/upa64s
drv/sparcv9/i2c
drv/sparcv9/ce
drv/sparcv9/ffb
drv/sparcv9/i2cadc
drv/sparcv9/scmi2c
drv/sparcv9/db21554
drv/sparcv9/sf
drv/sparcv9/bbc_beep
drv/sparcv9/i2cgpio
drv/sparcv9/disk_ata
drv/sparcv9/tod
drv/sparcv9/fcode
drv/sparcv9/Neide
drv/sparcv9/atata
drv/sparcv9/igs
drv/sparcv9/i8042
drv/sparcv9/kb_ps2
drv/sparcv9/kdmouse
drv/sparcv9/gfb
drv/sparcv9/us
drv/sparcv9/m64
drv/sparcv9/rootnex
drv/sparcv9/zs
drv/sparcv9/gfxp
drv/sparcv9/zsh
drv/sparcv9/afb
drv/sparcv9/cgsix
drv/sparcv9/wrsmd
drv/sparcv9/cpc
        hard link:   sys/sparcv9/cpc
drv/sparcv9/consbus
drv/sparcv9/echip
drv/sparcv9/gchip
drv/sparcv9/scman
drv/sparcv9/uflash
drv/sparcv9/lom
drv/sparcv9/lomp
drv/sparcv9/lomv
misc/consconfig
misc/forthdebug
misc/md5
misc/obpsym
misc/pcmcia
misc/platmod
misc/vis
misc/dadk
misc/gda
misc/snlb
misc/strategy
misc/bootdev
misc/cpr
misc/sparcv9/forthdebug
misc/sparcv9/i2c_svc
misc/sparcv9/md5
misc/sparcv9/obpsym
misc/sparcv9/pcmcia
misc/sparcv9/platmod
misc/sparcv9/sbd
misc/sparcv9/vis
misc/sparcv9/fcpci
misc/sparcv9/gptwo_cpu
misc/sparcv9/consconfig
misc/sparcv9/fcodem
misc/sparcv9/gptwocfg
misc/sparcv9/pcicfg.e
misc/sparcv9/bootdev
misc/sparcv9/cpr
misc/kgss/sparcv9/gl_kmech_krb5
sparcv9/genunix
sparcv9/unix
```

```
strmod/kbsm_ps2
strmod/vuidps2
strmod/kb
misc/kgss/gl_kmech_krb5
strmod/sparcv9/kbsm_ps2
strmod/sparcv9/vuidps2
strmod/sparcv9/kb
*
* Loadable Object Path = /kernel
*
ipp/dlcosmk
ipp/ipgpc
ipp/dscpmk
ipp/flowacct
ipp/tokenmt
ipp/tswtclmt
ipp/sparcv9/dlcosmk
ipp/sparcv9/ipgpc
ipp/sparcv9/dscpmk
ipp/sparcv9/flowacct
ipp/sparcv9/tokenmt
ipp/sparcv9/tswtclmt
genunix
drv/md
drv/bpp
drv/clone
drv/cn
drv/conskbd
drv/consms
drv/dad
drv/devinfo
drv/esp
drv/icmp
        hard link:   strmod/icmp
drv/pcic
drv/icmp6
        hard link:   strmod/icmp6
drv/ip
        hard link:   strmod/ip
drv/pcs
drv/ip6
        hard link:   strmod/ip6
drv/pem
drv/ippctl
drv/ipsecesp
        hard link:   strmod/ipsecesp
drv/stp4020
drv/isp
drv/iwscn
drv/keysock
        hard link:   strmod/keysock
drv/le
drv/lebuffer
drv/llc1
drv/lofi
drv/log
drv/mm
drv/openeepr
drv/options
drv/poll
drv/pseudo
drv/ptc
drv/ptsl
drv/random
drv/rts
        hard link:   strmod/rts
drv/pcelx
drv/sad
        hard link:   strmod/sad
drv/pcmem
drv/sd
drv/sgen
drv/spdsock
drv/st
drv/sy
drv/sysmsg
```

```
drv/tcp
        hard link:   strmod/tcp
drv/pcram
drv/tcp6
        hard link:   strmod/tcp6
drv/pcser
drv/tl
drv/uata
drv/udp
        hard link:   strmod/udp
drv/ecpp
drv/udp6
        hard link:   strmod/udp6
drv/wc
drv/xbox
drv/glm
drv/soc
drv/ssd
drv/se
drv/pcata
drv/qlc
drv/ses
drv/fcp
drv/ge
drv/fas
drv/qfe
drv/ifp
drv/fp
drv/arp
        hard link:   strmod/arp
drv/ipsecah
        hard link:   strmod/ipsecah
drv/pln
drv/audioens
drv/dbri
drv/rtvc
drv/hubd
drv/hid
drv/ohci
drv/scsa2usb
drv/usb_ac
drv/usb_as
drv/usb_mid
drv/usbprn
drv/usoc
drv/hme
drv/scsi_vhci
drv/audiocs
drv/fcip
drv/socal
drv/bofi
drv/nca
drv/skip_key
drv/screen
drv/aar
drv/atmip
drv/atmmb
drv/ba
drv/lane
drv/laner
drv/q93b
drv/qcc
drv/pf
drv/nf
drv/smt
drv/HSIP
drv/HSI
drv/tsalarm
drv/sparcv9/hubd
drv/sparcv9/cn
drv/sparcv9/conskbd
drv/sparcv9/consms
drv/sparcv9/dad
drv/sparcv9/devinfo
drv/sparcv9/esp
drv/sparcv9/icmp
```

```
        hard link:  strmod/sparcv9/icmp
drv/sparcv9/hid
drv/sparcv9/ohci
drv/sparcv9/scsa2usb
drv/sparcv9/usb_ac
drv/sparcv9/usb_as
drv/sparcv9/usb_mid
drv/sparcv9/iwscn
drv/sparcv9/keysock
        hard link:  strmod/sparcv9/keysock
drv/sparcv9/usbprn
drv/sparcv9/lebuffer
drv/sparcv9/llc1
drv/sparcv9/lofi
drv/sparcv9/log
drv/sparcv9/mm
drv/sparcv9/openeepr
drv/sparcv9/options
drv/sparcv9/poll
drv/sparcv9/pseudo
drv/sparcv9/ptc
drv/sparcv9/ptsl
drv/sparcv9/random
drv/sparcv9/rts
        hard link:  strmod/sparcv9/rts
drv/sparcv9/pcs
drv/sparcv9/pem
drv/sparcv9/usoc
drv/sparcv9/sgen
drv/sparcv9/spdsock
drv/sparcv9/st
drv/sparcv9/sysmsg
drv/sparcv9/tcp
        hard link:  strmod/sparcv9/tcp
drv/sparcv9/eri
drv/sparcv9/fcip
drv/sparcv9/ttymux
drv/sparcv9/uata
drv/sparcv9/fcp
drv/sparcv9/dcam1394
drv/sparcv9/ge
drv/sparcv9/fas
drv/sparcv9/hme
drv/sparcv9/stp4020
drv/sparcv9/pcmem
drv/sparcv9/hci1394
drv/sparcv9/pcelx
drv/sparcv9/pcic
drv/sparcv9/pln
drv/sparcv9/ssd
drv/sparcv9/audiocs
drv/sparcv9/audioens
drv/sparcv9/soc
drv/sparcv9/pcram
drv/sparcv9/pcser
drv/sparcv9/ecpp
drv/sparcv9/glm
drv/sparcv9/se
drv/sparcv9/pcata
drv/sparcv9/ses
drv/sparcv9/ifp
drv/sparcv9/socal
drv/sparcv9/scsi_vhci
drv/sparcv9/md
drv/sparcv9/fp
drv/sparcv9/qlc
drv/sparcv9/audiots
drv/sparcv9/dbri
drv/sparcv9/arp
        hard link:  strmod/sparcv9/arp
drv/sparcv9/clone
drv/sparcv9/sy
drv/sparcv9/udp
        hard link:  strmod/sparcv9/udp
drv/sparcv9/rtvc
drv/sparcv9/qfe
```

```
drv/sparcv9/bpp
drv/sparcv9/icmp6
        hard link:   strmod/sparcv9/icmp6
drv/sparcv9/ip
        hard link:   strmod/sparcv9/ip
drv/sparcv9/ip6
        hard link:   strmod/sparcv9/ip6
drv/sparcv9/ippctl
drv/sparcv9/ipsecah
        hard link:   strmod/sparcv9/ipsecah
drv/sparcv9/ipsecesp
        hard link:   strmod/sparcv9/ipsecesp
drv/sparcv9/bofi
drv/sparcv9/isp
drv/sparcv9/le
drv/sparcv9/sad
        hard link:   strmod/sparcv9/sad
drv/sparcv9/sd
drv/sparcv9/tcp6
        hard link:   strmod/sparcv9/tcp6
drv/sparcv9/tl
drv/sparcv9/udp6
        hard link:   strmod/sparcv9/udp6
drv/sparcv9/wc
drv/sparcv9/nca
drv/sparcv9/skip_key
drv/sparcv9/screen
drv/sparcv9/aar
drv/sparcv9/atmip
drv/sparcv9/atmmb
drv/sparcv9/ba
drv/sparcv9/lane
drv/sparcv9/laner
drv/sparcv9/q93b
drv/sparcv9/qcc
drv/sparcv9/pf
drv/sparcv9/nf
drv/sparcv9/smt
drv/sparcv9/HSIP
drv/sparcv9/HSI
drv/sparcv9/tsalarm
exec/elfexec
exec/intpexec
exec/aoutexec
exec/sparcv9/intpexec
exec/sparcv9/aoutexec
exec/sparcv9/elfexec
fs/autofs
fs/fifofs
fs/hsfs
fs/lofs
fs/mntfs
fs/procfs
fs/sockfs
fs/specfs
fs/tmpfs
fs/ufs
fs/udfs
misc/kgss/gl_kmech_krb5
fs/cachefs
fs/nfs
        hard link:   sys/nfs
fs/sparcv9/fifofs
fs/sparcv9/hsfs
fs/sparcv9/lofs
fs/sparcv9/mntfs
fs/sparcv9/procfs
fs/sparcv9/sockfs
fs/sparcv9/specfs
fs/sparcv9/tmpfs
fs/sparcv9/ufs
fs/sparcv9/autofs
fs/sparcv9/udfs
fs/sparcv9/cachefs
fs/sparcv9/nfs
        hard link:   sys/sparcv9/nfs
```

```
misc/consconfig
misc/dada
misc/des
misc/fssnap_if
misc/gld
misc/hpcsvc
misc/ipc
misc/krtld
misc/md5
misc/pcicfg
misc/pcihp
misc/rpcsec
misc/scsi
misc/seg_drv
misc/seg_mapdev
misc/sha1
misc/strplumb
misc/swapgeneric
misc/tlimod
misc/ufs_log
misc/md_hotspares
misc/md_mirror
misc/audiosup
misc/rpcsec_gss
misc/klmops
misc/amsrc1
misc/nfs_dlboot
misc/md_notify
misc/md_raid
misc/md_sp
misc/md_stripe
misc/diaudio
misc/md_trans
misc/klmmod
misc/kgssapi
misc/mixer
misc/busra
misc/hidparser
misc/fctl
misc/kbtrans
misc/usba
misc/nfssrv
misc/rsmops
misc/vlan
misc/mpxio
misc/phx
misc/sparcv9/dada
misc/sparcv9/des
misc/sparcv9/fssnap_if
misc/sparcv9/gld
misc/sparcv9/hpcsvc
misc/sparcv9/ipc
misc/sparcv9/krtld
misc/sparcv9/md5
misc/sparcv9/pcicfg
misc/sparcv9/pcihp
misc/sparcv9/rpcsec
misc/sparcv9/scsi
misc/sparcv9/seg_drv
misc/sparcv9/seg_mapdev
misc/sparcv9/sha1
misc/sparcv9/strplumb
misc/sparcv9/tlimod
misc/sparcv9/ufs_log
misc/sparcv9/hidparser
misc/sparcv9/klmops
misc/sparcv9/nfs_dlboot
misc/sparcv9/nfssrv
misc/sparcv9/rpcsec_gss
misc/sparcv9/s1394
misc/sparcv9/audiosup
misc/sparcv9/diaudio
misc/sparcv9/mixer
misc/sparcv9/consconfig
misc/sparcv9/kgssapi
misc/sparcv9/mpxio
```

```
misc/sparcv9/phx
misc/sparcv9/fctl
misc/sparcv9/busra
misc/sparcv9/swapgeneric
misc/sparcv9/kbtrans
misc/sparcv9/amsrc1
misc/sparcv9/usba
misc/sparcv9/md_hotspares
misc/sparcv9/md_mirror
misc/sparcv9/md_notify
misc/sparcv9/md_raid
misc/sparcv9/md_sp
misc/sparcv9/md_stripe
misc/sparcv9/md_trans
misc/sparcv9/klmmod
misc/sparcv9/rsmops
misc/sparcv9/vlan
sched/TS_DPTBL
sched/TS
sched/sparcv9/TS_DPTBL
sched/sparcv9/TS
strmod/authmd5h
strmod/authsha1
strmod/bufmod
strmod/connld
strmod/dedump
strmod/encr3des
strmod/encrdes
strmod/ldterm
strmod/pckt
strmod/pfmod
strmod/pipemod
strmod/ptem
strmod/redirmod
strmod/rpcmod
        hard link:  sys/rpcmod
strmod/atun
strmod/ttcompat
strmod/tun
strmod/ms
strmod/timod
strmod/tirdwr
strmod/hwc
strmod/usbms
strmod/usb_ah
strmod/usbkbm
strmod/bd
strmod/efs
strmod/spf
strmod/sscop
strmod/sparcv9/authsha1
strmod/sparcv9/bufmod
strmod/sparcv9/connld
strmod/sparcv9/dedump
strmod/sparcv9/encr3des
strmod/sparcv9/encrdes
strmod/sparcv9/pckt
strmod/sparcv9/pfmod
strmod/sparcv9/pipemod
strmod/sparcv9/ptem
strmod/sparcv9/redirmod
strmod/sparcv9/rpcmod
        hard link:  sys/sparcv9/rpcmod
strmod/sparcv9/usb_ah
strmod/sparcv9/usbms
strmod/sparcv9/ttcompat
strmod/sparcv9/tun
strmod/sparcv9/usbkbm
strmod/sparcv9/hwc
strmod/sparcv9/atun
strmod/sparcv9/authmd5h
strmod/sparcv9/ldterm
strmod/sparcv9/ms
strmod/sparcv9/timod
strmod/sparcv9/tirdwr
misc/kgss/sparcv9/gl_kmech_krb5
```

```
strmod/sparcv9/bd
strmod/sparcv9/efs
strmod/sparcv9/spf
strmod/sparcv9/sscop
sys/doorfs
sys/inst_sync
sys/kaio
sys/msgsys
sys/pipe
sys/pset
sys/semsys
sys/shmsys
sys/c2audit
sys/sparcv9/inst_sync
sys/sparcv9/kaio
sys/sparcv9/msgsys
sys/sparcv9/pipe
sys/sparcv9/pset
sys/sparcv9/semsys
sys/sparcv9/shmsys
sys/sparcv9/c2audit
sys/sparcv9/doorfs
*
* Loadable Object Path = /usr/kernel
*
exec/sparcv9/javaexec
fs/sparcv9/fdfs
fs/sparcv9/namefs
fs/sparcv9/pcfs
sched/sparcv9/RT_DPTBL
sched/sparcv9/FX
sched/sparcv9/FX_DPTBL
sched/sparcv9/IA
sched/sparcv9/RT
sched/sparcv9/FSS
sys/sparcv9/sysacct
sys/sparcv9/acctctl
sys/sparcv9/exacctsys
misc/bsafe2_kern_lib
misc/skip_bdc_rc2_cbc
misc/skip_bdc_rc4
misc/skip_bdc_rc4_128
misc/skip_fast_des_cbc
misc/skip_des_ede_k3
misc/skip_safer_128sk_cbc
misc/screen_dns
misc/screen_fail
misc/screen_ftp
misc/screen_ip
misc/screen_nfsro
misc/screen_normal
misc/screen_ping
misc/screen_pmap
misc/screen_raudio
misc/screen_rsh
misc/screen_sqlnet
misc/screen_stateless
misc/screen_tcp
misc/screen_ts7
misc/screen_ts8
misc/screen_udp
drv/sparcv9/sppp
drv/sparcv9/sppptun
        hard link:   strmod/sparcv9/sppptun
drv/sparcv9/dump
drv/sparcv9/fssnap
drv/sparcv9/kstat
drv/sparcv9/ksyms
drv/sparcv9/lockstat
drv/sparcv9/logindmux
drv/sparcv9/ptm
drv/sparcv9/pts
drv/sparcv9/pm
drv/sparcv9/tnf
drv/sparcv9/vol
drv/sparcv9/winlock
```

```
drv/sparcv9/llc2
drv/sparcv9/rsm
drv/sparcv9/screen_ipsec
drv/sparcv9/screen_skip
strmod/sparcv9/telmod
strmod/sparcv9/u8lat2
strmod/sparcv9/spppcomp
strmod/sparcv9/u8lat1
strmod/sparcv9/u8koi8
strmod/sparcv9/rlmod
strmod/sparcv9/spppasyn
drv/dump
drv/fssnap
drv/kstat
drv/ksyms
drv/lockstat
drv/logindmux
drv/ptm
drv/pts
drv/winlock
drv/pm
drv/vol
drv/sppptun
        hard link:   strmod/sppptun
drv/rsm
drv/tnf
drv/llc2
drv/sppp
drv/screen_ipsec
drv/screen_skip
exec/javaexec
fs/fdfs
fs/namefs
fs/pcfs
sched/FX
sched/FX_DPTBL
sched/IA
sched/RT
sched/RT_DPTBL
sched/FSS
strmod/spppcomp
strmod/rlmod
strmod/telmod
strmod/u8koi8
strmod/u8lat1
strmod/u8lat2
strmod/spppasyn
sys/acctctl
sys/exacctsys
sys/sysacct
misc/sparcv9/skip_bdc_rc4
misc/sparcv9/skip_bdc_rc4_128
misc/sparcv9/skip_fast_des_cbc
misc/sparcv9/skip_des_ede_k3
misc/sparcv9/skip_safer_128sk_cbc
misc/sparcv9/screen_dns
misc/sparcv9/screen_fail
misc/sparcv9/screen_ftp
misc/sparcv9/screen_ip
misc/sparcv9/screen_nfsro
misc/sparcv9/screen_normal
misc/sparcv9/screen_ping
misc/sparcv9/screen_pmap
misc/sparcv9/screen_raudio
misc/sparcv9/screen_rsh
misc/sparcv9/screen_sqlnet
misc/sparcv9/screen_stateless
misc/sparcv9/screen_tcp
misc/sparcv9/screen_ts7
misc/sparcv9/screen_ts8
misc/sparcv9/screen_udp
*
* System Configuration
*
  swap files
swapfile               dev  swaplo blocks   free
```

```
/dev/dsk/c1t0d0s1   136,1      16 1049312 1049312
*
* Tunable Parameters
*
 2449408       maximum memory allowed in buffer cache (bufhwm)
    1866       maximum number of processes (v.v_proc)
      99       maximum global priority in sys class (MAXCLSYSPRI)
    1861       maximum processes per user id (v.v_maxup)
      30       auto update time limit in seconds (NAUTOUP)
      25       page stealing low water mark (GPGSLO)
       5       fsflush run rate (FSFLUSHR)
      25       minimum resident memory for avoiding deadlock (MINARMEM)
      25       minimum swapable memory for avoiding deadlock (MINASMEM)
*
* Utsname Tunables
*
     5.9   release (REL)
  mopoke   node name (NODE)
   SunOS   system name (SYS)
Generic_112737-02   version (VER)
*
* Process Resource Limit Tunables (Current:Maximum)
*
0x0000000000000100:0x0000000000010000    file descriptors
*
* Streams Tunables
*
     9  maximum number of pushes allowed (NSTRPUSH)
 65536  maximum stream message size (STRMSGSZ)
  1024  max size of ctl part of message (STRCTLSZ)
*
* IPC Messages module is not loaded
*
*
* IPC Semaphores module is not loaded
*
*
* IPC Shared Memory module is not loaded
*
*
* Time Sharing Scheduler Tunables
*
60       maximum time sharing user priority (TSMAXUPRI)
SYS      system class name (SYS_NAME)
mopoke%
```

Determining How Long a System Has Been Up (uptime)

To find out how long a system has been up, type **uptime** and press Return. The time, number of users, and load average are displayed for the local system.

```
castle% uptime
  1:16pm  up  4:57,  1 user,  load average: 0.12, 0.06, 0.04
castle%
```

To find out when a system was booted, type **who -b** and press Return. The month, day, and time of the last boot are displayed.

```
oak% who -b
 . system boot Jul 14 08:49
oak%
```

Determining the System Date and Time (date)

To display the system date and time, type **date** and press Return. The system date and time are displayed.

```
castle% date
Sat July  1 13:17:03 WST 2000
castle%
```

Setting the System Date and Time (date)

Use the following steps to reset the system date and time.

1. Become superuser.
2. Type **date** *mmddhhmmyy* and press Return, where *mm* is the month, *dd* is the day, *hh* is the hour, *mm* is the minute, and *yy* is the year. The system date and time are reset according to the month, day, hour, minute, and year that you specify.

```
# su
Password:
# date
Sat Jul 1 16:07:01 WST 2000
# date 07011552
Sat Jul 1 15:52:00 WST 2000
#
```

Changing the System Time Zone (/etc/TIMEZONE)

The time zone is set in the `/etc/TIMEZONE` file. The available U.S. time zone variables are shown below. Look in the `/usr/share/lib/zoneinfo` directory for a complete list of time zone variables.

```
Alaska
Aleutian
Arizona
Central
East-Indiana
Eastern
Hawaii
Michigan
Mountain
Pacific
Pacific-New
Samoa
```

Use the following steps to change the system time zone.

1. Become superuser.
2. Edit the /etc/TIMEZONE file, change the TZ=*time-zone* variable, and save the changes. The time zone is reset.
3. Reboot the system.

The following example shows the /etc/TIMEZONE file for a system set to Australia West standard time. Note that /etc/TIMEZONE is now a symbolic link to /etc/default/init.

```
paperbark% more /etc/TIMEZONE
# @(#)init.dfl 1.5 99/05/26
#
# This file is /etc/default/init.   /etc/TIMEZONE is a symlink to this file.
# This file looks like a shell script, but it is not.  To maintain
# compatibility with old versions of /etc/TIMEZONE, some shell constructs
# (i.e., export commands) are allowed in this file, but are ignored.
#
# Lines of this file should be of the form VAR=value, where VAR is one of
# TZ, LANG, or any of the LC_* environment variables.
#
TZ=Australia/West
CMASK=022
LANG=C
paperbark%
```

The following example changes to U.S./Eastern.

```
oak% su
Password:
# vi /etc/TIMEZONE
TZ=US/Eastern;export TZ
:w!
# reboot
oak% date
Tue Jul 1 14:24:52 EST 2000
oak%
```

NOTE. You may need to make your text editor do a confirmed write of the file. For example, in vi use the command :w! to write the changes even if the permissions normally would not allow it.

Configuring Additional Swap Space (mkfile, swap)

To create and add additional swap space without reformatting a disk, you first create a swap file with the mkfile command. You can specify the size of the swap file in kilobytes (the default) or in blocks or megabytes by using the b and m suffixes, respectively. The swap file can either be on a local disk or be NFS-mounted. You then add the swap space with the swap command.

To list available swap files, type **swap -l** and press Return. A list of available swap files is displayed. The swap command replaces the SunOS 4.x swapon command.

```
drusilla% swap -l
swapfile            dev   swaplo blocks    free
swapfs               -         0  94520   93512
/dev/dsk/c0t3d0s1  32,25        8  65512   45048
drusilla%
```

Use the following steps to create a swap file.

1. Become superuser. You can create a swap file without root permissions, but it is a good idea to have root be the owner of the swap file so that other processes cannot access it.
2. Type **mkfile *nnn*[k|b|m] *file-name*** and press Return. The letter following the number you specify indicates kilobytes, blocks, or megabytes. The swap file of the size and file name you specify is created. The following example creates a 1-Mbyte swap file named SWAP.

```
oak% su
Password:
# mkfile 1m /files1/SWAP
#
```

Use the following steps to add the swap file.

1. Become superuser.
2. Type **swap -a *path-name*** and press Return. You must use the absolute path name to specify the swap file. The swap file is added and becomes available.
3. Type **swap -l** to verify that the swap file is added.

```
# swap -a /files1/SWAP
# swap -l
swapfile            dev   swaplo blocks    free
swapfs               -         0  94520   93512

/dev/dsk/c0t3d0s1  32,25        8  65512   45048

/files1/SWAP      -    8  2040   2040
#
```

Use the following steps to remove a specified swap file from use.

1. Become superuser.
2. Type **swap -d** *path-name* and press Return. When the swap file is no longer in use, it is removed from the list so that it is no longer available for swapping. The file itself is not deleted.

```
oak% su
Password:
# swap -d /files1/SWAP
# swap -l
swapfile             dev  swaplo
blocks    free
swapfs                -       0
94520  93512

/dev/dsk/c0t3d0s1   32,25      8
65512  45048
# ls -l /files1/SWAP
-rw-------   1 root    root       1048576 Jan 31 13:56 SWAP
#
```

When you create additional swap space, if you want the swap space to remain available when the system is rebooted, you must add the entry to the /etc/vfstab file. Use the following steps to add a swap file entry to the /etc/vfstab file.

1. Become superuser.
2. Edit the /etc/vfstab file and add the following line. Be sure the line follows the entry for the partition in which the swap file was created.

```
path-name - - swap - no -
```

The next time the system is rebooted, the swap file is added automatically.

The following example adds the swap file /files1/SWAP to the /etc/vfstab file after the entry that mounts the file system /files1.

```
/files1/SWAP - - swap - no -
```

Creating a Local Mail Alias (/etc/mail/aliases)

In a network environment, you probably have a central way to administer mail aliases. In addition, users frequently want to set up local aliases for use from their systems. Use the following steps to create mail aliases on a local system.

1. Become superuser.
2. Edit the `/etc/mail/aliases` file.
3. At the end of the file, under the Local Aliases category, type
   aliasname:username1,username2,... and press Return after the
   last *username*.
4. Save the changes.

For example, if you want to create an alias called `friends`, edit the
`/etc/mail/aliases` file and add an entry like the following.

```
friends:dexter@elm,ogden@willow,mary@maple
```

10

ADMINISTERING NETWORK SERVICES

This chapter contains information about checking on remote system status, logging in to a remote system, transferring files between systems, and administering the Network Information Service Plus (NIS+) databases. It also introduces the IPv6 Internet protocol, new in the Solaris 8 release, and describes how to display network and configuration information.

This chapter also provides information about the Secure Shell commands, *New!* new in the Solaris 9 release, that enable users to securely access a remote host on an unsecured network. It also contains brief instructions on creating and editing local network configuration files and on using the snoop command.

Configuring Systems for a Network   *New!*

When you install Solaris, network software is installed along with the operating system software. At installation time, certain IP configuration parameters are stored in appropriate files so that they can be read when the system boots.

The parameters that are supplied during network configuration are listed below.

- IP address of the network interface for the system.
- Host name of the system.

- NIS, NIS+, or DNS domain name in which the system resides, if applicable.
- Default router address.
- Subnet mask.

Configuring a Host for Local Files Mode

Use the following steps to configure TCP/IP on a system that runs in local files mode. You may need to use this procedure if you add a new network interface to your system after the initial Solaris software installation.

1. Become superuser.
2. Type **cd /etc** and press Return.
3. Create a file named **/etc/hostname.*interface*** or **/etc/hostname6.*interface*** for each network interface.

   The Solaris installation program creates this file automatically for the primary network interface. This file maps host names to interfaces for IPv4. For IPv6, you need one /etc/hostname.*interface* or /etc/hostname6.*interface* file for each system, for example, hostname.le0 or hostname6.le0.

4. Edit the /etc/hostname.*interface* or /etc/hostname6.*interface* file and type either the system's IP address or its host name.

NOTE. The Solaris installation program creates the default /etc/inet/hosts file for the local system. The old /etc/hosts name for this file is now a symbolic link to /etc/inet/hosts. If you are using IPv6, the installation program creates the default /etc/inet/ipnodes file.

5. Edit the /etc/inet/hosts file to add any IP addresses that you have assigned to any additional network interfaces in the local system along with the corresponding host name for each interface. If you are running IPv4, you do not need to create the /etc/inet/ipnodes file. If you have any IPv6 systems, copy all of the IPv4 IP addresses and host names from /etc/inet/hosts to the /etc/inet/ipnodes file. Add the IP addresses and host names for IPv6 systems only to the /etc/inet/ipnodes file.

NOTE. Put only the host name(s) and IP address(es) of network interfaces that are in each system in the /etc/inet/hosts file. DNS should handle all external host-name-to-IP-address mappings; you must, therefore, properly configure the /etc/nsswitch.conf and /etc/resolv.conf files to make this work. Follow this convention because you (as the system administrator) normally don't control the network or other systems on the network. If, for example, the owners of other systems or network equipment change their IP addresses or host names in DNS, the /etc/inet/hosts *file on each of the systems under your control would then be out of date and each system's network configuration would mysteriously no longer work.*

6. If the /usr file system is NFS mounted, also add the IP address or addresses of the file server to the /etc/inet/hosts file.

7. Edit the /etc/defaultrouter file and type the router's IP address. This file should contain an entry for each router that is directly connected to the network. The entry should be the IP address of an interface on the router that is on the same subnet as the system you're configuring.

8. Edit the /etc/inet/hosts file and type the name of the default router and its IP addresses.

9. If the network is subnetted, edit the /etc/inet/netmasks file and type the network number and netmask.

   If you have set up an NIS, NIS+, or LDAP server, you can type netmask information in the netmasks database on the server if server and clients are on the same network.

10. Reboot the system.

Checking on Remote System Status

This section describes commands you use to find out the status of remote systems: rup, ping, and rpcinfo -d.

Determining How Long a Remote System Has Been Up (rup)

To find out how long a system has been up and to determine the load average, type **rup *system-name*** and press Return. The host name, uptime, and load average are displayed.

```
oak% rup ash
ash    up 59 days,  3:42, load average: 0.12, 0.12, 0.01
oak%
```

You can also display a list of all remote hosts in the subnet by typing **rup** and pressing Return. If you display a list, you can use the options shown in Table 78 to sort the output.

Table 78   *Options to the rup Command*

Option	Description
-h	Sort the display alphabetically by host name.
-l	Sort the display alphabetically by load average.
-t	Sort the display by uptime.

In the following example, the output is sorted alphabetically by host name.

```
oak% rup -h
ash     up  1 day,    1:42,   load average: 0.00, 0.31, 0.34

elm     up 14 days,  0 min,   load average: 0.07, 0.01, 0.00

maple   up 32 days,  14:39,   load average: 0.21, 0.05, 0.00

oak     up  8 days,  15:44,   load average: 0.02, 0.00, 0.00
oak%
```

Determining Whether a Remote System Is Up (ping, rup, rpcinfo -p)

Use the following steps to determine whether a remote system is up and to log in to the remote system.

1. Type **ping *system-name*** and press Return.

    The message *system-name* is alive means the system is accessible over the network. The message ping: unknown host *system-name* means the system name is not known on the network. The message ping: no answer from *system-name* means the system is known on the network but is not up at this time.

2. Type **rup *system-name*** and press Return.

    Information about how long the system has been up and the load average is displayed.

3. Type **rpcinfo -p *system-name*** and press Return.

    Information about RPC services is displayed.

4. Type **rlogin *system-name*** and press Return.

    You are logged in to the remote system.

```
cinderella% ping drusilla
drusilla is alive
```

```
cinderella% rup drusilla
   drusilla     up  3 days,  15:10     load average: 0.07, 0.08, 0.09
cinderella% rpcinfo -p drusilla
program  vers proto port   service
100000    3   udp    111   portmapper
100000    2   udp    111   portmapper
100000    3   tcp    111   portmapper
100000    2   tcp    111   portmapper
100007    3   tcp   1029   ypbind
100007    3   udp   1025   ypbind
100021    1   tcp   1030   nlockmgr
100021    1   udp   1026   nlockmgr
100024    1   tcp   1028   status
100024    1   udp   1027   status
100021    3   tcp   1030   nlockmgr
100021    3   udp   1026   nlockmgr
100020    2   tcp   4045   llockmgr
100020    2   udp   4045   llockmgr
100021    2   tcp   1030   nlockmgr
100021    2   udp   1026   nlockmgr
100087   10   udp   1031   adm_agent
100011    1   udp   1034   rquotad
100002    1   udp   1037   rusersd
100002    2   udp   1037   rusersd
100012    1   udp   1041   sprayd
100008    1   udp   1043   walld
100001    2   udp   1046   rstatd
100001    3   udp   1046   rstatd
100001    4   udp   1046   rstatd
100068    2   udp   1049   cmsd
100068    3   udp   1049   cmsd
100083    1   tcp   4049
cinderella% rlogin drusilla
Password:
Last login: Mon Mar  2 10:31:55 from cinderella
drusilla%
```

You can also use `ping` with a system's IP address by typing
ping *IP-address* and pressing Return. The message *IP-address* is
alive means the system is accessible over the network. The message `ping:
no answer from` *IP-address* means the system is not available to the
network. The message `ping: unknown host` *IP-address* means the
system name is not known on the network.

```
oak% ping 129.144.52.119
129.144.52.119 is alive
oak% ping 129.137.67.234
ping: unknown host 129.137.67.234
oak% ping 129.145.52.119
ping: no answer from 129.145.52.119
oak%
```

Logging In to a Remote System (rlogin)

*NOTE. Starting with the Solaris 9 release, Secure Shell is
recommended for secure remote login. See "Secure Shell Commands"
on page 359 for more information.*

New!

Use the following steps to log in to a remote system.

1. Type **rlogin *system-name*** and press Return. You may be prompted for a password.

2. If you have a local account on that system, type your local password. Otherwise, type your NIS, NIS+, or LDAP password.

   Unless you have a home directory that is accessible on the remote system (because it is local on that system or because it is hard-mounted or automounted), you log in to the root (/) directory.

```
oak% rlogin ash
Password:
No directory!  Logging in with home=/
Last login: Tue Sep 17 13:54:28 from 129.144.52.119
Sun Microsystems, Inc. SunOS 5.8    Generic February 2000
ash%
```

Authentication for Remote Logins (rlogin)

The remote system or the network environment can perform authentication to establish who the user is for rlogin operations.

The main differences between these forms of authentication are in the type of interaction they require from the user and the way the authentication is established. If a remote system tries to authenticate a user, the user is prompted for a password unless the user is included in the /etc/hosts.equiv or .rhosts file on the remote system. If the network authenticates the user, no password is required because the network already knows who the user is.

New!

Network authentication relies on either a trusting network environment set up with your local nameservice and the automounter or one of the nameservices pointed to by the remote system's /etc/nsswitch.conf file.

NOTE. Network authentication usually supersedes system authentication.

New!

The rlogin command also interacts with the Pluggable Authentication Module (PAM) subsystem for authentication and may require configuration of the /etc/pam.conf file for authentication to work. For complete information on PAM, refer to the Sun *System Administration Guide: Security Services* or the "Using Authentication Services" chapter in the *Solaris Advanced System Administrator's Guide* available from Sun Microsystems Press and Prentice Hall.

Remote System Authentication

When the remote system tries to authenticate a user, it relies on information in its local /etc/hosts.equiv or .rhosts files. If the user's system or host name is included in the remote system's /etc/hosts.equiv file, authentication is automatic and the user can use the rlogin command without typing a password. Alternatively, authentication is automatic with the rlogin command when the user has a remote home directory with a .rhosts file that includes the user's system name and user name.

The /etc/hosts.equiv File   The /etc/hosts.equiv file contains a list of trusted hosts for a remote system, one entry per line. If a user tries to log in remotely with the rlogin command from one of the hosts listed in this file, and if the remote system can access the password entry for the user, the remote system enables the user to log in without a password.

A typical hosts.equiv file has the following structure.

```
host1
host2 user_a
+@engineering
-@marketing
```

When the /etc/hosts.equiv file contains an entry consisting of just a host name, such as the host1 entry above, the host is trusted and so is any user at that system.

If the user name is also mentioned, as in the second entry above, then the host is trusted only for that specified user.

A netgroup name preceded by a plus sign (+) means that all the systems in that netgroup are considered trusted.

A netgroup name preceded by a minus sign (-) means that none of the systems in that netgroup are considered trusted.

A single line of + in the /etc/hosts.equiv file indicates that every known host is trusted.

The /etc/hosts.equiv file presents a security risk, especially if it contains a + entry. If you maintain an /etc/hosts.equiv file on a system, include only trusted hosts in your network. Do not include any host that belongs to a different network or any systems that are in public areas. For example, do not include a host for which you do not have administrative control.

The .rhosts File   The .rhosts file is the user equivalent of the /etc/hosts.equiv file. It contains a list of host-user combinations instead of hosts in general. If a host-user combination is listed in this file, the specified user is granted permission to log in remotely from the specified host without having to supply a password.

> *NOTE. A* `.rhosts` *file must reside at the top level of a user's home directory.* `.rhosts` *files located in subdirectories are not consulted.*

Users can create `.rhosts` files in their home directories. Using the `.rhosts` file is another way to enable trusted access between an individual's user accounts on different systems without using the `/etc/hosts.equiv` file.

Unfortunately, the `.rhosts` file presents a major security problem. While the `/etc/hosts.equiv` file is under the control of system administrators and can be managed effectively, any user can create a `.rhosts` file granting access to whomever the user chooses without the system administrator's knowledge. The only secure way to manage `.rhosts` files is to completely disallow them.

Use the following procedures to search and remove `.rhosts` files.

1. Become superuser.
2. All on one line, type **find *home-directories* -name .rhosts -print -exec rm{} \;** and press Return.

   The `find` command starts at the designated directory and searches for any file named `.rhosts`. If any `.rhosts` files are found, the path is printed on the screen and the file is removed.

The following example removes all `.rhosts` files in the users' home directories located in the `/export/home` directory.

```
paperbark% su
Password:
# find /export/home -name .rhosts -print -exec rm{} \;
/export/home/ray/.rhosts
/export/home/des/.rhosts
#
```

Network Authentication

Network information is stored in NIS maps, NIS+ tables, or LDAP. Network authentication relies on one of the following two methods.

- A trusting network environment that has been set up with the user's local network information service and the automounters.
- One of the network information services pointed to by the `/etc/nsswitch.conf` file on the remote system that contains information about the user.

What Happens After You Log In Remotely

When you log in to a remote system, the in.rlogind daemon tries to find your home directory. If the in.rlogind daemon can't find your home directory, it assigns you to the root (/) directory on the remote system and the following message is displayed.

```
Unable to find home directory, logging in with /
```

When you invoke the rlogin command on your local host, inetd(1M) on the remote host invokes the in.rlogind daemon. The server checks the client's source port. If the port is not in the range 512–1023, the server aborts the connection. The server checks the client's source address. If an entry for the client exists in both /etc/inet/hosts and /etc/hosts.equiv, a user logging in from the client is not prompted for a password. If the address is associated with a host for which no corresponding entry exists in /etc/inet/hosts or if the host name is found in the NIS or NIS+ hosts map or in DNS, the user is prompted for a password, regardless of whether an entry for the client is present in /etc/hosts.equiv.

Once the source port and address are checked, in.rlogind allocates a pseudoterminal and manipulates file descriptors so that the slave half of the pseudoterminal becomes the standard input, standard output, and standard error for a login process.

The login process is an instance of the login(1) program invoked with the -r option. The login process then proceeds with the pam(3PAM) authentication process. If the login program finds your home directory, it sources both the .cshrc and .login files for the C shell or the .profile file for the Bourne shell. Therefore, your prompt on the remote system is your standard login prompt, and the current directory is the same as for a local login. For example, if your usual prompt is your system name followed by the percent (%) sign, such as paperbark%, when you log in to a remote system, the remote system name is displayed as the login prompt.

In the following example, user winsor remotely logs in to the system castle and displays the current working directory.

```
paperbark% rlogin castle
Password:
Last login: Tue Jun 20 14:02:01 from :0
Sun Microsystems Inc.   SunOS 5.7      Generic October 1998
You have mail.
castle% pwd
/export/home/winsor
castle%
```

Logging Out from a Remote System

You use the exit(1) command to log out from a remote system.

The following example shows the user winsor logging out from the system castle.

```
castle% exit
castle% logout
Connection closed.
paperbark%
```

Transferring Files Between Systems (rcp, ftp)

New!

NOTE. Starting with the Solaris 9 release, Secure Shell is recommended for secure remote copy and file transfer protocol. See "Secure Shell Commands" on page 359 for more information.

If the automounter is set up for your site, you can transfer files between systems by using commands such as cp and mv. This section describes how to use the rcp and ftp commands to transfer files between systems.

Using the rcp Command

To transfer a file from a remote system to your system with the remote copy command, type **rcp *system-name:source-pathname destination*** and press Return. If you have proper security to access the remote system, the file is copied to the destination you specify.

In the following example, the file quest is copied from the /tmp directory on the system ash to the current working directory on the system oak.

```
oak% rcp ash:/tmp/quest .
oak%
```

To transfer a file from a local system to a remote system, type **rcp *pathname system-name:destination-pathname*** and press Return. If you have proper security to access the remote system, the file is copied from the local system to the remote destination you specify.

In the following example, the file quest is copied from the current working directory on the system oak to the /tmp directory on the system ash.

```
oak% rcp quest ash:/tmp
oak%
```

If you want, you can rename the file as part of the destination path name. For example, to rename the file quest to questions and put it in the /tmp directory, type **/tmp/questions** as the destination path name.

Using the File Transfer Program (ftp)

Use the following steps to transfer files from your local system to a remote system by using the file transfer program.

NOTE. You may need to have an account on each system to use the file transfer program. Some systems allow read-only ftp *access to anybody who logs in as* anonymous *and types a login name at the password prompt.*

If you have an NIS, NIS+, or LDAP account, you can use your login name and network password to access a remote system by using ftp.

1. Type **ftp** and press Return.

   The ftp> prompt is displayed.

2. Type **open** *remote-system-name* and press Return.

   System connection messages are displayed, and you are asked for a user name.

3. Type the user name for your account on the remote system and press Return.

   If a password is required, you are asked to enter it.

4. Type the password (if required) for your account on the remote system and press Return.

   A system login message and the ftp> prompt are displayed.

5. Type **bin** to set binary format or **asc** to set ASCII format and press Return.

   The file type is set. ASCII is the default format.

6. Type **put** *local-filename destination-filename* and press Return to transfer a single file.

   File transfer messages and the ftp> prompt are displayed.

7. Type **quit** and press Return.

   A goodbye message and the command prompt are displayed.

The following example establishes an ftp connection from the system oak to the system elm, specifies ASCII format, puts the file quest from oak into the /tmp/quest directory on elm, and quits the session.

```
oak% ftp
ftp> open elm
Connected to elm
220 elm FTP server (UNIX(r) System V Release 4.0) ready.

Name (elm:ignatz): ignatz
331 Password required for ignatz.
Password:
230 User ignatz logged in.
ftp> asc
ftp> put quest /tmp/quest
200 PORT command successful.

150 ASCII data connection for /tmp/quest (129.144.52.119,1333).

226 Transfer complete.
ftp> quit
221 Goodbye.
oak%
```

You can use the send command as an alternative to the put command. You can copy multiple files by using the mput command. There is no msend command. See the ftp(1) manual page for more information.

NOTE. You must have an account on each system to use the file transfer program.

If you have an NIS, NIS+, or LDAP account, you can use your login name and network password to access a remote system with ftp. Use the following steps to transfer files from a remote system to your local system by using the file transfer program.

1. Type **ftp** and press Return.

   The ftp> prompt is displayed.

2. Type **open *remote-system-name*** and press Return.

   System connection messages are displayed, and you are asked for a user name.

3. Type the user name for your account on the remote system and press Return.

   If a password is required, you are asked to enter it.

4. Type the password (if required) for your account on the remote system and press Return.

   A system login message and the ftp> prompt are displayed.

5. Type **bin** to set binary format or **asc** to set ASCII format and press Return.

   The file type is set. ASCII is the default format.

6. Type **get *remote-filename destination-filename*** and press Return.

   File transfer messages and the ftp> prompt are displayed.

7. Type **quit** and press Return. A goodbye message and the command prompt are displayed.

The following example establishes an `ftp` connection from the system `oak` to the system `elm`, specifies ASCII format, gets the file `quest` from `elm`, puts it into the `/tmp/quest` directory on `oak`, and quits the session.

```
oak% ftp
ftp> open elm
Connected to elm
220 elm FTP server (UNIX(r)System V Release 4.0) ready.

Name (elm:ignatz): ignatz
331 Password required for ignatz.
Password:
230 User ignatz logged in.

ftp> asc
ftp> get quest /tmp/quest
200 PORT command successful.
150 ASCII data connection for /tmp/quest (129.144.52.119,1333).
226 Transfer complete.

ftp> quit
221 Goodbye.
oak%
```

NOTE. You can copy multiple files by using the `mget` *command. See the* `ftp`*(1) manual page for more information.*

Administering NIS+ Databases

NIS+ provides a central store of information for network resources such as hosts, users, and mailboxes. NIS+ replaces NIS (Network Information Service) and provides the following enhancements.

NOTE. LDAP is now scheduled to replace NIS+.

New!

- An organizational framework that is simpler to administer in large companies.
- Improved security.
- Improved distribution time to propagate changes through the network.

In addition, the Solaris Operating Environment provides a nameservice switch file, `/etc/nsswitch.conf`, that lets you use several different network information services at once. The `/etc/nsswitch.conf` file also lets you specify which service provides which type of information. In previous SunOS releases, selection of the nameservice was hard-coded into the services, which made it difficult to switch to a new nameservice. The `/etc/nsswitch.conf` file defines the order in which local files and network databases are searched for information. Describing how to set up NIS+ is beyond the scope of this book.

Using NIS+ Tables

NIS+ tables correspond to NIS maps. The Solaris Operating Environment provides 16 types of tables (shown in Figure 19) that store the network information used by NIS+.

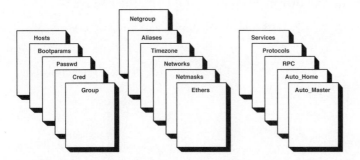

Figure 19   The 16 NIS+ Tables

Each table stores a different type of information about users, workstations, or resources on the network. For instance, the Hosts table stores the host name and network address of every workstation in the domain; the Bootparams table stores the location of the root, swap, and dump directories of the diskless clients in the domain.

Each domain can have its own set of these NIS+ tables, which store all the NIS+ information for that particular domain. Table 79 lists the 16 NIS+ tables and the information they store.

Table 79   NIS+ Tables

Table	Information in the Table
Hosts	Network address and host name of every workstation in the domain.
Bootparams	Location of the root, swap, and dump partition of every diskless client in the domain.
Password	Password information about every NIS+ principal (Nobody, Owner, Group, or World) in the domain, plus a pointer to the shadow file.
Cred	Credentials for principals who have permission to access the information or objects in the domain.
Group	Password, group ID, and members of every group in the domain.

Table 79   NIS+ Tables (Continued)

Table	Information in the Table
Netgroup	The netgroups to which workstations and users in the domain may belong.
Aliases	Information about the `sendmail` and e-mail aliases of individual users in the domain.
Timezone	The time zone of every workstation in the domain.
Networks	The networks in the domain and their canonical names.
Netmasks	The networks in the domain and their associated netmasks.
Ethers	The Ethernet address of every workstation in the domain.
Services	The names of IP services used in the domain and their port numbers.
Protocols	The list of IP protocols used in the domain.
RPC	The RPC program numbers for RPC services available in the domain.
Auto_Home	The location of all users' home directories in the domain.
Auto_Master	Automounter map information.

You can access information in NIS+ tables either by entry row or by column, as shown in Figure 20.

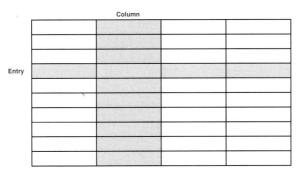

Figure 20   Entry Row and Columns in a Table

For example, if you want to find the network address of a workstation named `drusilla` in the `Hosts` database, you can ask a search program to look through the `hostname` column until it finds `drusilla`, as shown in Figure 21. The program then searches the `drusilla` entry row to find its network address, as shown in Figure 22.

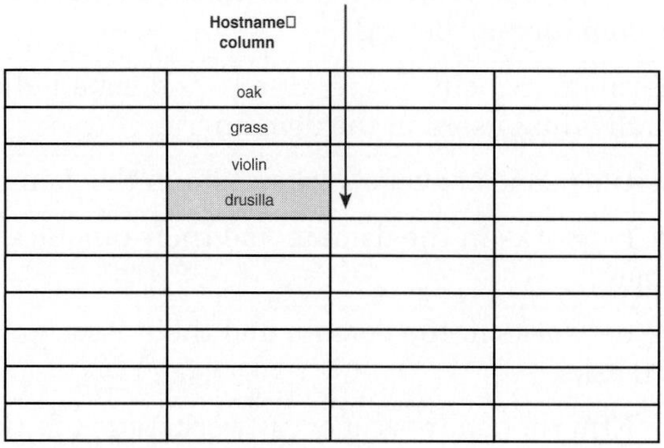

Figure 21   Searching the Hostname Column

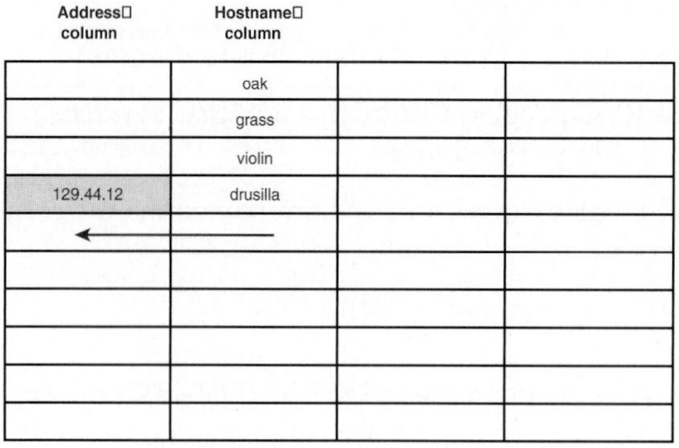

Figure 22   Finding a Network Address

You can use NIS+ commands to perform these types of searches for you. Table 80 lists the NIS+ administrative commands.

Table 80   NIS+ Administrative Commands

Command	Description
nistbladm	Display, add, modify, and delete information in an NIS+ table.
nisgrep	Search for information in an NIS+ table.
nismatch	Search for information in an NIS+ table.
niscat	Display the entire contents of an NIS+ table.

See the manual pages for information about how to use these commands.

NIS+ Security

NIS+ uses a security authorization model that is similar to the UNIX file system model. It specifies that each item in the namespace as well as each record, each column, and each row has associated with it a set of access rights that are granted to four broad classes of principals.

- The owner of the item.
- A group owner of the item.
- All other principals.
- nobody—the class of users not defined in the NIS+ domain or those users accessing NIS+ resources from NIS clients.

The specific access rights are different from the traditional read, write, and execute rights of file systems because of the nature of information services. Refer to your system manual for more information about NIS+ security.

Using SMC Computers and Networks Tool   *New!*

Starting with the Solaris 9 release, you can use the SMC System Configuration/Computers and Networks tool to administer computers and networks. With this tool, you can also create multihomed hosts and rename a computer.

Introducing the IPv6 Internet Protocol

Internet Protocol, version 6 (IPv6) was introduced in the Solaris 8 release. This new protocol version evolved from the current IPv4 version, which is also supported in the Solaris 8 Operating Environment. IPv6 adds increased address space and improves Internet functionality by use of a simplified header format, support for authentication and privacy, autoconfiguration of address assignments, and new quality-of-service capabilities. Networking commands in the Solaris 8 release have been amended to include support for both the IPv4 and IPv6 network protocols.

You can enable IPv6 on a system when you install the Solaris 8 software. If you answer yes to enable the IPv6 during the installation process, you do not need to enable IPv6 manually. Describing how to enable IPv6 manually is beyond the scope of this book. Refer to Sun's *System Administration Guide, IP Services*, for more information.

The IPv6 protocol changes are summarized below.

Expanded Routing and Addressing Capabilities

IPv6 increases the IP address size from 32 bits to 128 bits to support more levels of addressing hierarchy, provide more addressable nodes, and use simpler autoconfiguration of addresses.

A scope field improves the scalability of multicast routing to multicast addresses.

IPv6 supports three types of addresses: `unicast`, `anycast`, and `multicast`. The new `anycast` address is defined to identify sets of nodes, whereby a packet sent to an `anycast` address is delivered to one of the nodes. The use of `anycast` addresses in the IPv6 source route enables nodes to control the path over which their traffic flows.

IPv6 has no broadcast addresses. Multicast addresses are used instead.

Simplified Header Format

Some IPv4 header fields have been dropped or made optional to reduce the common-case processing cost of packet handling. Bandwidth cost of the IPv6 header is kept as low as possible, despite the increased size of the addresses. Even though the IPv6 addresses are four times longer than IPv4 addresses, the IPv6 header is only twice the size of the IPv4 header.

Improved Support for Options

IP header options are encoded to enable more efficient forwarding, less stringent limits on the length of options, and greater flexibility for introducing new options in the future.

Quality-of-Service Capabilities

A new capability enables the labeling of packets belonging to particular traffic flows for which the sender requests special handling, such as nondefault quality of service or real-time service.

Authentication and Privacy Capabilities

IPv6 includes the definition of extensions that provide support for authentication, data integrity, and confidentiality.

Showing Network Status (netstat)

You can use the netstat(1M) command to display the following network status information.

- A list of active sockets for each protocol.
- The state of the interfaces.
- The routing table.
- The multicast routing table.
- The state of DHCP on one or all interfaces.

The Solaris release supports both the IPv4 and IPv6 network interfaces. In the Solaris 8 release, the netstat command has been updated to include the IPv6 interfaces.

Displaying Status of Active TCP and UDP Ports

Use the netstat command with no arguments to display the status of active TCP and UDP ports. The following example shows the output of the netstat command with no arguments, to display the status of active TCP and UDP ports.

```
paperbark% netstat

TCP: IPv4
   Local Address        Remote Address     Swind Send-Q Rwind Recv-Q  State
-------------------- -------------------- ----- ------ ----- ------ -------
localhost.32786      localhost.32773      32768      0 32768      0 ESTABLISHED
localhost.32773      localhost.32786      32768      0 32768      0 ESTABLISHED
localhost.32789      localhost.32784      32768      0 32768      0 ESTABLISHED
localhost.32784      localhost.32789      32768      0 32768      0 ESTABLISHED
localhost.32792      localhost.32791      32768      0 32768      0 ESTABLISHED
localhost.32791      localhost.32792      32768      0 32768      0 ESTABLISHED
localhost.32795      localhost.32784      32768      0 32768      0 ESTABLISHED
localhost.32784      localhost.32795      32768      0 32768      0 ESTABLISHED
localhost.32798      localhost.32797      32768      0 32768      0 ESTABLISHED
localhost.32797      localhost.32798      32768      0 32768      0 ESTABLISHED
localhost.32813      localhost.32784      32768      0 32768      0 ESTABLISHED
localhost.32784      localhost.32813      32768      0 32768      0 ESTABLISHED
localhost.32816      localhost.32815      32767      0 32768      0 ESTABLISHED
localhost.32815      localhost.32816      32768      0 32768      0 ESTABLISHED
paperbark.32891      G3.ftp               17520      0 24820      0 ESTABLISHED
paperbark.8888       paperbark.32904      32768      0 32768      0 TIME_WAIT
paperbark.32905      paperbark.32779      32768      0 32768      0 TIME_WAIT

Active UNIX domain sockets
Address  Type       Vnode    Conn   Local Addr      Remote Addr
707f1d90 stream-ord 705b89e0 00000000 /tmp/.X11-unix/X0
707f1ea8 stream-ord 00000000 00000000
paperbark%
```

Displaying the Status of Network Interfaces

Use the -i option to the netstat command to display the status of network interfaces. The following example uses the netstat -i command on the system paperbark to display the status of network interfaces.

```
paperbark% netstat -i
Name  Mtu   Net/Dest    Address      Ipkts  Ierrs Opkts  Oerrs Collis Queue
lo0   8232  loopback    localhost    11787  0     11787  0     0      0
hme0  1500  paperbark   paperbark    8      0     5      0     0      0

paperbark%
```

Displaying Kernel Routing Tables

Use the -r option to the netstat command to display kernel routing tables, and use the -n option to display network addresses as numbers. The following example uses the netstat -r -n command to display the kernel's routing tables with the network addresses as numbers.

```
paperbark% netstat -r -n

Routing Table: IPv4
  Destination         Gateway              Flags Ref   Use    Interface
-------------------- -------------------- ----- ----- ------ ---------
172.16.8.0           172.16.8.22          U     1     0      hme0
224.0.0.0            172.16.8.22          U     1     0      hme0
127.0.0.1            127.0.0.1            UH    16    11150  lo0
paperbark%
```

Refer to the netstat(1M) manual page for more information.

Displaying Network Interface Parameters (ifconfig)

You can use the ifconfig command to display information about specific interfaces, assign an address to a network interface, or configure network interfaces. The /etc/rc2.d scripts run ifconfig at boot time to define the network address of each interface present on a system. You can also use ifconfig at a later time to redefine an interface address or other operating parameters. Refer to the ifconfig(1M) manual page for complete information. The following sections describe how to use the ifconfig command to display information about specific interfaces.

The ifconfig command has been modified in the Solaris 8 release to create the IPv6 stack and to support new parameters.

Displaying Information About All Interfaces on a System

Use the -a option of the ifconfig command to display information about all interfaces on a system. The following example shows the interfaces on the system paperbark.

```
paperbark% ifconfig -a
lo0: flags=1000849<UP,LOOPBACK,RUNNING,MULTICAST,IPv4> mtu 8232 index 1
        inet 127.0.0.1 netmask ff000000
hme0: flags=1000843<UP,BROADCAST,RUNNING,MULTICAST,IPv4> mtu 1500 index 2
        inet 172.16.8.22 netmask ffffff00 broadcast 172.16.8.255
paperbark%
```

The flags section shows the status of the interface. The mtu field tells you the maximum transfer size in octets. Information on the second line includes the IP address of the host you are using, the netmask currently being used, and the IP broadcast address of the interface.

The following example shows the interfaces on the system castle.

```
castle% ifconfig -a
lo0: flags=849<UP,LOOPBACK,RUNNING,MULTICAST> mtu 8232
        inet 127.0.0.1 netmask ff000000
le0: flags=863<UP,BROADCAST,NOTRAILERS,RUNNING,MULTICAST> mtu 1500
        inet 172.16.8.19 netmask ffff0000 broadcast 172.16.255.255
castle%
```

Displaying Information About Specific Interfaces

Use the following syntax to display information about the configuration of a specific interface.

```
ifconfig interface-name [protocol-family]
```

The following example displays information about the hme0 interface.

```
paperbark% su
Password
# ifconfig hme0
hme0: flags=1000843<UP,BROADCAST,RUNNING,MULTICAST,IPv4> mtu 1500 index 2
        inet 172.16.8.22 netmask ffffff00 broadcast 172.16.8.255
        ether 8:0:20:7d:79:d4
#
```

The flags section shows that the interface is configured UP, is capable of broadcasting, and not using trailer link-level encapsulation. The mtu field tells you that this interface has a maximum transfer size of 1500 octets.

Information on the second line includes the IP address of the host, the netmask currently being used, and the IP broadcast address of the interface. The third line gives the system address (in this case, Ethernet) of the host.

New! Displaying Packet Contents

You can use the snoop(1M) command to capture network packets and display their contents. You can display packets as soon as they are received or save them to a file. When snoop writes to an intermediate file, it is unlikely that you will lose packets under busy trace conditions. You can then use snoop to interpret the file. See the snoop(1M) manual page for more information about using the snoop command.

You must run snoop as root to capture packets to and from the default interface in promiscuous mode. In summary form, only data that pertains to the highest-level protocol is displayed.

Checking All Packets from Your System

Use the following steps to check all packets from your system.

1. Become superuser.
2. Type **netstat -i** and press Return.

   Review the output to determine the interfaces that are attached to the system.
3. Type **snoop** and press Return.

   Packet information is displayed.
4. Press **Control-C** to halt the process.

The following example traces packets during an FTP file transfer.

```
mopoke% netstat -i
Name  Mtu   Net/Dest    Address      Ipkts  Ierrs Opkts  Oerrs Collis Queue
lo0   8232  loopback    localhost    11197  0     11197  0     0      0
eri0  1500  mopoke      mopoke       537    0     9      3     0      0

mopoke% su
Password:
# snoop
Using device /dev/eri (promiscuous mode)
        mopoke -> G4        FTP C port=32830 PORT 172,16,8,25,128
           G4 -> mopoke     FTP R port=32830 200 PORT command suc
        mopoke -> G4        FTP C port=32830 STOR examples\r\n
           G4 -> mopoke     FTP-DATA R port=32834
        mopoke -> G4        FTP-DATA C port=32834
           G4 -> mopoke     FTP-DATA R port=32834
           G4 -> mopoke     FTP R port=32830 150 Opening BINARY m
        mopoke -> G4        FTP-DATA C port=32834 mopoke% netstat -i\nN
        mopoke -> G4        FTP-DATA C port=32834
           G4 -> mopoke     FTP-DATA R port=32834
           G4 -> mopoke     FTP-DATA R port=32834
        mopoke -> G4        FTP-DATA C port=32834
```

```
      mopoke -> G4          FTP C port=32830
          G4 -> mopoke      FTP R port=32830 226 Transfer complet
      mopoke -> G4          FTP C port=32830
          G4 -> 172.16.8.255 UDP D=631 S=631 LEN=76
          G4 -> 172.16.8.255 UDP D=631 S=631 LEN=118
          G4 -> 172.16.8.255 UDP D=631 S=631 LEN=107
^C#
```

Capturing snoop Results to a File

Use the following steps to capture `snoop` results to a file.

1. Become superuser.
2. Type **snoop -o** *filename* and press Return.

   Review the output to determine the interfaces that are attached to the system.
3. To inspect the file, type **snoop -i** *filename* and press Return.

Secure Shell Commands

New!

Secure Shell commands enable users to securely access a remote host on an unsecured network. Passwords, public keys, or both provide authentication. All network traffic is encrypted to prevent others from reading an intercepted communication or spoofing the system.

The Solaris 9 release provides the Secure Shell commands described in Table 81 to communicate among systems.

Table 81 Secure Shell Commands

Command	Description
scp(1)	Secure copy (remote file copy program).
sftp(1)	Secure file transfer program.
ssh(1)	Open SSH client (remote login program).
ssh-add(1)	Add RSA or DSA identities for the authentication agent.
ssh-agent(1)	Authentication agent.
ssh-http-proxy-connect(1)	
	Secure Shell proxy for HTTP.
ssh-keygen(1)	
	Authentication key generation.

Table 81   Secure Shell Commands (Continued)

Command	Description
`ssh-socks5-proxy-connect(1)`	
	Secure Shell proxy for SOCKS5.
`sshd(1M)`	Secure Shell daemon.
`ssh_config(4)`	
	SSH client configuration file.
`sshd_config(4)`	
	SSH server configuration file.

Users can be authenticated with an account password or with a public/private key pair stored on the local host in the user's home directory in the `.ssh` subdirectory. The remote host is provided with the public key, which is required to complete the authentication. Table 82 lists the default names for the identity files that store the public and private keys.

Table 82   Naming Conventions for Private/Public Keys

Private Key	Public Key	Cipher and Protocol Version
`identity`	`identity.pub`	RSA v1
`id_rsa`	`id_rsa.pub`	RSA v2
`id_dsa`	`id_dsa.pub`	DSA v2

Secure Shell supports two versions of the Secure Shell protocol: the original version 1 and the more secure version 2. Version 2 also amends some of the basic security design flaws of version 1. Version 1 use is discouraged, and the SSH server daemon's configuration file turns on only SSH v2 compatibility (see the `Protocol` line in `/etc/ssh/sshd_config`). Version 1 is provided only to assist users migrating to version 2.

Table 83 lists the authentication methods and local and remote host requirements.

Table 83   Authentication Methods for Secure Shell

Authentication Method	Local Host Requirements	Remote Host Requirements
Password-based (v1 or v2)	User account	User account

Table 83   Authentication Methods for Secure Shell (Continued)

Authentication Method	Local Host Requirements	Remote Host Requirements
RSA/DSA public key (v2)	User account Private key in `$HOME/.ssh/id_rsa` or `$HOME/.ssh/id_dsa` Public key in `$HOME/.ssh/id_rsa.pub` or `$HOME/.ssh/id_dsa.pub`	User account User's public key (`id_rsa.pub` or `id_dsa.pub`) in `$HOME/.ssh/authorized_keys`
RSA public key (v1)	User account Private key in `$HOME/.ssh/identity` Public key in `$HOME/.ssh/identity.pub`	User account User's public key (`identity.pub`) in `$HOME/.ssh/authorized_keys`
`.rhosts` with RSA (v1)	User account	User account Local host name in `/etc/hosts.equiv` `/etc/shosts/equiv` `$HOME/.rhosts` or `$home/.shosts`
`.rhosts` only (v1 or v2)	User account	User account Local host name in `/etc/hosts.equiv` `/etc/shosts/equiv` `$HOME/.rhosts` or `$home/.shosts`

`.rhosts` provides only weak security, and SSH in the Solaris 9 Operating Environment is, by default, configured to ignore `.rhosts` completely. `.rhosts` with RSA (v1) and password-based authentication (v1 or v2) provide medium security. RSA public key (v1) and RSA/DSA public key (v2) provide strong security. Password-based authentication is the default.

Benefits of SSH

SSH provides a secure replacement for the `rsh`, `rlogin`, `rcp`, `telnet`, and `ftp` commands. It automatically tunnels X11 traffic and allows authentication with passwords, Kerberos 4 and 5, and public keypairs.

With Secure Shell, you can log in to another host securely over an unsecured network, copy files securely between two hosts, and run commands securely on the remote host.

SSH Configuration

At boot time, the `/etc/init.d/sshd` script normally starts the `sshd` Secure Shell daemon. The daemon listens for connections from clients. When the user runs the `ssh`, `scp`, or `sftp` command, a Secure Shell session begins. A new `sshd` daemon is forked for each incoming connection to handle key exchange, encryption, authentication, command execution, and data exchange with the client. The client-side configuration files and server-side configuration files determine the session characteristics. After the authentication succeeds, the user can execute commands remotely and copy data between hosts.

Configuring Secure Shell Clients

The client-side characteristics of a Secure Shell session are usually governed by the systemwide configuration file `/etc/ssh/ssh_config`, which the administrator sets up. Users can override settings in the systemwide configuration file with the configuration in the user's `$HOME/.ssh_config` file. In addition, the user can override both configuration files on the command line.

The default `/etc/ssh/ssh_config` file is shown below.

```
# Copyright (c) 2001 by Sun Microsystems, Inc.
# All rights reserved.
#
# ident   "@(#)ssh_config   1.2   01/10/08 SMI"
#
# This file provides defaults for ssh(1).
# The values can be changed in per-user configuration files $HOME/.ssh/config
# or on the command line of ssh(1).

# Configuration data is parsed as follows:
#  1. command line options
#  2. user-specific file
#  3. system-wide file /etc/ssh/ssh_config
#
# Any configuration value is only changed the first time it is set.
# host-specific definitions should be at the beginning of the
# configuration file, and defaults at the end.

# Example (matches compiled in defaults):
#
# Host *
#    ForwardAgent no
```

```
#    ForwardX11 no
#    PubkeyAuthentication yes
#    PasswordAuthentication yes
#    FallBackToRsh no
#    UseRsh no
#    BatchMode no
#    CheckHostIP yes
#    StrictHostKeyChecking ask
#    EscapeChar ~
```

Lines have the format keyword arguments and are case sensitive.

Table 84 lists valid keywords and their descriptions.

Table 84   Valid Keywords for the ssh_config File

Keyword	Description
BatchMode	The argument must be yes or no. If set to yes, passphrase/password querying is disabled. This option is useful in scripts and other batch jobs for which no user is present to supply the password.
CheckHostIP	If this option is set to yes, ssh additionally checks the host IP address in the known_hosts file. This option enables ssh to detect if a host key changed because of DNS spoofing. If the option is set to no, the check is not executed.
Cipher	Specify the cipher to use for encrypting the session in protocol version 1; blowfish and 3des are the only valid values. Specify the ciphers allowed for protocol version 2 in order of preference. Comma-separate multiple ciphers. The default is 3des-cbc,blowfish-cbc,aes-128-cbc.
Compression	Specify whether to use compression. The argument must be yes or no.
CompressionLevel	
	Specify the compression level to use if compression is enabled. The argument must be an integer from 1 (fast) to 9 (slow, best). The default level is 6, which is good for most applications.
ConnectionAttempts	
	Specify the number of tries (one per second) to make before falling back to rsh or exiting. The argument must be an integer. This option can be useful in scripts if the connection sometimes fails.

Table 84   *Valid Keywords for the ssh_config FIle (Continued)*

Keyword	Description
DSAAuthentication	
	Specify whether to try DSA authentication. The argument to this keyword must be yes or no. DSA authentication is tried only if a DSA identity file exists. Note that this option applies to protocol version 2 only.
EscapeChar	Set the escape character. The default is tilde (~). You can also set the escape character on the command line. The argument should be a single character, ^, followed by a letter, or none to disable the escape character entirely (making the connection transparent for binary data).
FallBackToRsh	
	Specify that if connecting with ssh fails because of a connection-refused error (there is no sshd listening on the remote host), automatically use rsh(1) instead (after a suitable warning about the session being unencrypted). The argument must be yes or no.
ForwardAgent	Specify whether to forward the connection to the authentication agent (if any) on the remote system. The argument must be yes or no. The default is no.
ForwardX11	Specify whether X11 connections are automatically redirected over the secure channel and DISPLAY set. The argument must be yes or no. The default is no.
GatewayPorts	Specify whether remote hosts are allowed to connect to local forwarded ports. The argument must be yes or no. The default is no.
GlobalKnownHostsFile	
	Specify a file to use instead of /etc/ssh_known_hosts.
Host	Restrict the following declarations (up to the next Host keyword) to be those only for hosts that match one of the patterns given after the keyword. You can use asterisk (*) and question mark (?) as wildcards in the patterns. To provide global defaults for all hosts, use a single *. The host is the *hostname* argument given on the command line (that is, the name is not converted to a canonicalized host name before matching).

Table 84   Valid Keywords for the ssh_config FIle (Continued)

Keyword	Description
HostName	Specify the real host name to log in to. You can use this option to specify nicknames or abbreviations for hosts. Default is the name given on the command line. Numeric IP addresses are also permitted (both on the command line and in `HostName` specifications).
IdentityFile	Specify the file from which the user's RSA authentication identity is read. The default is `$HOME/.ssh/identity` in the user's home directory. Additionally, any identities represented by the authentication agent are used for authentication. The file name can use the tilde (~) syntax to refer to a user's home directory. You can specify multiple identity files in configuration files; all of these identities are tried in sequence.
IdentityFile2	
	Specify the file from which the user's DSA authentication identity is read. The default is `$HOME/.ssh/id_dsa` in the user's home directory. The file name can use the tilde (~) syntax to refer to a user's home directory. You can have multiple identity files specified in configuration files; all of these identities are tried in sequence.
KeepAlive	Specify whether the system should send keepalive messages to the other side. If the messages are sent, death of the connection or crash of one of the systems are properly noticed. However, connections die if the route is down temporarily, which can be annoying.

The default is `yes` (to send keepalives), which means the client notices if the network goes down or the remote host dies. This behavior is important in scripts, and many users also want it. To disable keepalives, set the value to `no` in both the server and the client configuration files. |
| LocalForward | Specify that a TCP/IP port on the local system be forwarded over the secure channel to a given *host:port* from the remote system. The first argument must be a port number, and the second must be *host:port*. You can specify multiple forwardings, and you can specify additional forwardings on the command line. Only superuser can forward privileged ports. |

Table 84   *Valid Keywords for the ssh_config FIle (Continued)*

Keyword	Description
LogLevel	Specify the verbosity level used when logging messages from ssh. The possible values are QUIET, FATAL, ERROR, INFO, VERBOSE, and DEBUG. The default is INFO.
NumberOfPasswordPrompts	
	Specify the number of password prompts before giving up. The argument to this keyword must be an integer. The default is 3.
PasswordAuthentication	
	Specify whether to use password authentication. The argument to this keyword must be yes or no. Note that this option applies to both protocol versions 1 and 2.
Port	Specify the port number to connect on the remote host. The default is 22.
Protocol	Specify the protocol versions ssh should support, in order of preference. The possible values are 1 and 2. Comma-separate multiple versions. The default is 1, 2, which means that ssh tries version 1 and falls back to version 2 if version 1 is not available.
ProxyCommand	Specify the command to use to connect to the server. The command string extends to the end of the line and is executed with /bin/sh. In the command string, for %h substitute the host name to connect, and for %p substitute the port. The string can be any valid command and should read from its standard input and write to its standard output. It should eventually connect an sshd(1M) server running on some system or execute sshd -i somewhere. Host key management is done by use of the HostName of the host being connected (defaulting to the name typed by the user). Note that CheckHostIP is not available for connections with a proxy command.
RemoteForward	
	Specify that a TCP/IP port on the remote system be forwarded over the secure channel to a given *host:port* from the local system. The first argument must be a port number, and the second must be *host:port*. You can

Table 84   Valid Keywords for the ssh_config FIle (Continued)

Keyword	Description
	specify multiple forwardings and give additional forwardings on the command line. Only superuser can forward privileged ports.
RhostsAuthentication	
	Specify whether to try `rhosts`-based authentication. Note that this declaration affects only the client side and has no effect whatsoever on security. Disabling `rhosts` authentication can reduce authentication time on slow connections when `rhosts` authentication is not used. Most servers do not permit `RhostsAuthentication`, because it is not secure (see `RhostsRSAAuthentication`). The argument to this keyword must be `yes` or `no`.
RhostsRSAAuthentication	
	Specify whether to try `rhosts`-based authentication with RSA host authentication. This authentication method is the primary one for most sites. The argument must be `yes` or `no`.
StrictHostKeyChecking	
	If this option is set to `yes`, `ssh` never automatically adds host keys to the `$HOME/.ssh/known_hosts` file and refuses to connect hosts whose host key has changed. This option provides maximum protection against Trojan horse attacks. However, it can be inconvenient if you do not have good `/etc/ssh_known_hosts` files installed, and you frequently connect new hosts. This option forces the user to manually add any new hosts. Normally, this option is disabled, and new hosts are added automatically to the known host files. The host keys of known hosts are verified automatically in either case. The argument must be `yes` or `no`.
UsePrivilegedPort	
	Specify whether to use a privileged port for outgoing connections. The argument must be `yes` or `no`. The default is `yes`. Note that setting this option to `no` turns off `RhostsAuthentication` and `RhostsRSAAuthentication`.

Table 84   Valid Keywords for the ssh_config FIle (Continued)

Keyword	Description
`User`	Specify the user to log in as. This option can be useful if you have different user names on different systems. Using this option means you do not need to enter the user name on the command line.
`UserKnownHostsFile`	
	Specify a file to use instead of `$HOME/.ssh/known_hosts`.
`UseRsh`	Use `rlogin` or `rsh` for this host. It is possible that the host does not support the `ssh` protocol. `ssh` immediately executes `rsh(1)`. All other options (except `HostName`) are ignored if you specify this option. The argument must be `yes` or `no`.
`XAuthLocation`	
	Specify the location of the `xauth(1)` program. The default is `/usr/openwin/bin/xauth`.

You determine the authentication method for a client by setting one of the following keywords to `yes`.

- `DSAAuthentication`
- `PasswordAuthentication`
- `RhostsAuthentication`
- `RhostsRSAAuthentication`

Configuring Secure Shell Servers

The server-side characteristics of a Secure Shell session are usually governed by the systemwide configuration file `/etc/ssh/sshd_config`, which the administrator sets up. Users can override settings in the system-wide configuration file with the configuration in the user's `$HOME/.ssh_config` file only if the user runs his own copy of the `sshd` daemon on a nonprivileged port. In addition, the user can override both configuration files on the command line.

The default `/etc/ssh/sshd_config` file is shown below.

```
# Copyright (c) 2001 by Sun Microsystems, Inc.
# All rights reserved.
#
# ident  "@(#)sshd_config  1.3  01/10/08 SMI"
#
# Configuration file for sshd(1m)

# Protocol versions supported
```

```
#
# The sshd shipped in this release of Solaris has support for major versions
# 1 and 2.  It is recommended due to security weaknesses in the v1 protocol
# that sites run only v2 if possible. Support for v1 is provided to help sites
# with existing ssh v1 clients/servers to transition.
# Support for v1 may not be available in a future release of Solaris.
#
# To enable support for v1 an RSA1 key must be created with ssh-keygen(1).
# RSA and DSA keys for protocol v2 are created by /etc/init.d/sshd if they
# do not already exist, RSA1 keys for protocol v1 are not automatically created.

# Uncomment ONLY ONE of the following Protocol statements.

# Only v2 (recommended)
Protocol 2

# Both v1 and v2 (not recommended)
#Protocol 2,1

# Only v1 (not recommended)
#Protocol 1

# Listen port (the IANA registered port number for ssh is 22)
Port 22

# The default listen address is all interfaces, this may need to be changed
# if you wish to restrict the interfaces sshd listens on for a multi homed host.
# Multiple ListenAddress entries are allowed.

# IPv4 only
#ListenAddress 0.0.0.0
# IPv4 & IPv6
ListenAddress ::

# Port forwarding
AllowTcpForwarding no

# If port forwarding is enabled, specify if the server can bind to INADDR_ANY.
# This allows the local port forwarding to work when connections are received
# from any remote host.
GatewayPorts no

# X11 tunneling options
X11Forwarding no
X11DisplayOffset 10

# The maximum number of concurrent unauthenticated connections to sshd.
# start:rate:full see sshd(1) for more information.
# The default is 10 unauthenticated clients.
#MaxStartups 10:30:60

# Banner to be printed before authentication starts.
#Banner /etc/issue

# Should sshd print the /etc/motd file and check for mail.
# On Solaris it is assumed that the login shell will do these (eg /etc/profile).
PrintMotd no
CheckMail no

# KeepAlive specifies whether keep alive messages are sent to the client.
# See sshd(1) for detailed description of what this means.
# Note that the client may also be sending keep alive messages to the server.
KeepAlive yes

# Syslog facility and level
SyslogFacility auth
LogLevel info

#
# Authentication configuration
#

# Host private key files
# Must be on a local disk and readable only by the root user (root:sys 600).
HostKey /etc/ssh/ssh_host_rsa_key
HostKey /etc/ssh/ssh_host_dsa_key
```

```
# Default Encryption algorithms and Message Authentication codes
Ciphers    aes128-cbc,blowfish-cbc,3des-cbc
MACS       hmac-sha1,hmac-md5

# Length of the server key
# Default 768, Minimum 512
ServerKeyBits 768

# sshd regenerates the key every KeyRegenerationInterval seconds.
# The key is never stored anywhere except the memory of sshd.
# The default is 1 hour (3600 seconds).
KeyRegenerationInterval 3600

# Ensure secure permissions on users .ssh directory.
StrictModes yes

# Length of time in seconds before a client that hasn't completed
# authentication is disconnected.
# Default is 600 seconds. 0 means no time limit.
LoginGraceTime 600

# Maximum number of retries for authentication
# Default is 6. Default (if unset) for MaxAuthTriesLog is MaxAuthTries / 2
MaxAuthTries      6
MaxAuthTriesLog   3

# Are logins to accounts with empty passwords allowed.
# If PermitEmptyPasswords is no, pass PAM_DISALLOW_NULL_AUTHTOK
# to pam_authenticate(3PAM).
PermitEmptyPasswords no

# To disable tunneled clear text passwords, change PasswordAuthentication to no.
PasswordAuthentication yes

# Use PAM via keyboard interactive method for authentication.
# Depending on the setup of pam.conf(4) this may allow tunneled clear text
# passwords even when PasswordAuthentication is set to no. This is dependent
# on what the individual modules request and is out of the control of sshd
# or the protocol.
PAMAuthenticationViaKBDInt yes

# Are root logins permitted using sshd.
# Note that sshd uses pam_authenticate(3PAM) so the root (or any other) user
# maybe denied access by a PAM module regardless of this setting.
# Valid options are yes, without-password, no.
PermitRootLogin no

# sftp subsystem
Subsystem    sftp    /usr/lib/ssh/sftp-server


# SSH protocol v1 specific options
#
# The following options only apply to the v1 protocol and provide
# some form of backwards compatibility with the very weak security
# of /usr/bin/rsh.  Their use is not recommended and the functionality
# will be removed when support for v1 protocol is removed.

# Should sshd use .rhosts and .shosts for password less authentication.
IgnoreRhosts yes
RhostsAuthentication no

# Rhosts RSA Authentication
# For this to work you will also need host keys in /etc/ssh/ssh_known_hosts.
# If the user on the client side is not root then this won't work on
# Solaris since /usr/bin/ssh is not installed setuid.
RhostsRSAAuthentication no

# Uncomment if you don't trust ~/.ssh/known_hosts for RhostsRSAAuthentication.
#IgnoreUserKnownHosts yes

# Is pure RSA authentication allowed.
# Default is yes
RSAAuthentication yes
```

Lines have the format keyword arguments and are case sensitive.

Table 85 lists valid keywords and their descriptions.

Table 85   Valid Keywords and Descriptions for sshd_config

Keyword	Description
AllowGroups	You can follow this keyword with a space-separated list of names of groups that are allowed to log in. If specified, login is allowed only for users whose primary group matches one of the patterns. You can use asterisk (*) and question mark (?) as wildcards in the patterns. Only group names are valid; a numerical group ID is not recognized. By default, login is allowed regardless of the primary group.
AllowTcpForwarding	
	Specify whether TCP forwarding is permitted. The default is yes. Note that disabling TCP forwarding does not improve security unless users are also denied shell access, because they can always install their own forwarders.
AllowUsers	Follow this keyword with a space-separated list of names of users who are allowed to log in. If specified, login is allowed only for a user whose name matches one of the patterns. You can use asterisk (*) and question mark (?) as wildcards in the patterns. Only user names are valid; a numerical user ID is not recognized. By default, login is allowed regardless of the user name.
Ciphers	Specify the ciphers allowed for protocol version 2. Comma-separate multiple ciphers. The default is 3des-cbc,blowfish-cbc,aes-128-cbc.
CheckMail	Specify whether sshd checks for new mail for interactive logins. The default is no.
DenyGroups	You can follow this keyword with a space-separated list of group names. Users whose primary group matches one of the patterns are not allowed to log in. You can use asterisk (*) and question mark (?) as wildcards in the patterns. Only group names are valid; a numerical group ID is not recognized. By default, login is allowed regardless of the primary group.

Table 85   Valid Keywords and Descriptions for sshd_config (Continued)

Keyword	Description
DenyUsers	You can follow this keyword with a space-separated list of user names. Login is disallowed for user names that match one of the patterns. You can use asterisk (*) and question mark (?) as wildcards in the patterns. Only user names are valid; a numerical user ID is not recognized. By default, login is allowed regardless of the user name.
DSAAuthentication	
	Specify whether DSA authentication is allowed. The default is yes. Note that this option applies only to protocol version 2.
GatewayPorts	Specify whether remote hosts are allowed to connect to ports forwarded for the client. The argument must be yes or no. The default is no.
HostKey	Specify the file containing the private RSA host key (default /etc/ssh_host_key) used by SSH protocols. The /etc/ssh/sshd_config file provides two HostKey lines, one for the v3 RSA key (/etc/ssh/ssh_host_rsa_key) and one for the v2 DSA key (/etc/ssh/ssh_host_dsa_key).
IgnoreRhosts	Specify that .rhosts and .shosts files are not used in authentication. /etc/hosts.equiv and /etc/shosts.equiv are still used. The default is yes.
IgnoreUserKnownHosts	
	Specify whether sshd ignores the user's $HOME/.ssh/known_hosts file during RhostsRSAAuthentication. The default is no.
KeepAlive	Specify whether the system should send keepalive messages to the other side. If they are sent, death of the connection or crash of one of the systems is properly noticed. However, connections die if the route is down temporarily, which can be annoying. On the other hand, if keepalives are not sent, sessions can hang indefinitely on the server, leaving "ghost" users and consuming server resources. The default is yes (to send keepalives), and the server notices if the network goes down or the client host reboots. This option avoids infinitely hanging sessions.

Table 85   Valid Keywords and Descriptions for sshd_config (Continued)

Keyword	Description
	To disable keepalives, set the value to no in both the server and the client configuration files.
KeyRegenerationInterval	
	Automatically regenerate the server key after *n* seconds (if it has been used). Regeneration prevents decryption of captured sessions by someone later breaking into the system and stealing the keys. The key is never stored anywhere. If the value is 0, the key is never regenerated. The default is 3600 (seconds).
ListenAddress	
	Specify the local address on which sshd listens. The default is to listen to all local addresses. Multiple options of this type are permitted. Additionally, the Ports options must precede this option.
LoginGraceTime	
	Disconnect the server after *n* seconds if the user has not successfully logged in. If the value is 0, there is no time limit. The default is 600 (seconds).
LogLevel	Specify the verbosity level used when messages from sshd are logged. The possible values are QUIET, FATAL, ERROR, INFO, VERBOSE, and DEBUG. The default is INFO. Logging with level DEBUG violates the privacy of users and is not recommended.
MaxStartups	Specify the maximum number of concurrent, unauthenticated connections to the sshd daemon. Additional connections are dropped until authentication succeeds or the LoginGraceTime expires for a connection. The default is 10. Alternatively, you can enable random early drop by specifying the three colon-separated values *start:rate:full* (for example, 10:30:60). For this example, sshd refuses connection attempts with a probability of 30 percent (*rate*/100) when there are currently 10 (from the start field) unauthenticated connections. The probability increases linearly and all connection attempts are refused if the number of unauthenticated connections reaches 60 (*full*).

Table 85   *Valid Keywords and Descriptions for sshd_config (Continued)*

Keyword	Description
PasswordAuthentication	
	Specify whether password authentication is allowed. The default is yes. Note that this option applies to both protocol versions 1 and 2.
PermitEmptyPasswords	
	When password authentication is allowed, it specifies whether the server allows login to accounts with empty password strings. The default is no.
PermitRootLogin	
	Specify whether root can log in with ssh. The argument must be one of yes, without-password, or no. The default is no. When this options is set to without-password, root can log in only through public key authentication; passwords are ignored. Note that the Secure Shell is integrated with the PAM subsystem. You can configure PAM to deny login access to root regardless of this setting. Root login with RSA authentication when the command option is specified is allowed regardless of the value of this setting. This setting might be useful for taking remote backups even if root login is normally not allowed.
Port	Specify the port number at which sshd listens. The default is 22. You can specify multiple options of this type.
PrintMotd	Specify whether sshd displays the contents of /etc/motd when a user logs in interactively. (On some systems, /etc/motd is also displayed by the shell or a shell startup file, such as /etc/profile.) The default is yes.
Protocol	Specify the protocol versions sshd supports. The possible values are 1 and 2. You must comma-separate multiple versions. The default is 2.
RhostsAuthentication	
	Specify whether authentication with rhosts or /etc/hosts.equiv files is sufficient. Normally, you should not permit this method because it is insecure. Use

Table 85   Valid Keywords and Descriptions for sshd_config (Continued)

Keyword	Description
	`RhostsRSAAuthentication` instead because it performs RSA-based host authentication in addition to normal `rhosts` or `/etc/hosts.equiv` authentication. The default is `no`.
`RhostsRSAAuthentication`	
	Specify whether `rhosts` or `/etc/hosts.equiv` authentication together with successful RSA host authentication is allowed. The default is `no`.
`RSAAuthentication`	
	Specify whether pure RSA authentication is allowed. The default is `yes`. Note that this option applies only to protocol version 1.
`ServerKeyBits`	
	Define the number of bits in the server key. The minimum value is `512`, and the default is `768`.
`StrictModes`	Specify whether `sshd` checks file modes and ownership of the user's files and home directory before accepting login. This behavior is normally desirable because novices sometimes accidentally leave their directory or files world-writable. The default is `yes`.
`Subsystem`	Configure an external subsystem (for example, a file transfer daemon). Arguments should be a subsystem name and a command to execute on subsystem request. The command `sftp-server`(1M) implements the `sftp` file transfer subsystem. By default, no subsystems are defined. Note that this option applies only to protocol version 2.
`SyslogFacility`	
	Give the facility code used when messages from `sshd` are logged. The possible values are `DAEMON`, `USER`, `AUTH`, `LOCAL0`, `LOCAL1`, `LOCAL2`, `LOCAL3`, `LOCAL4`, `LOCAL5`, `LOCAL6`, and `LOCAL7`. The default is `AUTH`.
`X11DisplayOffset`	
	Specify the first display number available for `sshd` X11 forwarding. This option prevents `sshd` from interfering with real X11 servers. The default is `10`.

Table 85   *Valid Keywords and Descriptions for sshd_config (Continued)*

Keyword	Description
`X11Forwarding`	
	Specify whether X11 forwarding is permitted. The default is `no`. Note that disabling X11 forwarding does not improve security in any way, because users can always install their own forwarders.
`XAuthLocation`	
	Specify the location of the `xauth`(1) program. The default is `/usr/openwin/bin/xauth`.

You determine the authentication method for a server by setting one of the following keywords to `yes`.

- `DSAAuthentication`
- `PasswordAuthentication`
- `RhostsAuthentication`
- `RhostsRSAAuthentication`
- `RSAAuthentication`

X11 Forwarding

The X Window system (also known as X11) lets you log in to a remote system, run X11 programs on that system, and, if the X11 server program running on your local system controls the monitor at which you are working, displays the X11 program output there. If you use the Solaris `rsh`, `rlogin`, or `telnet` commands without SSH to log in to that remote system, you need to perform the following manual steps for this process to work properly.

- Before you log in to the remote system by using `rsh`, `rlogin`, or `telnet`, run `xhost +remote-system` to give the remote system permission to send X11 datastreams from any X11 program to your local X11 server program.
- Once you log in to the remote system, set the `DISPLAY` environment variable to indicate the X11 server program to which all X11 client programs send their data streams (in this case, your X11 server program).

The Secure Shell automates the X11 forwarding process and secures it by encrypting the X11 datastreams as they pass over the network. Sun disables the X11 forwarding feature by default. You must enable it for both the client and server by making the following changes to both the local and remote systems.

In the `/etc/ssh/ssh_config` file, change

```
# ForwardX11 no
```

to

```
Forwardx11 yes
```

Be sure to remove the # comment character at the beginning of the line as well.

This change takes effect the next time you run `ssh`.

In the `/etc/ssh/sshd_config` file, change

```
X11Forwarding no
```

to

```
X11Forwarding yes
```

To make this change take effect, restart the Secure Shell daemon on both systems by running

```
# /etc/init.d/sshd stop
# /etc/init.d/sshd start
```

You can now use `ssh` to log in to the remote system. Run an X11 client such as `xterm` to verify that X11 Forwarding works properly. If the `xterm` window is displayed on your local X11 display, then everything is working.

Public Key Authentication with the Secure Shell

The examples in this section assume that you have a single home directory that is automounted on every system under your control at `/home/`*username*. By convention, this directory is referenced with the environment variable $HOME. If you have a unique account and home directory on every system that you log in to, then a reference to the $HOME/.ssh/ directory implies that this directory exists on every system (that is, you need to copy the contents of that directory to each unique home directory you have before the procedures in this section work).

The Secure Shell uses regular password authentication by default; that is, when you use ssh to log in to a remote system, you are asked to enter a password to authenticate your account identity. Once you enter the correct password, you are allowed to log in. The Secure Shell also allows you to use public key authentication instead of password authentication. Public key authentication has the following benefits.

- When set up properly, you can log in to a remote host without entering a password. That means you get all the benefits that .rhosts previously gave you without any of the liabilities.

- It is much more difficult to break a public key's passphrase than your regular UNIX password. Accounts are better protected when you disallow the use of the rlogin, rsh, telnet, rcp, and ftp commands at your site and use only the Secure Shell commands.

The first step in using public key authentication is to generate one or more public/private keypairs with the ssh-keygen(1) command. Refer to the ssh-keygen(1) manual page for detailed information on the different types of keypairs you can generate.

NOTE. You can have more than one keypair, and you can use each for a different purpose. For example, you can have one keypair for logging in as the root user on the Solaris systems on the manufacturing floor, and another for logging in as the backup administrator on the backup server, and so on. By default, the keypairs are stored in your $HOME/.ssh/ *directory when you create them.*

The following examples create several keypairs. In these examples, $HOME is /home/gmarler.

The following example creates a default 1024-bit RSA keypair. This keypair is treated as your default RSA keypair for use with the SSH v2 protocol. The public key is stored at $HOME/.ssh/id_rsa.pub, and the private key is stored at $HOME/.ssh/id_rsa.

```
[ns3:/home/gmarler]
$ ssh-keygen
Enter file in which to save the key(/home/gmarler/.ssh/id_rsa):
Generating public/private rsa key pair.
Enter passphrase(empty for no passphrase): Enter passphrase.
Enter same passphrase again: Enter passphrase again.
Your identification has been saved in /home/gmarler/.ssh/id_rsa.
Your public key has been saved in /home/gmarler/.ssh/id_rsa.pub.
The key fingerprint is:
md5 1024 d1:88:b9:5c:f1:28:0f:dd:6e:f3:fc:ea:af:3c:21:ed gmarler@ns3
```

The following example creates a 768-bit DSA keypair. This keypair is treated as your default DSA keypair for use with the SSH v2 protocol. The public key is stored as $HOME/.ssh/id_dsa.pub, and the private key is stored as $HOME/.ssh/id_dsa.

```
[ns3:/home/gmarler]
$ ssh-keygen -b 768 -t dsa
Enter file in which to save the key(/home/gmarler/.ssh/id_dsa):
Generating public/private dsa key pair.
Enter passphrase(empty for no passphrase): Enter passphrase.
Enter same passphrase again: Enter passphrase again.
Your identification has been saved in /home/gmarler/.ssh/id_dsa.
Your public key has been saved in /home/gmarler/.ssh/id_dsa.pub.
The key fingerprint is:
md5 768 1d:f0:f5:d5:bd:35:b1:ac:9a:2a:b9:7f:95:14:02:f0 gmarler@ns3
```

The following example creates a 512-bit RSA1 keypair (for use only with SSH protocol v1). This keypair is treated as your default RSA keypair for use with SSH v1 protocol—SSH v1 supported only the use of RSA keys. The public key is stored at $HOME/.ssh/identity.pub, and the private key is stored at $HOME/.ssh/identity.

```
[ns3:/home/gmarler]
$ ssh-keygen -b 512 -t rsa1
Enter file in which to save the key(/home/gmarler/.ssh/identity):
Generating public/private rsa1 key pair.
Enter passphrase(empty for no passphrase): Enter passphrase.
Enter same passphrase again: Enter passphrase again.
Your identification has been saved in /home/gmarler/.ssh/identity.
Your public key has been saved in /home/gmarler/.ssh/identity.pub.
The key fingerprint is:
md5 512 bb:e2:c5:25:4d:d1:89:23:83:9e:89:51:4f:d0:5b:86 gmarler@ns3
```

The following example creates a 2048-bit RSA keypair for use when you log in to remote systems as the root user.

```
[ns3:/home/gmarler]
$ ssh-keygen -b 2048 -f $HOME/.ssh/rootkey -C "Root Admin Keypair"
Generating public/private rsa key pair.
Enter passphrase(empty for no passphrase): Enter passphrase.
Enter same passphrase again: Enter passphrase again.
Your identification has been saved in /home/gmarler/.ssh/rootkey.
Your public key has been saved in /home/gmarler/.ssh/rootkey.pub.
The key fingerprint is:
md5 2048 44:e0:26:4d:6a:93:6c:5c:88:ac:0a:87:e1:d6:ad:8b Root Admin Keypair
```

The following example creates a 1024-bit RSA keypair, with no passphrase, for use in automated batch jobs to remote systems.

You would use this keypair in cron jobs or scripts that use ssh.

NOTE. Because the keypair is not protected by a passphrase, it is only as secure as the permissions on the files you store it in.

```
[ns3:/home/gmarler]
$ ssh-keygen -b 1024 -f $HOME/.ssh/nopasskey -C "Batch Jobs (no passphrase)"
Generating public/private rsa key pair.
Enter passphrase(empty for no passphrase): Press Return.
Enter same passphrase again: Press Return.
Your identification has been saved in /home/gmarler/.ssh/nopasskey.
Your public key has been saved in /home/gmarler/.ssh/nopasskey.pub.
The key fingerprint is:
```

```
md5 1024 21:56:cb:8e:fb:1f:d1:1c:14:50:f2:88:09:f7:39:93 Batch Jobs (no
passphrase)
```

Changing the Passphrase of a Private Key

Once you create keypairs, you can manipulate them in various ways. One
thing you may want to do fairly often is to change the passphrase on a
keypair. The following example changes the passphrase on the 2048-bit RSA
keypair created in one of the previous examples.

```
[ns3:/home/gmarler]
$ ssh-keygen -p -f $HOME/.ssh/rootkey
Enter old passphrase: Enter old passphrase.
Key has comment 'rsa w/o comment'
Enter new passphrase(empty for no passphrase): Enter new passphrase.
Enter same passphrase again: Enter new assphrase again.
Your identification has been saved with the new passphrase.
```

Using the Public Key in Each Keypair

The public key in each keypair is not used by the Secure Shell client. It is
used by sshd on a remote host whenever you try to use ssh to log in to that
remote host. But how does sshd on the remote host get access to your public
key?

When you use ssh to log in to a remote host, ssh on your local host
contacts sshd on the remote host and tells sshd which user you want to log
in as. sshd then looks into the .ssh subdirectory of that user's home
directory for the authorized_keys file. If any of the public keys stored in
that file match the private key you told ssh to use when logging in to the
remote host, the Secure Shell grants you access to that account.

The following example logs you in to a remote host as yourself with public
key authentication.

In this case, you're logging in as yourself, so you need to append one of
your public keys into your $HOME/.ssh/authorized_keys file. For this
example, assume that you are the user gmarler and use the key generated
in the first example above.

```
[ns3:/home/gmarler]
$ cat $HOME/.ssh/id_rsa.pub >>$HOME/.ssh/authorized_keys
```

Now you can try to log in to another host (that has the same home
directory automounted) with the private key (specifying it with the -i option
to ssh) that matches the public key you appended to the authorized_keys
file.

```
[ns3:/home/gmarler]
$ ssh -i $HOME/.ssh/id_rsa ns1.gmarler.com
Enter passphrase for key '/home/gmarler/.ssh/id_rsa': Enter key passphrase.
Last login: Thu Oct 10 18:57:07 2002 from dhcp101.gmarler
Sun Microsystems Inc.   SunOS 5.8      Generic February 2000
Sun Microsystems Inc.   SunOS 5.8      Generic February 2000
Agent pid 17661
[ns1.gmarler.com:/home/gmarler]
 $
```

NOTE. The passphrase you are asked for is NOT your login password, but the passphrase entered for the private key when the keypair was created (or last changed).

The following example logs in to a remote host as the root user with public key authentication.

In this case, you're trying to log in to a remote host as the root user, so you need to find some way to first log in to that host as root, then append the specific public key you want to use to that root's `authorized_keys` file (located at `/.ssh/authorized_keys` on that host). This time, use the key generated specifically for this purpose in the fourth example above.

NOTE. At this point you're already logged in to the remote host as root.

```
[ns1.gmarler.com:/]
# cat /home/gmarler/.ssh/rootkey.pub >>/.ssh/authorized_keys
[ns1.gmarler.com:/]
# exit
```

NOTE. Now you're back on your original system as the user `gmarler`.

```
[ns3:/home/gmarler]
$ ssh -i $HOME/.ssh/rootkey ns1.gmarler.com -l root
Enter passphrase for key '/home/gmarler/.ssh/rootkey': Enter key passphrase.
Last login: Thu Oct 10 23:15:47 2002 from ns3
Sun Microsystems Inc.   SunOS 5.8      Generic February 2000
Sun Microsystems Inc.   SunOS 5.8      Generic February 2000
[ns1.gmarler.com:/]
 #
```

Private Keys and Passphrases

You've probably noticed that a passphrase is usually applied to the private key in each keypair. You apply the passphrase to the private key so that if someone happens to steal your private keys (you don't care if someone takes your public keys; in fact, you want everyone to have them), the thief can't use them. Why not? Because each private key is encrypted with the passphrase you put on it and is useless until it is decrypted.

But, you have to enter a passphrase before using each private key to log in to a remote host, right? That would be true if you used each private key manually, as has been done so far. But that's where the `ssh-agent` program comes in.

The ssh-agent   The `ssh-agent` command has a simple and elegant purpose: it stores one or more of your decrypted private keys in memory so that `ssh` can use them without prompting you for the passphrase every time you use them. And, if you load all of your private keys into `ssh-agent`, `ssh` tries them all in sequence until it finds one that works. You don't have to specify a particular private key on the command line.

How do you use `ssh-agent`? Each user must configure his login environment to properly start and stop this program for every shell he invokes. The following example shows the necessary changes to `$HOME/.profile` if you use the `sh`, `ksh`, or `bash` shells.

```
# Set up SSH-Agent
if [ "$SSH_AUTH_SOCK" = "" -a -f /bin/ssh-agent ]; then
  eval `/bin/ssh-agent`
fi

# Kill the SSH-Agent when you log out…
trap '
   test -n "$SSH_AGENT_PID" && eval `/bin/ssh-agent -k`
' 0
```

The following example shows the changes needed to `$HOME/.login` and `$HOME/.logout` if you used the `csh` or `tcsh` shells.

```
$HOME/.login:
# Start SSH-Agent
eval `/bin/ssh-agent -c`

$HOME/.logout:
# Kill SSH-Agent
if ( "$SSH_AGENT_PID" != "" ) then
  eval `/bin/ssh-agent -k`
endif
```

Once you make these changes and log out and back in, each shell started inherits the environment variable settings that `ssh-agent` sets up (with the `eval` command) so that `ssh` knows how to communicate with `ssh-agent`. Also, the program is terminated whenever you log out, so you don't have hundreds of separate `ssh-agent` programs cluttering up the system.

Now that `ssh-agent` has been set up and automatically starts every time you log in, you need to know how to decrypt and load your private keys into it.

ssh-add   You use `ssh-add` to decrypt and load each private key into your `ssh-agent`. The following example loads all the private keys you generated earlier. You can load the first three default identity keys (RSA, DSA, RSA1) just by running the `ssh-add` command with no arguments, as shown in the following example.

```
[ns3:/home/gmarler]
$ ssh-add
Enter passphrase for gmarler@ns3: Enter passphrase.
Identity added: /home/gmarler/.ssh/identity(gmarler@ns3)
Identity added: /home/gmarler/.ssh/id_rsa(/home/gmarler/.ssh/id_rsa)
Identity added: /home/gmarler/.ssh/id_dsa(/home/gmarler/.ssh/id_dsa)
```

NOTE. This example worked this way only because the private keys all had the same passphrase. If they did not, then you would have to enter each passphrase when prompted.

Now load `rootkey` and `nopasskey`, as shown in the following example.

```
[ns3:/home/gmarler]
$ ssh-add $HOME/.ssh/rootkey
Enter passphrase for /home/gmarler/.ssh/rootkey: Enter passphrase.
Identity added: /home/gmarler/.ssh/rootkey(/home/gmarler/.ssh/rootkey)
[ns3:/home/gmarler]
 $ ssh-add $HOME/.ssh/nopasskey
Identity added: /home/gmarler/.ssh/nopasskey(/home/gmarler/.ssh/nopasskey)
```

Notice that `nopasskey` did not prompt for a passphrase because there is no passkey. It was simply loaded into the `ssh-agent`.

You can see which keys are loaded into this particular `ssh-agent` with the `ssh-add -l` command.

```
[ns3:/home/gmarler]
$ ssh-add -l
md5 512 bb:e2:c5:25:4d:d1:89:23:83:9e:89:51:4f:d0:5b:86 gmarler@ns3(RSA1)
md5 1024 d1:88:b9:5c:f1:28:0f:dd:6e:f3:fc:ea:af:3c:21:ed
 /home/gmarler/.ssh/id_rsa(RSA)
md5 768 1d:f0:f5:d5:bd:35:b1:ac:9a:2a:b9:7f:95:14:02:f0
 /home/gmarler/.ssh/id_dsa(DSA)
md5 2048 44:e0:26:4d:6a:93:6c:5c:88:ac:0a:87:e1:d6:ad:8b
 /home/gmarler/.ssh/rootkey(RSA)
md5 1024 21:56:cb:8e:fb:1f:d1:1c:14:50:f2:88:09:f7:39:93
 /home/gmarler/.ssh/nopasskey(RSA)
```

You have now resolved the problem of having to manually enter the passphrase each time you use `ssh`. Because you now have the rootkey loaded in the `ssh-agent`, try logging into the remote system as root again.

```
[ns3:/home/gmarler]
 $ ssh ns1.gmarler.com -l root
Last login: Thu Oct 10 23:16:11 2002 from ns3
Sun Microsystems Inc.   SunOS 5.8      Generic February 2000
Sun Microsystems Inc.   SunOS 5.8      Generic February 2000
[ns1.gmarler.com:/]
 #
```

Presto! No need to enter a passphrase again (except when you first log in to your account).

The Secure Shell Commands

The following section discusses the ssh, scp, and sftp commands.

NOTE. The examples for these commands use public key authentication, discussed above, instead of password authentication. You won't see the commands prompting for passwords here. If you don't set up public key authentication, then you will be prompted for your account's password.

ssh   The ssh command is a secure replacement for rlogin, rsh, and telnet. It takes the same parameters as rlogin and rsh (and many more), so migration to this tool is easy.

The following example logs in to a remote host as the root user.

```
[ns3:/home/gmarler]
$ ssh ns1.gmarler.com -l root
Last login: Thu Oct 10 23:51:09 2002 from ns3
Sun Microsystems Inc.   SunOS 5.8      Generic February 2000
Sun Microsystems Inc.   SunOS 5.8      Generic February 2000
[ns1.gmarler.com:/]
 #
```

The following example creates a tar archive datastream of the ./src directory and transmits it to another host (by logging in to that host as the current user with ssh) to be extracted in the /tmp directory.

```
[ns3:/home/gmarler]
$ tar cf - ./src | ssh ns1.gmarler.com "(cd /tmp; tar xf -)"
[ns3:/home/gmarler]
 $
```

scp   The scp command is a secure replacement for the rcp command. It takes parameters similar to those of rcp, but is more flexible. The following examples show some ways to use the scp command.

The following example copies the connect.sql file from the current directory to the /tmp directory on host ns1.gmarler.com, as the user gmarler.

```
[ns3:/home/gmarler]
$ scp connect.sql gmarler@ns1.gmarler.com:/tmp
connect.sql          100% |*****************************|    49        00:00
```

The following example logs in to host ns1.gmarler.com as user gmarler and copies the file /tmp/connect.sql to the /tmp directory on the local system.

```
[ns3:/home/gmarler]
$ scp gmarler@ns1.gmarler.com:/tmp/connect.sql /tmp
connect.sql        100% |*****************************|    49       00:00
```

The following example recursively copies the `./bin/` directory on the local system to the `/tmp/bin` directory on system `ns1.gmarler.com`, as user `gmarler`.

```
[ns3:/home/gmarler]
$ scp -r bin/ gmarler@ns1.gmarler.com:/tmp/bin
ksh                100% |*****************************| 1609 KB   00:03
patch              100% |*****************************|  349 KB   00:00
```

The following example logs in to host `ns1.gmarler.com` as the root user and copies the `/etc/passwd` file to the `/tmp` directory on the local system.

```
[ns3:/home/gmarler]
$ scp root@ns1.gmarler.com:/etc/passwd /tmp
passwd             100% |*****************************|   931     00:00
```

sftp   The `sftp` command is a secure replacement for the `ftp` command. It takes parameters similar to those of `ftp`, but is more flexible.

The following example uses `sftp` to connect to the host `ns1.gmarler.com` as the current user, changes to the `/tmp` directory on the local system, and downloads `connect.sql` from that system to `/tmp` on the local system.

```
[ns3:/home/gmarler]
$ sftp ns1.gmarler.com
Connecting to ns1.gmarler.com...
sftp > lcd /tmp
sftp > lpwd
Local working directory: /tmp
sftp > get /home/gmarler/connect.sql
sftp > quit
```

The following example uses `sftp` to connect to the host `ns1.gmarler.com` as the root user, changes to the `/tmp` directory on the local system, changes to the `/etc` directory on the remote system, and downloads the `passwd` file.

```
[ns3:/home/gmarler]
$ sftp root@ns1.gmarler.com
Connecting to ns1.gmarler.com...
sftp > lcd /tmp
sftp > lpwd
Local working directory: /tmp
sftp > cd /etc
sftp > pwd
Remote working directory: /etc
sftp > get passwd
sftp > quit
```

Common Administrative Uses for the Secure Shell

This section describes two common uses for SSH.

Transferring Files Between Systems Securely

Transferring Files Between Systems Securely   Quite often, you need to move files between systems. You can do so securely by using ssh instead of rsh. The following example copies the home directory of the user gmarler from system ns3.gmarler.com to ns1.gmarler.com. This action is done as the root user on ns3.gmarler.com, using public key authentication.

```
[ns3:/home/gmarler]
# cd /home
[ns3:/home]
# tar cf - gmarler | ssh ns1.gmarler.com -l root "(cd /home; tar xf -)"
```

Secure Root Login Without Allowing Passwords   You've already seen how to use public key authentication to allow authorized system administrators to log in to remote systems as the root user. This section describes how to make public key authentication the *only* way a user can log in to a system as the root user. To force such behavior, edit the /etc/ssh/sshd_config file on all systems and change the following line

```
PermitRootLogin yes
```

to

```
PermitRootLogin without-password
```

Once you have made the changes, restart the sshd daemon on each system with the following commands.

```
# /etc/init.d/sshd stop
# /etc/init.d/sshd start
```

Secure Shell on Pre-Solaris 9 Releases

The Secure Shell provided with Solaris 9 is a Sun-supported port of OpenSSH. If you want to use the Secure Shell on releases of Solaris before Solaris 9, go to the http://www.openssh.com/ Web site, download the source code, compile it, and install it on your pre-Solaris 9 systems.

For More Information

For more information, refer to *SSH, The Secure Shell: The Definitive Guide*, by Daniel J. Barrett and Richard E. Silverman, O'Reilly & Associates, Inc., 2001.

11

ADMINISTERING PRINTING

The printing service consists of the LP print service software, any print filters (programs that process data before printing) you provide, the hardware (the printer, workstation, and network connections), and the Solaris Print Manager tool that you can use to administer printing.

This chapter briefly describes the LP print service; it lists the files, daemons, and logs used by the LP print service; describes tools available for administering printing; provides steps for setting up print servers and clients; and describes the basic commands used for printing.

What's New in Printing in the Solaris 9 Release   *New!*

This section describes new printing features in the Solaris 9 Operating Environment

Changes to the LP Scheduler (lpsched)

Starting with the Solaris 9 release, the lpadmin command automatically starts the lpsched process only when local printers are added to a system and stops it when the last local printer is removed from that system. In previous releases, the lpsched process was automatically started at system boot regardless of whether local printers were configured on a system.

Administering the print subsystem from print clients, printing, and configuring new printers are not affected by this change.

USB Printer Support

With the Solaris Print Manager, you can set up a USB printer that is attached to a SPARC or IA system with USB ports. The logical device names for USB printers are `/dev/printers/[0...N]*`.

When you add a USB printer to a print server, on the Add New Attached Printer screen, select one of these devices for a USB printer under Printer Port.

The Solaris USB printer driver, `usbprn`, supports all USB printer-class compliant printers. See the `usbprn`(7D) manual page for a list of recommended PostScript printers. The `usbprn` driver is compliant with non-PostScript printers that use third-party PostScript conversion packages such as GhostScript. You can obtain conversion packages from the Solaris Software Companion CD, available at the following URL. `http://www.sun.com/software/solaris/binaries/package.html`

The Notes and Diagnostics sections of the `usbprn`(7D) manual page contains information and cautions about hot-plugging USB printers.

Printer Information Management with LDAP

In addition to managing printer information with the NIS, NIS+, NIS+ with Federated Naming Service, and `files` name services, starting with the Solaris 9 release, you can manage printer information with LDAP.

When managing printer information in the LDAP nameservice, consider the following.

- When the LDAP server is the Netscape Directory Server (NSDS), the default distinguished name is `cn=Directory Manager`. When the LDAP server is Sun Directory Server, the distinguished name can use a format like `cn=admin, dc=xyz, dc=com`. Solaris Print Manager uses the `ldapclient` command to determine the default LDAP server name. When more than one server is specified, the first one is automatically selected. See `ldapclient`(1M) for more information.
- Solaris Print Manager always displays printer entries from the current LDAP server. If this server is not the domain's LDAP master server, the list of printers displayed may not be the current list of printers. This mismatch can result when the LDAP replica server is out of sync with

the master. Replica servers can have various update replication agreements. For example, when a change is made on the master, replica servers may be updated immediately or only once a day.

- When the selected LDAP server is an LDAP replica server, any updates are referred to the master server and are updated there. The printer list could be out of sync with the master until the replica is updated from the master.

- Although users can use the `ldapadd` and `ldapmodify` commands to update printer entries in the directory, this practice is not recommended. The *printer-name* attribute must be unique within the `ou=printers` container. If the printer name is not unique, modifications done with Solaris Print Manager or the `lpset` command may not be predictable.

What's New in Printing in the Solaris 8 Release

This section describes new printing features in the Solaris 8 Operating Environment.

Solaris Print Manager

The Solaris Print Manager, previously available as part of the Solstice AdminSuite Package, is a Java-based graphical user interface that enables you to manage local and remote printers. You can use the Solaris Print Manager with LDAP, NIS, NIS+, NIS+ with Federated Naming Service (`xfn`), and `files` nameservices. You must be superuser to use this tool. See "Setting Up Printing Services" on page 411 for more information about the Solaris Print Manager.

Print-Naming Enhancement to the Nameservice Switch File

The Solaris release supports the `printers` database in the `/etc/nsswitch.conf` nameservice switch file. The `printers` database provides centralized printer configuration information to print clients on the network.

See "Print-Naming Enhancement" on page 409 for more information.

Methods for Enabling or Disabling Global Banner Page Printing

The Solaris 8 Operating Environment adds the `-banner` option with arguments of `always`, `never`, and `optional` to the `lpadmin` command. When banner page printing is set to `optional`, the banner is printed by default, but users can disable banner page printing by using the `lp -o nobanner` command. See "Controlling the Printing of Banner Pages" on page 423 and `lpadmin`(1M) for more information.

Solaris Print Package Redesign

This section describes the redesign of the Solaris print packages starting with the Solaris 2.6 release and the additional features that were added with that release.

Redesign of Print Packages

Starting with the Solaris 2.6 release, print packages have been redesigned to provide greater flexibility and modularity of print software installation and to enable installation of a smaller footprint for the print client.

Solaris 2.6 print software includes the following features.

- Redesign of print packages.
- Print protocol adapter.
- SunSoft print client.
- Network printer support.

The Solaris 2.6 print software has the following limitations.

- No support for print servers defined as S5 (the System V print protocol) in previous Solaris releases.
- No print filtering on print clients.

With the Solaris 2.6 redesign, the default is to install all the print packages. Print servers require installation of all packages, including both client and server. For print clients, you can choose to install only the print client packages. PostScript filter software is provided in its own print package. Table 86 describes the new set of print packages.

Table 86   Solaris Packages

Package	Base Directory	Description
SUNWpcr	root (/)	SunSoft Print—Client.
SUNWpcu	/usr	SunSoft Print—Client.
SUNWpsr	root (/)	SunSoft Print—LP Server.
SUNWpsu	/usr	SunSoft Print—LP Server.
SUNWPSF	/usr	PostScript filters.
SUNWscplp	/usr	SunSoft Print—Source compatibility.
SUNWppm	/usr/sadm/admin/bin	Solaris Print Manager (new in the Solaris 8 release).

The following print packages were removed from the Solaris 2.6 release.

- SUNWlpr—LP print service (root).
- SUNWlpu—LP print service—Client (usr).
- SUNWlps—LP print service—Server (usr).

Print commands from SUNWscpu have been moved into the SUNWscplp (SunSoft Print—Source Compatibility) package.

Print Protocol Adapter

The Solaris 2.6 print protocol adapter replaces the Service Access Facility (SAF), the network listener, and lpNet on the inbound side of the LP spooler with a more modular and modern design.

The print protocol adapter provides the following features.

- The complete BSD print protocol and extended Solaris functionality are implemented.
- Multiple spooling systems can coexist on the same host and have access to the BSD print protocol.
- Third-party application developers can extend the print protocol adapter to support other printing protocols such as Apple and Novell.

The new print protocol adapter is compatible with print clients set up in previous Solaris releases if the BSD protocol was used to configure these clients. If the BSD protocol was not used, you must modify the previous

Solaris print client configuration to use the BSD protocol by using Solaris Print Manager or the lpsystem command.

SunSoft Print Client

Starting with the Solaris 2.6 release, the SunSoft Print Client software is bundled with the Solaris Operating Environment as packages SUNWpcr and SUNWpcu. This software was previously released as an unbundled product. It was available on the Solaris Migration CD and as part of the Solstice AdminSuite suite of administration products.

The SunSoft Print Client software uses an NIS map, an NIS+ table, or a single file to provide centralized client administration in the Solaris 2.6 release. The Print Client software includes the following features.

- Replacing the /etc/lp directory structure with a configuration database that can be stored in a user file ($HOME/.printers), a system file (/etc/printers.conf), an NIS map (printers.conf.byname), or an NIS+ FNS context.
- Using a more streamlined implementation that provides reduced client overhead and quicker and more accurate responses to print status requests.
- Using the lpset(1M) command to create the printers.conf file.
- Reducing the size of the package (183 Kbytes total) from previous Solaris releases.
- Providing interoperability with the BSD protocol available with SunOS 4.x, Solaris 2.x, HP-UX, and other systems, as described in RFC-1179.

Enhanced Network Printer Support

Starting with the Solaris 2.6 release, print software provides better support for network printers than in previous Solaris releases. The following new features are included.

- A new interface script, /usr/lib/lp/model/netstandard, which is specifically designed to support network printers. This script collects the spooler and print database information needed to perform network printing and passes it to the print output module.
- A new print output module, netpr, is called from the netstandard interface script to print the print job. It opens a network connection to the printer, creates the correct protocol instructions, and sends the data to the printer. The netpr program currently supports two protocols: BSD print protocol and a TCP pass-through.

- New arguments to the `lpadmin -o` command to specify destination name, protocol, and time-out values for the network printer.
- Solaris Print Manager, now included in the Solaris 8 Operating Environment, can set up and manage network printers.

Print Administration Tools in the Solaris Environment

Starting with the Solaris 2.6 release, the Solaris Operating Environment printing software provides an environment for setting up and managing client access to printers on a network. The Solaris printing software contains the following components.

- *SunSoft Print Client software*, previously available only with the Solstice AdminSuite set of administration tools, enables you to make printers available to print clients by using a nameservice.
- *The LP print service commands*, a command-line interface used to set up and manage printers, provide additional functionality not available with the other print management tools.
- *The Solaris Print Manager*, a graphical user interface used to manage printers in a nameservice environment, is available with the Solaris 8 Operating environment.

NOTE. If you do not use the Solaris Print Manager to set up and manage printing, you must use some combination of the other components to completely manage printing in the Solaris Operating Environment.

Table 87 summarizes the features of the printing components, all of which are available in the Solaris 8 Operating Environment.

Table 87   Solaris Printing Component Features

Component	Graphical User Interface	Configure Network Printers	Manage Print Clients and Servers	NIS, NIS+, NIS+ (xfn), or LDAP Support
Solaris Print Manager	Yes	Yes	Yes	Yes
LP commands	No	Yes	Yes	No

Choosing a Method to Manage Printers

In the Solaris Operating Environment, adding printer information to a nameservice makes access to printers available to all systems on the network and generally makes printer administration easier because all printer information is centralized.

The Solaris print client software and Solaris Print Manager application offer a graphical solution for setting up and managing printers on a network. You can also use the lpadmin command to configure printers on individual systems.

You can accomplish most printing configuration tasks with Solaris Print Manager. However, if you need to write interface scripts or add your own filters, you can use the LP print service commands directly to accomplish these tasks.

Introducing the LP Print Service

The LP print service is a set of software commands that enable users to print files while they continue to work. The print service consists of the LP print service software and spooler—spool is an acronym for system peripheral operation off-line. The LP print service performs the following functions.

- Administers files and schedules local print requests.
- Schedules network requests.
- Filters files (if necessary) so that they print properly.
- Starts programs that interface with the printers.
- Tracks the status of jobs.
- Tracks forms mounted on the printer.
- Tracks print wheels that are currently mounted.
- Delivers alerts to mount new forms or different print wheels.
- Delivers alerts about printing problems.

Administering Files and Scheduling Print Requests

The LP print service has a scheduler daemon, called lpsched. The scheduler daemon updates the LP system files with information about printer setup and configuration, as shown in Figure 23.

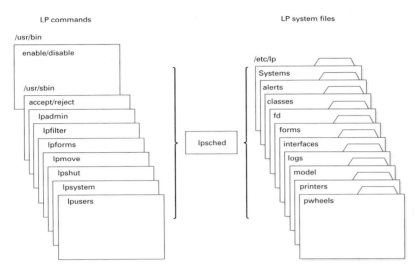

Figure 23   The lpsched Scheduler Updates the LP System Files

Starting with the Solaris 2.6 release, all the LP commands except for enable and disable have been moved from /usr/bin into /usr/sbin. The enable and disable commands are located in /usr/bin and /usr/lib/lp/local and are symbolically linked to the accept and reject commands.

The lpsched daemon also schedules all local print requests, as shown in Figure 24, regardless of whether the requests are issued by users from an application or from the command line. In addition, the scheduler tracks the status of printers and filters. When a printer finishes printing a request, the scheduler schedules the next request if one is in the queue.

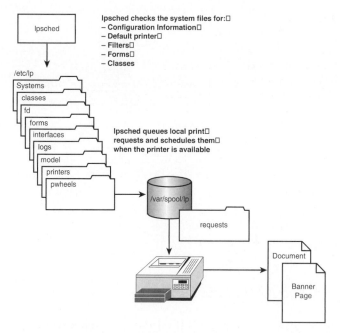

Figure 24   The lpsched Scheduler Schedules Local Print Requests

Each print client and print server must have only one LP scheduler running. Starting with the Solaris 9 release, the scheduler is started by the `lpadmin` command when a local printer is added to the system and stopped when the last local printer is removed from the system. Without rebooting the system, you can stop the scheduler with the `/usr/sbin/lpshut` command and restart the scheduler with the `/usr/lib/lp/lpsched` command. The scheduler for each system manages its own print requests. It waits for requests issued by the LP commands and then handles the requests in an appropriate manner.

Scheduling Network Print Requests

Starting with the Solaris 2.6 release, the `lpNet` daemon does not schedule network requests. Instead, network scheduling is handled by the `inetd` Internet services daemon. The `inetd` daemon listens for a request and starts `in.lpd`. Then, `in.lpd` looks at the request and loads `bsd_lpsched.so`. `in.lpd` passes the request through `bsd_lpsched.so` to `lpsched` for local printing.

Filtering Print Files

Print filters are programs that convert the content of a file from one format to another so that it can be printed. In network printing, print filters process the file on the print client before it gets transmitted to the server. The LP print service uses filters to perform the following tasks.

- Convert a file from one data format to another so that it can be printed properly on a specific type of printer.
- Handle the special modes of printing that users may request with the -y option to the lp command—for example, two-sided printing, landscape printing, draft- or letter-quality printing.
- Detect printer faults and notify the LP print service of them so that the print service can deliver alerts.

Not every print filter can perform all these tasks. However, because each task is printer-specific, it can be implemented separately.

A print filter can be as simple or as complex as needed. The Solaris Operating Environment provides print filters in the /usr/lib/lp/postscript directory to cover most PostScript printing situations in which the destination printer requires the data to be in PostScript format. You have to create and add filters to the system for non-PostScript printers.

Starting the Printer Interface Program

The LP print service uses a standard printer interface program to interact with other parts of the operating system to perform the following tasks.

- Initialize the printer port if necessary. The standard printer interface program uses the stty command to initialize the printer port.
- Initialize the printer. The standard printer interface program uses the terminfo database and the TERM shell variable to find the appropriate control sequences.
- Print a banner page if necessary.
- Print the correct number of copies specified by the print request.

The LP print service uses the standard interface program (found in the /usr/lib/lp/model directory) unless you specify a different one. You can create custom interface programs, but you must be careful that the custom program does not terminate the connection to the printer or interfere with proper printer initialization.

Tracking the Status of Print Jobs

The lpsched daemons on the print server each keep a log of every print request that is processed and note any errors that occurred during the printing process. This log is kept in the /var/lp/logs/lpsched file. Every night, the lp cron job renames /var/lp/logs/lpsched to a new file lpsched.*n* and starts a new log file. If errors occur or jobs disappear from the print queue, you can use the log files to determine what lpsched has done with a print job.

The following example shows the end of the /var/lp/logs/lpsched file.

```
# tail /varl/lp/logs/lpsched
06/01 14:51:50: Print services started.
06/01 16:52:27: Print services stopped.
06/02 15:43:44: build info: 01/08/00:18:06:11
06/02 15:43:44: Print services started.
06/02 17:04:25: Print services stopped.
06/04 10:34:00: build info: 01/08/00:18:06:11
06/04 10:34:00: Print services started.
06/04 16:53:05: Print services stopped.
06/05 09:34:59: build info: 01/08/00:18:06:11
06/05 09:34:59: Print services started.
#
```

Tracking Forms

The LP print service helps you track which forms are mounted on each printer and notifies you when it cannot find the description of how to print on a form. You are responsible for creating form descriptions and mounting and unmounting the paper form in each printer, either as part of setting up a printer or in response to alerts from the LP print service.

Users can specify the form on which they want a job to print. You (root) can mount a specific form and then tell the LP print service that the form is available and on which printer it is mounted. Alternatively, users can submit print requests specifying a particular form and requesting that the form be mounted. When the LP print service receives the request, it sends an alert message to the system administrator (root) requesting that the form be mounted.

Tracking Print Wheels

The procedure for tracking print wheels is similar to the procedure for tracking forms. Some printers (usually letter-quality printers) have removable print heads, such as daisy wheels or print balls, that provide a particular font or character set. A user can request a named character set. If that character set is not available, the LP print service notifies the system administrator (root) of the request. The job is stored in the print queue until the print wheel is changed.

Receiving Printing Problem Alerts

The LP print service performs sophisticated error checking. If a printing problem occurs, alerts are sent to the originator of a print request or to the system administrator, depending on the nature of the problem and what is required to fix it. Users are notified when a print request cannot be completed. Users can request notification by e-mail when a job is successfully completed. Administrators are alerted to problems with printers and to requests for filters, forms, or character sets.

For problems that require an administrator's attention, the LP print service default is to write an alert message to the system administrator's console window (that is, to the terminal on which root is logged in).

As the system administrator, you can change the policy to receive alert messages by e-mail or a program of your choice. Or, you can choose to receive no alerts when printing problems occur.

Understanding the Structure of the LP Print Service

The following sections explain the structure and directory hierarchy for the LP print service. The many files of the LP print service are distributed among several directories, as shown in Table 88.

Table 88   Directories for the LP Print Service

Directory	Description
/usr/bin	The lp, lpstat, enable, and disable commands.
/etc/lp	A hierarchy of LP configuration files.
/usr/share/lib	The terminfo database directory.
/usr/sbin	The accept, reject, lpadmin, lpfilter, lpforms, lpmove, lpshut, lpsystems, and lpusers LP commands.
/usr/lib/lp	The LP daemons, directories for binary files and PostScript filters, and the model directory (which contains the standard printer interface program).
/var/lp/logs	The logs for LP activities.
lpsched.*n*	Messages from lpsched.

Table 88   Directories for the LP Print Service (Continued)

Directory	Description
`/var/spool/lp`	The spooling directory in which files are queued for printing.
`requests.`*n**	Information about completed print requests.

*   Moved from `/var/lplogs` starting with the Solaris 2.6 release. Note that the `lpNet` log was removed completely from the `/var/lp/logs` directory because the `lpNet` daemon is replaced by `inetd`, starting with the Solaris 2.6 release.

User Commands

The `/usr/bin` directory contains the `lp` and `lpstat` commands, with which users submit and monitor print requests. The directory also contains the `enable` and `disable` commands used to enable and disable printers.

Users can customize their print requests by using options for the `lp` command, specifying forms, character sets, filters, titles, banners, and so forth. Table 89 summarizes the frequently used options for the `lp` command. These options can be used individually or combined in any order on the command line. When combining options, use a space between options and repeat the dash (-). For example, the following command specifies a destination printer, requests e-mail notification, and prints six copies of a file.

```
% lp -d printer-name -m -n6 filename
%
```

Table 89   Summary of Frequently Used lp Options

Option	Name	Description
`-d`	Destination	Specify a destination printer by name.
`-m`	Mail	Send e-mail to the user who submitted the print request when the file has been printed successfully.
`-n`	Number	Specify the number of copies to be printed.
`-t`	Title	Specify a title for a print request (printed only on the banner page).
`-o nobanner`	Option	Suppress printing of the banner page for an individual request.
`-h`	Header	Put a header on each page of the print request.

Table 89   *Summary of Frequently Used lp Options (Continued)*

Option	Name	Description
-c	Copy	Copy the file before printing.
-w	Write	Write a message to root's terminal when the file has printed successfully.

See the `lp(1)` manual page for a complete list of options.

LP Configuration Files

The scheduler stores configuration information in LP configuration files located in the `/etc/lp` directory. You can check the contents of these files, but you should not edit them directly. The LP administrative commands provide input for the configuration files in the `/etc/lp` directory. The `lpsched` daemon administers and updates the configuration files. You should use the administrative commands any time you need to update any configuration file. Table 90 describes the contents of the `/etc/lp` directory.

Table 90   *Contents of the /etc/lp Directory*

Name	Type	Description
alerts	Directory	Contains `form`, `jobdone`, `printer`, and `sendMsg` scripts for sending print system alerts to users.
classes	Directory	Contains files that identify classes provided by the `lpadmin -c` command.
fd	Directory	Contains descriptions of existing filters.
forms	Directory	Is the location in which to put files for each form. Initially, this directory is empty.
interfaces	Directory	Contains printer interface program files.
logs	Link to /var/lp/logs	Contains log files of printing activities.
model	Link to /usr/lib/lp/model	Contains the standard printer interface program.

Table 90   *Contents of the /etc/lp Directory (Continued)*

Name	Type	Description
printers	Directory	Contains directories for each (remote or local) printer setup. Each directory contains configuration information and alert files for an individual printer.
pwheels	Directory	Contains print wheel or cartridge files.

The `printers` directory has a subdirectory for each printer (local or remote) known to the system. The following example shows the subdirectories for the printers `pinecone` and `sparc1`.

```
% ls -l /etc/lp/printers
drwxrwxr-x 2 lp lp 512 Jan 23 23:53 pinecone
drwxrwxr-x 2 lp lp 512 Jan 11 17:50 sparc1
%
```

Within each of the printer-specific directories, the following files can describe the printer.

- `alert.sh`—Shell to execute in response to alerts.
- `alert.vars`—Alert variables.
- `configuration`—Configuration file.
- `users.deny`—List of users who are denied printer access.
- `comment`—Printer description.

The following example shows a typical configuration file for the printer pinecone, `/etc/lp/printers/pinecone/configuration`.

```
Banner: on: Always
Content types: PS
Device: /dev/term/b
Interface: /usr/lib/lp/model/standard
Printer type: PS
Modules: default
```

Printer Definitions

The LP print service uses the `terminfo` database to initialize a local printer; to establish a selected page size, character pitch, line pitch, and character set; and to communicate the sequence of codes to a printer. The `terminfo` database directory is located in `/usr/share/lib`.

Each printer is identified in the `terminfo` database with a short name. If necessary, you can add entries to the `terminfo` database, but it is a tedious and time-consuming process. Describing how to add entries to the `terminfo` database is beyond the scope of this book.

Daemons and LP Internal Files

The `/usr/lib/lp` directory contains daemons and files used by the LP print service, as described in Table 91.

Table 91   *Contents of the /usr/lib/lp Directory*

Name	Type	Description
bin	Directory	Contains files for generating printing alerts, slow filters, and queue management programs.
local	Directory	Contains LP executables for the local system.
locale	Directory	Contains locale information.
lpsched	Daemon	Manage scheduling of LP print requests.
model	Directory	Contains the standard printer interface program.
postscript	Directory	Contains all PostScript filter programs provided by the Solaris LP print service. These filters come with descriptor files in the `/etc/lp/fd` directory that tell the LP print service the characteristics of the filters and where to locate them.

LP Administrative Commands

The commands used to set up and administer the LP print service are in the `/usr/sbin` directory; they are listed in Table 92.

Table 92   *The LP Commands in the /usr/sbin Directory*

Command	Purpose
accept reject	Accept print requests into the printer's queue or reject print requests.

Table 92   The LP Commands in the /usr/sbin Directory (Continued)

Command	Purpose
lpadmin	Define printer names, printer types, file content types, print classes, printer devices, and printer comments; remove printers or print classes; specify fault recovery, interface programs (either custom or standard), printing options, banner/no banner; mount forms; mount print wheels or cartridges; define allow and deny user lists.
lpfilter	Add, change, delete, and list filters.
lpforms	Add, change, delete, and list forms.
lpmove	Move queued print requests from one printer to another.
lpshut	Halt the LP print service (the lpsched command, which starts the LP print service, is in the /usr/lib/lp directory).
lpsystem	Register print servers and print clients with the LP print service.
lpusers	Set queue priorities for users.

Log Files

The LP print service maintains two sets of log files: a list of current requests that are in the print queue (/var/spool/lp) and an ongoing history of print requests (/var/lp/logs/requests).

Print Queue Logs

The scheduler for each system keeps a log of print requests in the directories /var/spool/lp/requests/*system* and /var/spool/lp/tmp/*system*. Each print request has two files (one in each directory) that contain information about the request. The information in the /var/spool/lp/requests/*system* directory can be accessed only by root or lp. The information in the /var/spool/lp/tmp/*system* directory can be accessed only by root, lp, or the user who submitted the request.

The following example shows the contents of the /var/spool/lp/tmp/pine directory. See Table 93 on page 406 for an explanation of the LP requests log codes.

```
pine% ls /var/spool/lp/tmp/pine
20-0 21-0
pine% cat 21-0
C 1
D slw2
F /etc/default/login
P 20
t simple
```

```
U winsor
s 0x1000
```

These files remain in their directories only as long as the print request is in the queue. Once the request is finished, the information in the files is combined and appended to the `/var/lp/logs/requests` file, which is described in the next section.

Use the information in the `/var/spool/lp` logs if you need to track the status of a print request that is currently in the queue.

History Logs

The LP print service records a history of printing services in the `lpsched` and `requests` log files. These log files are located in the `/var/lp/logs` directory. You can use the information in these logs to diagnose and troubleshoot printing problems. The following example shows the contents of the `/var/lp/logs` directory.

```
# cd /var/lp/logs
# ls
lpsched.1       requests        requests.2
lpsched         lpsched.2       requests.1
#
```

The files with the `.1` and `.2` suffixes are copies of logs for previous days. Each day, the `lp cron` job cleans out the `lpsched` and `requests` log files; it keeps copies for two days.

The most important log file for troubleshooting is the `lpsched` log, which contains information about local printing requests.

The `requests` log contains information about print requests that have completed and are no longer in the print queue. Once a request is finished printing, the information in the `/var/spool/lp` log files is combined and appended to the `/var/lp/logs/requests` file.

The `requests` log has a simple structure, and you can extract data by using common UNIX shell commands. Requests are listed in the order in which they are printed and are separated by lines showing their request IDs. Each line below the separator line is marked with a single letter that identifies the kind of information contained in that line. Each letter is separated from the data by a single space.

The following example shows the contents of a `requests` log.

```
# pwd
/var/lp/logs
# tail requests.2
= slw2-20, uid 200, gid 200, size 5123, Thu Nov 18 01:24:01 EST 2000
```

```
z slw2
C 1
D slw2
F /etc/motd
P 20
t simple
U irving
s 0x0100
#
```

Table 93 shows the codes in the LP `requests` log.

Table 93   Codes in the LP requests Log

Character	Content of Line
=	The separator line. It contains the following items, separated by commas: the request ID, the user ID and group IDs of the user, the total number of bytes in the original (unfiltered) files, and the time the request was queued. The user ID, group IDs, and file size are preceded by the words `uid`, `gid`, and `size`.
C	The number of copies printed.
D	The printer or class destination or the word `any`.
F	The name of the file printed. The line is repeated for each file printed; files were printed in the order shown.
f	The name of the form used.
H	One of three types of special handling: `resume`, `hold`, and `immediate`. The only useful value found in this line is `immediate`.
N	The type of alert used when the print request was successfully completed. The type is the letter `M` if the user was notified by e-mail or `W` if the user was notified by a message to the terminal.
O	The `-o` options.
P	The priority of the print request.
p	The list of pages printed.
r	This single-letter line is included if the user asks for raw processing of the files (the `-r` option of the `lp` command).
S	The character set or print wheel (or cartridge) used.
s	The outcome of the request, shown as a combination of individual bits expressed in hexadecimal form. Although several bits are used internally by the print service, the most important bits are listed below.

Table 93   Codes in the LP requests Log (Continued)

Character	Content of Line
	`0x0004` Slow filtering finished successfully.
	`0x0010` Printing finished successfully.
	`0x0040` The request was cancelled.
	`0x0100` The request failed filtering or printing.
`T`	The title placed on the banner page.
`t`	The type of content found in the file(s).
`U`	The name of the user who submitted the print request.
`x`	The slow filter used for the print request.
`Y`	The list of special modes to give to the print filters used to print the request.
`z`	The printer used for the request. This printer differs from the destination (the `D` line) if the request was queued for any printer or a class of printers or if the request was moved to another destination.

Spooling Directories

Files queued for printing are stored in the `/var/spool/lp` directory until they are printed. Table 94 shows the contents of the `/var/spool/lp` directory.

Table 94   Contents of the /var/spool/lp Directory

File	Type	Description
`SCHEDLOCK`	File	Lock file for the scheduler. Check for this file if the scheduler dies and won't restart.
`admins`	Directory	Linked to `/etc/lp`.
`bin`	Directory	Linked to `/usr/lib/lp/bin`.
`fifos`	Directory	Contains pipes that convey networked print requests to and from the `inet` daemon.
`logs`	Link	Linked to `../lp/logs` where completed print requests are logged.
`model`	Link	Linked to `/usr/lib/lp/model`.

Table 94   Contents of the /var/spool/lp Directory (Continued)

File	Type	Description
requests	Directory	Contains a directory for each configured printer where print requests are logged until printed. Users cannot access this log.
system	Directory	Contains a print status file for the system.
temp	Link	Linked to /var/spool/lp/tmp/*printer-name*, which contains the spooled requests.
tmp	Directory	Contains a directory for each configured printer where print requests are logged until printed. Changes to existing print requests are also recorded in this log.

Using the SunSoft Print Client

This section describes how the SunSoft print client works. Starting with the Solaris 2.6 release, the SunSoft print client is provided as part of the Solaris Operating Environment. It was available previously only as an unbundled product.

A system becomes a SunSoft print client when you install the SunSoft print client software and enable access to remote printers on the system. The SunSoft print client commands have the same names and produce the same output as the print commands of the previous Solaris releases.

The SunSoft print client commands use a greater number of options to locate printer configuration information than in the previous Solaris Operating Environment, and the client communicates directly with the print server.

The print command locates a printer and printer configuration information in the following sequence.

1. It checks whether the user specified a destination printer name or printer class in one of the three valid styles.
2. If the user did not specify a printer name or class in a valid style, the command checks the user's PRINTER or LPDEST environment variable for a default printer name.

3. If neither environment variable for the default printer is defined, the command checks the `.printers` file in the user's home directory for the `_default` printer alias.

4. If the command does not find a `_default` printer alias in the `.printers` file, it then checks the SunSoft print client's `/etc/printers.conf` file for configuration information.

5. If the printer is not found in the `/etc/printers.conf` file, the command checks for any nameservice (NIS, NIS+, or LDAP).

The client does not have a local print queue. The SunSoft print client sends its requests to the queue on the specified print server. The client writes the print request to a temporary spooling area only if the print server is not available or if an error occurs. This streamlined path to the server decreases the print client's use of resources, reduces the chance for printing problems, and improves performance.

Printer Configuration Resources

This section describes the resources that the SunSoft print client commands use to locate printer names and printer configuration information.

The SunSoft print client commands can use a nameservice, which is a shared network resource, for storing printer configuration information for all printers on the network. The nameservice (NIS, NIS+, NIS+ with FNS, or LDAP) simplifies the maintenance of printer configuration information. When you add a printer in the nameservice, all SunSoft print clients on the network can access it.

The SunSoft print client software locates printers by checking the following resources.

- Atomic, POSIX, or context-based printer name or class.
- User's `PRINTER` or `LPDEST` environment variable for the default printer.
- User's `.printers` file for a printer alias.
- SunSoft print client's `/etc/printers.conf` file.
- Nameservice (NIS, NIS+, LDAP, or NIS+ with FNS).

Print-Naming Enhancement

The Solaris 8 Operating Environment supports the `printers` database in the `/etc/nsswitch.conf` nameservice switch file. The `printers` database provides centralized printer configuration information to print clients on the network.

With the `printers` database and corresponding sources of information in the nameservice switch file, print clients can automatically access printer configuration information without having it added to their own systems. Table 95 shows the default `printers` entry for each of the nameservice environments.

Table 95   Default printers Entries in the /etc/nsswitch.conf File

Nameservice	Default `printers` Entry
dns	`printers: user files`
files	`printers: user files`
ldap	`printers: user files ldap`
nis	`printers: user files nis`
nis+	`printers: user nisplus files xfn`

New! (beside dns/files rows)
New! (beside ldap row)

For example, if the nameservice is NIS, print client configuration information is looked up in the following order.

- `user`—The `$HOME/.printers` file for the user.
- `files`—The `/etc/printers.conf` file.
- `nis`—The `printers.conf.byname` table.

If the nameservice is NIS+, print client configuration information is looked up in the following order.

- `user`—The `$HOME/.printers` file for the user.
- `nisplus`—The `printers.org_dir` table.
- `files`—The `/etc/printers.conf` file.
- `xfn`—The FNS printer contexts.

Print Request Submission

Users submit a print request from a SunSoft print client by using either the `lp` or `lpr` command. The user can specify a destination printer name or class in any of three styles.

- *Atomic style*, which is the print command and option followed by the printer name or class and the file name.
  lp -d *printer-name filename*
- *POSIX style*, which is the print command and option followed by *server*:*printer* and the file name.
  lpr -P *server-name:printer-name filename*

- *Context-based style,* as defined in the *Federated Naming Service Guide* in the *Solaris Software Developer Answer Book.*
  ```
  lpr -d dept-name/service-name/printer-name filename
  ```

Summary of the SunSoft Print Client Process

The following list summarizes how the SunSoft print client process works.

1. A user submits a print request from a SunSoft print client by using a SunSoft print client command.
2. The print client command checks a hierarchy of print configuration resources to determine where to send the print request.
3. The print client command sends the print request directly to the appropriate print server. A print server can be any server that accepts the BSD printing protocol, including SVR4 (LP) print servers and BSD print servers such as the SunOS 4.x BSD print server.
4. The print server sends the print request to the appropriate printer.
5. The print request is printed.

Setting Up Printing Services

You need to decide which systems have local printers directly cabled to them and which systems connect to printers over the network. The system that has the printer connected to it and makes the printer available to other systems is called a *print server.* The system that has its printing needs met by a print server is called a *print client.*

Setting up printing services comprises three basic tasks.

- Setting up local printers.
- Setting up print servers.
- Setting up print clients.

You can have the following client/server combinations, as illustrated in Figure 25.

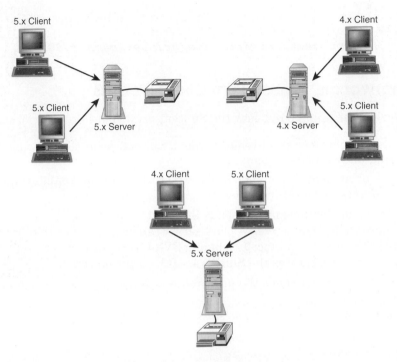

Figure 25   Print Client/Server Configurations

- SunOS 5.0 print clients with a SunOS 5.0 print server.
- SunOS 5.0 and SunOS 4.1 print clients with a SunOS 5.0 print server.
- SunOS 5.0 and SunOS 4.1 print clients with a SunOS 4.1 print server.

This section describes how to set up a Solaris print client.

Introducing Solaris Print Manager

In the Solaris 8 release, the Solaris Print Manager is the preferred method for managing printers because this Java-based graphical user interface centralizes printing information when used in conjunction with a nameservice. Using a nameservice to store printer configuration information centralizes printer information and makes printer information available to all systems on the network.

You can use Print Manager in the following nameservice environments.

- `files`.
- DNS.
- LDAP.

- NIS.
- NIS+.
- NIS+ with Federated Naming Service (xfn).

You can use the Solaris Print Manager to manage printer configuration information in the NIS+ nameservice without the underlying xfn application layer. Eliminating the underlying xfn application layer provides better performance when accessing printer configuration information. See "Converting Printer Configuration in NIS+ (xfn) to NIS+ Format" on page 420 for more information

You must be superuser or belong to a role that enables you to manage printing functions to use the Solaris Print Manager. See Chapter 6, "Administering Rights and Roles," for more information about roles.

Solaris Print Manager recognizes existing printer information on the printer servers, print clients, and in the nameservice databases. You do not need to convert print clients to use the new Solaris Print Manager as long as the print clients are running either the Solaris 2.6 release or compatible versions.

Using Solaris Print Manager to perform printer-related tasks automatically updates the appropriate printer databases. Solaris Print Manager also includes a command-line console that displays the lp command line for the add, modify, and delete printer operations. Errors and warnings are also displayed when Printer Manager operations are performed.

You can run Solaris Print Manager on a remote system with the display sent to the local system. See "Managing Printing Services" in *System Administration Guide, Volume II,* for instructions on setting the DISPLAY environment variable.

See printmgr(1M) for more information.

Starting Solaris Print Manager

The command to start Solaris Print Manager is /usr/sadm/admin/bin/printmgr&. If you use Solaris Print Manager frequently, you may want to add /usr/sadm/admin/bin to your path.

Use the following steps to access the Print Manager.

1. Become superuser.
2. Type **/usr/sadm/admin/bin/printmgr&** and press Return to start the Print Manager.

   The window that is displayed asks you to choose the naming service, as shown in Figure 26.

Figure 26   *Print Manager Select Naming Service Window*

3. Choose the appropriate nameservice from the Naming Service menu
   and click on the OK button.

   The Print Manager window is displayed, as shown in Figure 27.

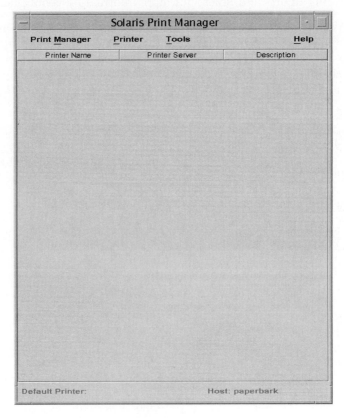

Figure 27   *Solaris Print Manager Window*

Adding Access to a Printer with the Print Manager

To add access to a printer, you need the following information.

- Printer name.
- Print server name.
- Description of the printer.
- Whether this printer is the default printer.

Use the following steps to add access to a printer.

1. Start the Print Manager (if necessary).

   See "Starting Solaris Print Manager" on page 413 for more information.

2. From the Printer menu, choose Add Access to Printer, as shown in Figure 28.

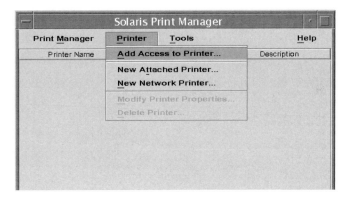

Figure 28   Printer Menu

The Solaris Print Manager Add Access to Printer window is displayed, as shown in Figure 29.

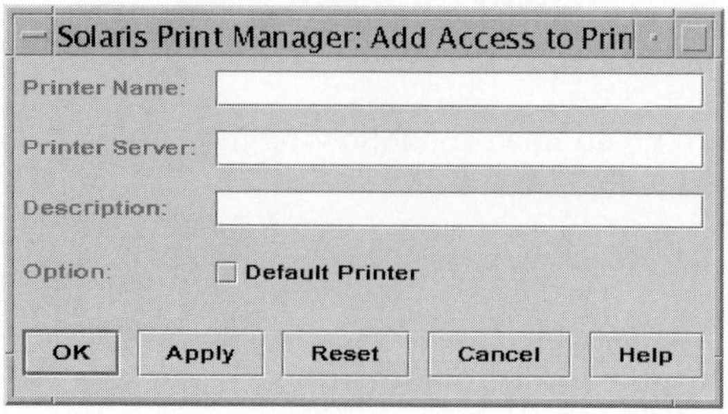

Figure 29   Solaris Print Manager Add Access to Printer Window

3. Type the printer name, name of the printer server, and description in the text fields. If you want this printer to be the default printer, click on the Default Printer check box.

4. Click on the OK button.

The printer is configured, the printer information is added to the list in the Solaris Print Manager window, and the relevant files are updated. The name of the default printer is displayed at the bottom of the window, as shown in Figure 30.

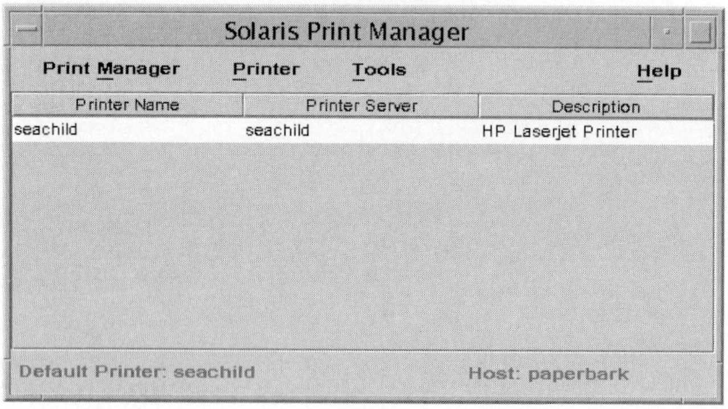

Figure 30   Solaris Print Manager Window

Adding a New Attached Printer with Print Manager

To add a new printer attached to a print server, you need the following information.

- Printer name.
- Description.

- Printer port.
- Printer type.
- File contents.
- Fault notification policy.
- Whether this printer is the default.
- Whether to always print banners.
- User access list.

Once you have physically attached the printer to the computer, use the following steps to make the printer available to the local computer.

1. Start the Print Manager (if necessary).

   See "Starting Solaris Print Manager" on page 413 for more information.

2. From the Print menu, choose New Attached Printer, as shown in Figure 31.

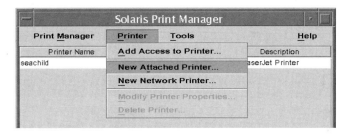

Figure 31   *Choose New Attached Printer from the Print Menu*

The New Attached Printer window is displayed, as shown in Figure 32.

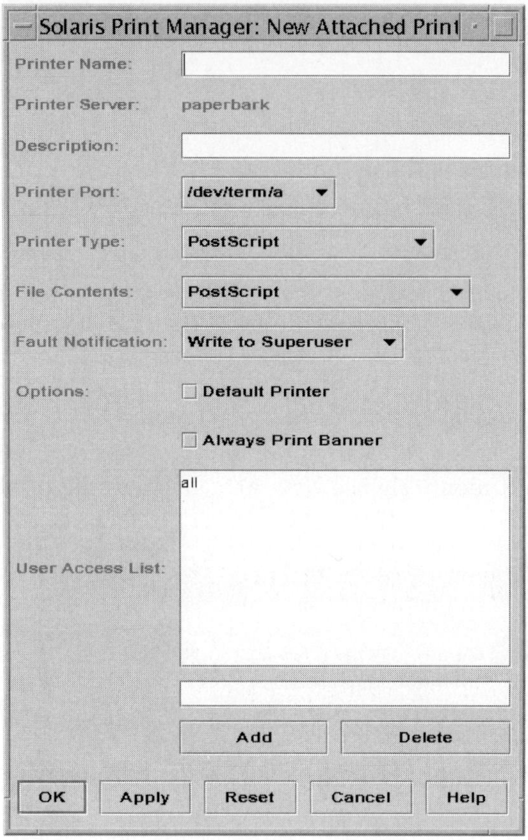

Figure 32   *Add New Attached Printer Window*

Click on the Help button if you need help with details about values that are required for the text fields.

3.   Fill in the form and click on the OK button.

The printer is added to the Print Manager, and the appropriate databases and files are updated.

Adding a New Network Printer with Print Manager

To add a new network printer, you need the following information.

- Printer name.
- Description.
- Printer type.

- File contents.
- Fault notification policy.
- Destination.
- Protocol.
- Whether this printer is the default.
- Whether to always print banners.
- User access list.

Use the following steps to add a new network printer.

1. Start the Print Manager (if necessary).

    See "Starting Solaris Print Manager" on page 413 for more information.

2. From the Printer menu, choose New Network Printer, as shown in Figure 33.

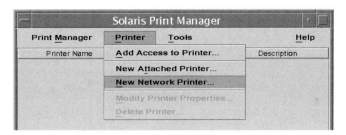

Figure 33   Choose New Network Printer from the Printer Menu

The New Network Printer window is displayed, as shown in Figure 34.

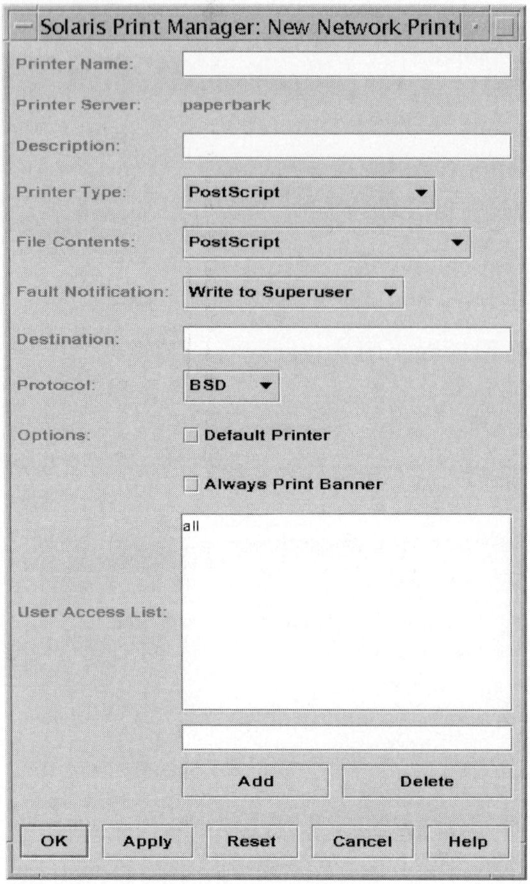

Figure 34   New Network Printer Window

Click on the Help button if you need help with details about values that are required for the text fields.

3. Fill in the form and click on the OK button.

The printer is added to the Print Manager, and the appropriate databases and files are updated.

Converting Printer Configuration in NIS+ (xfn) to NIS+ Format

This section describes how to convert printer configuration information in NIS+ (xfn) format to NIS+ format. You can run the following conversion script only on a system running the Solaris 8 Operating Environment.

1. Log in as superuser on the NIS+ master.
2. Copy the following conversion script and name it something like `/tmp/convert`.

```
#!/bin/sh
        #
        # Copyright (C) 1999 by Sun Microsystems, Inc.
        # All Rights Reserved
        #
        PRINTER=""
        for LINE in `lpget -n xfn list | tr "\t " "Control A Control B?"` ; do
         LINE=`echo ${LINE} | tr "Control A Control B" "\t " | sed -e 's/^
\t//g'`
          case "${LINE}" in
           *:)
            PRINTER=`echo ${LINE} | sed -e 's/://g'`
            ;;
           *=*)
            lpset -n nisplus -a "${LINE}" ${PRINTER}
            ;;
          esac
        done
```

3. Type **chmod 755 /tmp/convert** and press Return.

   The script is executable.
4. Type **/tmp/convert** and press Return.

Setting Up a Print Server (Solaris Operating Environment)

This section describes how to add a network printer by using LP commands.

You need the following information to set up a Solaris print server.

- Printer name.
- Server name.
- Network printer access name, sometimes qualified by a port name.
- IP address for the printer.
- Protocol. The print subsystem uses the BSD print protocol and raw TCP to communicate with the printer. In general, the TCP protocol is more generic. The printer vendor documentation provides the information about which protocol to use.
- Time-out value. The `timeout` option specifies the amount of time in seconds to wait between successive attempts to connect to the printer. The default is 10 seconds. Some printers have a long warm-up time, so a longer time-out is advised.
- Printer type. The default is PostScript.
- File content type. The default is PostScript.

- Fault notification policy for this print server. The default is write to superuser.

Use the following steps to set up a print server.

1. Set switches and ensure appropriate cabling.

   Consult the printer vendor installation documentation for information about hardware switches and cabling requirements.

2. Connect the printer to the network and turn on the power to the printer.

3. Get an IP address and select a name for the printer node.

   These procedures are equivalent to those for adding any new node to the network.

4. Become superuser.

5. Type **lpadmin -p** *printer-name* **-v /dev/null** and press Return.

   This step defines the printer name and the port device the printer uses. The device to use is /dev/null.

6. All on one line, type **lpadmin -p** *printer-name* **-i /usr/lib/lp/model/netstandard** and press Return.

   This step defines the interface script the printer uses.

7. All on one line, type **lpadmin -p** *printer-name* **-o dest=***access-name:port* **-o** protocol=*protocol* **-o timeout=***value* and press Return.

   This step sets the printer destination, protocol, and time-out values.

8. All on one line, type **lpadmin -p** *printer-name***-I** *content-type* **-T** *printer-type* and press Return.

   This step specifies the file content type and the printer type.

9. Type **cd /etc/lp/fd** and press Return.

   The current working directory is in the filter directory.

10. Type **for filter in *.fd;do** and press Return.

11. At the > prompt, type **name=`basename $filter .fd`** and press Return.

12. At the > prompt, type **lpfilter -f $name -F $filter** and press Return.

13. At the > prompt, type **done** and press Return.

    You have installed filters.

14. Type **accept** *printer-name* and press Return.

    The printer is able to accept requests.

15. Type **enable *printer-name*** and press Return.

    The printer is able to print the requests.

16. Type **lpstat -p *printer-name*** and press Return.

    This step verifies that the printer is configured correctly.

17. Set up any print clients that should have access to this printer.

The following example sets up a print server by supplying the following information.

- Printer name: seachild
- Network printer access name: nimquat:9100
- Protocol: tcp
- Time-out: 5
- Interface: /usr/lib/lp/model/netstandard
- Printer type: PS
- Content types: postscript
- Device: /dev/null

```
# lpadmin -p seachild -v /dev/null
# lpadmin -p seachild -i /usr/lib/lp/model/netstandard
# lpadmin -p seachild -o dest:nimquat:9100 -o protocol=tcp -o timeout=5
# lpadmin -p seachild -I postscript -T PS
# cd /etc/lp/fd
# for filter in *.fd;do
  > name=`basename $filter .fd`
  > lpfilter -f $name -F $filter
  > done
# accept castle
destination ` `castle' ` now accepting requests
# enable castle
printer ` `castle' ` now enabled
# lpadmin -p castle -D "PostScript printer"
# lpstat -p castle
  printer castle is idle. enabled since Thu Sep 15 08:45 1997.
available
#
```

Controlling the Printing of Banner Pages

A banner page identifies the person who submitted the print request, the print request ID, and the date and time the request was printed. Banner pages also have a modifiable title to help users identify their printouts.

By default, the print service forces banner pages to be printed. However, starting with the Solaris 8 Operating Environment, by using the new -o banner= option to the lpadmin command, you can specify whether a banner is always printed, never printed, or is optional. Behavior of banner page printing is summarized in Table 96.

Table 96   Behavior of Banner Page Printing

Command	Behavior of Banner Page Printing	Overridden
lpadmin -p *printer* -o banner or lpadmin -p *printer* -o banner=always	Required and printed.	If you are root or lp, the nobanner argument is honored. The nobanner argument is ignored for all other users.
lpadmin -p *printer* -o nobanner lpadmin -p *printer* -o banner=optional	On by default but can be disabled for each print request with the lp -o nobanner command.	N/A.
lpadmin -p *printer* -o banner=never	Disabled.	No.

Making Banner Pages Optional

When you specify optional, the banner is printed by default but users can disable banner printing with the lp -o banner command.

Use the following steps to make banner pages optional.

1. Become superuser or lp on the print server.
2. Type **lpadmin -p *printer* -o banner=optional** and press Return.

   The banner page setting is entered in the /etc/lp/printers/*printer*/configuration file on the print server.
3. Type **lpstat -o *printer* -l** and press Return.

   Review the output to verify that the Banner not printed line is displayed.

The following example makes banner pages optional for the printer seachild.

```
seachild% su
# lpadmin -p seachild -o banner=optional
```

```
# lpstat -p seachild -l
printer seachild is idle. enabled since Thu Jan  3 18:20:22 PST 2000.
 available.
         Content types: PS
         Printer types: PS
         Description:
         Users allowed:
                (all)
         Forms allowed:
                (none)
         Banner not required
         Character sets:
                (none)
         Default pitch:
         Default page size:
 #
```

Turning Off Banner Pages

Use the following steps to turn off the printing of banner pages.

1. Become superuser or lp on the print server.

2. Type **lpadmin -p *printer* -o banner=never** and press Return.

   The banner page setting is entered in the /etc/lp/printers/*printer*/configuration file on the print server.

3. Type **lpstat -o *printer* -l** and press Return.

   Review the output to verify that the Banner not required line is displayed.

The following example turns off banner pages for the printer seachild.

```
seachild% su
# lpadmin -p seachild -o banner=never
# lpstat -p seachild -l
printer seachild is idle. enabled since Thu Jan  3 18:20:22 PST 2000.
 available.
         Content types: PS
         Printer types: PS
         Description:
         Users allowed:
                (all)
         Forms allowed:
                (none)
         Banner not printed
         Character sets:
                (none)
         Default pitch:
         Default page size:
 #
```

Setting Up a PostScript Print Client with LP Commands

This section describes how to set up a Solaris print client to print on a SunOS 4.x print server that has a PostScript printer installed. You must complete the following tasks so the print client can use the printer connected to the print server.

- Identify the printer and server system to which the printer is connected.
- Define the characteristics of the printer.
- Set up the print filters.

You must have a network that enables access between systems to set up print clients. If your network is running NIS or NIS+, follow the appropriate procedures for enabling access between systems. If your network is not running NIS or NIS+, you must include the Internet address and system name for each print client in the /etc/hosts file on the print server. You must also include the Internet address and system name of the print server in the /etc/hosts file of each print client system.

Before you start, you need superuser privileges on the print client system. You also need the name of the printer and the name of the print server system. You do not need to specify a printer type or file content type for a printer client. If no printer type is specified, the default is unknown. If no file content type is specified, the default is any, which allows both PostScript and ASCII files to be printed on a PostScript printer.

Use the following steps to set up a PostScript print client.

1. Become superuser on the print client system.
2. Type **lpsystem -t bsd *server-system-name*** and press Return. The print server system is identified as a BSD (SunOS 4.x) system.
3. Type **lpadmin -p *printer-name* -s *server-system-name*** and press Return. The printer and the server system name are registered with the client LP print service.
4. Type **cd /etc/lp/fd** and press Return.
5. Type **lpfilter -f download -F download.fd** and press Return.
6. Type **lpfilter -f dpost -F dpost.fd** and press Return.
7. Type **lpfilter -f postio -F postio.fd** and press Return.
8. Type **lpfilter -f postior -F postior.fd** and press Return.
9. Type **lpfilter -f postprint -F postprint.fd** and press Return.

10. Type **lpfilter -f postreverse -F postreverse.fd** and press Return.

    The PostScript filters are installed.

11. Type **accept** *printer-name* and press Return.

    The printer is now ready to begin accepting (queuing) print requests.

12. Type **enable** *printer-name* and press Return.

    The printer is now ready to process print requests in the print queue.

13. (This step is optional but recommended.) Type **lpadmin -d** *printer-name* and press Return.

    The printer you specify is established as the default printer for the system. You should define a default printer even if only one printer is configured for a system.

14. Type **lpstat -t** and press Return. Check the messages displayed to verify that the printer is accepted and enabled.

15. Type **lp** *filename* and press Return. If you have not specified a default printer, type **lp -d** *printer-name* *filename* and press Return.

    The file you choose is sent to the printer.

If you want to set up Solaris print clients and print servers in addition to setting up the LP print system, you must also configure the port monitors by using the Service Access Facility. See "Understanding the Service Access Facility" on page 312 for information on how to set up the port monitors. If you use the Solaris Print Manager, the port monitors are configured for you automatically. To set up a Solaris print client, in place of step 2 in the procedure described above, type **lpsystem** *server-system-name* and press Return. The print server system is identified as a Solaris system.

Using Printing Commands

The following sections describe how to use lp to submit requests from a command line. When a request is made, the LP print service places it in the queue for the printer, displays the request ID number, and then redisplays the shell prompt. The lp command has many options that can modify the printing process, as summarized in Table 89 on page 400. For a complete list of options, see the lp(1) manual page.

Printing to the Default Printer

When the LP print service is set up with a default printer, users can submit print requests without typing the name of the printer. Type **lp *filename*** and press Return. The file specified is placed in the print queue of the default printer, and the request ID is displayed.

The following example prints the /etc/passwd file.

```
pine% lp /etc/passwd
request id is pinecone-8 (1 file)
pine%
```

Printing to a Printer by Name

Regardless of whether a default printer has been designated for your system, you can submit print requests to any printer that is configured for your system. To submit a print request to an individual printer, type **lp -d *printer-name filename*** and press Return. The file specified is placed in the print queue of the destination printer, and the request ID is displayed.

The following example prints the /etc/passwd file on the printer acorn.

```
pine% lp -d acorn /etc/passwd
request id is acorn-9 (1 file)
pine%
```

If you submit a request to a printer that is not configured on your system, an informational message is displayed, as shown in the following example.

```
pine% lp -d thorn /etc/passwd
UX:lp: ERROR: Destination "thorn" is unknown to the
            LP print service.
pine%
```

Requesting Notification When a File Has Been Printed

When you submit a large file to be printed, you may want the LP print service to notify you when printing is complete. You can request that the LP print service notify you either by an e-mail message or by a message to your console window.

To request e-mail notification, use the -m option when you submit the print request. Type **lp -m *filename*** and press Return.

To request that a message be written to your console window, use the -w option when you submit the print request. Type **lp -w *filename*** and press Return.

Printing Multiple Copies

You can print more than one copy of a file. When you request more than one copy, the file is printed the number of times you specify by the -n option to the lp command. The print request is considered as one print job, and only one banner page is printed if banner printing is enabled. To request multiple copies, type **lp -n*number filename*** and press Return.

The following example prints four copies of the /etc/passwd file.

```
pine% lp -n4 /etc/passwd
request id is pinecone-9 (1 file)
pine%
```

Determining Printer Status

Use the lpstat command to find out about the status of the LP print service. You can check on the status of your own jobs in the print queue, determine which printers are available for you to use, or determine request IDs of your jobs if you want to cancel them.

The Status of Your Print Requests

To find out the status of your own spooled print requests, type **lpstat** and press Return. A list of the files that you have submitted for printing is displayed.

In the following example, on the system pine, one file is queued for printing to the printer pinecone.

```
pine% lpstat
pinecone-10            fred         1261   Mar 12 17:34 on pine
pine%
```

The lpstat command displays one line for each print job, showing the request ID followed by the name of the user who spooled the request, the output size in bytes, and the date and time of the request.

Availability of Printers

To find out which printers are configured on your system, type **lpstat -s** and press Return. The status of the scheduler is displayed, followed by the default destination and a list of the systems and printers that are available to you.

In the following example, on the system `elm`, the scheduler is running, the default printer is `pinecone`, and two network printers are available.

```
elm% lpstat -s
scheduler is running
system default destination: pinecone
system for pinecone: pine
system for acorn: oak
elm%
```

Display of All Status Information

The `-t` option for `lpstat` gives you a short listing of the status of the LP print service. To display a short listing of all status information, type **lpstat -t** and press Return. All available status information is displayed.

In the following example, no jobs are in the print queue. When files are spooled for printing, the status of those print requests is also displayed.

```
elm% lpstat -t
scheduler is running
system default destination: tom
system for slw2: bertha
system for slw1: bertha
device for tom: /dev/term/b
slw2 accepting requests since Thu May 11 11:01:54 EDT 2000
slw1 accepting requests since Sat May 27 16:26:38 EDT 2000
tom accepting requests since Sat Jun  3 14:25:41 EDT 2000
printer slw2 is idle. enabled since Thu May 11 11:01:55 EDT 2000. available.
printer slw1 is idle. enabled since Thu May 27 16:26:38 EDT 2000. available.
printer tom is idle. enabled since Sat Jun  3 14:25:41 EDT 2000. available.
character set usascii
character set english
character set finnish
character set japanese
character set norwegian
character set swedish
character set germanic
character set french
character set canadian_french
character set italian
character set spanish
character set line
character set security
character set ebcdic
character set apl
character set mosaic
elm%
```

The `-l` option for `lpstat`, when used with one of the other options, gives you a long listing of the status of the LP print service. To display a long listing of all status information, type **lpstat -t l** and press Return. All available status information is displayed.

In the following example for the same system, additional information is displayed. When files are spooled for printing, the status of those print requests is also displayed.

```
{:44} lpstat -tl
scheduler is running
system default destination: tom
system for slw2: bertha
system for slw1: bertha
device for tom: /dev/term/b
slw2 accepting requests since Thu May 11 11:01:54 EDT 2000
slw1 accepting requests since Sat May 27 16:26:38 EDT 2000
tom accepting requests since Sat Jun  3 14:25:41 EDT 2000
printer slw2 is idle. enabled since Thu May 11 11:01:55 EDT 2000. available.
        Content types: any
        Printer types: unknown
        Description:
        Users allowed:
                (all)
        Forms allowed:
                (none)
        Banner not required
        Character sets:
                (none)
        Default pitch:
        Default page size:

printer slw1 is idle. enabled since Sat May 27 16:26:38 EDT 2000. available.
        Content types: simple
        Printer types: unknown
        Description: Located in ia lab
        Users allowed:
                (all)
        Forms allowed:
                (none)
        Banner not required
        Character sets:
                (none)
        Default pitch:
        Default page size:

printer tom is idle. enabled since Sat Jun  3 14:25:41 EDT 2000. available.
        Form mounted:
        Content types: PS
        Printer types: la100
        Description: hi
        Connection: direct
        Interface: /usr/lib/lp/model/standard
        After fault: continue
        Users allowed:
                (all)
        Forms allowed:
                (none)
        Banner required
        Character sets:
                usascii
                english
                finnish
                japanese
                norwegian
                swedish
                germanic
french
        canadian_french
                italian
                spanish
                line
                security
                ebcdic
                apl
                mosaic
```

```
            Default pitch: 10 CPI 6 LPI
            Default page size: 132 wide 66 long
(More information not shown in this example)
```

Display of Status for Printers

You can request printer status information for individual printers by using
the -p option to lpstat. This option shows whether the printer is active or
idle, when it was enabled or disabled, and whether it is available to accept
print requests.

   To request status for all printers on a system, type **lpstat -p** and press
Return. In the following example, two printers are idle, enabled, and
available, as shown in the following example. If one of those printers had
jobs in the print queue, those jobs would also be displayed.

```
elm% lpstat -p
printer pinecone is idle. enabled since Sat Jan  1 18:20:22 PST 2000.
 available.
printer acorn is idle. enabled since Thu Mar  2 15:53:44 PST 2000. available.
elm%
```

   To request status for an individual printer by name, type
lpstat -p _printer-name_ and press Return.

Display of Printer Characteristics

To see all of the characteristics for a printer, use the -p option together with
the -l (long) option to lpstat. This command can be especially useful for
finding the printer type and content type.

   To show characteristics for all printers on a system, type **lpstat -p -l**
and press Return. A table shows all the configuration information that is
used by the LP print service for each printer.

   In the following example, all the fields are blank except for the content
type and the printer type of the printer pinecone.

```
elm% lpstat -p pinecone -l
printer pinecone is idle. enabled since Sat Jan  1 18:20:22 PST 2000.
 available.
        Content types: PS
        Printer types: PS
        Description:
        Users allowed:
                (all)
        Forms allowed:
                (none)
        Banner not required
        Character sets:
                (none)
        Default pitch:
        Default page size:
elm%
```

Summary Table of lpstat Options

You can request different types of printing status information by using the lpstat command. Table 97 summarizes the frequently used options for the lpstat command. Use these options individually or combine them in any order on the command line. When you combine options, use a space between options and repeat the dash (–). For example, to show a long list of status for an individual printer, type **lpstat -p _printer-name_ -l** and press Return. See the lpstat(1) manual page for a complete list of options.

Table 97   *Summary of Frequently Used Options to the lpstat Command*

Option	Description
-a	Accept. Show whether print destinations are accepting requests.
-c	Class. Show classes and their members.
-d	Destination. Show default destination.
-f	Forms. Show forms.
-o	Output. Show status of output.
-p [*list*] [-D] [-l]	Printer/description/long list. Show status of printers.
-r	Request. Request scheduler status.
-R	Show position of job in the queue.
-S	Sets. Show character sets.
-s	Status. Show status summary.
-u [*username*]	User. Show requests by user.
-v	Show devices.

Cancelling a Print Request

Use the cancel command to cancel a print request while it is in the queue or while it is printing. To cancel a request, you need to know its request ID. The request ID always includes the name of the printer, a dash, and the number of the print request. When you submit the print request, the request ID is displayed. If you do not remember your request ID, type **lpstat** and press Return. Only the user who submitted the request or someone logged in as root or lp can cancel a print request.

Cancelling a Print Request by ID Number

To cancel a print request, type **cancel** *request-ID* and press Return. A message is displayed telling you that the request is cancelled. The next job in the queue begins printing.

In the following example, two print requests are cancelled.

```
elm% cancel pinecone-3 pinecone-4
request "pinecone-3" cancelled
request "pinecone-4" cancelled
elm%
```

Cancelling by Printer Name a File That Is Currently Printing

You can also cancel just the job that currently is printing (if you were the submitter) by typing the printer name in place of the request ID. Type **cancel** *printer-name* and press Return. A message is displayed telling you that the request is cancelled. The next job in the queue begins printing.

In the following example, the currently printing job has been cancelled.

```
elm% cancel pinecone
request "pinecone-3" cancelled
elm%
```

As system administrator, you can log in as root or lp and cancel the currently printing job by using the printer name as the argument for the cancel command.

12

RECOGNIZING FILE ACCESS PROBLEMS

This chapter describes how to recognize problems with search paths, permissions, and ownership.

Users frequently experience problems—and call on a system administrator for help—because they cannot access a program, a file, or a directory that they could formerly access. Whenever you encounter such a problem, investigate one of the following areas.

- The user's search path may have been changed.
- The directories in the search path may not be in the proper order.
- The file or directory may not have the proper permissions or ownership.

This chapter briefly describes how to recognize problems in each of these areas and suggests possible solutions.

Recognizing Problems with Search Paths

If a user types a command that is not in the search path, the message `Command not found` is displayed. The command might not be found because the command is not available on the system or the command directory is not in the search path.

If the wrong version of the command is found, a directory with a command of the same name is in the search path. In this case, the proper directory may be found later in the search path or may not be present at all.

To diagnose and troubleshoot problems with search paths, use the following procedure.

1. Display the current search path.

New!

2. Edit the file in which the user's path is set (`.login` for the C shell, `.profile` for the Bourne and Korn shells). Add the directory or rearrange the order of the path.

New!

NOTE. For the C shell, always check both the `.cshrc` *and* `.login` *files to make sure the path information is set all in one place. When you find path information in the* `.cshrc` *file, move it to the* `.login` *file. Duplicate entries can make the search path harder to troubleshoot and make search times less efficient for the user.*

3. Source the file to activate the changes. See "Sourcing Bourne and Korn Shell Dot Files" and "Sourcing C Shell Dot Files" on page 437 for more information.

4. Verify that the command is found in the right place.

5. Execute the command.

The tasks you use to follow this procedure are described in the following sections.

Displaying the Current Search Path

To display the current search path, type **echo $PATH** and press Return. The current search path is displayed.

```
cinderella% echo $PATH
/sbin:/usr/sbin:/usr/bin:/etc
cinderella%
```

Setting the Path for Bourne and Korn Shells

The path for the Bourne and Korn shells is specified in the user's $HOME/`.profile` file in this way.

```
PATH=/usr/bin:/$HOME/bin:.;export PATH
```

The dot (`.`) at the end of the path specifies that the current working directory is always searched last.

Sourcing Bourne and Korn Shell Dot Files

When you have changed information in the `.profile` file, you must source
the file to make the new information available to the shell. To source the
`.profile` file, type **. .profile** and press Return.

```
$ . .profile
$
```

Setting the Path for the C Shell

Specify the path for the C shell in the user's `$HOME/.login` file (with the
`setenv PATH` environment variable) in this way.

```
setenv PATH (/usr/bin $home/bin .)
```

The dot (`.`) at the end of the path specifies that the current working
directory is always searched last.

Sourcing C Shell Dot Files

When you have changed information in the `.login` file, you must source the
file to make the new information available to the shell. To source the `.login`
file, type **source .login** and press Return.

```
castle% source .login
castle%
```

Verifying the Search Path

When you have changed a user's path, use the `which` command to verify that
the shell is finding the proper command. The `which` command looks in the
`.cshrc` file for information. The `/bin/which` command is a C shell script.
Any configuration files in a user's home directory that affect the C shell also
may affect the `which` command. To ensure accurate results, use the `which`
command in a C or `tcsh` shell. Alternatively, from the Korn or `zsh` shell you
can use the `whence` command instead of the `which` command.

To verify the search path, type **which *command-name*** and press Return. If
the command is found in the path, the path and the name of the command
are displayed.

The following example shows that the OpenWindows executable is not in
any of the directories in the search path.

```
oak% which openwin
no openwin in . /home/ignatz /sbin /usr/sbin /usr/bin /etc/home/ignatz/bin
  /bin /home/bin /usr/etc
oak%
```

The following example shows that the executable for OpenWindows is found among the directories in the search path.

```
oak% which openwin
/usr/openwin/bin/openwin
oak%
```

If you cannot find a command, you can often look at the manual page to find its path name. For example, if you cannot find the `lpsched` command (the LP printer daemon), the `lpsched`(1M) manual page tells you the path is `/usr/lib/lp/lpsched`.

Executing a Command

To execute a command, type ***command-name*** and press Return. The command is executed if it is in the search path. You can always execute a command that is not in the search path by typing the full path name for the command.

Recognizing Problems with Permissions and Ownership

When users cannot access files or directories that they used to be able to access, the most likely problem is that permissions or ownership on the files or directories has changed.

New!

Frequently, file and directory ownerships change because someone edited the files as root. When you create home directories for new users, be especially careful to make the user the owner of both the home directory and the dot (`.`) files in the home directory.

Another way access problems can arise is when the group ownership changes or when a group of which a user is a member is deleted from the `/etc/groups` database.

Changing File Ownership

NOTE. You must own a file or directory (or have root permission) to be able to change its ownership. If the

{_POSIX_CHOWN_RESTRICTED} *configuration option is enabled (the default), you must be superuser to change ownership of a file, even if you own it. See "Changing File Ownership or Permissions (chown, chmod, chgrp)" on page 77 for more information.*

Use the following steps to change file ownership.

1. Type **ls -l** *filename* and press Return. The owner of the file is displayed in the third column.
2. Become superuser.
3. Type **chown** *new-owner* *filename* and press Return. Ownership is assigned to the new owner you specify, in this case, ignatz.

```
oak% ls -l quest
-rw-r--r--  1 fred    staff     6023 Aug  5 12:06 quest
oak% su
Password:
# chown ignatz quest
# ls -l quest
-rw-r--r--  1 ignatz   staff     6023 Aug  5 12:06 quest
#
```

Changing File Permissions

You use the chmod command to change file permissions. You can change permissions in two ways. If you use letters, use the following syntax.

```
chmod [who] operator[permission(s)] file-name
```

For *who*, you can specify u, g, or o (for user, group, or other). You can specify a to change all operators. If you do not specify who the permissions are for, permissions are changed for all three groups. The operator is either + to add permission or – to take away permission. The permissions are r, w, or x, for read, write, or execute. See the chmod(1) manual page for more information.

For example, to grant read, write, and execute permissions to everyone, type **chmod +wrx** *filename* and press Return.

```
oak% chmod +wrx kookaburra
oak% ls -l kookaburra
-rwxrwxrwx 1    janice    staff    54 Jul 7  11:33  kookaburra
oak%
```

To grant read and execute permissions to everyone, type **chmod +rx** *filename* and press Return.

```
oak% chmod +rx kookaburra
oak% ls -l kookaburra
-r-xr-xr-x  1    janice    staff    54  Jul 7  11:34  kookaburra
oak%
```

Another way to change the permissions to read and execute only would be to deny write permission to everyone. Type **chmod -w** *filename* and press Return.

```
oak% chmod -w kookaburra
oak% ls -l kookaburra
-r-xr-xr-x  1    janice    staff    54  Jul 7  11:35  kookaburra
oak%
```

To change ownership for a specific group, type the letter for the group followed by the operator and the permission. In the following example, read, write, and execute permissions have been granted for the owner to the file kookaburra.

```
oak% chmod u+wrx kookaburra
oak% ls -l kookaburra
-rwxr-xr-x  1    janice    staff    54  Jul 7  11:36  kookaburra
oak%
```

To deny execute permissions to group and other, type **chmod go-x** *filename* and press Return.

```
oak% chmod go-x kookaburra
oak% ls -l kookaburra
-rwxr--r--  1    janice    staff    54  Jul 7  11:37  kookaburra
oak%
```

With the chmod command, you can also use a numeric argument that describes the user class and permission to change as a sequence of bits. Table 98 shows the octal values for setting file permissions. You use these numbers in sets of three to set permissions for owner, group, and other. For example, the value 644 sets read/write permissions for owner and read-only permissions for group and other.

Table 98   Octal Values for File Permissions

Value	Description
0	No permissions.
1	Execute-only.
2	Write-only.
3	Write, execute.

Table 98   Octal Values for File Permissions (Continued)

Value	Description
4	Read-only.
5	Read, execute.
6	Read, write.
7	Read, write, execute.

Use the following steps to change permissions on a file.

1. Type **ls -l** *filename* and press Return.

   The long listing shows the current permissions for the file.

2. Type **chmod** *nnn* *filename* and press Return.

   Permissions are changed according to the numbers you specify.

NOTE. You can change permissions on groups of files or on all files in a directory by using metacharacters such as * and ? in place of file names or in combination with them.

The following example changes the permissions of a file from 666 (read/write, read/write, read/write) to 644 (read/write, read-only, read-only).

```
oak% ls -l quest
-rw-rw-rw-  1 ignatz    staff    6023 Aug  5 12:06 quest
oak% chmod 644 quest
oak% ls -l quest
-rw-r--r--  1 ignatz    staff    6023 Aug  5 12:06 quest
oak%
```

Changing File Group Ownership

If a file has an incorrect group owner, users of the group won't be able to make changes to the file. To change file group ownership, you must either be a member of the group, owner of the file, or root.

To change the group ID for a file, type **chgrp** *gid* *filename* and press Return. The group ID for the file you specify is changed. With the Solaris Operating Environment, the ls -l command shows the owner and the group for the file. You can display only the group owner by using the ls -lg command.

```
$ ls -lg junk
-rw-r--r-- 1 other 0 Oct 31 14:49 junk
$ chgrp 10 junk
$ ls -lg junk
-rw-r--r-- 1 staff 0 Oct 31 14:49 junk
$
```

New!   The group ID is found in the group database indicated by the `group` entry in the `/etc/nsswitch.conf` Nameservice Switch configuration file or the local `/etc/group` file.

GLOSSARY

archive

A copy of files, on secondary media, that have been removed from the system because they are no longer active.

autoconfiguration

The automatic loading of kernel modules as they are needed.

auto_home

The indirect automount map that you use to add home directories to the automounter.

automounter

Software that can automatically mount several different types of file systems, for example, NFS, LOFS, HSFS, when a user changes that file system; unmounts the file system when it is no longer in use.

backing-store

A bitmapped file created by the `fssnap` command, that contains copies of presnapshot data that has been modified since the snapshot was taken.

New!

backup schedule

The schedule you establish for a site to determine when you will regularly run the `ufsdump` command at different levels to back up user files and essential file systems. See *full backup, incremental backup*.

443

bang

> An exclamation point (!) that acts as a single-character UNIX command or as a separator between the routes of a UUCP e-mail address.

BIOS

> Basic Input/Output System (BIOS) is the firmware interface on a PC.

boot block

> An 8-Kbyte disk block that contains information used during booting. Block numbers point to the location of the boot program on that disk. The boot block directly follows the disk label.

booting

> The process of powering up a system, testing to determine which attached hardware devices are running, and bringing the operating system kernel into memory and operation at the run level specified by the boot command.

Bourne-Again shell

> A Bourne-shell-compatible language interpreter that executes commands read from the standard input or from a file. bash incorporates useful features from the Korn and C shells.

Bourne shell

> The default shell for the Solaris Operating Environment. The Bourne shell is a small shell for general-purpose use. It also provides a full-scale scripting language that you can use to develop shell scripts to capture frequently performed commands and procedures.

C shell

> A shell completely different from the Bourne and Korn shells with its own C language syntax. The most important advantages of the C shell are command history, command editing, and aliases.

cache

> A small, fast memory area that holds the most active part of a larger and slower memory.

CDE

> Common Desktop Environment is a windowing system based on the Motif graphical user interface.

core file

> An image of the state of a software program when it failed; used for troubleshooting. A core file can be created by any program, including the operating system kernel.

crash

> A situation when a system panics and dies. See also *hang*.

crash dump

> A core file image of the operating system kernel; saved in the swap partition when a system crashes. If crash dumps are enabled, the core image is written from the swap partition to a file.

cylinder group

> One or more consecutive disk cylinders that include inode slots for files.

cylinder group map

> A bitmap in a UFS file system that stores information about block use and availability within each cylinder group. The cylinder group replaces the traditional free list.

daemon

> A type of program that, once activated, carries out a specific task without any need for user input. Daemons typically are started when the system is started and don't die until the system shuts down. Daemons run in the background and do not generally require direct interaction with a user or system administrator. They handle day-to-day tasks for the system, such as printing (lpd), logging (syslogd), e-mail (sendmail), and serial port monitoring (ttymon).

disc

> An optical disc, a CD-ROM, or a DVD-ROM.

disk

> A hard-disk storage device.

diskette

> A nonvolatile storage medium used to store and access data magnetically. Solaris Operating Environment supports 3.5-inch, double-sided, high-density (DS, HD) diskettes.

diskless client

> A system with no local disk drive that instead relies on an NFS server for the operating system, swap space, file storage, and other basic services.

disk quotas

> A mechanism for controlling how much of a file system's resources any individual user can consume. Disk quotas are optional and must be configured and administered to be used.

DNS domain

> A hierarchical directory structure for e-mail addressing and network address naming. Within the United States, top-level domains include com for commercial organizations, edu for educational organizations, gov for governments, mil for the military, net for networking organizations, and org for other organizations. Outside the United States, top-level domains designate the country. Subdomains designate the organization and the individual system.

domain addressing

> Using an address contained in the Domain Naming System (DNS) to specify the destination of an e-mail message.

DS, HD

> Double-sided, high-density signifies the type of 3.5-inch diskettes supported by the Solaris Operating Environment.

dump

> The process of copying directories, by using the ufsdump command, onto media (usually tape) for off-line storage.

DVD

> Digital Versatile Disc or Digital Video Disc uses the UDFS format for storing information.

dynamic reconfiguration

> The capability, available on certain SPARC servers, to remove and replace hot-pluggable system I/O boards in a running system, eliminating the time lost in rebooting.

e-mail

> Electronic mail. A set of programs that transmit mail messages from one system to another.

environment variable

> A system- or user-defined variable that provides information about the operating environment to the shell or a program.

file system

> A hierarchical arrangement of directories and files organized on a portion of a magnetic or optical disk.

Flash archive

New!

> A file that contains a snapshot of all of the software on a master system. You use the Flash archive to replicate this installation configuration on clone systems of the same architecture.

Flash installation

New!

> A feature that enables you to create a base configuration on a master system and then create a Flash archive file to replicate that configuration on clone systems of the same architecture.

floppy diskette

> See *diskette*.

free list

> See *cylinder group map*.

full backup

> A complete, level 0 backup of a file system, done with the `ufsdump` command. See *incremental backup*.

fully qualified domain name

> The complete domain name that contains all the elements needed to specify one particular system in the world. See also *DNS domain*.

gateway

> A system that handles e-mail traffic between different communications networks.

GID

> The group identification number used by the system to control access to files and directories owned by other users.

group

> The sources of group account information used by Solaris. The sources are specified by the group entry in the Nameservice Switch configuration file.

group ID

> See *GID*.

hang

> A condition in which a system does not respond to input from the keyboard, a mouse, or the network.

home directory

> The part of the file system that is allocated to an individual user for private files.

hosts

> The sources of information used to map host names or host name aliases to IP addresses. The sources are specified by the hosts entry in the Nameservice Switch configuration file. The hosts entry in the Nameservice Switch configuration file is the only one that can specify dns in addition to the files, nis, nisplus, and ldap nameservices.

hot-plugging

> The ability to physically add, remove, or replace system components while a system is running. See *dynamic reconfiguration*.

incremental backup

> A partial backup of a file system that is performed by the ufsdump command. The backup includes only those files in the specified file system that have changed since a previous backup at a lower level. See *full backup*.

initialization files

> The dot files (files prefixed with .) in a user's home directory that set the path, environment variables, windowing environment, and other characteristics to enable users to use the system.

init state

> One of the seven initialization states, or run levels, a system can be running in. A system can run in only one init state at a time.

inode

> An entry in a predesignated area of a disk that describes the location of a file on that disk, the size of the file, the time and date it was last used, and other identification information.

input variables

> The environment variables that CDE's dtsearchpath reads.

IP address

A unique Internet protocol number that identifies each system in a network.

IPv4

Internet Protocol, version 4 is the default protocol for the Solaris 7 and earlier releases.

IPv6

Internet Protocol, version 6 adds increased address space and improves Internet functionality to the IPv4 protocol by use of a simplified header format, support for authentication and privacy, autoconfiguration of address assignments, and new quality-of-service capabilities.

kernel

The master program set of Solaris software that manages all the physical resources of the computer, including file system management, virtual memory, reading and writing of files to disks and tapes, process scheduling, printing, and communications over a network.

Korn shell

A shell that uses the same syntax as the Bourne shell but provides more built-in functions that can be defined directly from the shell as well as a sophisticated form of command editing.

LDAP   *New!*

Lightweight Directory Access Protocol is an industry-standard nameservice for accessing directory servers. LDAP is one of the nameservices provided by Solaris. Naming information is stored in containers on the LDAP server.

Live Upgrade   *New!*

An installation tool that enables you to create one or more duplicates of an existing boot environment. While the original system is still running, you can either upgrade or reinstall the inactive boot environment. You can also add patches to the inactive boot environment. Activate one of the duplicate boot environments and reboot. The original boot environment remains available if needed for failure recovery.

login name

The name that is assigned to an individual user to control user ID access to a system.

manual pages

Online technical references for each Solaris command.

metacharacter

> A symbol used in file names and extensions to represent another character or string of characters. An asterisk (*) matches any number of characters. A question mark (?) matches a single character.

monitor

> The program in the OpenBoot PROM that provides a limited set of commands that can be used before the kernel is available. See *OpenBoot PROM*.

mount point

> A directory in the file system hierarchy at which another file system is attached to the hierarchy.

New! *Nameservice Switch configuration file*

> The configuration file, /etc/nsswitch.conf, that specifies which nameservice database to search. Nameservices include files, NIS, NIS+, LDAP, and DNS.

netmask

> A setting that determines how many and which bits in the host address space represent the subnet number and how many and which represent the host number. See also *subnet mask*.

NFS

> The default Solaris distributed file system that provides file sharing among systems. NFS servers can also provide kernels and swap files to diskless clients.

NFS failover

> The process of selecting an alternate NFS server for a particular file system from a list of servers, each of which contains an identical copy of the file system. Normally, the next NFS server in the sorted list is used unless it fails to respond.

NIS

> One of the nameservices provided by Sun that enables centralization of configuration information for user and group accounts, printing, e-mail aliases, the automounter subsystem, and some network security. In the process of being replaced by LDAP.

NIS+

> One of the naming services supported by Solaris, intended as a replacement for NIS. Incorporates all of the features of NIS, adds better security, and fewer limitations in the size of information that can be stored, and allows delegation

of administrative subdomains. Slated to be replaced by LDAP in the Solaris 10 timeframe.

OpenBoot PROM

Programmable read-only memory is a chip containing permanent, nonvolatile memory and a limited set of commands used to test the system and start the boot process.

OpenWindows

A windowing system based on the OPEN LOOK graphical user interface.

parse

To resolve a string of characters or a series of words into component parts to determine their collective meaning. Virtually every program that accepts command input must do some sort of parsing before the commands can be acted on. For example, the `sendmail` program divides an e-mail address into its component parts to decide where to send the message.

partition

A discrete portion of a disk, configured with the `format` program. Also referred to as *slice*.

passwd

The source of user account information used by Solaris. The sources are specified by the `passwd` entry in the Nameservice Switch configuration file.

path

The list of directories that are searched to find an executable command.

path name

A list of directory names, separated with slashes (/), that specifies the location of a particular file.

port

A physical connection between a peripheral device (such as a terminal, printer, or modem) and the device controller.

port monitor

A program that continuously watches for requests to log in or requests to access printers or files. The `ttymon` and `listen` port monitors are part of the Service Access Facility.

power cycling

Turning off the power to a system and then turning it on again.

preen

To run `fsck` with the `-o p` option, which automatically fixes any basic file system inconsistencies normally found when a system halts abruptly but does not repair more serious errors.

process

A program in operation.

remap

To make use of a new server with NFS client failover. Through normal use, the clients store the path name for each active file on the remote file system. During remapping, these path names are evaluated to locate the files on the new server.

root

The highest level of a hierarchical system. As a login ID, the user name of the system administrator or superuser who has responsibility for an entire system. Root has permissions for all user files and processes on the system. See also *superuser*.

run level

See *init state*.

runaway process

A process that progressively uses more and more CPU time.

server

A system that provides network services such as disk storage and file transfer; a program that provides such a service.

Service Access Facility (SAF)

The part of the system software that is used to register and monitor port activity for modems, terminals, and printers. SAF replaces `/etc/getty` as a way to control logins.

shell

The command interpreter for a user, specified in the `passwd` database. The Solaris Operating Environment supports the Bourne (default), C, and Korn shells. The Solaris 8 Operating Environment also provides the freeware Bourne Again, TC, and Z shells.

slice

An alternative name for a partition. See also *partition*.

snapshot

New!

A read-only image of a file system created by the fssnap(1M) command; can be used to back up a file system while the file system is mounted.

Solaris Management Console

New!

A collection of network-aware system administration tools.

spooling directory

A directory in which files are stored until they are processed.

spooling space

The amount of space that is allocated on a print server for storing requests in the printer queue.

stand-alone system

A system that has a local disk and can boot without relying on a server.

state flag

A flag in the superblock that the fsck file system check program updates to record the condition of a file system. If a file system state flag is clean, the fsck program is not run on that file system.

subnet mask

A setting that determines the bits in the host IP address bytes that are applied to subnet addresses and those applied to host addresses. See also *netmask*.

superuser

A user who is granted special privileges by supplying the correct password with the su command or when logging in as root. For example, only the superuser can edit major administrative files in the /etc directory. See also *root*.

swap file

A disk partition or file used to temporarily hold the contents of a memory area until they can be loaded back into memory.

symbolic link

A file that contains a pointer to the name of another file.

system

> A computer with a keyboard and terminal. A system can have either local or remote disks and can have additional peripheral devices such as CD-ROM players, DVD-ROM players, tape drives, diskette drives, and printers.

tcsh

> An enhanced and completely compatible variation of the Berkeley UNIX C shell, csh(1); can be used as an interactive login shell and a shell script command processor. It includes a command-line editor, programmable word completion, spelling correction, a history mechanism, job control, and a C-like syntax.

UFS

> UNIX file system is the default disk-based file system for the Solaris Operating Environment.

UID

> The user identification number assigned to each login name. UID numbers are used by the system to identify, by number, the owners of files and directories.

Universal Disc Format file system

> The UDFS file system is the industry-standard format for storing information on the optical media technology called DVD (Digital Versatile Disc or Digital Video Disc).

user account

> An account set up for an individual user in the passwd database; specifies the user's login name, UID, GID, login directory, and login shell.

user ID

> See *UID*.

user mask

> The setting that controls default file permissions that are assigned when a file or directory is created. The umask command controls the user mask settings.

New! *virtual device*

> A virtual device contains a snapshot of a file system, created by the fssnap(1M) command. The virtual device looks and acts like a real device to existing Solaris backup commands.

virtual memory

A memory management technique that is used by the operating system for programs that require more space in memory than can be allotted to them. The kernel moves only pages of the program currently needed into memory; unneeded pages remain on the disk.

zombie

A child process that has terminated but whose parent process has not properly reaped the child's exit status by calling one of the `wait` system calls (such as `waitpid`(1)). Zombie processes take up valuable process slot resources, and if you get enough of them, you won't be able to start any new processes. Zombie processes are removed from the process table when a system is rebooted. You can also use the `preap`(1) command, new in the Solaris 9 release, to force a defunct process to be reaped by its parent.

zsh

A UNIX command interpreter that you can use as an interactive login shell and as a shell script command processor. The Z shell most closely resembles the Korn shell with enhancements. The Z shell provides command-line editing, built-in spelling correction, programmable command completions, shell functions (with autoloading), a history mechanism, and a host of other features.

INDEX